Praise for *Dick Hamer*

'It's a great story — really well told. We can all be ever grateful for Dick Hamer's remarkable legacy, and grateful, too, for Tim Colebatch's passionate record of how "Hamer made it happen".'

— Ted Baillieu, premier of Victoria, 2010–2013

'*Dick Hamer* is one of the most compelling books on Australian politics I have read. The narrative is strong and the prose is fluent. The book makes me realise how, in writing the modern history of the nation, we too often focus on federal politics, forgetting that most of the political decisions that shaped human lives were made far from Canberra.'

— Geoffrey Blainey, *Australian Book Review*

'Tim Colebatch's book is a fine, fair, candid biography … Hamer comes over as one of the best of them.'

— Robert Murray, *Quadrant*

'Colebatch has done an excellent job … Hamer comes across as a person and politician of considerable charm and manifest integrity.'

— Ross Fitzgerald, *The Australian*

'A glimpse into another age … when a courteous, thoughtful, urbane man who "argued for what is right over what was popular at the moment", as Colebatch puts it, was the most popular premier in the country … Hamer was a remarkable man … he stands as a reminder of what the Liberal party, and states, once were.'

— Gay Alcorn, *The Guardian*

'(One of) the 20 best books of 2014 … Colebatch chronicles how Hamer decriminalised homosexuality, abolished capital punishment, championed equal opportunity, gave Melbourne an arts hub — all done with courtesy and and integrity. A true liberal.'

— *The Australian Financial Review*

'Tim Colebatch has written a fascinating account of one of Australia's most remarkable post-war leaders. Dick Hamer is the forgotten reformer of the 1970s … he restored Victoria's position as the nation's pre-eminent progressive state.'

— George Megalogenis, author of *The Australian Moment*

'Colebatch brings a shrewdness of judgment to the biographical task, as well as a deep knowledge of Victoria's political history … In his commitment to public service, his vision for Victoria and his unfailing courtesy, (Hamer) represented the best of the tradition that had shaped him.'

— Judith Brett, *Inside Story*

'Tim Colebatch has combined meticulous research with fluent writing to produce a book which is as much a social and political history of Victoria as a biography.'

— Richard Thomas, former press secretary to Dick Hamer

'Dick Hamer was ahead of his time. In 1972, when Australia was clamouring for change, he had already developed environmental, equal-opportunity, and arts policies that threw off years of social conservatism under his predecessor.

'Dick Hamer also embodied democracy with great decency, openness, and a genuine commitment not seen today.

'We should be grateful to Tim Colebatch for this biography. His account says as much about Victoria as it does about the Hamer government. He is right to assert that, apart from the Kennett years, all subsequent Labor and Liberal governments have governed in the same direction. May it ever be thus.'

— Steve Bracks, premier of Victoria, 1999–2007

'A great political biography — arguably the best produced in Australia in the last 40 years …

'There's a lot in this biography that explains what is wrong with Australian politics today. It should be compulsory reading for all those opportunists who hang around the offices of politicians seeking to make a career for themselves, with no commitment to anything but personal ambition.'

— John Cain, premier of Victoria, 1982–1990

DICK HAMER

Tim Colebatch is a political and economic journalist. Born in Melbourne in 1949, he studied arts and economics at the University of Melbourne. From 1971 to 2013, he wrote for *The Age* and observed the Hamer era at close quarters. He was in turn the paper's environment writer, chief investigative reporter, editorial writer, and columnist before becoming its Washington correspondent, economics writer, and ultimately economics editor and columnist for 20 years. His journalism has won many awards.

To my mother, Betty Colebatch,
who taught me to read
and encouraged me to write

DICK HAMER

the liberal Liberal

TIM COLEBATCH

SCRIBE
Melbourne • London

Scribe Publications
18–20 Edward St, Brunswick, Victoria 3056, Australia
2 John St, Clerkenwell, London, WC1N 2ES, United Kingdom

First published by Scribe 2014
This edition (with minor corrections) published 2015

Indexed by Olive Grove Indexing Services
Typeset in Minion Pro by the publishers

Printed and bound in Australia by Griffin Press

The paper this book is printed on is certified against the Forest Stewardship Council® Standards. Griffin Press holds FSC chain of custody certification SGS-COC-005088. FSC promotes environmentally responsible, socially beneficial and economically viable management of the world's forests.

National Library of Australia Cataloguing-in-Publication data

Colebatch, Tim, author.

Dick Hamer: the liberal Liberal / Tim Colebatch.

9781925321067 (paperback)
9781925113396 (e-book)

1. Hamer, Rupert, Sir, 1916-2004. 2. Liberal Party of Australia. Victorian Division.
3. Premiers–Victoria–Biography. 4. Politicians–Victoria–Biography.
5. Victoria–Politics and government–1976-1990.

994.506092

scribepublications.com.au
scribepublications.co.uk

Contents

Part IV: The Hamer Years: 2

Coda

Appendices

‘There is a sort of enthusiasm in all projectors, absolutely necessary for their affairs, which makes them proof against the most fatiguing delays, the most mortifying disappointments, the most shocking insults; and, what is severer than all, the presumptuous judgement of the ignorant upon their designs.’

— *Edmund Burke*

Preface to this edition

Dick Hamer was premier of Victoria from 1972 to 1981. He had been out of politics for almost 30 years, and was no longer with us, when I decided to write this book. It raises the question: why bother? Why should Australians today be interested in what some state political leader did all those years ago?

A short answer is that Hamer was a successful politician who had integrity, intelligence, and foresight. Today, that sounds like an oxymoron. There are still some of them around, certainly, mercifully — New South Wales premier Mike Baird is a standout among today's leaders — but they are becoming a threatened species.

Hamer was a thoroughly good man who had an acute political mind, and the courage and conviction to take the lead in reform of a state that for so long had worked on the principle of 'Do what you're told.' He led an uneven team, but a critical mass of first-rate ministers became the drivers of change, and made the Hamer government a landmark in far-sighted, compassionate, and decent government.

The times are right to recall that landmark age. In recent times, we have seen an alarming moral and intellectual decline in Australian politics. Our leaders and their media hit-squads no longer try to persuade us with facts and logical argument, as Hamer did, but with misrepresentation of opponents, crass spin, and three-word slogans. Hamer's policy focus was on the long-term interests of Victorians. Today's leaders try to artificially manufacture issues and make decisions in their own short-term political interests — or the interests of those funding their party.

Australians are seeing through this, and growing cynical about politics. This is dangerous for our future.

In the past five years, Australians have voted at 12 federal, state or territory elections. At eight of those 12 elections, they have thrown out the government, coalition or Labor; in a ninth (South Australia), Labor clung on as a minority government, although the coalition won 53 per cent of the two-party vote. Of 12 governments seeking re-endorsement, Australians voted to re-elect just three. That is clearly a vote of no confidence in the way politics now operates.

Politics does not have to be like this. It was not always like this. Dick Hamer won re-election three times. He was re-elected for a simple reason: people trusted him. He was the last Liberal premier anywhere in Australia to win more than two terms. With few exceptions — Mike Baird; Katy Gallagher, when she was chief minister of the Australian Capital Territory; Colin Barnett, when the West Australian economy was booming — today's political leaders have not won that trust.

The distrust is felt towards both sides of politics; as I wrote this, not long before Malcolm Turnbull deposed Tony Abbott as Liberal leader and prime minister, opinion polls told us that voters disapproved of both Tony Abbott and Bill Shorten by 2:1 majorities. But the brunt of their distrust fell on the Liberals and Nationals.

Since 1982, when the long reign of the Victorian Liberals under Sir Henry Bolte, Dick Hamer, and Lindsay Thompson finally ended, Labor has been in power for most of that time in Canberra, and in every single state of Australia. In Hamer's time, the coalition was the natural party of government. It is now the natural party of opposition.

Since 1982, the coalition has spent just 11 years out of 33 in power in Victoria and NSW. In Queensland, it has been in opposition for 20 of the past 25 years. Despite John Howard's success, it has won just five of the past 12 federal elections, and only 11 of the past 32 elections in the three largest states. In both Victoria and Queensland, coalition governments have now lost power after just one term, previously a rare event. The polls consistently suggested that in 2016 the Abbott government would have met the same fate.

The Liberals were not always accustomed to failure. Dick Hamer and Malcolm Fraser were the last of a long generation of Liberal leaders, federal and state, who dominated Australian politics from 1950 to 1980. Hamer was from the urban left of the party, while Fraser in those days was seen as head of the rural right. But the Liberal Party was then a broad church, one where liberals and conservatives alike could feel at home. Since then it has drifted sharply to the right, especially at federal level, to the point that Hamer publicly opposed many of the Howard government's policies, and Fraser eventually left the party.

The Liberal Party was not always the party it is now. It was founded in 1909 by the archetypal Australian liberal, prime minister Alfred Deakin, who persuaded the free trade party to merge with his protectionists in opposition to the rising force of Labor. Over the decades, the party then went through two changes of name and various splinterings before Robert Menzies welded the broken pieces back together in 1944.

Menzies insisted that it be named the Liberal Party, not the Conservative Party, as in Britain. At its formal launch in Sydney, he declared: 'Liberalism proposes to march down the middle of the road.' At its inaugural meeting in Canberra, he warned his colleagues: 'On far too many questions we have found our role to be simply that of the man who says "no" … There is no room in Australia for a party of reaction. There is no useful place for a policy of negation.'

Menzies became increasingly conservative as he got older, and became stricken with pain and disability. He wrote to his beloved daughter Heather Henderson: 'I am compelled to recognise that the world has moved on, and that I perhaps have not moved with it'. But when he retired as prime minister, respected journalist Alan Reid wrote that to call him a conservative was to stretch the meaning of the word to the limit. 'On his record, probably the most accurate description of him within the framework of domestic politics is that he is a cautious reformer', Reid wrote. And the man Menzies wanted to succeed him as the member for Kooyong was Dick Hamer.

In his memoir, *Afternoon Light*, Menzies explains that why he and his colleagues chose to call themselves Liberals:

> We took the name 'Liberal' because we were determined to be a progressive party, willing to make experiments, in no sense reactionary but believing in the individual, his rights and his enterprise, and rejecting the Socialist panacea.

It was Menzies whom the young Dick Hamer admired in politics, and who inspired him to join the Liberal Party. This statement of his aims fits Hamer and his key ministers perfectly. They were Liberals, but reformers. They came from the centre-right of politics, and governed from there. They were modern: far more modern in their outlook than some Liberal leaders today.

The reforms Hamer and his ministers introduced in Victoria have lasted because they responded to permanent shifts in social values: equal opportunity for women, protection of the environment, protection of historic buildings and precincts, protection of consumer rights, promotion of the arts. Hamer was comfortable with driving these reforms, because they enlarged the freedom of the individual, and conserved the best things Victoria had inherited from the past.

Hamer was an instinctive feminist long before feminism became a political force. He encouraged women to enter politics, opened up the Victorian public service to women, and pushed through legislation to abolish sexual discrimination in the workplace, which became a landmark reform when airline tycoon Sir Reginald Ansett was forced to back down on his refusal to hire female pilots.

This reform exemplifies why Hamer matters to Liberals today. It embodied the principle of freedom: freedom of opportunity for women. Yet his was the only Liberal government to pass such legislation. His contemporary in Western Australia, Sir Charles Court, blocked repeated private member's bills to provide equal opportunity in WA. In 1983, Tasmania's Liberal premier, Robin Gray, even abolished the office of the state's equal-opportunity advisor.

Similarly, Hamer was an instinctive environmentalist. For him, it was entirely natural that a conservative party should act to conserve the best of the environment, and to head off environmental damage before it happens. The Conservative Party in the United Kingdom has done just that in moving strongly to tackle global warming, as have its counterparts on the centre-right in France, Germany, the Netherlands, and most of Europe. Only in the United States, Canada, and Australia is global warming a left/right issue.

Hamer backed an outstanding conservation minister, Bill Borthwick, in making his Liberal government the nation's leader on environmental legislation and practice: from tackling pollution, to reviewing the whole state to set aside a critical mass of each ecosystem as national parks, and in making environmental-impact studies mandatory for major developments. An equally outstanding planning minister, Alan Hunt, used both guile and the law to protect the best of state's built heritage, and to implement Hamer's 'green wedges' policy of channelling Melbourne's fringe development along areas served by rail.

As a minister, Hamer had already won a protracted battle to stop the Housing Commission demolishing Melbourne's inner-suburban terraces to build high-rise flats. As premier, he met a resurgent Labor Party head-on by himself leading the reforms that Liberal governments too rarely make: legalising homosexual behaviour, abolishing the death penalty, and massively expanding funding for the arts and cultural facilities.

He and his team left many legacies to Melbourne: the underground rail loop, the Victorian Arts Centre, the Eastern Freeway, the freeway linking the Monash Freeway to City Link, the big outer-suburban parks along the Yarra, Maribyrnong, and Dandenong Creek, and the start of the network of bike paths and parks down the city's creeks.

Hamer was a human being, and thus imperfect. Like many leaders, he stayed on too long. He was too willing to trust others, and sometimes that trust was abused; his post-political life shows a surprising commercial naivety beneath his political savvy. He was reluctant to give offence, and could be less than frank at such times; he spent too little time with the team he led, and had no real interest in economics. This book does not try to present him as anything but a real person, who was elected to lead a government and to grapple with the myriad issues that those years produced.

What does stand out about Dick Hamer is that he was genuine. He thought for the long term, and governed for the future as well as the present. He cared about society, and the way it held together. He made Victoria a better place for all who came after him.

Acknowledgements

This book had its genesis in another time. In 1979, the editor of *The Age*, Michael Davie, asked me to write a 2,000-word profile of the premier, Dick Hamer, for the paper's state-election coverage. I warned him that Hamer's daughter Sarah and her husband, John Brenan, were close friends of mine; he thought that would not get in my way. Hamer duly gave me a long interview one Saturday at his home. I worked hard on the article, and it received appreciative reviews. 'Why don't you write a biography of him?' some people suggested. I thought about it, looked at all the other things I was already doing, and decided to leave it for someone else.

Some 30 years later, at dinner one night, Sarah mentioned that no one had ever written a biography of her father. Hamer himself twice drew up outlines for an autobiography, but went no further. In the 1980s, a young Louise Asher began work on a biography, but then took a job in Sydney as research officer to future New South Wales Liberal leader Peter Collins. Her work on the book stopped and, ultimately, as her own political career developed wings, she passed on her material to Christopher Sexton, a young lawyer who had just written an acclaimed biography of the microbiologist Macfarlane Burnet. Sexton himself had known Hamer at Trinity College in the 1980s, where Hamer, a Fellow of the college, sometimes dined after his retirement. Sexton went on to conduct some hours of interviews with Hamer, but decided he didn't want to write an official biography. Later, Hamer's elder daughter, Julia, recorded many hours of interviews with her father when he was in his early eighties, but mostly about his life before he entered politics.

After that dinner with the Brenans, early in 2009, I thought hard. The Hamer years had transformed Victoria. They marked the transition between its past and its present, for a variety of reasons, but one of them was the lasting impact made by Hamer's own priorities and style. Malcolm Turnbull was then federal leader of the Liberal Party, and Ted Baillieu its state leader. Both were liberals, broadly in the same political stream as Hamer. I thought it might be useful to see what lessons Hamer's career held for other liberals who led the Liberal Party. The year 2010 was full of elections, but I arranged to take several months off in 2011; in my ignorance, I thought that would be enough time to research and write the book.

This turned out to be the first of four long breaks, amounting to a year of full-time work. There were mountains of material for me to read and to digest, dozens of people to interview, and vast amounts of material to be collated and ordered into a coherent story that could hold a reader's interest. I quickly realised that this would not be a work of political theory, but an empirical study of one individual who was the product of his genes, his times, his family, and all the influences on him. I wished for more time. I envied Robert Caro, who has spent the last 40 years researching and writing his still-unfinished biography of US president Lyndon Baines Johnson; his fifth and final volume is yet to come. I have left many fields unploughed; the Public Records Office of Victoria finally made Hamer government papers available in 2013, too late to be much help to me, and I would have loved to have had time to read the records of the Victorian Liberal Party, now in the University of Melbourne's archives. I suspect they could be valuable in helping us understand how political parties really work.

Instead, I spent many hours at the National Library reading thousands of pages of the diaries of Peter Howson, a former federal minister and a prominent insider in Victorian Liberal politics from the 1950s to the 1980s. Howson has not had a good press, but his disciplined habit of recording his thoughts on events every night meant that, as Professor Alan (A.G.L.) Shaw told him in 1973, all future historians of his period will owe him a debt. I am very conscious of mine.

Many people generously shared their thoughts and memories of Dick Hamer with me. I would like to thank Richard Alston, Louise Asher, Ted Baillieu, Bruce Baskett, Bill Baxter, Gracia Baylor, John Bayly, Dame Beryl Beaurepaire, Muffie Borthwick, Steve Bracks, Allison Brouwer, Alan Brown, Murray Byrne, John Cain, Sue Calwell, Joan Chambers, Philip Chubb, Jim Clarke, Geoff Coleman, Brian Costar, Digby Crozier, Brian Dixon, Trisha Dixon, Bernie Dunn, Bill Ebery, Eugene Falk, Warwick Forge, Brian Goldsmith, Harry Gordon, Phil Gude, Jim Guest (surgeon), James Guest (ex-MLC), Athol Guy, John Haddad, Ian Hamilton, Bob Hare, Tom Harley, Don Hayward, Charles Hider, Ralph Howard, Neville Hughes, Alan Hunt, Glyn Jenkins, Barry Jones, Brian Joyce, Jeff Kennett, Yolanda Klempfner, Rob Knowles, Prue Leggoe, Jane Lennon, Lou Lieberman, Peter McArthur, Daryl McClure, Frank McGuire, Robert Maclellan, Ian Macphee, Fay Marles, Richard Mulcahy, Robert Murray, John Poynter, Bruce Reid, Peter Ross-Edwards, Christopher Sexton, Lawrie Shears, Dennis Simsion, Russell Skelton, Haddon Storey, Ted Tanner, John Taylor, Noel Tennison, Richard Thomas, Murray Thompson, Yvonne Thompson, Noel Turnbull, Robin Usher, Evan Walker, Graeme Weideman, David White, and David Yencken for the time and hospitality they gave me in remembering the events and impressions they formed so many years ago. Writing this list, it saddens me that Murray Byrne, Alan Hunt, and Peter Ross-Edwards, three men I greatly respected, are no longer here to see the book their memories helped me write.

Several favours were of enormous help. Muffie Borthwick lent me her husband's entire collection of *Hansard* from 1972 to 1981. On issues about which my memory had rusted away, or which I had never understood in the first place, time and again Bill's set of *Hansards* proved invaluable as a document of the key issues of the time, of the details, and the nuances of positions taken by different sides. Bruce Baskett, state political correspondent of *The Herald* from

1972 to 1977, lent me his scrapbooks of everything he wrote in those years, which helped clarify many issues. Tom Harley lent me his papers from the period. Sadly, Louise Asher's research material from the 1980s was lost somewhere in the sands of time. But Christopher Sexton passed on his interviews with Hamer in the 1990s to me, and has kindly allowed me to quote from them. My parents-in-law, Frank and Norah Toohey, gave me a welcoming home away from home on my frequent trips to Melbourne. I am very grateful to all of them.

Ian Smith, whose public criticism of Hamer precipitated his early retirement, politely declined to be interviewed. I am grateful to Jim Clarke, the then editor of the *Warrnambool Standard*, for giving me a recording of his fateful interview with Smith.

Authors traditionally thank the staff of the libraries they have worked in, and I thank the librarians of the National Library of Australia, the State Library of Victoria, and the Public Records Office of Victoria for their help. It is less traditional to thank online sources of information; but these days, they are equally important to an author. I had a lot of help from the Parliament of Victoria's biographies of former MPs at parliament.vic.gov.au/re-member; and from the *Australian Dictionary of Biography*, at adb.anu.edu.au. Two sites were invaluable: the National Library's wonderful search engine for newspapers and books, Trove, at trove.nla.gov.au — and Wikipedia, surely one of the greatest philanthropic ventures of our time.

For more than 40 years, including Hamer's time as premier and deputy premier, I was a journalist on *The Age*, and I am deeply in its debt for the opportunities it gave me, and for its help in writing this book. In those days my beats ranged from state politics to environmental and planning issues, investigative reporting, and editorial commentary. I had several long interviews with Hamer at his home for *The Age*. It was typical of him that while my reporting often caused him problems, especially on the Housing Commission land deals, he never held it against me, but accepted that it was a journalist's job to hold governments to account. I have plagiarised my old articles shamelessly for this book. John Langdon, Maria Paget, and Michelle Stillman of *The Age* library gave me invaluable assistance in locating files and photographs, even though we never found the delightful Tandberg cartoon we were looking for.

Henry Rosenbloom, my friend from university days, agreed to publish the book for the public good, although it will probably not pay its way. For his generosity, support, and understanding of the countless delays which prolonged its writing well past two deadlines, I will always be grateful.

I am also conscious of old debts. The two ministers I dealt with most in the Hamer years were Bill Borthwick, the minister for conservation, and Alan Hunt, the minister for planning. Starting out as a sceptic, I grew to admire both of them deeply. In different ways, they were shrewd, honest, passionate men: men of principle who had their feet on the ground, cared about ordinary people, and cared about the future. They knew the limits of what was possible, but they thought and acted for the long-term good of Victorians, not for short-term political gain. To me they epitomised what was best about the Hamer government. They set the standard by which I have judged all ministers since.

This is not an official biography. Nonetheless, the Hamer family was most helpful in providing me with memories, photographs, and materials. I am especially grateful for the time I spent with Lady April Hamer: she was eternally self-deprecating, eternally generous. The early chapters of this book rely heavily on the hours of interviews that Julia Hamer recorded with her father in the late 1990s; this would be a lesser book without her invaluable contribution. Sarah Brenan scanned the four volumes of diaries her father wrote between 1939 and 1941, and sent them to me. Nothing has added more to my understanding of Dick Hamer than the 1,160 pages of those diaries, which are a free and frank record of his life and thinking. Julia and Sarah, their brothers Chris and Alastair Hamer, Dick's sister-in-law Barbara Hamer, son-in-law John Brenan, and niece Kate Patrick all read drafts of the early chapters and gave me valuable insights into Dick and the Hamer family. I am equally grateful to John Haddad, Haddon Storey, and Richard Thomas, who read various chapters of the book and made helpful comments.

Sarah Brenan, my old friend Sal, has been my guide and inspiration in writing this book. Without her, it would not have been written. I hope it justifies her trust.

Last, but never least, I thank Mary Toohey for her patience, forbearance, love, and understanding over the years in which this book has claimed most of my spare time. Mary, you may now have your husband back.

***

For this paperback edition, minor corrections have been made where errors have been found. I am grateful to Brian Goldsmith, the nightclub owner who became Hamer's best friend in his years after politics, for pointing out that it was Hamer himself who decided they should pour money into jojoba bean plantations — a decision that proved costly for them both. Dr John Dwyer, counsel for the pilot Deborah Lawrie (then Wardley), corrected the record on her legal battle with Sir Reginald Ansett.

Introduction

On 12 September 1972, in the ornate green chamber of Victoria's Legislative Assembly, a new premier rose to deliver the state's budget. He looked unexceptional — a middle-aged man of medium height, in a grey suit with a blue tie, his dark hair brushed back and starting to grey. Yet what he had to say was very different from the budget speeches delivered by any Victorian premier before him:

> In the last two decades the world has seen perhaps the most dramatic period of growth in terms of the development of resources and rising material living standards in the whole of the history of mankind. Yet more and more the world over, people are calling into question the validity of this material growth as an end in itself. Growth for what, and at what cost, are the questions people — and in particular, young people — are asking. What is the profit, they say, in steadily expanding and improving man's supply of material things, if the things of the spirit are dimmed, and the very environment in which we live is threatened?
>
> These are proper questions for all of us. Indeed, it is not for the first time in the history of man that they are being asked, although the urgency of the asking is perhaps greater. Economists gave us the concept of 'Gross National Product', and interest has centred on the rate at which that grows. Is it time to think more about 'Gross National Wellbeing'? Is it time that our proper concern with growth

> should be tempered with a greater emphasis on the very essence of the quality and purpose of life itself — of the relationship of man to his environment and the world in which he lives? …
>
> The quality of living, and the endeavour to preserve the very ability of man to live, must become the increasing concern of all peoples and all Governments. To emphasise quality is not to ignore quantity. It is simply to acknowledge that henceforth the two will need to go hand in hand.[1]

To Victorians, the message was clear: they had a new government, with a new premier. The Liberal Party was still in power, but it was now a different Liberal Party. For 17 years, Victoria had been led by an outspoken, earthy, chain-smoking farmer, Sir Henry Bolte, a pragmatic conservative who embodied the rural Australia of his time. But his was an Australia that was passing. At the federal level, after 23 years in power, the Liberal–Country Party coalition was heading for defeat. A new wave of political values was sweeping across Australia, demanding a new kind of government, with new priorities. In Victoria, the Liberal Party put itself on the crest of that wave, pledging to deliver the new priorities of a new Australia.

The leader that their MPs chose to replace Bolte with could hardly been more different from him. Dick Hamer had served loyally under Bolte as a minister for ten years, but whereas Bolte epitomised the conservative rural wing of the party, Hamer epitomised its liberal urban wing. Bolte loved shooting ducks, betting on the races, and watching sport on TV. Hamer loved the opera, the theatre, and meditative walks in parks. Bolte had left school early, and became a farmer. Hamer won the Supreme Court prize as dux of the Melbourne University law school, and became senior partner in a city law firm. Bolte was shrewd, incisive, authoritarian, gregarious, rough, and at times bullying, and had been forged with old Australian values and prejudices. Hamer was trusting and tolerant, a private man, gentle and invariably courteous, cosmopolitan, always open to new ideas. As future Labor minister Race Mathews put it, 'It felt like a change of government without a change of party.'

This book is about that government, and the man who led it. Dick Hamer was to be premier of Victoria for almost nine years. He became the man who set the state on a new direction — one which (the Kennett years aside) it has been on ever since. In his low-key way, as much by his personal example as by his use of power, he fostered a new political culture in Victoria — one that spread tolerance, inclusiveness, love of the arts, and concern for the environment, good planning, and looking after those in need. Hamer belonged to the Liberal Party, but he was essentially a politician of the centre.

The phrase that epitomised his priorities was 'the quality of life'. Hamer and his government changed laws and planning schemes to conserve the best of Melbourne's old buildings, its inner suburbs of terrace houses, the forests of the Dandenongs, and the farmland and bush of the Yarra Valley and Mornington Peninsula. He ended the city's sprawl, fostering the growth of regional cities, and channelling Melbourne's outer-suburban growth along defined corridors around railway lines, and separated by 'green wedges' of farms and bushland. With the Board of Works, his government created large new parks in the outer suburbs, and bike paths along the creeks and rivers. He built the theatres and concert hall of the Arts Centre on the Yarra's south bank, and regional arts centres and galleries throughout the state. He subsidised artists and performances, local history and libraries, care services for the elderly, and groups restoring local environments: he encouraged volunteers to do what the state could not afford to do. His government removed the laws against homosexuality, and the laws that allowed hangings. He helped to make Melbourne and Victoria a centre for things of the mind.

His leadership also saw a remarkable change in style. Bolte and his longtime deputy, partner, and tower of strength, Sir Arthur Rylah, loved to verbally rough up their opponents. Hamer never did that; indeed, until he was under pressure in later years, he rarely criticised the Labor Party at all. He preferred to campaign on his own merits, trusting that voters would make their own comparisons, and prefer him and his party. Bolte would overstate his case; Hamer would understate his. It was an unusual style in politics, and one that won respect and affection across the political spectrum. Steve Bracks, the Labor premier from 1999 to 2007, in some ways followed Hamer's style of government with similar success. There were strong echoes of it also in the understated style of a future Victorian Liberal premier, Ted Baillieu.

Much went wrong in the later years of Hamer's government, as we shall see. Yet Hamer was an unusually successful politician. He won three consecutive elections, the first two with record majorities — lifting the Liberal vote far higher than it had ever been in Bolte's time — until the enthusiasm that had greeted the new leader wore away. Party unity began to crack, and eventually to shatter. Victorians liked Hamer personally, but many concluded that as a leader he was too diffident, too much the instinctive democrat to assert authority. A continuing scandal over Housing Commission land purchases eroded voters' confidence. Factors beyond his control ended the long economic boom: factories shut down, and unemployment and inflation rose. Hamer won a third election in 1979, but only just avoided being forced into a coalition government with the National Party. The premier tried to tackle the worsening economic conditions, but failed to persuade either his party or the community to support his solutions: a casino-cum-convention centre in Melbourne, a plan to turn the Latrobe Valley's brown coal into oil, and a subsidised power price to attract Alcoa's aluminium smelter to Portland. As Labor lifted its game to provide a credible alternative, Liberal ministers and backbenchers grew restive, and frustrated ambitions rose to the top. A senior minister issued a suicidal challenge to the premier's authority, and Hamer decided to retire early, in conditions that would have been humiliating were it not for the extraordinary dignity he displayed at the lowest point of his career.

Most political careers end in a fall. But Dick Hamer's fall saw an outpouring of public emotion, even anger. How could this most decent of men have been treated so badly by his own side, people asked, after all he had done for the state? More than 1,000 letters poured in to Dick and April Hamer from Victorians grateful for what he had stood for: decency, fairness, openness, and far-sighted planning for the future. This most gentle of political leaders had changed Victoria, by his example, as well as by his policies. Bolte's Victoria now seems the Victoria of another age. Hamer's Victoria is the Victoria of today. His government was a turning point in the state's history, and in its character.

Hamer's political career ended in 1981, but his public life continued for another generation. His last political statement was a letter to *The Age* at Christmas 2003, urging the Howard government to release asylum-seekers from mandatory detention. One day in March 2004, aged 87, he took a siesta after lunch, and never woke up. Victorians from all sides of politics expressed their admiration for a man who seemed to embody much of what Melbourne was about: a city of the arts; a city of many cultures; a city of parks and gardens; a city of tolerance and creativity. Premier Steve Bracks, another courteous, understated leader from the political centre, named the city's concert hall Hamer Hall, as a lasting memorial to the leader who built it. To many who see politics as a grubby, second-rate theatre of mudslinging and opportunism, Dick Hamer's example and dedication to the public good seem to shine out as a lighthouse of idealism.

It is to explore this man and his legacy that this book has been written. It is not a hagiography: as readers will find, I see him as a man not perfect, but admirable. Walk out into Melbourne today, and it bears his imprint. But what shaped his values, to make them so different? How did he, a liberal, get elected to lead a solidly conservative party? Does his career hold lessons for us today, or was it just the product of his own times?

To help answer those questions, the book takes a detour into Victorian political history, some of which is now virtually forgotten. But I have long felt that to understand Hamer's approach as premier, you had to understand Bolte, the old leader he was reacting against. And to understand Bolte, and the importance he placed on loyalty, you had to understand the lessons he drew from the 30 years of instability that preceded him, as well as the background to the Labor Party split that helped keep him in office for 17 years.

It is a surprising fact that, 40 years after Hamer became premier, he remains the last Liberal premier anywhere in Australia to have won three elections in a row. To do so was more difficult for him than for his predecessors, because he was premier during a time of dramatic social transformation. In his time, Australia passed from an era of conservative hegemony — think of Sir Robert Menzies in Canberra, Bolte in Victoria, Sir Robert Askin in New South Wales, Sir Frank Nicklin and Sir Joh Bjelke-Petersen in Queensland, Sir Thomas Playford in South Australia, Sir David Brand in Western Australia — to one of Labor dominance, particularly at state level. In the 30-plus years since Hamer retired, the only Liberal who has lasted eight years as leader of a government is John Howard. Labor has had seven of them: Neville Wran, John Cain, John Bannon, Bob Hawke, Bob Carr, Peter Beattie, and Mike Rann.

The reason for the conservative hegemony in the late 1950s and 1960s was obvious: the Labor Party split in two, and it took half a generation for the impact of that split to fade. But why Labor has become so dominant at state level since 1980 is a question that has received too little serious analysis. This book is not the place for it, but one lesson that leaps out of the Bolte–Hamer era is that, in its prime, the Liberal Party was a broad church — broad enough to embrace Bolte and Hamer in turn as its leaders. Its leaders were men (almost all of them) who came into politics after wartime service in the military, followed by successful careers in business, a profession, or on the land. They learned the lessons of life through war and practical experience — not as career conservatives who joined the right wing of student politics at university, and then became professional political apparatchiks. The Liberals of old were doers, who came from the mainstream of society. Their party was a party of the centre-right, which drew as much of its inspiration from the centre as from the right. Deakin, Bruce, Menzies, Bolte, Fraser, Hamer: in different ways, they all exemplify this. This book is the story of how one of the finest in that tradition came to lead the party, and what he did when he was given that chance.

Part I

Before Politics

CHAPTER ONE

Beginnings

Dick Hamer was born into a world of privilege. Relative to other Victorians, even relative to other Victorian premiers, he grew up surrounded by the good things of life. His main childhood home was in St Georges Road, Toorak, one of Melbourne's most affluent streets, in a house with almost as many servants as family members. His brother David admitted that he (David) didn't know how to make a bed until he got married. Dick grew up as the oldest son in a large and loving family. He was given the best education Australia could offer, studying first at Melbourne Grammar's junior school, then as a boarder at Geelong Grammar, and finally in the law school of the University of Melbourne. In an age when beach houses were rare, his family built their own at Frankston, and had it landscaped by the great Edna Walling. His summers were spent mucking about there, or sailing with cousins at their beach house in Portsea. His diary as a young lawyer records a delightfully busy upper-middle-class life, in which work and study mingled with an endless stream of parties, dinner dances, nights at concerts, the theatre, films, and the ballet, and weekends on the links at the Royal Melbourne Golf Club. When he graduated as dux of the Melbourne University law school, winning the Supreme Court prize, his parents rewarded him by buying him a new car. When he signed up for World War II, he quickly became an officer.

But privilege is only part of the story of Dick Hamer's formative years. From his family, and from his school and university, he also learned an ethic of community service. And a household of four bright children, not to mention his peers at Geelong Grammar and the university, placed him in a highly competitive environment. Family, church, school, university, and sibling rivalry nurtured in the Hamer children the values of hard work, self-discipline, sympathy for others, and personal integrity.

Their father, Hubert Hamer, was a successful lawyer, the senior partner in the city law firm of Smith and Emmerton. Yet Hubert's father had died when he was 15, forcing him to leave school to find work. Hubert's main client was the Commercial Bank of Australasia, which he served as legal advisor for decades; but he also worked tirelessly on a pro bono basis, doing unpaid legal work for hospitals and charities. His wife, Nancy, was vice-president of the Queen Victoria Hospital for 40 years, then briefly president before handing over to her daughter-in-law Margaret, who was its president for a decade until it was merged into the Monash Medical Centre. Nancy was an ambitious, talented woman, a generation younger than her husband, who channelled her energy into charity work. Yet she had grown up as an orphan, brought up successively by her grandmother and two aunts, always the extra child in a family with her cousins. Hubert and Nancy's children became achievers with a strong streak of social responsibility. All four became successful in their fields. Two, Dick and David, went into politics, where they shunned point-scoring and focussed on policies.

The Hamers were not rich: theirs was an upper-middle-class family whose money came from work, not inherited wealth. Yet there was something of *noblesse oblige* about their values. They typified many families who gave time, money, and energy to build the great institutions of Melbourne and other cities. Dick used to say that he and his siblings were brought up to believe that 'to make a living wasn't all there is to life'. It was important to look after themselves, certainly, but it was also important to look after the community they lived in. Their uncles included one of Melbourne's most remarkable doers, George Swinburne, a successful engineer who introduced gas and hydraulic pumps to Melbourne, but later gave away much of his fortune to found (and fund) the technical college that is now Swinburne University. Swinburne's close friend Sir William McPherson, an industrialist-turned-politician, decided as premier in 1928 that the state could not afford to pay for Nancy Hamer's request for a new wing for the Queen Victoria Hospital. Instead, McPherson decided to pay for it himself — provided that she and the hospital kept it secret until after the coming state election, lest anyone think he had done it to buy votes.

Many Australians, rich, middling, and poor, lived by the same values. In an age when we look to government to provide the services the community needs, we forget that in earlier times those services were provided by the generosity of individual Australians giving their own time and money. There is no better example of this than the Queen Victoria, which absorbed the energies of three generations of the Hamer family. In the 1880s and 1890s, as the first generation of women doctors in Melbourne emerged from university, they found themselves shunned by the conservative male doctors who ran the hospitals. Women doctors were denied career opportunities, so they decided to set up their own hospital. Dick's grandmother Sarah Hamer joined the inaugural committee, which set up a 'Women's Shilling Fund', to which all women were asked to donate a shilling (10 cents in those days, but more like $10 today in buying power), or more if they could afford it. The appeal won widespread support after Queen Victoria 'expressed her personal wish that all funds raised for the occasion [of her Diamond Jubilee in 1897] should be used for the welfare of women and children'. Boosted by Her Majesty's wish, the appeal raised £3,162/11/9 — enough to buy a vacant city building and equip it as a hospital. The 'Queen Vic' became the first hospital in the British Empire to be 'run by women, for women'. Successive appeals to the public developed it into one of the major hospitals of Melbourne, and it kept expanding until the old era of honorary medical work gave way to state-funded health care, and it became part of the new Monash Medical Centre.

The important role of philanthropy and volunteers in the development of Melbourne's institutions is outside the scope of this book. The Hamer/Swinburne family was just one of many that contributed to it. And in the Hamer family's history, one can see an evolution from religious idealism to civic idealism.

Dick Hamer inherited English ancestry on his father's side; Scots, on his mother's. The Hamers were a Lancashire family, centred around Bolton, north-west of Manchester. In the early 19th century, Dick's great-grandfather Samuel Hamer moved to the expanding northern suburbs of London to pursue his business and his two great interests: music, and the Congregational Church. He married the daughter of a renowned Congregationalist minister, the Rev. William Jones, of Bolton. Their son, Daniel Jones Hamer, born on 14 February 1844, inherited his father's love of music and the church.

The Congregationalists were a small non-conformist denomination with a distinctive belief in religious democracy. Each congregation ran itself. The church was a federation of autonomous congregations. Not surprisingly, its members became pioneers in social progress. Harvard University was founded by Congregationalists, early settlers in Boston who wanted to train ministers who could show them the way to a better world. In Australia, the Congregationalists became the first church to ordain female ministers. In 1977, most of the congregations merged with the Presbyterians and Methodists to create the Uniting Church of Australia, although a small number remain independent.

At the age of 17, Daniel Jones Hamer left his job in his father's firm to study theology in Lancashire, aided by scholarships. He went to Cambridge, taking out a degree in music, and then launched himself into the world as a Congregationalist minister. He became a rising young force as a preacher, organist, composer, and ardent campaigner for removing the special privileges of the Church of England (the cause known as disestablishmentarianism). Where other ministers recoiled from broader political issues, Daniel flung himself into them, becoming a strong supporter of Gladstone's Liberal Party. A tribute published after his death noted that: 'Mr Hamer took an active part in all the movements of his time — social, municipal and political — which seemed to him to tend towards progress.' He was particularly committed to the campaign to give all adult males the right to vote — a basic right granted in 1848 in France, and in 1857 for Victoria's Legislative Assembly, yet resisted in Britain until 1919. He later told his Melbourne flock that by the time he left England, he had only one Tory left in his congregation, 'and he was a fair way to conversion'. How that was received in conservative Collins Street was not recorded.

Daniel married Sarah Harman, a young woman from Kent slightly older than himself. As we have seen already, Sarah Hamer, too, had strong views, and later became politically active. They had two children: Ethel, born in 1868, and Hubert, born in 1870. Daniel was a minister in Wolverhampton, in the West Midlands, when his growing reputation led to an invitation from the other side of the world: the wealthy congregation of the Collins Street Independent Church in Melbourne, Australia, invited him to be its new minister. After some soul-searching, he accepted, in part because he thought that Hubert's health would benefit from Australia's warmer climate.

He arrived in March 1882, aged 38, to take up the most important position in his church in what was then Australia's most important city. Victoria was growing rapidly, and had close to a million inhabitants, almost half of them living in its booming capital. It was the decade of 'marvellous Melbourne'. Grand new buildings, public and private, including St Paul's Cathedral, were rising in the city. The Paris end of Collins Street was largely created in the 1880s. New suburbs sprawled out along the rapidly growing railway lines, leading to a frenzy of speculation that would end in disaster in the 1890s. The Independent Church itself (these days, renamed as St Michael's) stood proudly on the corner of Collins and Russell streets, its polychrome brickwork a mark of modernity compared with its beautiful but more old-fashioned neighbours, the Scots Church opposite and the Baptist Church halfway down the hill. All three were designed by Joseph Reed, the great architect of 19th-century Melbourne, who created many of the landmarks of those exuberant times: the Melbourne Town Hall, the Exhibition Buildings, Rippon Lea, the old ANZ Bank building on Queen Street, and Ormond College, to name a few.

Politically, Victoria in 1882 had finally put to rest the bitter war that had raged for two decades between radicals and conservatives over tariffs to protect industry, and land reform to break the squatters' grip. The shrewd leadership of James Service had brought both sides together in a coalition government that accepted the radicals' changes, and shifted the focus to developing the city and the state. It was a time of wealth, optimism, and rapid change.

The Rev. Jones Hamer, as he was known, was strongly sympathetic to Australia's democratic ethos. But in other respects, he found himself out of tune with the times, and with his congregation. An intense, educated, puritanical man, he waged a campaign around Australia against the widespread practice of running raffles and bazaars to raise funds for new church buildings. In an articulate speech that was widely reprinted, he raised the bar for his flock very high, warning them against fundraising methods that 'involve the principle of gambling, and are utterly demoralising and discreditable'. 'The success attending such attempts,' he wrote, 'is more fatal than failure, because it hinders the growth of true feeling and conviction.' One suspects that his grandson, who was to stake his premiership on trying to build a casino in Melbourne, would have disagreed, politely but firmly.

The Rev. Hamer also stirred up widespread controversy by denouncing mixed education. This was an issue that Victoria had settled a decade earlier, when the Francis government's Education Bill of 1872 ended support for church schools to establish its own system in which primary education would be 'free, compulsory and secular'. The Rev. Hamer reopened the debate, declaring to the Congregational Union that educating boys and girls in mixed schools was 'a fruitful source of evil'. He became the talk of the town when he claimed that 11 children had presented to a doctor in a single day 'suffering the effects of immorality'. The newspapers tried in vain to find a doctor who would corroborate this claim. The Rev. Jones Hamer declined to present his evidence, citing confidentiality, and instead widened his attack. At a meeting of the Society for the Promotion of Morality, chaired by the chief justice, Sir William Stawell, he moved:

> That this meeting, strongly impressed with the conviction that more stringent legislation in the interest of public health and morality is imperatively necessary, would respectfully urge the Government to initiate such legislation early in the next session of Parliament.[1]

The motion was seconded by the retired headmaster of Melbourne Grammar School, Dr J.E. Bromby, and passed unanimously. One wonders what the canny James Service made of it. The mover's own grandson, as premier almost a century later, would have raised a quizzical eyebrow and moved on to the next item.

But grandfather and grandson were never to meet. The Rev. Jones Hamer drove himself hard to live up to his own high standards as well as his responsibilities as the leader of his church in Victoria. Late in 1885, he suffered a physical breakdown. On doctors' advice, and his congregation's pressure, he was persuaded to take a long holiday with his family. He sailed with them to New Zealand to recuperate, but, only six weeks later, he contracted pneumonia in Rotorua, and died there on 7 March 1886. He was just 42.

His death deprived his children of their father and their means of support. In a subtly critical obituary, the *Illustrated Australian News* noted that 'since he resided in Melbourne, Mr Hamer was continuously in receipt of £1,400 per annum, the largest salary paid to any minister of his rank in the colony'. It praised his intellect, intense earnestness, and unsparing sense of duty. But it also reported that 'he had failed to inspire that profound feeling of affectionate appreciation' enjoyed by his Church of England counterpart, Bishop Moorhouse. Church attendance at Collins Street had fallen, it said, in part because 'he had a habit of thought which was somewhat too profound for any but students to thoroughly grasp', leading to him 'impressing the few without attracting the many'.His followers, however, mourned him deeply, and published a posthumous volume of his sermons under the title *Salt and Light*. They praised his habit of appealing to his listeners' intellect and spirituality rather than to their emotions; his work for missions; and, in particular, his efforts to combat religious scepticism and to 'guard the young against being carried away by its fallacies'.

The death of her husband left Sarah Hamer with two teenage children, far from her own family. Her first need was to find another source of income to help pay the bills, so she decided to take in a lodger at their house in Kensington Road, South Yarra. The successful applicant was a young engineer fresh from England, who, with his uncle, had come to introduce Melbourne to the new technologies of gas and hydraulic power. His name was George Swinburne.

Let us detour briefly to meet one of the most engaging of the men who made Melbourne what it is. Tall, gangly, prodigiously bright, voraciously interested in everything, well organised, and persuasive, Swinburne grew up in Newcastle-on-Tyne. He never went to university, but learned engineering as an apprentice, then moved to London to work with his uncle, John Coates, on the new technologies that were transforming Western cities: gas, which lit city streets, and hydraulic power, which pumped water stored underground to power lifts in city buildings. In 1886 they moved to Melbourne, where their business proved a roaring success. Their underground network of water pipes enabled the young city to start building upwards; by 1889 the APA insurance company had built a 53-metre-high 12-storey building on the corner of Elizabeth Street and Flinders Lane: on one report, it was initially the third-tallest building in the world. Coates then moved to Canada, but Swinburne stayed in Melbourne, where he headed the Colonial Gas Association, became chairman of the National Mutual insurance house, joined the Collins House group of mining investors, pursued a range of business interests, and became one of the founders of the State Electricity Commission, helping to pioneer the work that turned Victoria's wet brown coal into a fuel able to power the state.

Swinburne chose to stay on in Melbourne because he had fallen in love with his landlady's daughter, the young Ethel Hamer. On 17 February 1890, they were married in the Collins Street Independent Church. They bought a large, luxurious home, 'Shenton', in Kinkora Road, Hawthorn, set in a big garden, including a tennis court and putting green. Sarah eventually moved in nearby, and 'Shenton' became the centre of Hamer family life for decades.

And Swinburne went into politics. Initially, he stood for Hawthorn council in protest against its reckless plan to generate its own electricity, which Swinburne argued would be small-scale and expensive. He was soon mayor, and then, from 1901 to 1913, MLA for Hawthorn. In 1904 he formed an unlikely partnership with Sir Thomas Bent, a leader widely seen as unprincipled, vulgar, and corrupt — 'Bent by name, bent by nature' — and yet, Swinburne's biographer Sir Frederic Eggleston argues persuasively, a rather more complex, shrewd, and successful premier than his reputation suggests.[2]

Swinburne became his minister for agriculture and water supply, and set about planning sweeping reforms to Victoria's water industry. The long Federation Drought hit Victoria hard. The state had few large water storages and hundreds of small, inefficient local authorities. Private landholders owned the streams running past their land, and by now Alfred Deakin's visionary irrigation schemes from the 1880s lay in financial ruin. Swinburne analysed the problems, and decided there was no alternative to radical change: he proposed nationalising all the state's rivers and streams, setting up a central body of experts, the State Rivers and Water Supply Commission, to plan large, low-cost storages, and to lift decision-making from short-term parish-pump priorities to long-term social and economic goals. In many ways, his solution was similar to the reforms advocated by economists today to try to ensure effective decision-making on infrastructure. His plan met with instant resistance, but Swinburne sat down with his opponents to patiently argue his case. Eventually, his trustworthiness, energy, sharp mind, and persuasiveness paid off. He won support from all sides for his blueprint, which was to last Victoria until the 1980s.

The Water Bill done, he turned his attention to Collingwood's infamous SP bookie, John Wren. Swinburne was the driving force behind the Bent government's crackdown on illegal gambling in general, and Wren's Collingwood tote in particular. Wren hit back, financing a relentless but unsuccessful campaign to unseat Swinburne in 1908. As Bent's erratic behaviour finally eroded his support, other

MPs urged Swinburne to take the premiership. He refused: Bent had been loyal to him, and Swinburne's heart was in policy issues, not politics. When Bent fell in 1909, Swinburne fell with him. He was never a minister again.

But he had many other interests to pursue. The most enduring was a plan he and Ethel had devised, after he got talking with some unemployed Richmond youths he encountered on a Saturday-afternoon walk along the Yarra with his close friend Sir William McPherson (whose company, McPherson's Pty Ltd, was Australia's biggest manufacturer of nuts, bolts, and machine tools). The Swinburnes decided to set up a college where unemployed young working-class men could learn the skills that would earn them a living. As Ethel Swinburne put it in a speech she recorded in 1960, at the age of 92: 'The idea we had was to help the young people growing up around us to find the best and fullest way of life.' The Eastern Suburbs Technical College opened its doors in 1909, with a £2,000 donation by the Swinburnes, more from McPherson and other friends, and with George as founding president. It expanded rapidly as students flocked in. Swinburne struck a deal with the government that he and Ethel would pay half the cost of new buildings if the government paid the other half. While Swinburne was overseas in 1913, the council renamed it, against his wishes, as Swinburne Technical College. Over his lifetime, he and Ethel gave roughly £20,000 to the college. It kept growing, and today it is the Swinburne University of Technology, with 32,500 university and TAFE students.

In 1913, Swinburne quit politics, handing his seat to McPherson (who later became Victoria's treasurer and premier). He played a range of roles in business and government, and stood unsuccessfully for the Senate. Then, in 1928, with McPherson as premier fighting to win support for unpopular but necessary belt-tightening measures, Swinburne agreed to help him by standing for the Legislative Council seat of East Yarra. There was, however, already another Nationalist (Liberal) in the field: a brilliant young lawyer, Robert Gordon Menzies, the rising star of the Victorian bar. The party wisely stayed neutral, as the 33-year-old Menzies and the 67-year-old Swinburne fought out a mutually respectful contest. With fears of a financial crisis looming, it was a one-sided contest: Swinburne defeated Menzies by 9,127 votes to 5,461. But his time in the council was short. Just three months later, as he was sitting in the chamber waiting to speak, that fountain of energy suddenly cut out: he collapsed and died in his seat. Amid widespread public grief, Menzies won the by-election to replace him, went straight into the ministry, and in 1930 moved down to the Legislative Assembly. He handed over the East Yarra seat to fellow barrister Clifden Eager, who held it for 28 years until, in 1958, he in turn lost it to Swinburne's nephew, Dick Hamer.

The biography of Swinburne by Eggleston and E.H. Sugden, then Master of Queens College, depicts a man of unusual energy, humanity, curiosity about new things, and the ability to decide what matters most and to do it, or to inspire others to do it. Aptly summed up as 'a practical visionary,' he was a man who would have stood out in any age. Eggleston paints a memorable picture of Swinburne on the move:

> Excessively tall and very thin, no figure was better known in Melbourne's streets; always busy, always in a hurry, striding along at a great pace, with body bent forward, obviously intent on a mission, his despatch case full of papers, he communicated enthusiasm and compelled others to work with him. He would hurry from one interview to another, always brief and businesslike, going rapidly to the point; with his information and the inspiration of his imagination and ideas, he illuminated it and passed on, putting one subject aside as he took up another. What was most impressive was the spring of his mind on to an idea, the rapidity with which he could reduce a tangled mass of facts to a coherent scheme.[3]

And we cannot but warm to the tall, moustachioed, bright-eyed man we farewell at the end of Sugden's final chapter:

> There was always something in him of the eternal boy ... After a visit to him in his home, one came away with the certain knowledge that

> the visit of a friend, however undistinguished, was to him a genuine delight. And as he took you to the door and wrung your hand and said 'So glad to see you, man', you knew that he meant it, as he meant everything he did in his fine and useful life.[4]

Sarah Hamer, who had been widowed earlier, threw herself into doing good works. In an age when government provided few welfare services, she became head of the Victorian Children's Aid Society, and of the local ladies' auxiliary of the London Missionary Society. She taught women's bible classes at the Independent Church, served as vice-president of a charity for needy mothers, and frequently spoke out on women's role in society. She joined the committee of largely feminist women who banded together in 1896 to raise money to build the Queen Victoria Hospital. She later became president of the Hawthorn branch of the Australian Women's National League, a conservative group that eventually merged into the Liberal Party. Sarah became a role model for generations of Hamer women, who were more than usually active in society, more than usually activist in redefining what it meant to be a woman, and more than usually educated, liberal and, in their own way, liberated.

At the time of his father's death, Hubert Hamer was studying at Scotch College, a Presbyterian school, since the Congregationalists had no schools of their own. He was an outstanding student — in 1884, he won every prize in his year — and had set his sights on studying law at Melbourne University. But his father's death forced him to leave school to find work. In July 1886, he began work as an articled clerk to Harry Emmerton, senior partner of the city law firm of J.M. Smith and Emmerton. It was the start of a 40-year partnership between these two men, born a generation apart. In a strange parallel, it was matched by a 40-year partnership between Harry's daughter Mabel, better known as Dame Mabel Brookes, queen of Melbourne society for decades, and Nancy Hamer, Hubert's wife. From the 1930s to 1970, they served as president and vice-president respectively of the Queen Victoria Hospital, over a period in which it grew rapidly.

Hubert made the most of his opportunity at Smith and Emmerton. By day he learned the solicitor's trade, and in the evening he went up to the university to study law in the articled clerks' course. He graduated in 1892, and soon afterwards Emmerton, impressed by his intellect and work ethic, took him into the partnership. He became a respected figure in the Melbourne legal profession, and over time, took over the firm's most important account, as solicitor to the Commercial Bank of Australasia. In 1925–26, he served as president of the Law Institute, and for many years chaired its ethics committee, dealing with ethical breaches and financial failures by lawyers.

Hubert remained a bachelor until his mid-forties, probably due to his shyness and his desire to establish a sound financial foundation before building a family. He became very good at rifle shooting and billiards. In his late teens, he had taken a year off to work on a property in Queensland owned by the Brookes family (who owned Australian Paper Mills, and were clients of the firm), where he developed into a crack shot. Rifle shooting became a passion, as did organising the Hawthorn Rifle Club and the Metropolitan Rifle Clubs Association. He became one of Melbourne's best billiards players: in 1909, he was in the final three in the Victorian amateur championship when he had to pull out to work on an important legal case (in which he represented his brother-in-law George Swinburne in a successful libel suit against *The Age*). He played the organ at the Independent Church; he made a long overseas trip in 1912–13 to see the world; he read and re-read the classic 19th-century British novelists such as Sir Walter Scott, Charles Dickens, and W.M. Thackeray; and he served as honorary legal advisor to the Royal Children's Hospital and other charities. A conservative in a mostly liberal family, he was a man of orderly mind. Dick recalled that his father used to put coloured bands on the legs of his chooks in order to tell them apart.

Dick Hamer remembered his father as 'very conscientious … a very reserved man … a man of almost quixotic high principles'. Hubert was intensely private; a man with little hair and a jowly, brooding face. The prime characteristic that struck other people was his silence. April Hamer, who married Dick, says she never had a real conversation with him in almost a decade of being part of the family. Barbara Hamer (née McPherson, granddaughter of Sir William), who married David Hamer, found him intimidating. 'He was always a rather formidable man,' she says. 'He didn't say very much.' Her most treasured memory of him was that during the war, by then in his mid-seventies, this respected city solicitor spent his spare time making camouflage netting for the troops.

As he became established as a partner, Hubert built himself a house in Kew, but 'Shenton' remained the centre of family life, especially as George and Ethel had four daughters: Muriel, Gwen, Edith, and Margaret. Hubert was a frequent visitor, and gradually became captivated by one of Muriel's friends, Nancy McLuckie. Born in 1890, Nancy was a generation younger than Hubert, and an extrovert with spirit, ambition, and drive. Theirs would be a union of opposites.

Nancy had had a disturbed childhood. Four days after her birth, her mother died from complications of the delivery. Her father, James McLuckie, a police magistrate in north-east Victoria, hired a governess to raise Nancy and her elder sister Jenny, but James too died when Nancy was only three. Her grandmother, Janet Houston McLuckie, a Scottish migrant, then raised the girls at her home in Yarrawonga. But when Nancy was six, her grandmother decided the girls should grow up with children their own age, and sent them to live with her daughter, Jessie Wilson, and her husband and four children. According to family legend, the girls subsequently discovered that their father had invested some money to pay for their education, and insisted they be sent to boarding school in Melbourne. They became boarders at the Presbyterian Ladies College (PLC), then in Victoria Parade where the Dallas Brooks Centre now stands. According to David Hamer's unpublished autobiography, Nancy also moved home again, to spend the holidays with her mother's sister, Mary Palmer, and her Palmer cousins in Geelong. One of them was Rupert Palmer, known as Dick.

At PLC, Nancy became a close friend of Muriel Swinburne. As a boarder, she was often invited out to the Swinburne home, where she also got to know Muriel's uncle Hubert. Slowly, a friendship formed between these two very unlike people. Nancy had excelled at school, but did not even think of going to university — instead studying nursing. Her daughter Alison recounted: 'She survived her first three months spent in an old men's ward, and after that was inured to new experiences.' Eventually, after the resourceful Nancy became a qualified nurse working at the Royal Melbourne Hospital, Hubert proposed. On 3 August 1915, when Nancy was 25, and Hubert almost 45, they married at the St Kilda Presbyterian Church.

Nancy moved into 'Appin', the house Hubert had built in Gellibrand Street, Kew, next to the Kew Gardens on Cotham Road. It was there, on 29 July 1916, that she gave birth to her first child. He was christened Rupert James, but, from the start, he was called Dick. Both his name and his nickname came from Rupert Palmer, Nancy's cousin, who had been killed at Gallipoli on 8 May 1915. Like Nancy, Rupert had moved while still young to Melbourne, where he became a customs agent, and lived in Hawthorn and St Kilda before enlisting. The few possessions found in his kit at Gallipoli included a book of poetry.

Dick was the first of four children. His brother Alan was born just 16 months later, and the two grew up, in Dick's words, 'almost like twins' — although with the older 'twin' setting the rules for their games. Alan went on to become Victoria's Rhodes Scholar in 1938, took out a first-class degree in chemistry at Oxford, was recruited into wartime research of munitions, and wanted to join the RAF, but instead was sent home to develop munitions for Imperial Chemical Industries, as clever chemists were in shorter supply than clever pilots. He spent his life working for ICI, and rose to become its joint managing director in Australia, in an era when it was one of the country's biggest manufacturers. He also became a legend in Melbourne's Real (Royal) Tennis Club, one of the few in the world where the ancient game is still played.

Their younger sister, Alison, who became Alison Patrick, went on to become a post-war pioneer in combining work — teaching history at the University of Melbourne, and carrying out her own research

— with raising four children. That choice was not open to women a generation earlier, but the war had opened up the workforce to them, and she seized the opportunity. In an engagingly frank memoir, 'Born Lucky', published in the anthology *The Half-Open Door*, Alison gives the credit for this to her mother's cleaning lady, Sylvia, who moved in with the Patricks to look after the children. Alison was in her forties before she felt free to accept a full-time position at the university, but then became head of the history department, and her studies of the politics of the French Revolution won praise from scholars worldwide.

The youngest brother, David, born in 1923, left school at 13 to join the navy. He topped his year in naval college, and went off to war in the same convoy that took Dick to the Middle East. In 1944, he was lieutenant on the cruiser HMAS *Australia* when it became the victim of the first-ever kamikaze attack by Japanese pilots. The plane crashed into the bridge of the ship, taking out the captain, senior officers, and navigation system. David, just 21, took command, restored control, got the navigation system working, steered a path to safety, and saved the ship. He was recommended for a Victoria Cross, but this was downgraded to a Distinguished Service Cross after the US warned that awarding the first VC ever to a naval officer would signal to the Japanese how effective their kamikaze attacks had proved. David later fought in the Korean War, became director of Naval Intelligence, and commanded a destroyer squadron before he, too, entered politics. He became the Liberal MP for Isaacs from 1969 to 1974, and from 1975 to 1977, and then a Liberal senator for Victoria from 1978 to 1990, arguing the case particularly for parliamentary reform and stronger accountability. His exceptionally candid *Memories of My Life*, distributed within the family, is invaluable for its entertaining description of the childhood years of these four extremely bright children.

CHAPTER TWO

Childhood

Dick Hamer's childhood seems to have been largely idyllic. Hamer always took a rosy view of life, but the hours of interviews his daughter Julia recorded with him in his early eighties suggest that he grew up happy and innocent, in a world that gave him love and assurance, opportunities to play and learn, and stimulation to develop his thinking and abilities.

His most important relationship in childhood was with his mother, Nancy. Her children agree that she was the dominant personality in a home in which her withdrawn husband provided the income and she provided the direction. 'As far as I can remember, she ran things; my father was a remote figure,' David Hamer recalled. In his disarmingly frank memoir, David painted a complex picture of his mother: supportive yet demanding, ensconced in charity work yet fiercely ambitious, taking no nonsense from her children, yet not without her own vanity. She was christened Elizabeth Annie, and grew up as Lizzie, but cast off that name to become successively Anne, Nan, and finally Nancy. 'She used to suggest that she was born in 1892,' David tells. 'This can't be true, for her mother died on 8 May 1890.' The house next door in Kew was a Catholic hostel that housed unmarried women who had 'got in the family way'. Perhaps to keep her boys from asking unwelcome questions, Nancy persuaded Hubert to move to Toorak. And apart from a year they spent minding 'Shenton' while the Swinburnes went to Europe, Toorak remained her home for the rest of her life.

All who knew Nancy agree that she was a formidable woman, with strong ambitions for her boys. She thrived in an era in which the wives of well-off men ran charities, and raised funds for them by staging balls, garden parties, and other society events to which their friends came and gave generously. You went to their charity do's, and they came to yours. As honorary secretary, committee member, vice-president, and briefly president of the Queen Victoria Hospital over almost half a century, Nancy did a lot of fundraising. In return, this gave her entrée to ministers, to Government House, and to high society. The National Library's Trove website shows that, on average, Nancy was mentioned 20 times a year in the social pages of *The Argus*, Melbourne's conservative morning paper. (That Hubert somehow financed all this, and their children's education, is a tribute to his financial management). In 1955, Nancy's long service to the hospital was recognised with the award of an O.B.E.

She loved her eldest son, and he loved her. As a soldier in the war, the letter home he wrote each week was addressed not to both parents, but to 'Mother'. In his diary, he described his beloved April and his mother as 'the folk nearest my heart'. In his old age, he told his daughter Julia that his mother had been 'a very lovely person. We always thought she was beautiful, and I think in a way she was. She had a remarkable memory: mention a person's name, and she would tell you who they married, how many children they had, and so on.' In the old sense of the term, Nancy was 'socially conscious': she liked having a position in society that meant she knew people who mattered, and she was proud when her boys came to be among them. When Alison's schooldays ended and she 'came out' in society, she was one of the select few whose debutante ball was held at Government House. Dick recalled his mother rising at 5.00 a.m. to polish the blackwood furniture; he speculated that her passion for such things might have been due to growing up an orphan with no home of her own. 'Her main interests were the house, playing bridge with her friends, the Queen Victoria Hospital, and going to social events,' he said. 'She loved to talk, endlessly. She didn't read much, although she liked to be up with the latest novel.'

(Nancy's relationship with Alison, her only daughter, was more complex, judging from Alison's all-too-brief memoir. The mother pushed the daughter to do well, teaching her to read before she went to school, engaging a Frenchwoman to converse with her for an hour a week so she could grow up speaking polished French, and sending her to school nearby at St Catherine's, as it upgraded its academic credentials. Nancy's efforts succeeded too well for her own taste. Alison grew up brainy, not beautiful — not the way her mother wanted her to be. The girl always had her nose in a book, she wanted to have the last word in every argument, and she lacked her mother's looks and social grace. 'There's something you want to remember,' Nancy told Alison in her student days. 'Men don't like clever women.')[1]

Photographs of Nancy, even in her eighties, reveal a woman poised and immaculately dressed. Her daughters-in-law remember her with a certain awe. 'Nancy was very strong, a feisty character, shrewd, and articulate,' April Hamer recalls. 'She talked a lot, and was very outgoing. She had a very strong mind, and, to some extent, Dick modelled himself on her.' Barbara Hamer, David's future wife, who was a toddler when they first met, says Nancy was 'the model lady we all wanted to be. She never seemed to put a foot wrong. Her forte was her charm: she had a knack of making people, even children, feel they were the people she most wanted to see. But she was also machinating: she wanted all her children to "marry well". Money was something of an obsession for her.'

It was while staying at 'Shenton' that Nancy had an experience that must have shaken even her sang-froid. Driving one night along Toorak Road, South Yarra, she knocked down and killed a 21-year-old cyclist. A witness testified that the man appeared to be drunk and was swerving across the road; the doctor who treated him said he smelt strongly of alcohol. The coroner exonerated her from any blame. At the time, Hubert was about to become president of the Law Institute. It appears the children were never told.[2]

Hubert Hamer, by contrast, formed part of the background to his boys' lives. He was 45 when his first son was born, and 53 at the birth of his last. 'My father always seemed to me an old man,' Dick told his daughter Julia. 'I don't remember much, except that he was a presence … They were a wonderful couple, but she had him twisted around her little finger. She ran the house.' David Hamer wrote that: 'In a way, I never had a father, just a sort of grandfather … He did not pay much attention to me.' A thickset, reticent Victorian man, Hubert rarely engaged in the kind of physical play for which fathers are renowned. Occasionally, he joined the boys in backyard cricket on the old asphalt tennis court, or took the elder boys rifle shooting (in which Dick inherited his father's skill; in 1940, training for war in the Adelaide Hills, he came second in a group of 60 soldiers on the shooting range).

Dick's best memory of Hubert was of him reading aloud to his children after dinner. He read them Sir Walter Scott's Waverley novels, thought to be good for boys. 'Dad would read us three or four chapters a night,' Dick told Julia. 'He'd be sitting in a great leather armchair, and we'd be sitting on the floor. It was hard to concentrate —Walter Scott has rolling prose, long sentences … But that was his idea of being a good father: to bring us up on Walter Scott. Later we started doing Dickens.'

Dick thought his father 'old-fashioned' and 'very conservative'. In political arguments around the dinner table, Hubert typically would take a conservative position; Dick, a liberal one. Dick's diary in later years reveals that on some issues his father was quite out of touch; in 1939, he was convinced that King George VI had considerable influence on the choice of ministers in Britain. An article in the *Melbourne University Magazine* so enraged him that he wanted to have the author interned. And while Dick was anti-Hitler, his father was anti-German (although in 1939–40, Dick mused sadly that, among his family and friends, he was the odd one out in seeing Germans as normal people).

Yet Alison's memoir is more sympathetic, showing that Hubert also had a liberal, modern streak:

> Our home environment [was] literate and articulate, although not at all intellectual … Our father insisted on precision in the use of

> words and punctuation; he expected us to ask questions and to be entitled to explanations; he had a very clear mind. In my first week of geometry, he found me trying to learn a theorem by heart, and took the book away. *Never* learn by heart, he said, get a grasp of the argument; and he showed me what it was. But such interventions were rare … He gave us all maximum credit for being able to do or appreciate what he could not … I was his only daughter; many of my interests were beyond him; he watched my career with mild appreciative astonishment.[3]

Both parents held the liberal view that their children should be free to choose their own careers. At the age of 13, David took them at their word and announced that he planned to leave Geelong Grammar School to go to the Naval College. They were aghast, but after Hubert was told there were just 12 places for 390 applicants, they let him sit the entry test. 'My mother says they only let me sit because they didn't think I would get in,' David wrote. He not only got in, but ended up topping his year.

For some years, Hubert headed the Law Institute's ethics committee, and Dick recalled that 'some of the cases he dealt with distressed him greatly'. He and Nancy could be generous: when her former nanny Emma kept being evicted from houses for failing to pay the rent, Hubert bought her a modest cottage for £150, to ensure she would always have a roof over her head.

When the Swinburnes returned in late 1925 after a year overseas, the Hamers moved out of 'Shenton' and back to Toorak. The legendary secretary of the Attorney-General's Department, Sir Robert Garran, who had played a key role in the fight to create a federation, sold them his home at 35 St Georges Road, Toorak. On 1 January 1901, Garran, 33, became Australia's first (and, for a while, only) public servant when Alfred Deakin chose him to head the department and write Australia's first legislation. A quarter of a century later, he became one of the first public-service chiefs to move to the new capital of Canberra. His old home became the Hamers' family home for a decade. While not a large house by Toorak standards, it was, in Alison's affectionate memory, fine for them:

> We lived in a roomy house in Toorak, with a third of an acre of garden: there was a loft above the disused stables, there were lawns and a decayed tennis court for ball games, there were climbable trees. Half a load of bricks, surplus from the garage, had been left by the builders on our parents' instruction — 'the children will use them for something'. We did. The Edwardian house had a long wide hall with bedrooms on one side and library, drawing room and nursery on the other, ending in swing doors with bathroom, dining room, kitchen and maids' rooms beyond. We had a nurse and there was a cook and a maid, but family life was lived on the hall side of the swing doors. The nursery was for small children and for homework; Mother's drawing room was used for family singing on Sunday nights to Dad's accompaniment; the library is where I remember being read to, where we played games and had afternoon tea by the winter fire …

The children had their own bedrooms; but as David recalled, they usually slept in adjoining sleepouts open to the air, which Nancy believed were healthier for them. The household also included a gardener. By coincidence, Dick's childhood home was just two doors up the road from number 39, which, more than a generation later, was the childhood home of another future premier, Ted Baillieu. As happens so often in St Georges Road, both houses have since been demolished.

Next door, at number 33, lived a national hero: General Sir John Monash, commander of Australian forces in World War I, and by then chairman of the State Electricity Commission. Monash was close to George Swinburne, and quickly made friends with the Hamers. 'He was a marvellous old man,' Dick recalled. 'He loved getting us in on Sunday evenings, making us look at his slides, explaining things. He was a very kindly man, and I remember him with great affection.'

His daughter and grandchildren, the Bennett family, lived with him, and David Hamer and David Bennett became best mates.

The most important person in Dick's early life, after Nancy, was his brother Alan. 'I don't remember a time when Alan wasn't there,' Dick recalled. 'We were virtually brought up as twins … I was very close to my brother.' Alan and Dick shared a room, they shared games, they shared schools, and they shared their lives. Younger brother David recalled enviously: 'Dick and Alan were known as "the boys", and were a separate unit'. Alison had similar memories, 'My two elder brothers lived in each other's pockets,' she wrote. Until the end of the 1920s, only Dick and Alan ate weekday dinners with their parents; Alison and David took their meals in the nursery, being allowed to join the family dinner table only on Sundays. Perhaps that was because the two younger Hamers kept trying to out-talk each other. 'Verbal battles were constant,' Alison recalled, 'I spent much time vainly struggling for the last word, especially with my young brother, who had inexhaustible stamina, and an all-too-ready tongue'. David agreed, writing: 'There were a lot of fights … She was very vulnerable because she had plaits, which were painful (I was told) when pulled.'

With Dick and Alan, by contrast, the competition was below the surface. Dick said he could not recall them ever having a serious difference. Alan, the last survivor of the four Hamer siblings, agreed when interviewed for this book: 'He and I got on very well. We did a lot of things together, and I can't remember any fights. But we were competitive at sport!' Barbara Hamer recalls Nancy telling her that Dick and Alan never fought. It was an important sign for the future. From the outset, Dick's instinct was to work with his younger brother, not to pick on him. It may have helped that, as a boy, Dick was small, and that Alan quickly outgrew him. While Dick was good at sport, Alan was better, winning a University blue in football (as well as a Rhodes scholarship to Oxford). The anecdotes suggest that, from early on, Dick already had the calm, unflappable manner that was to characterise him throughout his career. As a child, he had already that bedrock of quiet self-confidence that became his deepest strength in politics.

Dick and Alan sometimes would gang up verbally against the smaller fry. 'I was a good deal sat on by my brothers,' wrote Alison, 'without malice, and for my own good … I knew that my snubbing brothers were utterly with me when I needed them.' (Much later, Dick would take his young sister onto the dance floor at parties to get her noticed.) But while Dick and Alan were a team, Dick was the boss. He was the first-born son; and in their games, he took charge, assigned the roles, and made the rules. David recalls one special day when he and Alison were allowed to join 'the boys':

> There was a big pile of bricks and timber near the garage, and the boys (with 'assistance' from me) built a large ship on the lawn, with a deck, bridge and funnel. Dick, as the eldest, stood on the bridge with a steering wheel, and Alan was in the engine room stoking up a fire, some of the smoke from which came out the funnel. Every few minutes Alan would emerge from the engine-room, red-faced, take a few deep breaths, and then dive back to stoke the boiler. Alison was preparing the lunch (no nonsense about feminism in those days) of sandwiches and lemonade. I was the dogsbody — the lookout (I was very industrious at seeing enemy ships) and the deckhand — letting imaginary mooring ropes go and throwing out the anchor. We had a great time, except when we had to clear up the mess afterwards.[4]

Then there were holidays. Between the wars, the roads were poor, ships expensive, and airline travel had barely begun. Even well-off families like the Hamers rarely travelled far from home. Sometimes Nancy took them to stay with her Wilson cousins in Yarrawonga. Their one big trip was a family holiday to Sydney and the Southern Highlands. Most holidays, though, were spent at their beach house at Frankston. It was then the only house on a cliff overlooking Daveys Bay. Dick recalled: 'We used to spend a lot of time playing in the creek [Kackeraboite Creek, which divides Frankston from Mount Eliza]. We had a canoe and went down to the beach and did some fishing. We really didn't get around that much.'

One wonders whether the Edna Walling-designed garden left a lasting influence on the premier who, 50 years later, made Victoria 'the Garden State'. In their study of Edna Walling, Trisha Dixon and Jennie Churchill note that it was among her first gardens to focus on native plants, revelling in 'the relaxed and informal atmosphere indigenous plants can create, and their eminent suitability for seaside gardens'. Edna Walling herself wrote: 'The plants were nice and thick, the ground was well covered, and there was an air of wildness about the garden. It was the sort of garden in which you could garden if you wanted to, but if you didn't, it would not matter'.

The centre of wider family life was 'Shenton'. Every weekend, Hubert would take his family over to visit and dine with his mother (until her death in 1924), his sister Ethel, her husband George, their daughters, and other friends. Christmas dinner was always held at 'Shenton', with as many as 50 relatives and friends joining the celebrations. In 1939, when Dick was a young lawyer, his diary shows that the Hamers routinely went to 'Shenton' on Saturday evenings for dinner. Aunt Ethel, by then in her late sixties, was still running charities — the Victorian Children's Aid Society (now absorbed into OzChild), the International Club for women from foreign countries, the Victorian Association of Braille Writers — and keeping an eye on the college. She introduced Dick to Japanese art, argued with him about Wordsworth, and recommended books, as they listened to classical music, played bridge, and just chatted. In the middle of the war in 1940, one entry in Hamer's diary records simply: 'Went to Aunt Ethel's, where reason and calm always prevails.'

And, it seems, an unconventional frankness. Dick's sister, Alison, recalled that, like many girls in the 1930s, she had grown up almost ignorant of the facts of life:

> I had the sketchiest possible grasp of pregnancy and childbirth; the details of sexual relationships were a closed book to me. I resented this, it made me feel inadequate. Oddly enough, the only person to discuss family pregnancies and problems with me was my father's much-loved, formidable elder sister, who had much astringent

> commonsense. She was born in 1868 and lived till 1960, and my acquaintance with her makes me distrust every generalisation about Victorian women that I have ever heard; she fitted the stereotypes so deceptively well in some ways, and was so far beyond them in others.

Another side of Aunt Ethel that endeared her to her nephews was her prowess at golf. 'There used to be a putting green at 'Shenton', and Aunt Ethel was devastating,' David Hamer wrote ruefully. 'She could have out-putted any of the famous pro golfers you see on television these days, though I doubt if the high-heeled shoes she wore would be acceptable on many greens.'

Three of the four Swinburne children were a generation older than their Hamer cousins. In 1915, the same year as her uncle Hubert married her schoolfriend Nancy, Muriel (Mu) married a young barrister, Russell Martin. He ultimately became Mr Justice Martin of the Supreme Court of Victoria, and was affectionately known by the Hamer children as 'Uncle Justice'. The Martin boys, Bryan (or 'Digger') and Colin, became Dick's real cousins and playmates. They were roughly the same age as Dick and Alan, and the four of them spent most of the summer together, either at the Hamer's beach house in Frankston, or the Martins' at Portsea, sailing or playing golf.

Summer was often spent with the extended family. Nancy Crowe, their cousin on their mother's side, was a year older than Dick, and a keen horsewoman. One year, she led Dick and Alan in riding their horses down to Gull's Way from Melbourne. Dick's unfortunate horse barely survived the climb up Oliver's Hill. Cousins often came to stay at Frankston, and one time there were 16 people staying in the house. Later, Nancy rented out the Frankston house and moved their summer base, too, to Portsea. After Marg Swinburne, the youngest of the four daughters, married Yarrawonga farmer Ron Browning, the whole Hamer/Swinburne clan spent Christmas 1939 at their farm.

Sunday morning was not the best time to be one of the Hamer children, 'We were marched off to Sunday school, up to the Presbyterian Church,' Dick recalled without enthusiasm. Hubert grew up a Congregationalist; Nancy, a Presbyterian. George Swinburne was a Methodist, and the Hamer children went to Anglican schools. The denominations were confused, but the influence of Christian teaching on Dick was profound: indeed, it was almost certainly the most profound influence on his values. His was the Christianity of the Sermon on the Mount and the Good Samaritan. His core beliefs in life stemmed from the Gospels: giving support and compassion to those in need, doing good service to others, welcoming strangers, and turning the other cheek to those who do you wrong. Yet whether he really believed in God is not clear. As we will see, he was sceptical by the end of his schooldays. The diaries show that as a young adult he was interested in theological issues, but went to church only when staying with April's family, or when military duty demanded it. He ended up agnostic rather than atheist, but religion played no part in his adult life. Nancy, too, eventually drifted away. In later years she spent Sunday mornings preparing the family's weekly lunch together. One of her grandchildren recalls that at her funeral in 1984, it was obvious that she and the vicar had never met.

The darkest side of life that Dick experienced as a child was at Melbourne Grammar School. It was his third school. He and Alan began as boys in the first grade of a girls' school, Ruyton, near their home. (In the 1970s, during the school's centenary celebrations, a photo of the little Hamer boys learning how to knit was published on the front page of *The Age*.) They then went to Trinity Grammar for two years, but from third grade they went to Wadhurst, the junior school of Melbourne Grammar. The principal was Melbourne Sydney Caffin, whom Hamer described as 'a martinet'. Caffin taught Latin, and, Hamer recalled in retirement, was always looking for opportunities to hit the boys with his cane. 'He would line the boys up along the wall, and cane the last six who couldn't answer his questions,' Hamer told his daughter Julia. The school's headmaster, R.P. ('Lofty') Franklin was no better: when a group of young boys harassed some girls on the tram on the way home, Franklin gave each of them 30 cuts on the back. 'He was sadistic,' Hamer concluded. 'I don't think little boys could have done anything all that bad. What can you do to a girl on a tram when you're a boy of ten?'

Dick had no complaints about the academic standard at Wadhurst, although its approach was learning by rote. The Hamer boys were bright and industrious; they brought home armfuls of prizes every year. In Dick's final year, he just missed out on being dux of Wadhurst, and won prizes for spelling, history, and geography. Future High Court judge Keith Aickin, a classmate, made do with a general proficiency prize. The corporal punishment did not faze Dick unduly; everyone got caned, so everyone accepted it, he said: 'In my experience, it doesn't seem to have been detrimental.' A generation later, he and Alan sent their sons to Melbourne Grammar.

But Nancy and Hubert looked for an alternative, and found it at Geelong Grammar School. Traditionally a boarding school for the sons of Western District graziers, it was being woken from a long lethargy by its chairman, Donald Mackinnon. Mackinnon steered through the appointment of a new headmaster, a 30-year-old Englishman, James Darling, now seen as having been the outstanding Australian headmaster of his generation. Darling was an intellectual, and a former member of the British Labour Party. Mackinnon was a Liberal, and Geelong Grammar was deeply conservative, but Mackinnon and his council overlooked Darling's youthful fling with the Left, and commissioned him to transform the school into a place of academic and artistic excellence. To speed the transformation, they established scholarships to attract Victoria's best and brightest students. Hubert believed that the old English model of private boarding schools was 'good for the soul'; but with Australia sinking into the Depression, he agonised over the cost of sending two boys to boarding school. Dick and Alan solved his problem by winning scholarships.

Corio was Dick's home for the next five years, and a happy home it was. In interviews later in life, he named Darling (later Sir James) as one of the prime influences on his development. How much Darling really changed his direction, and how much he simply reinforced the way Dick was already heading, it is impossible to know. But his headmaster became a man Dick respected deeply, learned from, and was affirmed by, in a way that would have been impossible had he stayed at Melbourne Grammar. And the impact of Darling was magnified by the new teachers he recruited to replace the old regime. By the end of the 1930s, Geelong Grammar was widely seen as the best school in Australia, and wealthy families in Sydney and Adelaide as well as Melbourne sent their sons there.

In 1930, by the time Dick and Alan arrived at Corio, Australia and the world had sunk into the Great Depression. There was economic and social devastation everywhere. We have no reliable measure of how many people became unemployed, but, at its worst, 25 per cent of union members were out of work. The population of Melbourne had reached 1 million by 1929, but then shrank back well below that as unemployed people moved to the country to shoot rabbits, or seek work in return for food and shelter. Even the law firm of Smith and Emmerton suffered. In the mid-1930s, having to support three boys studying away from home, Hubert and Nancy leased out 35 St Georges Road, and moved with Alison to rent two adjoining apartments in Orrong Road until better times came.

Dick's new school and its headmaster were very unlike the old ones. In a 2008 oration in Darling's honour, former Geelong Grammar teacher and school historian Michael Collins Persse gave an interesting picture of Darling's values and work:

> Like Shaftesbury, like Gladstone, like his own early mentor William Temple, he carried his Christianity into every area of life, whether public or private. It had not, however, come easily. His natural tendency — evident still in his mid-nineties — was that of an active and questing intellect seeking an intelligible faith rather than a natural faith seeking intellectual justification. His greatest service at Geelong lay in the education of boys to a sense of responsibility for others and to a sensitive awareness of the needs of the world in which many of them were to play leading parts.
>
> Darling accepted the school's conventional overlay, but began at once to activate a range of interests and concerns to renew the school's independent spirit. He took over early in the Depression and stirred the social conscience of the school. Much work

> was done by the boys in Geelong (where Apex was founded in 1931 with Darling's help, and a boys' employment centre), and employment was given at the school to many who would otherwise have remained without work in those dark days.
>
> Thus, through the 1930s, a remarkable series of buildings was achieved, including substantial music and art schools, and a new senior boarding house. In addition, the school was swept into drama on an unprecedented scale, with Shakespearean productions and pageant-plays. Music, art and the manual crafts were brought in from the fringes of the school curriculum and made central to a degree, unique in Australia and rare even in Britain at the time.[5]

Darling had come from the English public school system. He himself had been a student at Repton School, founded in 1557; his two headmasters there, William Temple and Geoffrey Fisher, each went on to become Archbishop of Canterbury. (Fisher's son Charles later became headmaster at Corio.) Weston Bate, in his history of Geelong Grammar, *Light Blue Down Under*, describes Darling as 'tall, thin, energetic and ambitious':

> He … had, if not a philosophy of education, at least a set of ideas, ideals and prejudices that had as their centre the concept of the civilized man, who played games for the love of them, who studied without cramming, who valued music, art, literature, religion, politics and history above material success. Temperamentally he was an entrepreneur, prepared to take risks, but prepared also to work hard to minimize them, a strategist who kept his eye on the whole chess board.

Dick Hamer became a young exemplar of the 'civilized man' Darling was hoping to create. But the 13-year-old Hamer found his first experience of moving from the comfort of Toorak to the icy winds of Corio far from uplifting. 'It had a reputation as a great rowing school, but that's about it,' he told Julia. 'The conditions were primitive. Throughout my time there, all the showers were cold, even in the depths of winter. You'd get up in the morning and have these really freezing showers. Corio is open to every wind that blows, but particularly to the cold winds from the south and south-west. It's a cold place.'

In 1930, Geelong Grammar had just 370 students, of whom 330 were boarders. The boarding house was the social unit. Dick was in Manifold House, where all the boys in their year slept in the same dormitory: 'great big dormitories, with 20 or 30 beds each,' Dick said. 'But we slept all right, nothing kept us awake, except one night when one of the kids had an epileptic fit and his head got stuck between the iron bars of the bedhead. The bars had to be cut to free him.' James Guest, a school friend who later became one of Melbourne's leading surgeons, says Geelong Grammar in the 1930s was largely free of the bastardisation that has plagued other boarding schools. 'I had no experience of fagging or bullying in my time at Corio,' he recalled. 'In our group, it was a very happy life.'

Darling believed in keeping the boys busy. Dick recalled:

> You had classes all day till half past three. Then you turned out for sport, and you played that until half past five. Then you had dinner, and after that you had prep, where once again, you sat at desks for two hours. You'd had it by then!

But there were lots of activities to stimulate the boys' interests and develop their artistic abilities. In 1931, the school staged a dramatisation of Virgil's *Aeneid*. In 1933, Darling went further, putting on a production of Thomas Hardy's *The Dynasts*, which Hardy had thought impossible to stage. Darling invited senior boys to perform play readings in his study after dinner; in one of them, Dick was Shylock in *The Merchant of Venice*. Dick sang in the school choir, played fife in the school band, played piano, and conducted his house choir in the choral competition. While outshone by Alan on the sporting field, he played in the first XI in cricket and the first XVIII in football. He also went into the cadet corps, ending up at the top as a cadet lieutenant. He told Julia he was never bored:

> Mr Jennings, the master of the Middle School, made us run a little shop so kids knew how commerce operated. There were quizzes, lectures, and visiting speakers. Most kids down there had a bike, and on Saturdays you could go out on bike rides in a party with friends. You had to be back by dark: that was the only requirement. One Saturday we rode down to Lorne: we only just got down there before we had to turn back again!
>
> We had chapel every Sunday, and after that there was religious discussion. After lunch we were all sat down for an hour to write home. Sunday afternoon was free, but there was no sport, so you spent it walking, reading, or swimming.

Dick liked every subject, but his strength was in languages. After year 10, the smart students were expected to take the classics course. Alan rebelled and did science, but Dick took the usual route. He sat the Leaving exams twice, as Darling preferred his boys to do. In 1933, he won first-class honours in Latin, and seconds in French and ancient Greek; in 1934, he won firsts in all three. Forty years later, in 1974, he was probably the last MP in state parliament to interrupt debate with an interjection in Latin. He also studied maths, English, and Greek and Roman history, but missed out on honours. In 1933, the exhibition in Greek and Roman history went to a Melbourne Grammar boy — Manning Clark, later to be a friend of Hamer's and the author of the six-volume work *A History of Australia*.

Geelong Grammar finally separated the Hamer boys. They were in different classes and doing different subjects. 'Alan had his group of friends, and I had mine,' Dick recalled. His best friends became lasting friends, particularly Jim Guest, later honorary surgeon at the Alfred Hospital; Ross Cameron, who also went into medicine; the livewire Randal Deasey, later Archdeacon of Essendon; and David Hay, later administrator of Papua New Guinea and head of the Department of External Territories at the time PNG entered its transition to independence. All were school or house prefects with him. In 1934, Hamer and Hay were named jointly as dux of the school.

Jim Guest recalls that even as a 14-year-old, Dick had the unflappable manner that characterised him later in politics:

> He was already like that on the day I first met him. Even then, he seemed a very calm, considered personality. He didn't get fussed or flustered. He always seemed to be in control of the situation. He knew what he was capable of.
>
> And he was a very good scholar, intellectually bright. He didn't waste time. He used to carry a little book in his pocket, and if he had half an hour spare, he'd take it out and start reading. He was really diligent, he always buttoned down to it. I thought he would end up as Chief Justice, or something like that.[6]

Dick ended his schooldays as a school prefect and captain of Manifold House. It became his job to keep order in his house, and he had the right to cane boys when necessary. That happened just once, he told Julia, when he was awoken one night and told that three boys had dragged an unpopular boy out of bed, thrown him in a bath of cold water, and pinned him there by putting the wooden bathmat on top of him and sitting on it. 'I exercised my prerogative and beat all three of them,' he told Julia. 'The boy had made himself obnoxious, no doubt about that, but the punishment was really sadistic.' There were times when Dick was premier when a similar readiness to wield the birch on junior colleagues might have helped.

Darling and Hamer formed a strong bond. In 1937, when Alan won the Rhodes Scholarship for Victoria, Darling wrote to Nancy Hamer offering his congratulations, but could not resist adding: 'Dick is still my pick (of the boys), if not perhaps in mere ability, for absolute solid goodness and niceness.' Dick, in turn, was very appreciative of his headmaster, and the changes he wrought 'to enlarge our vision' by introducing the boys to music, art, and drama. 'It was a revolutionary time,' he concluded. 'Some changes came off; some didn't.' There are important similarities between the reforms that Darling introduced at Geelong Grammar, and those that Hamer himself introduced years later as premier. But they had one brief, spectacular falling out, which reveals the young Hamer's independent mind. Darling took the sixth form (final year) for English, and on one occasion he told the class to write an essay on the miracles performed by Jesus Christ. Hamer recalled:

> I wrote an essay, which I still believe, about how the miracles were all explicable as legends that build up around a character. If you took them seriously, they look more like a magician's tricks. Why turn water into wine? Why raise one person from the dead? Why create all those loaves and fishes?
>
> I got a colossal blast from JRD. Honestly, I felt that all heaven was falling on me. He really took me to task for impiety ... for throwing doubt on the miracles. 'You can't mean this!,' he said. 'It's in the Bible!' I said: 'Sir, it's only an essay'. He said: 'It's a question of faith. If you have faith, then all miracles are possible. So what you're exhibiting is a lack of faith!' I said: 'Yes, I suppose that's it.' I was overall a believer, but with considerable scepticism about some of the stuff that seemed to me beyond belief.[7]

Years later, when Dick briefly tried his hand at fiction, aiming to turn his army experience into a novel, 'Shadows in the Grass', his fictional alter ego, Hugo, is quizzed by an army clerk registering his details:

> — 'Religion?'
> — 'None.'
> — 'I'll put down C. of E.'

The official army registration form for R.J. Hamer, filled out at Caulfield Racecourse on 29 April 1940, shows his religion as 'C. of E.'

CHAPTER THREE

From law to war

As a schoolboy, Dick Hamer dreamed of becoming a diplomat. In an era when slow communications gave ambassadors real power, he told his daughter Julia much later, 'the diplomatic service seemed to me a wonderful way of getting around to other countries … while playing an active part [in the nation's affairs]'. But his father, Hubert, wanted his eldest son to join him in the family law firm, and Dick gave way: 'I didn't resist the idea of going into the law. Everything led to it in a way: the Latin, the study of logic. And it was a good course then, a much broader course than it is now. We didn't have to spend a year studying tax law.' But he drew the line when his father urged him to follow his own example by becoming an articled clerk straight from school. Dick insisted on going to university. And in the Hamer way, he made it happen by winning a senior government scholarship and a residential scholarship to Trinity College. 'That forced my father's hand,' he later recalled. 'He didn't press it after that.' The first scholarship paid his university fees for a year, and the second allowed Dick to go on enjoying a prestigious, congenial setting for his student life. Alan and Alison later also won scholarships to Trinity.

Melbourne University in the 1930s was small and socially select. The historian Brian Fitzpatrick summed up the campus in the 1920s as 'a resort for the sons and some daughters of gentlemen, and a few others'. A decade later, student numbers had doubled, but their composition was much the same. 'The students … were overwhelmingly drawn from the middle and upper classes of Melbourne's then small population and simple society,' wrote university historians John Poynter and Carolyn Rasmussen. 'Most had attended private schools … 60 per cent came from … the relatively well-off, the top 10 per cent of Victorian breadwinners.' Almost three-quarters of the student body were male, and the females generally studied arts. Male students wore suits on campus; female students wore hats, dresses, handbag, gloves, and stockings. (In 1938, one female fresher was censured by the Committee of Melbourne University Women for appearing on campus with her hair in plaits.) Entry was open to all, but few students from working-class families could afford to pay the fees. One of the few was Hamer's future political opponent and friend Jack Galbally, who broke the unwritten rules for 'University men' by working at night and weekends to pay his way through law school.

The university of the 1930s looked very different than it does today. To quote one of Hamer's contemporaries, Diana Dyason:

> The campus as I first knew it had the air of an English village centred round its pond 'the lake', not large nor overly clean. It had as a central building focus [the old] Wilson Hall, flanked by Moreton Bay fig trees. All these with the quad making the equivalent of a village church and its manse. The commons were the oval and the hockey fields. There was a sense of space … In your mind's eye, you would have to eliminate almost all of today's buildings.[1]

Trinity College was the centre of Hamer's world. It was even more select: most of its students came from Melbourne Grammar or Geelong Grammar. Its warden, 'Jock' Behan (later Sir John), was a generation older than Darling, with none of his reformist drive. 'He was the least charismatic figure you could imagine,' Hamer recalled. 'He was a very grey, ghostly figure, tall and gaunt. His opening remark to us as freshers was that two things were absolutely sacrosanct: the fire equipment, and the young ladies of Janet Clarke Hall' (Trinity's sister college next door). As a student, Behan had topped the law school in 1903, but Hamer found that as the college's law tutor, he was 'little help ... He couldn't quote any legal cases after the turn of the century.' But, in one way, he changed the young Hamer profoundly:

> I owe Jock Behan the beginning of my love of classical music. After chapel on Sunday morning, he would invite people over to the Warden's Lodge for a music session [listening to 78 rpm records]. I knew every word of the Gilbert and Sullivan operettas, but this was the first time I remember being taken with that kind of music. He regarded Beethoven as the greatest creator who ever walked on earth.[2]

By the end of his college days, so did Hamer, and it remained his view for the rest of his life.

Trinity men spent most of their time in college. Almost all of Hamer's best friends from university were from Trinity, not the Law School. They included his old schoolfriends Jim Guest, Randal Deasey, and Ross Cameron, and new friends, mostly from Melbourne Grammar: the historians A.G.L. Shaw and Manning Clark, fellow law student Finlay Patrick, Dave Kimpton, and future diplomat Keith (Mick) Shann. Deasey, whose father was the vicar of Christ Church, Geelong, was the imp of the group. At college, the future Archdeacon of Essendon was the main initiator of a string of student pranks — 'japes' as Hamer called them — that livened things up. The night before Archbishop Head was to bless the new gates of Janet Clarke Hall, for instance, the gates mysteriously disappeared, and, after a series of false leads from anonymous phone calls, turned up in the archbishop's own garden. The foundation stone of the college's Behan Building also disappeared the night before it was to be unveiled, and was later discovered buried in the long-jump pit. And one foggy Sunday night, when Royal Parade was being converted from cable trams to electric trams, with barriers and detour signs blocking the centre roadway, Deasey, Dick, and Alan Hamer and others snuck out and rearranged the detour signs so that all traffic coming down Royal Parade was directed into Trinity College, around the oak tree and onto the open field known as the Bulpadock, which, in those days, housed the college cows. 'It was pandemonium,' Jim Guest recalls. 'There must have been 50 or 60 cars, and they didn't know where they were. Then a number of us took torches out to show them how to get out.' One hopes they saw the joke.

The Melbourne University law school had an academic staff of just two: Professor (later Sir) Kenneth Bailey, and Professor (later Sir) George Paton. Most of the lectures were given in the evenings by busy barristers who headed up to university after a day in court. This meant that law students had a lot of free time, which suited Dick's wide-ranging interests. Deasey owned a 1908 Metallurgique they called 'the Urge': an open-roof tourer that had to be cranked up to start. It cost only £5 to buy, but a fortune to keep on the road. Dick played squash, sometimes golf, and turned out for Trinity in inter-collegiate sports. He was a regular in the first XI in cricket: while he hardly distinguished himself, in 1935 he kept up one end while, at the other, Manning Clark hit what *The Argus* called a 'flawless' 184 against Newman College. Hamer, Clark, and Guest played football in the second XVIII, in a spirit of great fun, judging from the gear they donned for the team photo. Dick continued his military service, joining the Melbourne University Rifles; interestingly, his superiors rated him as 'efficient' in only two of his four years in the unit. He appeared in supporting roles in college and university plays. He read, he talked and listened, no doubt flirted with girls, drank and partied, and enjoyed the university experience. He became secretary of the Trinity College Dialectical Society and the college's debating club, and twice won prizes at their annual dinners. In 1937, the judges in their wisdom gave the President's medal for oratory to Clark, and the Leeper prize for oratory to Hamer.

A serious power struggle between warden and students in 1934 had ended with Dr Behan sending down the entire committee of the social club and effectively making the college 'dry'. Students were allowed to have gramophones, but not radios. They were not allowed female visitors after dark. Despite all these restrictions, Hamer remembered college life as 'very hearty' and full of fun:

> We used to stay up until inordinate hours talking about everything under the sun. It was just accepted that around 10.30 p.m., you abandoned preparatory work for the next day's classes, and would go to someone's study, break out the biscuits and coffee, and chat until two or three in the morning. It was great to me, that was what college life ought to be. You had different people from all sorts of faculties exchanging ideas and comments.

Social life was also busy, if more formal than in later years. No Trinity man owned a pair of jeans, but everyone owned a dinner suit. Dating was rare, but dances were common; and in Melbourne society in the 1930s, Dick told his daughter, people never ran out of excuses to hold parties:

> In those days, girls used to have elaborate coming-out parties when they were 17 or 18. I think we were regarded as available swains; there was often no apparent reason for inviting us, but we were always invited. We used to have dance programs with little pencils attached, so you would dance with a lot of different partners in a night. We all loved dancing.

But Dick also worked hard. Unlike Alan and Alison, he did not win an exhibition until the very end, when he took out the big one: the Supreme Court prize for the top student in the Law School. It may not be entirely coincidence that his best academic results came in his final year, 1938, after Alan had one-upped him by winning Victoria's Rhodes Scholarship and going to Oxford. 'Dick was a huge worker,' Jim Guest recalled. 'He used to go over to the Library in the cloisters, the main University Library at that time, and work there until ten. He was a hard worker with a good brain.' Dick told Julia he used to spend hours at a time in the Law Library. 'We had to study all sorts of cases and extract the principles from them. It would take hours, and you would make pages and pages of notes.'

Until final year, Dick's best results in fact were in his arts subjects, despite stiff competition. In second year, he won second-class honours in constitutional and legal history, coming third behind Clark and A.G.L. Shaw, two of Australia's future historians. He won a first in modern political institutions, but was pipped for the top mark by George (G.B.) Kerferd, great-grandson of the premier of the same name; like Clark and Shaw, Kerferd went on to Oxford, and ended up a renowned writer on the history of philosophy. A year later, Hamer won first-class honours in political philosophy, but was pushed into second place by an 18-year-old prodigy named Zelman Cowen. Forty years later, they would meet again as premier and governor-general. In economics, Hamer got honours, but Shaw, initially an economic historian, took the exhibition.

The subjects that interested Hamer most were those taught by Macmahon Ball, the dynamic young lecturer on international politics. It was the late 1930s, the time of Hitler, Stalin, the Spanish Civil War, Munich, and Japan's war with China. The great issues of his times stirred Hamer's mind in ways that legal subjects could not:

> I was studying the Constitution, and studying the dictatorships, and asking what was the alternative. It taught you to value what you had, and what you were part of … A lot of people were attracted by the theoretical basis of communism, but they didn't know how terrible it was in practice. We knew it was an oppressive regime, but even we didn't know about the liquidation of 20 million Russians. We had Fascism in Italy, Nazism in Germany. Japan carried out a massacre in Nanjing that wiped out 300,000 people. It was a time of fear, and anticipation. We thought everybody was taking it all a bit too calmly.

Macmahon Ball later became Australia's ambassador to post-war Japan before returning to take up a chair at the university. He had a profound influence on Hamer, focussing his students on understanding the causes of political movements. As a politician, Hamer was unusual in trying to understand what motivated opposition to his policies, and to find a way of coming to terms with it. In a 1979 interview, Hamer praised Ball as 'a very enlightened man, and one I've always admired. I'm sure he had a big influence on a whole generation of political science students, guiding them to a liberal approach to affairs of government, and a strong distrust of dictators of any kind.'[3]

Hamer took no part in student politics, which in any case were mostly passive. The vice-chancellor, Raymond Priestley, who had been recruited from England, derided alarmist claims by some MPs of radicalism on campus, writing that he did not know of 'any university (that) has a student body less politically and socially conscious than Melbourne'. One rowdy debate on the Spanish Civil War ended with some students being thrown into the university lake; but then, it was not unusual for students to be thrown into the lake. Diana Dyason recalled that: 'Generally an anti-jingoistic, anti-militaristic attitude seemed to dominate the campus.' That certainly sums up Hamer's pre-war views in the diaries he began keeping from 1939, if not what he later told the world he had thought.

It was probably Randal Deasey who thought up the most famous of their pranks. The night after the 1938 Munich agreement, when British prime minister Neville Chamberlain agreed to Hitler annexing western Czechoslovakia in return for the Nazi leader pledging no further territorial claims, a group of Trinity men snuck down to St Paul's Cathedral and stuck a gas mask on the statue of Matthew Flinders on Swanston Street. As premier, later, Hamer explained it as their warning to Melbourne that war was coming. Maybe it was, but it was not Hamer's view in 1939, when his diaries show that up to the last minute, he believed that Britain and Germany would (and should) pull back from the brink.

Hamer's diary in 1939 reflects a view that Germany should (and could) be appeased by allowing it to expand across eastern Europe. He was probably one of few Australians at that time who had read *Mein Kampf*, Hitler's credo, and understood why Germans had turned to Nazism. He felt strongly that the terms of the 1919 Treaty of Versailles had been unjust to Germany, and had wrecked its economy, creating a mass of resentment that Hitler rode to power. He believed that Britain and France had no interests in eastern Europe, and no reason to defend it from German expansion; rather, they should draw the line against German expansion to the west. And he assumed that Hitler did not really want a war with the West. Hamer was not alone in these views, either on the campus or in the community. Both sides of Australian politics leant towards appeasement rather than war. This was also the view of the best-informed Australian of that time, S.M. (later Lord) Bruce, the former prime minister who was our high commissioner in London from 1933 to 1945. In World War I, Bruce spent four horrendous months in the trenches in Gallipoli, winning a Military Cross for bravery before being invalided out with a shattered knee that hampered him all his life. Bruce was pro-appeasement because he knew what war was like; he was determined to avoid it, and assumed that, in the end, Germany's leader shared that view. We know now that he, Chamberlain, Australian prime minister Robert Menzies, opposition leader John Curtin, and the young Dick Hamer, at the time, all got Hitler wrong. Those who condemn them for that from this distance can be congratulated on their perfect 20/20 hindsight.

There was never any doubt that Dick would go into the family law firm. After graduating in early 1939, he became articled clerk to his father, and, as his diary records, was entrusted with a series of minor cases and tasks, and occasionally major ones. One day he went to serve a writ on the owner of an engineering shop, and found himself threatened, sworn at, and finally hit with a block of wood. On another, he spent the day conferring with 'Ned' Herring, KC (later Sir Edmund, and Victoria's chief justice), who appeared for the CBA in a big contested case. He went to the Titles Office to check land titles for conveyancing clients; he spent a Saturday morning drawing up wills. He appeared before the Full Court pro bono for the Royal Children's Hospital over a contested will after a daughter challenged her mother's decision to leave money to the hospital. He resumed study, with his close friend, squash partner, and future brother-in-law Finlay Patrick, taking on litigation and accounting, to upgrade their degrees to Master of Laws. He made a couple of appearances before the Law Students Society, where the previous winner of the Supreme Court prize, his old Wadhurst schoolmate Keith Aickin, set a 'most ingenious' problem for Dick to argue at a moot court against a fellow student. Dick won the case, and wrote prophetically of Aickin, the future High Court judge: 'He will go far at the bar, if his health can stand it. He has a clear, logical and fair mind.'

It was around this time that Hamer started writing a diary. He was inspired in this by the diary of Samuel Pepys, the 17th-century navy official whose diary became an invaluable record of how people lived in the London of his time. Dick wrote in his diary each night to record what he did, thought, and felt. When he began, he was a 22-year-old young man about town, straight out of university, learning the law, falling in love, and revelling in the social, cultural, and sporting life of the Melbourne of 1939. He kept writing for two-and-a-half years and 1,140 pages, until, as a 25-year-old army officer in the midst of war, he suddenly stopped.

The diaries give an invaluable insight into his mind. They help to explain why, 40 years later, he handled the pressures and issues confronting him as premier in the ways he did. They also paint an absorbing picture of his life in peace and war. They begin as the life of an active, happy, energetic, intelligent young man, grappling intellectually with big issues, and making the most of the social opportunities opening up before him. His life in 1939 was a whirl of legal work, study, concerts, ballets, theatre, films, restaurants, parties, golf, squash, long walks, military training, trips to the snowfields, beaches, and countryside, innocent and serious relationships with girls, and endless family gatherings. How he managed to fit it all in is amazing; sometimes he went to three events a night, then wrote about all of them when he got home.

There are memorable moments. One day in the street, he throws a punch to stop a thief who stole a woman's handbag, and is sorely disappointed when it fails to knock the man down. At a gathering one night, 22-year-old Dick Hamer gets into an argument with the 75-year-old artist Rupert Bunny about 1930s architecture (Hamer, for; Bunny, against). He goes to hear the great Artur Schnabel perform Beethoven's 4th Piano Concerto in the Melbourne Town Hall, with the Melbourne Symphony Orchestra conducted by George

Szell. Another night, he goes to hear Szell conduct the MSO in, of all places, the Hawthorn Town Hall; surely one of the few times that venue hosted one of the world's great conductors. And he has a brief, unreciprocated, crush on Rupert Bunny's bossy niece, Tchili Reid, which ends when she sails off to study art in Paris.

The law was not Dick's main interest. By midyear, the drumbeats of war were growing louder. Hamer supported the Menzies government's decision in June to set up a compulsory national register for young men; indeed, despite his opposition to war, he supported the government on every action it took to prepare for war. As July turned into August, with German troops taking up position to attack Poland, he became very worried about what lay ahead. 'Intolerable suspense,' he wrote on Thursday 24 August. The next morning, he got up early to hear Britain's foreign secretary, Lord Halifax, speak on the radio; and at night in his diary, he denounced Britain's decision to take a stand against Nazi aggression, writing with unusually intemperate passion. Unlike some other young Australians, Hamer never saw war as an adventure or opportunity for heroism. To him, war was the enemy of civilisation, bringing death and destruction to the people and to 'the beauties of Berlin, London and Paris. I simply don't think anything is worth that'. One night, his analysis of the European situation concludes with a single word, written with great force on the page: 'Hell!'

But just three days after penning his passionate denunciation of Britain's decision to stand by Poland and risk a world war, Dick did something remarkable. On the Monday morning, 28 August, he reported to 6th Battalion headquarters to sign up for a further three years in the army reserves. He knew by doing so it meant that if war came, he would be called up immediately to fight in it. In his mind, his intellectual opposition to war was one thing; his duty to his country was another. He fervently opposed Australia going to war; but if it did, he would be on the frontline to fight for it. It is hard to read the sequence of entries in his diary without feeling deep admiration for this young man.

For now Dick had someone else to live for. He had fallen in love, deeply in love, with one of Alison's friends from St Catherine's. April Mackintosh was just 18, a beautiful, golden-haired girl with blue eyes, a gentle manner, a love of the arts, and an inquiring mind. Dick first really noticed her at her debutante ball, on 7 March 1939:

> I remember this stunning young slender blonde. She was in white, and she was a bit scared, which I liked. But she liked company, and she was very bright and intelligent, and nice to talk to. And we all liked dancing.

Like Alison, April was a fresher at Melbourne University, studying history. She, too, had grown up in Toorak, although by 1939 her family had moved to South Yarra, which gave Dick an ideal excuse to drive her to university each morning with Alison in his new Hillman. One night, Alison invited her to come to a Melbourne Symphony Orchestra concert on the Hamer family tickets. Randal Deasey also had a spare ticket, and had invited Dick to sit with him. Yet someone managed to arrange things so that Dick sat with April, and Randal sat with Alison. Dick was a born organiser.

April was the younger of two daughters, in a family with an unusual mix of ancestries. Her grandfather, James Mackintosh, arrived from Inverness in 1854, ended up in Echuca, and made a fortune by setting up sawmills in the 1860s when, as the local Crown Lands bailiff put it, for a 10-shilling licence, a sawmill owner could get 'permission to cut timber on the Crown lands of the colony where and how he pleased'. A pier of river red gum cost 5 shillings to cut and haul out of the forest, yet could be sold for £7 in Melbourne. Echuca became Victoria's second-biggest port, and James Mackintosh became its mayor, and seriously rich. In the mid-1870s, he paid £80,000, a huge sum then, to buy 'Wharparilla' station, with 21,852 acres of 'splendid land' along the Murray. But then one of his sons drowned while swimming in the river. James gradually withdrew from Echuca, sold his farm and business, took a world tour with his friend Simon Fraser (grandfather of Malcolm), stood unsuccessfully for state parliament, and moved to Melbourne, where he built an ornate Italianate mansion, 'Verulam', on seven-and-a-half acres on Mont Albert Road in Canterbury. (The house, now called 'Parlington', is classified by the National Trust.) Norman, his youngest son, was born in 1879, and went to school across the road at Camberwell Grammar. On leaving school, Norman went into insurance, eventually becoming 'superintendent' of the Australian and New Zealand operations for the London-based giant, Sun Insurance. He also became president of the Royal Melbourne Hospital, and was in charge when it finally moved in to its new home in Parkville, which had been occupied in wartime by the US army.

April's mother, Rena Dillon Bell, came from a prominent pioneer and political family in New Zealand. Rena's grandfather, Francis Dillon Bell, and his future father-in-law, Abraham Hort, both arrived in the new colony in 1843: Bell, an Englishman raised largely in France, came as a young agent for the New Zealand Company, while Hort, a merchant and elder of the Jewish community in London, was sent to be the patriach of a new Jewish community in Wellington. Dillon Bell married Margaret Hort in a civil ceremony in 1849, after the Anglican priest refused to officiate at an inter-religious wedding. Already bilingual in French and English, he learned to speak Maori fluently, negotiated land purchases from the tribes, became minister for native affairs, then Speaker of the parliament, and finally Sir Francis Dillon Bell, New Zealand's agent-general in London. An obituary noted that he was politically constrained by his 'faculty of [*sic*] seeing both sides of a question — a fact of which his opponents took undue advantage'. His eldest son, also Sir Francis Dillon Bell, was New Zealand's leading barrister before turning to politics, where he was briefly prime minister, and, for much longer, a reforming attorney-general. The *New Zealand Dictionary of Biography* calls the younger Sir Francis 'the supreme example of a Tory radical in New Zealand politics ... Bell's aloofness from party strife, his Roman sense of responsibility, and his magnanimous approach to public issues ... entitle him to the rank of statesman ... On questions involving individual liberty and welfare, he was often found on the left.' When April was a girl, her great-uncle was often acting prime minister of his country. This description of his politics bears an uncanny resemblance to those of the man she was to marry.

Her mother, Rena, grew up in Perth, where her father, Arthur Bell, a civil engineer, had become superintendent of public buildings. Eventually he suffered a nervous breakdown, the family returned to Wellington, and it was there that Rena met Norman Mackintosh. They married in the middle of World War I, in February 1917, with a reception at the home of her illustrious uncle. The bride wore 'a dainty frock of cream Georgette'; the groom wore a khaki uniform. The best man was missing because the army refused him leave from camp. Within two months, Norman was on a ship to France and Rena was pregnant with their first daughter, Anne. But in 1919 Norman returned; in 1921, April was born; and later that year the family settled in Melbourne, where they stayed.

'My father was a big, genial, sweet-natured optimist,' April told an interviewer years later. 'My mother was small, highly strung, deeply sensitive, almost neurotically pessimistic, shy, and introspective. She had a sense of exile, of always being in exile.' But Rena was also 'essentially creative' and passed that on to her daughters. 'She intensely loved all the arts and all things French, that great flowering of literature and music which was the aesthetic climate of her own lifetime … We learned French from a very early age.' Rena's daughters grew up reading Anatole France, Oscar Wilde, Proust, and Yeats: a very cool, modern reading list compared to that of the Hamer household. Anne, the elder daughter, was delicate but intense, 'passionate and outspoken and very quick-tempered'. Ballet was her first passion: as a young woman, she danced in the Ballets Russes and the Borovansky Ballet in Melbourne. In 1940, she married John Elder, a young lawyer then in the army, and bore and raised two children, David and Cathie. As Anne Elder, she took to poetry late in life, publishing two much-praised volumes, *For the Record* (1972) and, posthumously, *Crazy Woman* (1976).[4]

In 1939, April Mackintosh became one of Dick Hamer's two obsessions. The other was the threat, and finally the outbreak, of a second world war.

On 1 September, German troops invaded Poland. On 3 September, Britain declared war on Germany. That night, Menzies broadcast to the nation:

> Fellow Australians: it is my melancholy duty to inform you, officially, that in consequence of a persistence by Germany in her invasion of Poland, Great Britain has declared war upon her, and that, as a result, Australia is also at war.

Private Hamer listened to the broadcast at home with his family after returning from all-day manoeuvres with his unit on the Mornington Peninsula. A week of training in the 6th Battalion had already muted his opposition to Britain's actions. Within a month it would disappear entirely.

The Australian army in September 1939 was far from ready for war; in fact, Hamer was not called up until April 1940. But for those eight months, his time became divided between learning legal skills at Smith and Emmerton and learning intelligence skills with the 6th Battalion. Serious military training began in October 1939, when Dick and his friend John MacLeod spent a month in camp at Mount Martha. Training camps with the Melbourne University Rifles had been a joke, in Dick's eyes — a day of training at Point Nepean being a prelude to the real business of 'a vigorous party at night in the Portsea Pub'. Even this camp had something of that spirit about it: the army was short of rifles and bayonets, so the troops were issued with broomsticks for parades. But Dick threw himself into learning the ropes of intelligence work. His quick mind soaked it up. He led a team of three who were given a truck and the task of surveying the beaches from Rye to Point Nepean, and along the back beaches to Point Leo, 'some of the loveliest coast in Victoria, without houses,' he wrote in his diary, 'just vast stretches of beach and tossing sandhills for mile after mile … We had wonderfully interesting and intricate work to do: recces, reports, sketches, which kept us busy until 10 at night.' His mindset was still passionately anti-war, but he accepted that it was inevitable, and saw intelligence work as a way of saving lives, by avoiding dangers and working out how to win battles through 'the tactics that achieve so much more than frontal assault ... Intelligence, I regard as essentially protective'.

At the end of this camp, Dick faced a choice that could have changed his life. His commanding officer at the camp was Gordon Oldham, who in 1942 was to become deputy director of Australia's first spy unit, then given the innocuous title of the Inter-Allied Services Department. Dick rated Oldham very highly, 'unbeatable as an officer,' and was seriously tempted when Oldham invited him and John to join the 6th Division's intelligence headquarters. But, as for many of the young Australians who fought in World War II, to Dick, the idea of a desk job at home, even in Intelligence HQ, was no match for the cause of going abroad to put your body on the line to fight for your country. Dick and John decided to wait until the army was recruiting for overseas service. One wonders what Dick Hamer might have become had he joined Oldham, and followed him into directing spying and sabotage operations. He certainly would have become a different politician.

In mid-November he was back at Smith and Emmerton for another six weeks, appearing in court, acting in a Christmas revue organised by actor-academic Keith Macartney, sitting exams for his Master of Laws, moving house, walking in rapture through the Botanic Gardens in the evenings, playing golf with John MacLeod, going sailing with Uncle Justice and his cousins, and going to Yarrawonga for the Swinburne clan's family Christmas at the Brownings' farm, then to Barwon Heads for New Year's Eve. And, every chance he had, he spent time with April.

As 1940 began, he was back into uniform, and back to Mount Martha — this time as Sergeant Hamer, for a three-month camp. Now his intelligence work became more intensive, including planning a six-day trek that took the brigade on manoeuvres from Mount Martha to Rosebud, Flinders, Point Leo, and back to Mount Martha: '60 miles in five days, much laughter, many curses, great and valuable experience.' Hamer had to plan the route of the march and pick the campsites. In each battle, his intelligence men were also cast as the enemy. Every second weekend, he and John would head off either to Portsea, to the Martins' beach house, or back to Melbourne, but his pre-war life was receding into the background.

He spent one last month as a civilian in Melbourne. He took over some litigation from his father at Smith and Emmerton, went repeatedly to the Ballets Russes with April, visited relatives, took out his LL.M. degree, spent as much time as he could with his 'wondrously beautiful' beloved, and worried mightily about the future as the Nazis invaded Norway and Denmark. 'Impossible to be detached when all that one loves, admires and respects in England is in such fearful danger,' he wrote in his diary. His military service meant he had chalked up only nine of the 12 months required for admission as a barrister and solicitor; but Hubert, now nearing 70, was pulling strings on his behalf:

> Dad has been tremendously active trying to see that I am admitted before I leave for abroad. This calls for an amendment of the rules, as in 1914–18, allowing those who have done six months' articles to be admitted before they enlist — and admitted before they leave. Dad has drafted a proviso setting out his proposal … Dad has discussed it with the Chief Justice, Sir F. Mann, Uncle Justice, and the three solicitors on the Council for Legal Education, and finds them most sympathetic.
>
> I know it is one of Dad's chief worries, and that he wants me to take over the business as soon as may be: yet I must go to this war. I don't want to, in fact I'm sick with fear, not so much of death, as of being crippled or blinded or affected in some other way so that I become a burden on others: and I'm afraid, too, of what may happen at home while I'm away … It is clear to my mind, unpleasant though it may be, that this is an all-in war, in which industry and business must be kept going as far as possible: and I am one of those who can best be spared for the fighting forces. I have finished a University course, & have not properly begun a career or built up a business. For this is a final & decisive struggle for the survival of the Empire and of Australia as a member.[5]

On Anzac Day, the phone call finally came, requiring Dick and John MacLeod to report for military service on the following Monday, at Caulfield Racecourse. Their first experience of the AIF was depressing: long queues, officious clerks, ill-fitting uniforms left over from World War I, and then an obdurate refusal to allow them to leave to take up their posts at army headquarters. 'John was furious from 11 am onwards, and it was as much as I could do to keep my composure,' Dick wrote. 'Finally I had to see the camp commandant to secure our release.' When they eventually got to HQ, they were given the job of deciphering messages. Exciting at first, it soon became laborious and 'soul-destroying'. After waiting three hours for something to do, the first message Dick was given to decipher was from an army photographer who had dropped his camera down a ravine and wanted a replacement. Dick and John were relieved when, after a fortnight, they were given orders to prepare to sail for the Middle East.

'There was a round of farewell parties. People were giving us useful things like portable stoves,' Dick recalled later. In his diary he wrote:

> Mother and Alison were terribly upset, and I am afraid it is a shock to Dad, who was hoping I'd be admitted before I left … I feel not at all excited, but emptied of feeling … I must leave all my friends and loved ones, all my castles in the air, for a time unknown, perhaps for ever … I pray I may have mental & spiritual resilience to adapt myself … to whatever changes befall. Meanwhile I am sick with fear at what may happen to my family, at leaving them and my beloved April.

Dick and April found time to squeeze in two more visits to the Ballets Russes, in which Anne Mackintosh was now performing. They took a Sunday drive along the Acheron Way with Alison and Dick's college friend Finlay Patrick, who by then were a couple. Nancy threw a farewell party for 150 of Dick's friends at their new home in Evans Court, Toorak; the previous weekend, she had thrown another farewell party for David. At one farewell, Dick got into another argument with jingoistic friends about Germany, which fired him up into a passionate diary entry on the need to ensure that this war, unlike the last one, ended in a peace that was just to the vanquished:

> [The Treaty of] Versailles was a vindictive peace, and another such will inevitably produce another war in the next generation: we are avowedly fighting to secure a world order in which peace, happiness and justice prevail … We are avowedly fighting, not the German people, but Hitlerism; because we don't believe that Hitler represents the true will and genius of Germany … Civilisation cannot afford to lose the mighty artistic & intellectual potentialities of the German nation … It has the very slenderest hope of being achieved, but I do believe that it is the only true means to permanent peace, and that men of good sense & understanding must realise that. But passion and anger blind the eyes to the ultimate. In war, foresight is scarcely an asset.

It was a classic example of Hamer at his best, in the way that Australians would come to know him: an individual with a sharp, clear mind, thinking for the long term, never losing his sense of humanity, and arguing for what was right over what was popular at the moment. The Dick Hamer of 1940 was the same as the Sir Rupert Hamer who, in 2003, challenged the Howard government to end mandatory detention of asylum-seekers, and to treat them as the refugees they were.

But this farewell proved a false start. They sailed from Melbourne on a Saturday, spent Monday in Adelaide, disembarked at Fremantle on the Friday, and then were sent home again. For while they were at sea, Italy entered the war, and it was feared that Italy's North African colonies could create problems for Allied ships heading that way. After two days in Perth, sleeping on a concrete floor in the Poultry and Pigeon pavilion at the showgrounds, they were put on the train back to Melbourne, 'back to see all those people who had given us farewell parties the week before'. Hamer was then sent on a three-week course at an intelligence school at Narellan, in the southern highlands of New South Wales. By happy coincidence, Mr and Mrs Mackintosh had booked a holiday in Sydney to console April over Dick's departure. Dick (and friends) became part of the holiday, heading to Sydney each weekend, staying in hotels offering cheap rates to soldiers, and touring the harbour and other sights with April.

His next stop was the army camp at Broadmeadows, to do another intelligence course. While he waited for his next assignment, he was summoned to appear before the Full Bench of the Supreme Court. He was surprised to find that it had convened solely in order to admit him as a barrister and solicitor. Dick was in his sergeant's uniform, the first soldier to be admitted under the new rules that his father had initiated, and he was besieged by journalists and photographers. It wasn't the last time this was to happen, or the last time he was to allow himself to be the subject of a gimmicky photo, when a photographer got him to pose 'with my cap perched rakishly on the back of the head, and a foaming tankard in the right hand — hardly appropriate for the latest recruit to the legal profession'.

On 2 August, his unit was ordered to embark for the Middle East. A day later, that order was countermanded: instead, Hamer was transferred to become the intelligence officer of a new South Australian battalion, the 2/43rd, then assembling for training at Woodside in the Adelaide Hills. He would also be commissioned as a lieutenant. There was just time to attend a dinner to celebrate his parents' silver wedding anniversary, and an engagement dinner for Anne Mackintosh and John Elder. Then he was off in the train to Adelaide, on 'a cold and gloomy night, which suited my mood'. He asked April not to come to say goodbye.

His mood brightened when he got to the Adelaide Hills and met the men with whom he would share the next year or more. Woodside, he wrote, was the most beautiful location he had seen for an army camp: 'surrounded by rolling grassy hill slopes and wooded valleys, dotted with small rustic villages. This quiet and gracious countryside reminds me again of rural England ...' In the five months he spent there, he never tired of praising the landscape.

Nor did he tire of his men. At division headquarters, he had worked in a small group. Now he had to lead a team of 30 men, servicing a battalion of 1,000 or so, and with 60 men under his charge in the sleeping hut. Until now, Hamer had spent practically all his life among the social elite from which he came: in Toorak, in private schools, and at university and college, the legal profession, and the golf club. At Woodside, for the first time in his life, he found himself thrust amid ordinary working-class or rural Australians who comprised the bulk of the Australian infantry's forces. For the first time, the future politician met his future electorate, and he liked it:

> I find I can rub along with them very well, because they are frank and open, and simple in their tastes, with a strong element of humour and a desire to play games of every kind. They are not difficult to handle, provided that their sacred right to grumble and blaspheme is recognised. An arrogant & bullying manner may produce obedience, but will fail to induce true loyalty or co-operation. It is better to be as far as possible one of them, to share in their discussions, be sympathetic to their just complaints, & take in good part the chaff which they pour upon me unceasingly: retaining nevertheless a hint of firmness, refusing to be drawn into criticism of superior officers, and pulling them up short when the fun and high spirits goes too far. Above all, one should observe the supreme military principle of setting the men an example, & never ordering them to do something which you are unwilling or afraid to do yourself. The men appreciate firmness, if it is allied with justice, and authority allied with sympathy and common humanity.
>
> The men here seem in most respects to be typical Australian soldiers: bold, independent and forthright: resourceful in action, with a true soldier's dash and initiative: simple-natured, quick to appreciate fairness and proper treatment, equally quick to resent bombast, inefficiency and hypocrisy: in morals, distinctly low: in speech, distinctly coarse: in converse, rather circumscribed to the inexhaustible topics of drink and women: in wit and humour, simple

> and obvious, but most ready: likeable, brave and reliable. And I would rather have them with me in battle than any other soldiers on earth.

Hamer was to voice similar thoughts frequently in Palestine and Tobruk. He was not one of the boys; he never could be. But he respected them — more than that, he admired them, and the deeper the trouble they faced at Tobruk, the deeper his admiration for the character of the typical Aussie battler. He loved their sense of humour, their unpretentiousness, their ability to pick out falseness, and their bravery, initiative, endurance, and good humour under stress. The things that divided him from them were to do with different cultures and interests — above all, the unabashed sexism of their attitude to women. Hamer had grown up in a family of female achievers, and had made friends with many more at university. His mother's life had focussed on a hospital that was entirely run and staffed by women. He was an instinctive feminist in a pre-feminist age, and he could never accept his men's practice of bombarding women of any age or occupation with wolf whistles and lewd jokes. He was unforgiving when the same culture was displayed by his commanding officer.

One of the more unexpected sides of his new role was to find that his troops consulted him on romantic matters. Three times in a month, he was asked (and agreed) to be best man at weddings of his men. At 24, he sometimes found himself cast by his men as a marriage guidance counsellor, being asked for advice on problems he had never experienced personally. At the very least, this suggests that the men trusted Hamer and respected his judgement. He also guided his men through the grim task of drawing up their wills.

At the operational level, the lack of proper equipment for training was a frustration. The men of the intelligence section had to learn to draw maps and sketches of the terrain, but were supplied with no compasses, protractors, or sketching materials. In mock battles they were always cast as the enemy, but had no blank ammunition to fire with, so they had to wave a red flag to signify a rifle shot. Dick fumed about this in his diary, but eventually, being Australian, settled for irony: 'I am determined to see through the task of making bricks without straw, and with improvised clay.'

The serious work was to devise and lead courses to equip his men with the skills they would need for intelligence work. When sketchpads finally arrived, he took the men out into the hills so they could learn to accurately depict the terrain on which battles would be fought. One who was particularly good at it was John Dowie, later an artist and sculptor in Adelaide, whose sculptures now stand in every capital city. Hamer planned mock battles to build the fighting skills of the whole battalion, including a three-day trek through the hills featuring a surprise attack at midnight. 'It was our fate during all these encounters to be continually beaten, harried, chased and finally captured,' he wrote. 'But it is a great tactical experience for me, which I am glad to get, and excellent training for my section' (even if after the first trek, he roasted them for 'lack of imagination and common sense'). As the enemy, he was able to quickly spot any weaknesses in the attackers' tactics or execution. He had to organise billets in farmers' sheds each night for the men, and warn the farmers that battles were to be fought on their land. For all the community goodwill towards the troops, this must have sharpened his negotiating skills. The men constantly staged campfire concerts at night; they could also sniff out any dance in the neighbourhood, and persuade the farmers' daughters to come along with them.

In the first month, he and some friends headed for Adelaide every weekend, staying in hotels and going out to nightclubs and dance venues with Adelaide girls he knew. One night, he recounted to Julia years later, they ended up at an illegal casino, run by the uncle of one of his men. But as the training became more serious, his free time largely disappeared, and instead he banked up leave to head back to Melbourne, and his own girl. His first visit home was 'the happiest four days of my life'; his second, supposedly his final leave before embarking for the front, was 'the happiest ten days I have ever spent'. For Christmas 1940, he snuck in a third visit home. The Victorian Railways was booked out, so Dick took his first plane ride, 'on a big DC-2, 14-passenger liner, wonderfully comfortable'. But the visit was bittersweet: he had just a few days with April before leaving again. She was still only 19. And he told her that, as deeply as he loved her, and much as he wanted to marry her when the war was over, he did not want to tie her down with an engagement, but would rather leave her free to 'taste a brimming cup of life and happiness' with whomever she met. Between the lines, he was warning the girl he loved that he might not come back, or might come back permanently disabled. It exemplifies Dick's unselfishness, and willingness to put others' interests ahead of his own — albeit allowing no room for April's own views. An ordinary reader of his diary might be relieved to know that, before the war ended, he finally relented and married the girl of his dreams, with whom he would spend 60 happy years.

The 2/43rd Battalion embarked from Melbourne on 29 December 1940 on the luxury cruise liner the *Mauretania*, as part of an escorted convoy of some of the world's great passenger ships, including the *Queen Mary*, all requisitioned for military use. The escort included HMAS *Canberra*, on which Midshipman David Hamer, 17, was making his maiden voyage as a naval officer. The two brothers caught up when their ships were in Fremantle; they would not see each other again for four years. In both Melbourne and Fremantle, thousands lined the streets to cheer them off. They were bound first for Colombo, where Dick, like most Australians travelling abroad in those times, had his first sight of another country — a pleasant one, with two nights dining and dancing in the luxury of the Galle Face Hotel, with John MacLeod's aunt Mrs Walsh showing him around. (Sadly, Dick did not bring along Mary Bateman, the young masseuse whom he had taken a shine to on the ship. For, in one of those odd coincidences of wartime, Mary later met John MacLeod, fell in love with him, and, in 1944, married him in Brisbane.)

From Colombo, the cruise liners went back to Australia, while the troops climbed onto less valuable ships for the risky passage to Suez. When they got there, the ships spent some days tied up before the men were allowed to disembark. Officers, however, were free to explore the town; Hamer remonstrated in vain to his superiors at the injustice of this double standard. Finally, the men were allowed off the ship, and a train took them to Palestine, where they were to be trained until needed for duty. While they were at sea, a joint British–Australian force had invaded Libya, then an Italian colony, seized the eastern port of Tobruk, taken Libya's second-biggest city, Benghazi, and pushed the Italians right back to the fortress of Tripoli, in the west. It was a rare victory for the Allies at that stage, and the men of the 2/43rd were itching to get to the frontline to join them.

Lieutenant Hamer was far less keen. First, he felt the troops were not ready; all the mock battles so far had been at company level, and it was not until mid-March that he was given approval for the whole battalion to take part in a battle. Second, he was tired and frustrated: all the battalion's administration had now been loaded on his shoulders, on top of his intelligence work. This included censorship of every letter sent home to ensure that it gave away no information of use to the enemy. Dick found reading other people's mail and censoring it to be distasteful (and time-consuming).

The positive side was that he grew fascinated by the country he found himself in. He wanted to explore the Holy Land while he had the chance, and quickly understood the explosive situation being created by the gradual Jewish takeover of an Arab land. Few colleagues shared his interest. To them, the Arab communities around them were filthy, unhygienic, poverty-stricken dumps, and the biblical sites of no interest. When Dick organised a Sunday bus tour to Jerusalem and the Dead Sea, only 30 soldiers out of hundreds in his battalion signed up, mostly from his own section. He made the mistake of diving into the Dead Sea, and emerged with eyes and mouth stinging from its high salt content.

Dick's next excursion was a weekend in Tel Aviv with some brother officers. They asked a taxi owner there to recommend a nightclub and find them some girls who could be their dancing partners:

> He nodded sagely when we explained our wishes, but he evidently misunderstood, for the girls he sought out for us, though ravishingly beautiful, soon proved to have the wrong idea … the dancing and the visiting of night clubs to them were merely a prelude. As soon as

> this became evident, I gently explained to Marie from Marseilles, in my halting French, that I was certainly not coming home with her; and she graciously explained to me, with many charming nuances, that this was a Saturday night, and therefore her most lucrative evening, and though she was enjoying my company immensely, would I please take her home after a few more dances?

Poor Marie: she had probably never met an Australian soldier who had declined to spend the night with her. Hamer's next trip was a guided tour of the biblical sites of Jerusalem with the battalion's padre. There wasn't much danger of that trip going off the rails. While essentially agnostic, Dick had grown up steeped in Christianity; he found the tour 'one of the most interesting days I have ever spent,' and wrote 12 pages in his diary describing it in detail.

At last, the order came to embark for Libya. They would be stationed in Tobruk, replacing the 6th Division, which Churchill had decided to send to Greece as a futile gesture of British solidarity against the impending Nazi attack. Their own task, they were told, would be to guard the 14,000 Italian prisoners who had been taken captive during the Anglo–Australian blitz across Libya. Dick was sent on early in a car of senior officers who formed the advance party. One decided that the battalion needed a sewing machine, so they detoured to Cairo, toured the Pyramids, lunched at Cairo's famed Shepheard's Hotel, and then had to race to catch up with the buses they were supposed to be leading. Lunch at Shepheard's would be the last luxury that Dick Hamer would enjoy for months.

CHAPTER FOUR

Tobruk

Lieutenant R.J. Hamer arrived in Tobruk on 24 March 1941, on what was seen as a low-key mission. The Italians were far away in Tripoli, at the other end of Libya. The German general Erwin Rommel had joined them there; the Allies knew the Germans were shipping in troops and equipment, but since the British navy was busy shipping its own troops and equipment to Greece, they had no idea how many German tanks had arrived in Libya, and assumed there were few. The Allies thought the Germans might try a land assault, but not before May, and not on a scale to cause alarm. Hamer's superiors decided that two of the brigade's three battalions would be enough to guard both the town and the 14,000 Italian prisoners, while the third battalion would embark on a month's training in desert warfare. The task set for the 2/43rd was to survey the defences of Tobruk left by the Italians, decide what improvements were needed, and build them. Despite the damage Tobruk had suffered during the earlier fighting, Hamer was enchanted at first sight. 'Tobruk is as beautiful as Bardia,' he wrote in his diary, 'situated on a jutting tongue of land, with a large landlocked harbour — now filled with the wreckage of ships, submarines and airplanes destroyed by the R.A.F. … the same graceful town of white villas and large public buildings, badly damaged by bombing … but still retaining its outward charm.'

A surprise was awaiting him. He was moved out of intelligence to become the battalion's adjutant, or right-hand man to its commanding officer, Lieut-Col. William Crellin. It was a big jump for a relatively junior subaltern: the adjutant was a central figure in the command structure, and the post was normally held by a captain. His predecessor, Captain Ivan Hare, had fallen out with Crellin, and wanted to return to the frontline; his wish was granted, and Hamer had been chosen to replace him. Sadly, 18 months later, Hare was killed in the final push at El Alamein after displaying such 'great initiative, energy and courage' that he was posthumously awarded the Military Cross. Hamer was 'astounded' by his promotion, regretted leaving his colleagues and intelligence work, but concluded: 'I think I will like the job, because it gives opportunities for organisation, and allows one to take some part in planning the tactics of the Battalion … [to] be concerned vitally in all the unit's operations.'

It would, however, take him out of the action. His superiors had now cast him as part of the brain of the Australian army, not its muscle. While everyone in Tobruk during the siege was at risk from the bombardment of bombs, shells, and bullets, Hamer's involvement in combat missions was now to plan them. He had gone to war expecting to be on the frontline, but he was promoted out of it before he even started. From then on, while he spent much of the war in combat zones, he himself was never directly in combat, but was always planning, analysing, ensuring that orders were carried through, instructing and being instructed. The army, with good reason, put him where his quick, thorough mind would be best employed. But one of the 'what ifs?' one might ask is: had Dick Hamer's army experience been on the frontline, would he have become a different politician? Would he have been more ruthless, more willing to dispatch those trying to dispatch him, less tolerant of opponents and more ready to act quickly to seize his chance?

In Palestine, Hamer had speculated in his diary on the possibility of a German counter-attack. But it came sooner than anyone expected. On the day he arrived in Tobruk, something was stirring at the far end of Libya: Rommel and his Afrika Korps began their advance. They began on a small scale, as Berlin had ordered; even Rommel had no plan for what followed. But he had nearly 300 tanks, the dominant weapon of desert warfare. He had many more planes than the British, and much better artillery. He quickly realised that he had an overwhelming superiority in weaponry. As the overstretched Australians retreated before his advance, Rommel decided to ignore orders, and to sweep all the way to Egypt. By the end of March, his troops had pushed into eastern Libya. On 3 April, they took Benghazi, its biggest city. That night, Hamer wrote in his diary:

> The logical situation seems to me one of rear guard action right back here to Tobruk. Once armoured forces have inferior forces on the move, there is no stopping short of an anti-tank stronghold.

He was proved right. The Australians retreated all the way back to Tobruk, with Rommel's men in hot pursuit. By the night of 5 April, the mood in the garrison had become very grim: an attack was thought imminent. With characteristic Australian logic, Tobruk's commander, Major-General Leslie Morshead, ordered that the troops be given beer: one (longneck) bottle for every two soldiers — with instructions that once each bottle was empty, it was to be filled with kerosene and fitted with a grenade, to make it an anti-tank Molotov cocktail. Writing at 4.00 a.m. after a sleepless night, Dick was full of foreboding. The Australians were brave but, he wrote, did not have the tanks or weapons to hold out such an enemy: 'an attempt to defend Tobruk can end only in our own destruction'. But morning came with no attack, and no tanks yet in sight. The Australians regrouped. They now had four brigades to defend the city with, backed by British artillery and armoured units, an Indian contingent that excelled in night patrols, and many damaged Italian tanks and equipment that the salvage crews were working to fix. On 10 April, Hamer inspected the lines in the 2/43rd's sector, and concluded that, despite some weaknesses, 'overall, the defences here are solid … we will be difficult to dislodge'.

The fighting began on Good Friday, 11 April, when a long line of German tanks sent the sand flying as they took up positions around the 45-kilometre-long semi-circular line of ditches and barbed-wire fences that formed Tobruk's outer defences. On the opening day,

Dick had two close shaves: first, he was knocked off his bicycle by the force of a German shell landing on the road. Then, in the evening, a truck he was in was hit by 'a whole salvo of shells' that shattered the windscreen, punched a hole just below where he was sitting, and left one mudguard looking 'like a colander'. But no one was hit, and the truck kept going. Such escapes became commonplace as the shells, bombs, and bullets kept raining down on them. On Easter Sunday, another volley of shells hit the battalion HQ as Hamer and his superiors were sitting down to lunch. Lunch went on.

The Germans launched their first serious attack in the early hours of Easter Monday. Their engineers blew up the wire on the southern flank, and their tanks began rolling in. But instead of seeing the Australians retreating before them, the Germans were confronted by a battle plan they had never faced before. The Australians stayed in their trenches and their camouflaged dugouts, letting the tanks roll over them, neither firing nor retreating. The German tanks kept going, crossing even the inner 25-kilometre Blue Line of defences. But once they got deep into Allied territory, they were suddenly hit with everything the Allies had: tank guns, mortar shells, machine guns, and Molotov cocktails, and coming from all directions, not least the rear. Meanwhile, as the German infantry attempted to follow in the wake of the tanks, the troops who had stayed hidden now emerged to fire everything they had at them. German tanks and infantry alike were forced to retreat, with heavy losses. A German report by Colonel Olbrich of Rommel's 5th Tank Regiment, later captured by the Allies, blamed the fiasco on poor intelligence:

> The Intelligence gave out before the attack that the enemy was exhausted, that his artillery was extremely weak, and that his morale was very low. Before the beginning of the third attack, the Regt. had not the slightest idea of the well-designed and executed defences, nor of a single battery position, nor of the terrific number of anti-tank guns. Also, it was not known that he had heavy tanks …
>
> 39 tanks went into battle.
>
> 17 tanks were shot to pieces.

> 2 officers are missing or wounded.
> 21 NCOs and men are missing.
> 10 NCOs and men are wounded.
> This means a total loss of 50%.
>
> Sgd: Olbrich.[1]

The failure of the Easter Monday attack was the first reverse the Germans had suffered in Africa. Hamer analysed it repeatedly, in his diary and for his troops, drumming home the key features of Morshead's strategy (which foreshadowed Muhammad Ali's 'rope a dope' tactic in the boxing ring years later). But he sharply disagreed with Morshead's willingness to sacrifice his men's lives by sending them out on night patrols with orders to attack a post, just to create a nuisance. The 2/43rd was ordered to carry out such a raid the next night, an order that Crellin and Hamer 'put into effect with serious misgivings'. Their fears were well founded. The following day, Hamer recorded the costs: 'The patrol ran straight into the enemy,' he wrote. Five men were missing, killed, or captured; 'one of them is Corporal Mayman, a very fine and likeable fellow'.

> I sat up all night waiting for that patrol: I would have liked to be with them: not for the excitement, so much as because I believe that one should not order others to do what one is not prepared to do oneself. In a sense, I feel responsible for the casualties, & I can easily perceive that the worst part of this job is going to be the shuffling of pawns, the sending of men into danger without the chance of being able intimately to share it.[2]

It was a recurring theme in Hamer's Tobruk diary. Morshead took pride in his strategy of 'aggressive defence', of continual night patrols, including attempts to seize German posts, to put the attackers themselves on the defensive and keep them on edge. Hamer agreed with the strategy; but, like others, felt Morshead was prone to order attacks that put his troops in mortal danger without clear objectives and/or adequate planning and support. It left a deep imprint on him. Fifty years later, he told interviewer Christopher Sexton:

> They told us afterwards it was a feint, but we didn't know that at the time. How they expected one company of 120 men to break through the German cordon wasn't clear, and what they expected us to do after that wasn't clear either ... I was young and eager, I suppose, and I thought it was the kind of operation that was not worth losing people for ... You've got no hope [of achieving the objective]. You lose a lot of good men, and no one expects any advantage out of it, except in a strategic sense ... [It] always used to upset me.[3]

This was just one example of many futile tactics used in the war. The 9th Division was in Tobruk only because the 6th Division had been sent to Greece with an objective that Hamer soon realised was impossible with the resources available. In six weeks of fighting, the Germans killed, captured, or wounded almost 40 per cent of Australia's 6th division, for what Churchill knew would be only a futile gesture he thought would show the world that Britain had 'stood by' the Greeks. A few months later came the heartbreaking story of the 2/21st Battalion, sent to the Indonesian island of Ambon to halt the Japanese advance. Its commanding officer, Lieut-Col. Leonard Roach, a career officer with a Military Cross from the previous war, warned army HQ in Melbourne repeatedly that he could not stop the Japanese with the resources he had been given. For his honesty, he was cashiered, and allowed no further part in the war. In just five days, the Japanese then crushed the ill-equipped Australians; in all, 661 Australian soldiers, the majority of the battalion, died there or in captivity. The general who cashiered their commander and sent them to their deaths, Lieutenant-General Vernon Sturdee, ended up being given a knighthood.

One should not make too much of Hamer's criticisms. He was not alone: many officers at Tobruk privately criticised Morshead's willingness to sacrifice troops and tanks for futile shows of defiance. Dick admired the Australian troops, broadly supported Morshead's leadership, and was fully committed to the task he had been given. He was just as likely to complain in his diary about the 'spiritless' approach of the enemy (sometimes German units; sometimes Italian) who did less night patrolling than the Australians. Morshead had set a goal that 'no man's land would be our land'. Australian units were sent out constantly to engage with the enemy at night, usually in low-key raids, but sometimes in larger battles. It was in those forays, Hamer argued, that men were often sent out to face enemy fire with no clear objectives or means to achieve them.

Immediately after the 15 April fiasco, Hamer and his commanding officer decided to plan their own attack rather than wait for HQ to send them more orders like that. Hamer drew up a plan to try to 'clean up' two valleys occupied by the enemy, using two companies with tank and artillery support. A month later, Morshead visited the battalion and told Hamer his plan had been approved — but with some modifications. The next day, Lt. Hamer sat in on a meeting with the top brass, at which the revised plan was outlined. He was alarmed: the changes had made a simple plan complex, removed the element of surprise, exposed his troops to attack before they could launch their own attack, and left them vulnerable on the east, while the complexity of the revised plan meant there was 'much possibility of it going astray'. But, surrounded by brigadiers and colonels who gave it their instant endorsement, Hamer said nothing. 'As the only subaltern at the conference, and since the commanders of artillery, tanks and machine guns all approved of the plan, I did not voice my doubts,' he wrote that night. 'I discussed the plan (later) with the C.O., but he felt it too late to make any big changes.'

His fears were right. The attack failed, and for the reasons he had foreseen. The noise of the tanks moving to take up position alerted the enemy. Then the tanks got lost, and turned up in the middle of the infantry. Thanks to the tank noise, the Germans had time to get their own tanks into position, and the Allied attack had to be called off. Two Australians were killed, one of them a friend of Dick's, and two tanks and three weapons carriers were destroyed. Dick did not write in his diary for two nights, then resumed with the words: 'Even warfare becomes monotonous after a time.' Among other things, he reported having had another close shave with death, this time when he'd been machine-gunned by a Messerschmitt. He didn't bother adding any more after that: being shot at, bombed, and shelled was now an ordinary part of life in Tobruk.

The defiance of Tobruk was the first moral victory of the war for the Allied armies. Part of the reason was that Australian and British morale stayed high throughout the siege, despite the appalling conditions they were living in, the incessant bombardment, and their relentless workload. Morshead ordered that troops be kept busy constantly, to keep their minds on the job rather than run the risk of having idle time filled in by complaints and defeatism. A key factor, surely, was the cheeky, irreverent Australian character, which turned deprivation into a joke, and defence into attack, and seemed to take nothing seriously. A classic example was a depot known as Cantoneria 31, on the road to Derna. An advertising signwriter serving with the engineers, Sapper 'Doc' Dawes, painted a two-storey wall at Derna with a big ad for Victoria Bitter. On a second wall, he painted one of the signs ubiquitous in those days along Victoria's railways, '9,256¼ miles to Griffiths Bros. Teas'. And on a third wall, he painted a huge ad for Abbot's Lager, signing off: 'a good drink … but bloody hard to get'. The Derna depot was later abandoned to Rommel, who briefly used it as his headquarters. What did he make of the artwork decorating it? It should have warned him that this enemy was a bit unusual.

The most famous example was the troops' response when Nazi radio propagandist William Joyce (known to Allied troops as Lord Haw-Haw) disparaged them as 'the poor desert rats of Tobruk' living in their trenches and underground caves. The Australian and British soldiers quickly christened themselves the Rats of Tobruk. Their limestone caves, reinforced with concrete, were actually a godsend in the heat of the Libyan summer, and invisible to the bombers overhead. (Both sides usually slept under cover during the heat of the day, and fought at night.) A lot of work was done in the caves, while elaborate manoeuvres were undertaken to make it appear that the 43rd battalion HQ was in a building that was in fact abandoned: the Germans wasted many shells on that empty building. Constant deception of the enemy was another unusual feature of Morshead's strategy. To protect the crucial water-distilling plant, for example, the artists painted a huge crack down the middle of its wall; thinking it abandoned, the Nazi bombers left it alone.

But Tobruk survived only because the Royal Navy controlled the Mediterranean. By day, German planes controlled the air. By night, British ships controlled the sea. Each night, a convoy led by destroyers would speed at a rate of 40 knots from Egypt to Tobruk, laden with supplies and, sometimes, reinforcements. When they got to Tobruk, Hamer recalled, they would have only an hour to load and unload, often just heaving supplies onto the wharf, before turning around and getting back to the safety of port before dawn. The British also provided the tank and artillery regiments, which had proved crucial in the Battle of Easter Monday. But the soldiers the enemy feared most, Hamer wrote, were the Gurkhas of the Indian army, who excelled in night patrols. 'They were extremely adept at creeping up on people undetected,' he recalled later. 'They would knife the sentries without a sound and then bring back their ears to prove it.'

Hamer was quick to see the significance of Tobruk's defiance. 'While we hold Tobruk,' he wrote in his diary, 'we not only hold a considerable (German) force back from the easterly drive, but we make it impossible for the whole strength of enemy AFVs [armoured fighting vehicles] to be concentrated for the thrust into Egypt … This is the first time that the Panzer division has been checked in any real way and not only checked, but badly beaten.' It was only when he finally captured Tobruk in June 1942, after the Australians had been relieved by South Africans, that Rommel felt able to attack Egypt. But by then the Allies had been reinforced so much that their troops and tanks greatly outnumbered his.

Hamer by now used his diary almost entirely to record the progress of the battle for Tobruk, and of the war in general. Tobruk was virtually a town without inhabitants: most of its residents had fled when the fighting started, and the only non-soldiers left were 1,300 refugees dependent on Allied food rations, and organised into work groups. The Italian prisoners had been sent to Egypt on the British ships at night; some ended up in Australia. Unlike Palestine, Tobruk offered no opportunity for tourism; the most refined cultural experience on hand was a swim in the Mediterranean. It was also a town without women: despite strong protests from 2/4th AGH (Australian General Hospitals) commander Dr Norman Speirs, all the field hospital's nurses and masseuses (physiotherapists) had been ordered out on 7 April, on the grounds that Tobruk under fire would be 'no place for a woman'. The only moments when Dick's old life broke through were when letters came, or when *The Bulletin* arrived in town each week. He read it avidly: one day he took a break from the war all around him to write down his response to an article on Banjo Paterson's poetry; another day, to an article on what the British Labour party might do if it won power.

The war dominated his thoughts. When Germany attacked Russia on 22 June, Dick predicted correctly that it would end in 'disaster' for the Nazis. 'I do not expect the Russians to crack,' he wrote:

> The Red Army is colossal in size and equipment … Russia is an enormous country, and this is the greatest test the German Army has faced … If the Russians can hold out till the winter — no matter if the Germans reach the gates of Leningrad, Moscow and Odessa — that doom is half-accomplished. This will be the fiercest, bloodiest war in history.

It was an extraordinarily accurate forecast from a young lieutenant who, at this stage, had never set foot in Europe. But Hamer's mind was constantly analysing the lessons of everything happening in the war, from the small skirmishes of daily combat to the grand strategic moves of the dictators and army chiefs. His views sometimes wavered, and he was not always right, but he usually was. The probing, objective mind that had cracked the secrets of Latin at school, and the law at university, was now acquiring formidable military knowledge. He was learning by doing, and learning by thinking about what others did. It served him well as he moved up the ladder to higher responsibilities.

At the start of May, Rommel made a second attempt to seize Tobruk, this time from the south-west. He succeeded in taking an area of the outer defences known as the Salient, and its dominant feature, a rare hill rising above the flat desert landscape, known to the Australians as Hill 209. But Rommel could advance no further. The Germans had suffered colossal losses of men, tanks, and planes. Rommel had become overstretched, and on 3 May Hitler ordered him to halt the assault. Morshead ordered repeated attempts to retake Hill 209, leading to serious Australian losses, but without success. Two attempts by the British to break the siege from the Egyptian side also failed. The two armies settled into a stalemate that was to last for a year.

The 2/43rd's biggest battle was still ahead. On 9 July, it took its turn in the Salient, taking up positions so close to enemy lines 'you could hear the Germans talking 200 yards away'. Three weeks later they received orders that left Dick alarmed and angry:

> Our unit is to do a Company attack in a week's time. It has been ordered by Brigade, none of whose staff has ever seen the objective, or the terrain. We are to attack R7, the right flank of the enemy position in the Salient. It is very strongly held with MGs [machine guns] and mortars, and the enemy day discipline is so good that we have been able to pinpoint very few of his positions: it is one of his vital points, and to attack the enemy at his strongest point with an inadequate force is repulsive to my spirit. We have been promised strong artillery support, but it is really only a short concentration, fired without observation, on uncertain targets. Heavy casualties are certain, and I have no real hope of success: further, there are certain to be booby traps thickly strewn near the post, which our recce patrols can't get close enough to locate, or our engineers to delouse … And to attack this with one weak company, of whom 40 are newly arrived reinforcements, and 7 minutes artillery preparation! …

> I am absolutely opposed to the project, and I have put up these arguments to the C.O., but he, of course, hasn't seen the ground doesn't visit his troops or his positions nearly enough — and in the presence of Brigadiers and such, he is as meek as a chicken — won't fight for his troops — I feel very sickened and disheartened.

A day later, his 25th birthday was spent in conferences on the attack. He wrote that he was 'still full of misgivings, but an order is an order, and I must, for my part, see to it that the plan is as thorough as possible.' Having won agreement to have all the forward units open fire at once to disguise which one was launching the real attack, he planned with split-second timing which actions would be taken by each of the units involved at each moment. He concluded by noting: 'Mac [possibly the company's commanding officer, Captain Lewis McCarter], is confident, but I don't share it.'

The young lieutenant was right again. The attack failed, and failed badly. While 20 men got right up to the final ditch of the German defences, they were the last survivors of a company of 138 that had launched the attack. Hamer's diary records the grim toll, along with some reflection of what the Australian brass was portraying as a triumph:

> 138 men went into battle, 30 killed and 77 wounded: all the officers wounded, all but one of the NCOs killed or wounded. It was an epic of heroism and courage, magnificent even in failure … It was a glorious day for the unit, but let there be an end to this futile nibbling at enemy strongpoints. Let us go the whole way: attack him in strength, with adequate forces, in a task which has some prospect of success, or let us reserve our energy and eagerness.

For the only time in writing 1,160 pages of diaries, Hamer tore out a page he had written. One can only imagine what he had entered there about his superior officers. Even the official history of the war, which rarely criticised any commander's decisions, conceded: 'It had been a costly attack.'

Hamer was no pacificist: he believed that, in war, an enemy is there to be attacked. The diary records him suggesting targets for raids, or better ways of carrying them out. Fifty years later, he told Sexton:

> It was dog eat dog, and the only way to bring an end to the whole thing was to defeat them. It was them or us. There wasn't room for too much sentiment. You recognised them as fellow human beings, but you knew they had the same motivation, and if they had the chance, they'd do the same. You just had to do it.

But he had come up against one of the recurring problems of big organisations: the desire of senior executives to curry favour with their distant superiors by being seen to *do something* — even if it was something poorly thought out, and that wasted the lives of the young men under their command. Armies are highly vulnerable to this weakness, since soldiers are required to follow orders, even at the cost of their own lives. The commander reluctant to waste his men's lives in futile show fights, like Lieutenant-Colonel Roach on Ambon, risks being seen by his superiors as a coward, as 'lacking the will to fight'. The commander who sacrifices his men for nothing, by contrast, wins praise for being 'willing to fight', a man who takes risks and shows initiative. There is a parallel in today's world: executives in business and government who propose cutting jobs to save money are seen by their superiors as showing initiative and resourcefulness. Executives who give priority to ensuring that services are done well are seen as barriers to efficiency.

In Tobruk, Hamer visited the frontlines constantly to get a better sense of his troops' experience, and to learn what were the real opportunities and obstacles ahead. In later life, he told people he sometimes went on night patrols to gain a better understanding of what they involved. No such patrols, however, are recorded in his diary. By contrast, senior officers rarely visited the frontlines. Hamer believed that decision-making suffers when the decision-makers get out of touch with those who have to put their decisions into effect.

(Decades later, as premier, if Hamer had a spare half-hour in a country town, he would pop in to some state government office to ask how it was coping.) His Tobruk diary frequently records that his men are keen to take on the enemy rather than sit in trenches waiting. But as someone who valued human life deeply, he believed the Diggers' will to fight should be reserved for well-planned, adequately resourced missions with 'some prospect of success'. He would soon be put into a position where his views would carry more weight, and under a commander with a track record of standing up to his superiors.

But we are jumping ahead. The battle for R7 had an epilogue, perhaps the most extraordinary moment in Hamer's wartime experience. Let his diary tell the story:

> The most remarkable events were reserved for the full light of day [that is, after the Australians had retreated and the fighting stopped]. Many of our dead and wounded were still lying out near R7, and I suggested to the Doc that since both sides were respecting the Red Cross, we should try to get them in. So we organised three trucks with large white flags and the Geneva cross, and Sgt. Tuit [the head of the stretcher-bearers] went out by the gap, with his heart in his mouth. I intended him to stop well short, but he drove up to within 200 yards of R7, and went forward on foot until he was stopped by a German doctor, who came out of the post and indicated that there were mines in his path.
>
> Then followed an amazing scene. Our SBs [stretcher-bearers] tended our wounded, 7 of whom were still there, collected our dead, and brought them all back. German SBs actually brought some of our wounded out of the post, and handed them over to our people. Others, with the aid of a peculiar instrument resembling a long divining rod, cleared tracks through the minefield to allow our casualties to be reached. The German officer in charge of the post came and talked to Tuit, had him a delicious lemon drink brought from the post, and let him look through his binoculars, which Tuit says were really magnificent. All day our trucks worked, brought in 30 dead and 9 wounded: not a shot was fired by either side; Germans

> walked round R7 in the open, where previously it was impossible to see a trace of them. German ambulances were at work, too, all the morning; and tonight, the truce is over, machine guns rattle again, their mortars boom and crash, and the work of mutual destruction begins once more.

Sgt. Tuit and his stretcher-bearers were actually a Salvation Army band from Adelaide. Tuit was the bandmaster, and they were in Tobruk as the regimental band. But since Tobruk had no time for band recitals, they had been retrained as stretcher-bearers. When Tuit finally took his leave by saluting the humane German officer, he noted that the officer responded, not with the Nazi salute, as Hitler required, but with the former salute of the *Reichswehr*, the old German army.

The Battle of R7 was the most searing encounter that the 2/43rd faced in Tobruk. Three days later, they were relieved for a spell in Tobruk's rest camp, and Hamer for one sorely needed it. 'For a week, I have had about 3 hours' sleep in 24, always by day and always interrupted,' he wrote. 'I feel thoroughly exhausted ... Had a glorious swim in the Harbour this evening, and felt really clean again.' Then they returned to the more peaceful eastern front, from where they watched with glee as the defenders shot down Messerschmitts attempting dive-bombing raids; for once, he wrote, 'we were spectators, not the targets'. In quiet moments, he and his successor as intelligence officer, James Hardy, snuck off for a swim at the beach. Their days in Tobruk were nearing an end; British and Polish units were arriving to relieve them. Finally, on the night of 17–18 October, the 2/43rd climbed onto the fast ships when they arrived on their night run, and were taken back to Egypt. As they waited on the beaches of Tobruk, Hamer, who by then rarely wrote in his diary, penned his final thoughts:

> I can scarcely realise that we are to leave this place — our time here has passed quickly: it has been interesting and useful. Apart from the 2 August show, we have had no serious reverses; we have had

> many spectacular little successes. The unit has made the most of its chances, has shown itself tough, sensible and reliable, and I am proud to be its adjutant.
>
> It is clear that the failure to take Tobruk threw all the German Africa Corps plans out of gear. Sufficient armoured forces, artillery and infantry were concentrated here to make the advance into Egypt impossible. With its perimeter defence, Tobruk had no flank to be turned, and attempts to break through were prohibitively costly …

Four days later, on 21 October, Dick began his diary entry by recording that he was now in Palestine, 'in a comfortable camp with cinema, well-stocked canteen, hot showers and a mess. From my office I can see the rich green pastures and the trees and the distant hills — so long looked for and sorely missed'. He began recounting the voyage, and got as far as recalling his first meal in safe waters: 'a luxurious breakfast of bacon and eggs: no air attack: a lazy morning in the sunlight on the deck …' He did not finish the sentence. He never wrote in his diary again. Was it that experiencing peace and normality confronted him, as if for the first time, with the full horror of what he had been living through for the previous seven months?

Tobruk had changed him. Never had he experienced life with such intensity. Never had he confronted death and trauma on such a scale. Never before had he been under fire constantly, or played a part in so many decisions that meant life or death for others. Years later, he told me it was a turning point in his life. Above all, he learned to think for himself, to argue his case as logically and persuasively as he knew how — but if he failed to convince his superiors, to knuckle down to try to make their decision work. He had gone to war as a bright young law graduate, a social butterfly, and a cultural dilettante. He emerged from it as a highly disciplined, experienced administrator, used to weighing up decisions quickly and choosing the best course of action. Independent thinking, loyal teamwork, skilful administration: it was a combination that would take Dick Hamer to the top of Victorian politics.

CHAPTER FIVE

From El Alamein ...

On his return to Palestine in October 1941, Lieutenant R.J. Hamer was promoted to captain, and to a more senior post. While his colleagues were given some leave, many of them 'going down to Cairo, to the fleshpots,' Hamer was seconded to a ten-week course in Palestine, at a staff school for junior officers. He was to remain on secondment for the rest of the war: on the books of the 2/43rd, but never with his battalion. From here on, he was promoted to posts at increasingly higher levels of headquarters. He was sent on the staff course to equip him for his new position — as brigade major for the 20th Brigade. In effect, he was promoted from chief of staff to a lieutenant-colonel, to chief of staff to a brigadier. And not just any brigadier, but a man he had come to admire in Tobruk, and who clearly admired him. He was Brigadier Windeyer, later Justice Sir Victor Windeyer of the High Court.

Windeyer was then 41. The fourth generation of one of Australia's most prominent legal dynasties, he was a leading Sydney barrister. Later, he would spend 14 years on the bench of the High Court, where he became one of the most lucid judges in its history. Born in 1900, he had finished school in time to sign up for World War I, but too late to take part. Instead, he acquired his military skills in the Sydney University Regiment, becoming its part-time commander in 1937 while working as a barrister. When war broke out, he took command of the 2/48th Battalion. Its tracks moved in parallel with those of the 2/43rd: training together at Woodside, embarking together for Palestine, and sent together to defend Tobruk. With only a few hundred Australian officers in Tobruk, the two lawyer-soldiers got to know each other well.

Years later, Hamer singled out Windeyer as his outstanding commander in the war, ranking him with Sir James Darling and Professor Macmahon Ball as one of the three men who most influenced his development. In a history of the New Guinea campaign, *Bravery above Blunder*, the former chief of general staff, Lieutenant-General John Coates, summed up Windeyer's leadership style as 'precise, unruffled and resolute … firm, fair and friendly'. He made a point of keeping his men informed at all times, was thorough in everything he did, and was respected by those serving under him. The official war history notes that: 'His deliberate speech and contemplative manner, unusual in a military leader, masked a competent and determined personality.' He and his new right-hand man had something in common.

Their first assignment was easy: defending Syria against the risk of a German invasion from the north through Turkey. It was easy because no Germans came. The *Wehrmacht* had been overstretched by Hitler's ambitious decision to invade Russia; it was suffering such heavy losses that it had no troops to spare for a new front in the Middle East. Had the Germans been able to invade, Hamer probably would have ended up in a German prison camp. Half a century later, he told Christopher Sexton: 'We had 3,000 men to guard 3,000 square [kilometres].' They were based in Aleppo, one of the world's oldest cities, which Hamer thought 'a very romantic place, dominated by a medieval castle'. French was the *lingua franca* between Syrians and Europeans, so Hamer's modest facility in French was valuable. But their stay in Syria would be short.

Back in Australia, the September 1940 election left prime minister Menzies heading a minority government, reliant on two Victorian independents. The younger Menzies lacked the people skills he developed later. In August 1941, he was dumped by his own side, and Country Party leader Artie (later Sir Arthur) Fadden took over. Six weeks later, the two independents transferred their support to

Labor leader John Curtin, and he became prime minister. Just two months later, Japan attacked Pearl Harbour and began its rapid sweep through South-East Asia, brushing aside the small garrisons of the colonial powers. Curtin insisted that the Australian divisions in the Middle East be brought home to defend the country against the risk of Japanese attack. British prime minister Winston Churchill (correctly) saw the risk of the Japanese invading Australia as remote, and fought to at least keep some of the divisions in the Middle East, or send them to fight in Burma or Java. In another of those pointless shows of support that prime ministers and generals make in wartime, a token 3,000 Australian troops were sent to Java, where they were soon defeated, captured, and sent to Japanese prisoner-of-war camps. More than a third of them never came back. Curtin and Churchill agreed, however, that the 9th Division would be left in the Middle East until replacement units could be sent. The replacement units never came. The division ended up staying in the Middle East throughout 1942, and won eternal glory by playing a decisive role in the decisive battle that effectively ended the war in Africa.

In early 1942, both sides rearmed and replenished their North African armies: the British by sea, the Germans mostly by air. But Hitler's focus on the Russian front allowed the British to gain the upper hand in tanks, men, and weaponry. Rommel decided to launch an all-out attack before it was too late: his offensive began on 26 May, and by 21 June he had retaken Tobruk. The Afrika Korps then pushed into Egypt, heading for Cairo. British commander General Claude Auchinleck massed his forces at El Alamein, where topography created a relatively narrow passage between the Mediterranean to the north and the marshy Qattara Depression to the south. The 20th Brigade, by then in Lebanon, was ordered to head to Egypt — but in secret, without alerting the enemy. Captain Hamer was put in charge of the deception:

> When the Division was rolling on its way by military trucks to Egypt, mostly by night, I was left behind in Tripoli with about 20 men, with instructions to make it look as though they were all still

> there. We left all the tents up. We went buzzing around in trucks all the time, sending sand flying up. We had to keep the radios on all the time. But it was all futile. We were the only troops in the Middle East with brown boots; everyone else had black boots ... So as the troops drove down into Palestine in the trucks, with their boots showing, everyone saw it was us.[1]

The first battle of El Alamein in July 1942 halted the German advance. Three weeks later, the British launched a counter-attack, but it too was halted. The ensuing stalemate worked for the British. A third of the German ships sent to supply Rommel were sunk by the Royal Navy, while the British increased their superiority in tanks, weapons, and manpower. Desperately short of fuel, Rommel launched a fresh attack on 30 August, but had to abandon it after three days. The 20th Brigade was then ordered to launch a counter-attack to seize an enemy position by the coast, but that too failed. Amid the ongoing stalemate, Captain Hamer used intelligence reports and air photography to prepare what Australia's official war history called 'a brilliant analysis ... [that] built up a composite picture of the order of battle and the defensive lay-out in front of the brigade'. His analysis was circulated to the upper echelons of Britain's Eighth Army, now led by General Bernard Montgomery. Like Churchill, 'Monty' was one of the new style of leaders, with a great PR flair for instilling a sense of confidence and leadership around him. Hamer was assigned to show him around when he called on the 20th Brigade, and ended up with mixed feelings: 'Monty was a very egocentric little man, who didn't like fighting battles unless he was sure he could win,' he recalled. 'But he was a master of deceit: he created the impression he was going to attack in the south, and when the Germans pushed a lot of their forces there, he attacked through the middle. And because British intelligence had broken the German codes, Monty knew exactly when German attacks were coming.'

The final battle began on 23 October. Hamer described the opening as being like a battle from World War I. 'More than 1,000 Allied guns opened up at 9.30 p.m., followed by an infantry assault on the same narrow front,' he said. 'We broke through the enemy's forward lines, and held our positions for several days. Monty's forces used our position as a springboard for the final assault.' The losses on both sides were colossal. The official history reports that by the afternoon of the 24th, the 2/13th battalion, one of the three in Hamer's brigade, was 'practically without officers'. The battalion endured five consecutive nights of battle with no sleep. By dawn on the 26th, the Allies had already lost 6,140 men in just over two days. But on the Axis side the losses were far worse. Rommel, who had been in a sanatorium when the battle started, returned to find his units shredded to pieces. 'Rivers of blood were pouring out over miserable strips of land,' he wrote. It had become a war of attrition, and given the Allies' two-to-one advantage in tanks and manpower, it could end only one way. By 1 November, Rommel knew the battle was lost, but Hitler refused permission to retreat. By 4 November, Montgomery was down to 500 tanks of his original 1,100, but Rommel was down to just 25 tanks, with no more fuel. More than 50,000 men had been killed or wounded, almost three-quarters of them on the Axis side. Rommel then defied his Fuehrer and ordered a retreat, but too late. With little motor transport, he abandoned his Italian allies and half of his own men, to try to get a critical mass to safety. Even that ultimately proved futile: the German troops not killed or captured at El Alamein were taken on the long, slow retreat west. The Allies recaptured Tobruk in December. By 23 January they had taken Tripoli, and the Germans retreated into the mountains of Tunisia. Hitler finally sent Rommel substantial reinforcements, but that only swelled the number of German and Italian captives taken to a phenomenal 230,000 by the time the guns fell silent, on 12 May 1943.

El Alamein was like a World War I bloodbath. Even on the winning side, one in four Australians who took part were killed, wounded, or captured. In 12 days, some 620 Australians were killed — more troops than the country was to lose during the entire Vietnam War. But unlike the battles of World War I, El Alamein proved decisive. Together with the Russian victory at Stalingrad in the winter of

1942–43, it was the turning point of the war. After those two epic losses, Hitler was living on borrowed time.

For Hamer, El Alamein ended another phase of his army life: he was once again taken out of his unit, and sent back to school. At the start of 1943, the 9th Division went home at last. But within days of Rommel's retreat, Hamer was sent, unwillingly, to Haifa, to another course in planning and intelligence work at a British staff college. He did not get back to Australia until the middle of April 1943. He had been away for 28 months, and had lived through experiences utterly different from anything in his earlier life. April was now 22. She had graduated some time earlier, and was working as a researcher for the Prices Commission, under Professor Douglas Copland. Much had changed in their lives during their long separation, but their relationship had endured. In Palestine, Dick noted in his diary: 'April is yet to miss a mail, and neither have I.' Every week of the war, they wrote to each other. In Tobruk, when Dick's existence was a daily battle of life and death, he broke off from recording the battles to write: 'Lovely letter and birthday telegram from April the memory of her sweetness and love is my support.' His former reluctance to tie her down now seemed precious. On 11 May, they announced their engagement.

The army had an unwelcome surprise for him. The 20th Brigade was training for jungle warfare on the Atherton Tablelands, but Hamer was sent to Darwin, to be brigade major for the 23rd Brigade. This was a brigade originally formed from units of the civilian militias, and was dedicated to garrison duties only. It was the last brigade any red-blooded soldier wanted to be assigned to; Dick described it as 'a repository for officers who had been made redundant in Papua New Guinea, people who got blamed when things went wrong'. Eventually, the brigade was sent to PNG, but even there, only to patrol areas where there was no fighting. Fortunately, his appointment lasted only six weeks. By now promoted to major, his next job was in the headquarters of the 9th Division. A former colleague at 20th Brigade HQ, Lieutenant-Colonel the Rev. R.J. (Tim) Barham, asked for Dick to join him in a new unit being set up to plan the campaign to retake New Guinea from the Japanese.

They were ordered to plan in detail an invasion by sea, to take the coastal port of Lae. The Australian army had not made a landing by sea since Gallipoli in 1915. Other Allied troops had made some landings during the four years of the war, but mostly where they faced little resistance. The engineers had a unit of specialists on amphibian landings, but the army had no corporate knowledge to help it plan what Australia's official war history was to term 'the largest amphibious operation yet undertaken in the South-West Pacific'.

Hamer's job was to work out the exact logistics of the landing: 'how to load ships so that things come out in the right order at the other end'. After three weeks in Cairns, they flew to Milne Bay, in the south-east of Papua, to complete the planning. Their instructions were to land the troops east of Lae, then map out a detailed blueprint that would see them come around behind the Japanese to cut them off from escaping into the jungle. It would not be easy. To quote from the official war history:

> Dense jungle, interspersed with patches of kunai (grass) 8 to 10 feet high and mangrove swamps near the coast, covered the coastal plain. Between Red Beach and Lae, 16 miles away, the advancing division would have to cross five rivers and a large number of small streams … There were no roads in the area, only native paths. The two landing beaches were about 20 yards wide and of firm black sand, but behind them was a swamp from which there were few exits.[2]

The detailed planning for these operations was left to each division, which annoyed the Americans at General Douglas MacArthur's headquarters. Lieutenant-General Stephen Chamberlin complained to MacArthur that the Australian planning staff was 'undoubtedly new to the game'. So they were, but they were smart, and it turned out that their plans worked. Some losses were sustained while troops crossed the deep, fast-flowing Busu River under enemy fire, but Lae fell in 16 days. Dick's team was immediately ordered to plan a second landing further up the coast at Finschhafen. This attack was to be carried out by Hamer's old brigade, led by Windeyer. It began only six days after the fall of Lae, allowing little time for preparation; more things went wrong, including a thoroughly muddled landing in which different units got to the beaches mixed up with each other. On 25 September, Japanese planes bombed the 9th Division's mobile headquarters, and a number of senior officers were killed; but, yet again, Hamer escaped. Within 11 days, Finschhafen too had fallen. The pattern was then repeated around the coast, up to Sio in the north-east. Major Hamer, the future politician, thought it an excellent example of lateral thinking, making the most of scarce resources:

> The strategy was to seize the areas you needed as bases. You'd take one, then other areas up the coast, on the way to the Philippines. It was a very good strategic plan. If you'd just fought your way all along the coast, you'd have spent years doing it. But if you use your mobility, your ships and planes, you take what you need, clear a perimeter protection around it, and on to the next one.

For the first time in his army career, Hamer's role was recognised publicly, with an announcement that he had been mentioned in dispatches. But his work was interrupted by the common enemy of both the Australian and Japanese armies in that jungle: malaria. He spent Christmas 1943 in a field ambulance unit. After three weeks, he was discharged, but far from cured. In mid-February, the team was relieved, and flew back to Townsville, after seven months in PNG. Two weeks later, Hamer was granted a month's leave, and headed to Melbourne for an important event.

The bride was radiant. *The Argus* reported that she wore 'a gown of ivory georgette over satin, and limousine lace veil', and carried a bouquet of matching tuberoses. The groom was yellow. He was still suffering from jaundice, and wore a khaki serge uniform. But it was a happy wedding at Christ Church, South Yarra, on the Saturday evening of 4 March 1944. Dick's old friend from Trinity, the Rev. J.D. McKie, officiated. The best man was his brother Alan, who had come home from Britain to put his chemical knowledge to use in developing Australia's munitions industry. April's sister Anne, now Mrs John Elder, was matron of honour, and the reception was at the Elders' home in Toorak. It had been almost five years since Dick and April had started going out together; their marriage was to last for 60 years. Their wedding night was spent at the Windsor Hotel. But Dick recalled that, in a gesture of brotherly love, 'Alan arranged for us to start our honeymoon at 4 a.m. on the Sunday morning.' They flew to Tasmania, by then the only state that Dick had not seen in his travels with the army. They spent a fortnight touring the island and, somehow, April managed to get sunburnt in Tasmania in March.

They spent another fortnight together, back in Melbourne, before Dick returned to his unit. Three significant developments took place in that time. To his surprise, he was greeted home by a public notice in the morning papers:

> Messrs. J.M. Smith and Emmerton, of 480 Bourke Street, have pleasure in announcing that they have Admitted into Partnership Major Rupert James Hamer, LL.M., A.I.F.[3]

Dick's entire legal experience was nine months as an articled clerk. He commented later, '[I was] the most ill-qualified, inexperienced partner you could ever have in a law firm.' But Hubert was then 73, and perhaps desperate to lock Dick in as his successor — as well as rewarding him for his military service.

Second, Dick was not the only Hamer getting married. He stayed in Melbourne long enough to see Alison marry his old friend Finlay Patrick at the Melbourne Grammar chapel on 5 April. They had been a couple almost as long as Dick and April; Fin, too, had just returned from Papua New Guinea, after service in the Middle East, and was moving to army headquarters.

A third big change awaited Dick when he flew back to Melbourne for a brief visit in May: April was pregnant. It was not unusual after a honeymoon, but he felt devastated that he would not be there to help her through it. By the time he saw her again, their son Christopher was almost a year old.

The 9th Division was re-forming in the Atherton Tablelands, with many changes of personnel, and a new period of training ahead. But Dick was moved on again, summoned to a higher headquarters. In London, with victory against Germany in sight, the Combined Operations Headquarters was turning its mind to Japan. CHQ comprised officers from all three services: the British Army, Royal Navy, and the Royal Air Force. Its role, among other things, was to plan amphibious landings, and it wanted to learn from the Australians' success in carrying out landings to wrest control from the Japanese in Papua New Guinea. CHQ aimed to plan its own landings to wrest South-East Asia from Japanese control and, ultimately, to invade Japan itself. It asked the Australians to send one of their planners to the War Office to share the lessons of Australia's experience in coping with the jungles, the Japanese, and the tropical conditions, which were so different from those of North Africa and Europe. The army decided to send Major Hamer.

He left Australia in September, heading first to Washington, by ship and plane, to exchange views with his counterparts at the Pentagon. It was his first visit to America, and his first experience of racial discrimination:

> I went by bus to see George Washington's home at Mount Vernon. Under the law of the state of Virginia at the time, coloured people were required to sit in the back of the bus. I was really shocked.

The Pentagon in those days was the only building in Virginia exempt from state laws requiring separate toilets and dining rooms for whites and blacks. As late as the 1950s, houses in the white suburbs of Washington carried caveats forbidding their sale to blacks.

Dick crossed the Atlantic in an RAF bomber, flying from Montreal to Glasgow: his first sight of Britain was through teeming rain. He was then flown to London in another RAF plane, with a woman pilot. Male pilots were mostly carrying out bombing runs over Germany, and the RAF had trained female pilots to fly the planes at home. Hamer was impressed. He would quote that frequently in 1978 when he took on airline tycoon Sir Reginald Ansett over Ansett's refusal to hire women pilots.

Hamer spent the rest of the war in London. The CHQ office was in Whitehall, in Richmond Terrace, an 1820s building that was once a row of town houses. London by then was safe from German air raids, and the main danger was from V2 rockets fired across the Channel. Combined Operations had sites on the Welsh and Scottish coasts, where it was training units for eventual landings. Hamer's job was to advise on training for landings in Asia and the Pacific, so he spent a lot of time in the training camps. He lectured to British officers, explaining the landings in PNG and the lessons to be learned from them. He also became drawn into the unit's own work, using his expertise on loading and unloading ships to help plan the crossing of the Rhine, as the Allies closed in on Germany. At CHQ he was impressed to notice how many women were working in the office — one of the big social changes the war had unleashed.

As a young articled clerk in 1939, Dick had dreamed of going to London and touring Europe. Like young Australians today, he had sketched out a plan: he would work in Melbourne for two or three years, save as much money as he could, get a free passage to Europe by working as assistant purser on a ship, and then travel with Alan around Europe in the summer of 1941 before returning home. But in 1944–45, his experience in London must have felt like an anti-climax. He had spent much of the previous four years in combat zones, planning daily battles on the frontlines in Tobruk, El Alamein, and New Guinea. His desk job in Whitehall must have seemed humdrum by contrast, devoid of adrenalin. He lived in a bedsitter in Chelsea, saw the sights, and went out sometimes, but this was no time to be a tourist. His army mates were fighting battles at the other end of the world. His young wife was raising their baby without him. He longed to go home.

The war in Europe ended on 8 May 1945. But the war against Japan continued, and, with it, so did Hamer's work. On 28 May, Churchill broke up the all-party coalition that had served as his government, and called a general election for 5 July. One of Hamer's friends at CHQ stood as a Conservative candidate for a seat around Hammersmith, and Dick volunteered to help him out. It was his first adult experience of a political campaign, and it whetted his appetite for more.

On 15 August 1945, Japan surrendered, and the war was over. 'I was in Edinburgh at the time, visiting one of the Scottish training camps,' Hamer remembered. 'I heard it on George Street. The whole town went mad that night, it was unbelievable!' The young Australian had made a good impression at CHQ. He was offered a post teaching at the staff college at Sandhurst, attached to the Royal Military Academy, but he had had enough. He had spent five years away from April. 'Christie' (Christopher) was now ten months old. 'I rejected (the offer) and went home on the first ship available,' he recalled. It was the *Dominion Monarch*, filled with hundreds of New Zealanders returning from prisoner-of-war camps in Germany. He sailed out on 31 August, and reached Australia on 5 October. The army still had need of him: he had to serve another six weeks to help in dismantling the armed forces. In all, he served for 2,027 days, not counting his militia camps, and had spent almost four years overseas. He had just turned 23 when he signed up; now, he was nearing 30. He went in as a young law graduate. He came out as a trained, experienced administrator. Looking back later, he mused:

> Before the war, I was pretty carefree, everyone was, and perhaps even a bit self-centred. It sobered me down, [but] it wasn't just the war. It was service in a unit, and in other countries. It gave you tremendous perspective, and pushed you towards a more positive and constructive approach.[4]

Six years of wartime service was one of the defining experiences that made Dick Hamer the man he became.

CHAPTER SIX

... to East Yarra

On 3 November 1945, still in army uniform, but back in Melbourne, Dick Hamer danced around the crowded ballroom of Government House with his young wife April and a host of old friends from school and college days. The governor and his wife were hosting a ball for 'the younger generation' to thank them for their defence of their country. It might have seemed like old times. This was the same ballroom where his sister Alison had made her debut seven years earlier, and much the same crowd of friends was there. But nothing in 1945 would be the same as it was before the war.

All over Australia, everyone was deliriously glad to see the boys come back, but had nowhere to put them. 'There had been no building for six years, and no provision of building materials,' Hamer remembered. 'Everything was in short supply. There was a limit of 10½ squares [about 100 square metres] on new houses. You weren't allowed to build anything bigger.' Finding a home of your own became one problem. The men who had spent years away at war now had to get used to a whole lot of other things: sharing a home with a wife and children, getting a job, and going to work each day, doing the same repetitious tasks. Many found the adjustment hard to make.

The newlyweds bore the brunt of the housing shortage. After the honeymoon was over, and Dick returned to Queensland, April Hamer had moved in with her sister Anne in Balwyn. Anne's husband, John Elder, was also away at the war. April's first son, Christopher, was born in November 1944, and Anne's first son, David Elder, was born a few months later. Then John Elder came home from the war, and then Dick came home, too, and the house got crowded. April had been used to getting up in the night to go to Chris when he cried. To Dick, after sleeping through air raids and shell bombardments, a crying baby was no problem; even babies had to learn self-discipline. He stopped her getting up. 'Dick said: "No, wait. Give him more time",' April recalled. 'He let it go on for hours, until eventually Chris stopped.' Chris learned that it was not worth crying at night any more. The intelligence officer used to training soldiers was now training babies.

They moved out to Kooyong, to share a house with Alison and Fin Patrick and their young daughter, Kate. But that, too, began to get crowded. Both April and Alison were soon pregnant with their second children. Julia Hamer was born in July 1946, and James Patrick three months later. They then found themselves a house through barter. April's grandmother, Katie Bell, the widow of Arthur, had left them her flat in Toorak. As Dick told the story:

> We offered the flat to the headmistress of St Catherine's, who had been living in an apartment near Scotch. We knew people who had a house we liked in South Camberwell, and they wanted to move nearer to Scotch. So it was a triple move, and we moved into 10 Kerr Crescent, South Camberwell.[1]

Getting a house was one problem; getting to grips with the law was another. Dick went from being an expert in military logistics to being a novice trying to master complex legal problems — and, worse, a novice who was officially a partner in the firm. The ladder of legal knowledge was a steep one, although fortunately there was also a lot of work that was fairly straightforward:

> There were just three of us [partners]; law firms then were quite small. And there was a professional relationship between client and lawyer. If he wanted a will drawn up, you drew it up. If he had a contract to write, you'd do it. If he wanted to buy a house, you did the conveyancing.

The Commercial Bank of Australasia remained the firm's big client. Hubert, now 75, was the senior partner. The other partner, Henry Wollaston, son of the first head of the Department of Trade and Customs, Sir Harry Wollaston, was only five years younger. It was a race against time for them to pass on to Dick the legal knowledge they had acquired over their lifetimes. On 8 May 1948, Hubert's time ran out. He was 77, and he had been with Smith and Emmerton for 61 years. His death left a big gap in Dick's life.

Like many ex-servicemen who had spent the war shouldering responsibilities for their country, Hamer wanted to get involved in planning its future. His father had locked him into joining the family law firm. But as early as 1939, he had thought about making his career in politics. He and his friend John MacLeod discussed joining the Young Nationalists (who later became the Young Liberals). While he was attracted to the idea of being an independent, in practice, he wrote in his diary, independent candidates were 'inevitably crushed by the weight of the two or three great parties'. In any case, Dick judged, the Young Nationalists 'have a liberal policy, & are reasonably free, & are certainly active, & are clearly the fighting force of the UAP' (the United Australia Party, which became the Liberal Party five years later). He mused that while it was impossible these days to become prime minister at 24, as the younger Pitt had done, 'a start can be made, & John & I decided to make it'.

In fact, they didn't: they joined the army instead. But it is clear from his diary that while Hamer's views were broadly in the centre of the political spectrum, his leaning was always to the Liberal side, and to Menzies in particular. The Labor Party appears in his diaries as an alien body, a bunch of bumbling triers controlled by the trade unions, and unable to understand the modern world. Hamer believed in free markets, not socialism. He did respect Ben Chifley, who succeeded Curtin as Labor's prime minister; but that was respect for Chifley the man, and his good-humoured, unpretentious honesty with voters, rather than for his policies — such as bank nationalisation, which Hamer had good reason to oppose. Hamer also respected John Cain senior, for 20 years Labor's leader in Victoria.

It is worth noting that Hamer was born in the same month, in the same suburb, as Gough Whitlam. Both were the sons of lawyers; both went to private schools; and both became lawyers. Ideologically, they were not far apart — the biggest difference between them was over Federalism, the form of government, rather than its goals. But while Whitlam joined the Labor Party, Hamer could never have made his home there. Both he and April had grown up with close political relatives, George Swinburne and Sir Francis Dillon Bell, in the centre-right, on the Liberal side. Hubert Hamer was distinctly conservative; in 1902, he signed a petition supporting the Kyabram Reform Movement, and Hamer's diary shows that his father's views were well to the right of his own. Dick came from the Liberal class, in an age when politics was far more tribal and less ideological than it is now. Menzies had reformed the UAP as the Liberal Party in 1944, and Hamer now decided to get behind him. He later told interviewer Christopher Sexton:

> The Liberal Party had just started, it was getting going, and it attracted a very large number of returned men, all of whom had the same general approach. They'd spent the best years of their young lives fighting for certain principles, and defending them. They wanted to make sure that was reflected in the local scene, and it went on from there.[2]

Late in life, he told his daughter Julia:

> The main feeling was that you'd spent five-and-a-half years of your life defending something, and you wanted to see it flourish. To me, it would flourish better under a system of free enterprise. But I also foresaw that any compassionate government would need to have its other wing, looking after people who had been left behind, with economic handicaps or physical handicaps. I liked the idea of branches meeting and forming policies. I think that's an admirable way of doing things, and shows a true democratic spirit.

He and some friends set up a South Camberwell branch of the Liberal Party. Dick became president, and branch meetings were held in his house until growing numbers of members forced them to move to the local tennis club. He joined the Liberal Speakers' Group, and, in an age when political campaigns were waged by public meetings in draughty halls, Hamer learned the art of political speaking on the road. In the 1946 federal election, he travelled the length and breadth of Victoria to spruik the Liberal cause: from South Warrnambool to the Ringwood Town Hall, from the Oddfellows Hall in Eaglehawk to the Newport Church of Christ (where the handful of Liberal supporters in Newport were given Dick and his brother-in-law Fin Patrick as a double bill). Usually he was a warm-up act, a no-name supporting speaker to get the crowd going for the politician giving the keynote speech. His efforts were rewarded a year later when he was elected to the Liberals' state executive, where he joined the public relations and political education committee, headed by the formidable Dame Elizabeth Couchman, already 71, but destined to live to 106. R.G. (later Lord) Casey was another member, as was future prime minister John Gorton and the Toorak newsagent Horace Petty (later Sir Horace), who eventually became a colleague in state cabinet. In 1948, Dick made his first bid to win preselection, for Toorak; but in a Melbourne Cup field, barrister Ted Reynolds KC won the race, only to quit politics after just four years.

State politics had never interested Hamer in his youth. In 1,160 pages of his diaries, there is only one reference to a state issue — a proposed revision of land tax by veteran Country Party premier Sir Albert Dunstan (for whom Hamer, like most of Melbourne's intelligentsia, had little respect. ('[Dunstan] was absolutely thick; he just ambled through life,' he told Julia). Even in the first half of 1939, the political commentary in his diary was overwhelmingly on international politics; his friend Keith 'Mick' Shann (Australia's ambassador to Indonesia during the *konfrontasi* of the 1960s) had already embarked on a diplomatic career, and had Dick felt free to follow his own wishes, he probably would have done the same. He would have been a superb diplomat.

But once he had come back from the war to his family, and his law practice, it was another matter. Now his interests turned to how government provided services to people needing them. And it became clear to him that most of the services touching people's lives were state, not federal, responsibilities. In the 70 years before the Whitlam government turned every issue into a federal issue, the lines of responsibility were far more clear-cut. Schools were funded entirely by the states. Universities and training were also under state control. The states ran the hospitals, built and maintained the roads, ran the public transport. They were in charge of providing water, sewerage, and housing. The federal government primarily ran the economy, defence, and foreign affairs, and provided welfare payments. A second factor in Hamer's mind was that being in federal politics required long absences from home, and constant commuting to Canberra. By contrast, you could be a state politician and still be there for your family. This was what Dick set out to do.

He stood again in 1949 for the seat of Kew, but lost to another solicitor and former Trinity man, seven years older than him: Arthur Rylah. He stood again in 1955 for Balwyn, but lost to Alex Taylor. But by then he was a fixture on the state executive, well known and well respected, so winning a seat would be a matter of time.

Another interest now took a key role in his crowded life. After the war, the alliance between the Soviet Union and the West quickly disintegrated, as Stalin turned eastern Europe into a grim network of totalitarian states under Soviet control. In 1948, the ageing dictator ordered local communists around the world to foment strikes and revolutions. In Australia, amid a wave of communist-led strikes, the army responded by re-establishing part-time militia units as the Citizens Military Forces (CMF), and inviting ex-servicemen back to lead them. The old Victorian Scottish Regiment, first founded in 1896, was revived; Dick Hamer, of Scots ancestry on his mother's side, was invited to become one of its officers. He accepted, and for the next 12 years the military duties and social life of the regiment became his main pastime outside work, family, and the Liberal Party. His son, Chris, recalled:

> Their HQ was a drill hall in Burwood Road, Hawthorn. The Scottish tradition was heavily emphasised, and the regiment made a magnificent sight on parade in their green jackets, 'Black Watch' tartan kilts and sporrans with white gaiters, swinging past after a full pipe band with bagpipes and drums, led by the drum major twirling his baton. At formal dinners, a haggis would be ceremonially piped in to the table for the diners to enjoy.
>
> Every Friday evening there was Highland dancing at the drill hall, where the ladies in white dresses and the gentlemen in their kilts would dance eightsome reels, strathspeys and the occasional Highland Fling until late at night. April and Dick made many lifelong friends at the regiment, including Dick's first commanding officer, Ian Lowen and his wife Meryl, and the Taylors, Howard and Pat. (Alison's husband) Fin Patrick was also an officer in the regiment, and became CO after Dick.
>
> The regiment spent two or three weeks each summer at training camp at Puckapunyal, going on manoeuvres, practising on the firing range and swanning about in tanks. Families were invited to visit for an open day and picnics on one weekend. While watching Howard Taylor climb into a tank on one of these occasions, [I] was able to verify that the regiment maintained the old Scottish tradition of wearing nothing under their kilts.[3]

There was a serious side to it, however. In 1951, the Menzies government reintroduced national service, and the regiment took responsibility for training some of the 'nashos'. Dick worked hard at it. He was promoted to lieutenant-colonel, awarded an efficiency decoration for his work, and finally became the regiment's commanding officer.

Inevitably, he also became senior partner at Smith and Emmerton. It was a 'general practice' law firm, but Hamer concentrated on commercial law, looking after the CBA's business. Criminal law was not his game; clients charged with criminal offences were sent to other firms. Apart from the CBA work, he developed a specialty in helping ex-servicemen set up small businesses such as newsagencies.

'Some of them needed help in ensuring they got a good deal, and I handled all the court cases they got involved with — a lot of them, to do with motor accidents,' he recalled. He acquired first-hand experience of some of the nitty-gritty issues where law reform was needed — issues that were to confront him later in parliament. He also threw himself into other tasks, some inherited from Hubert: he became the honorary solicitor for and a board member at the Royal Children's Hospital and the Swinburne Technical College; he ran an annual conference for the Old Geelong Grammarians association; and he was secretary of the Trinity College counterpart, the Union of the Fleur de Lys. How did he find time for it all?

In 1949, their third child, Sarah, was born, and Kerr Crescent, too, was starting to get crowded. A generation earlier, their mothers had nannies to look after the children for them. Now April, like everyone else, had to do it all herself. As she put it, 'servants went with the war'. She made dresses: dresses for herself, dresses for the girls, dresses to be sold through a charity organised by a group of Melbourne University women. They moved again, to the house that would become their home for almost half a century: 39 Monomeath Avenue, Canterbury. They named it 'Wharparilla', after the family farm on the Murray where Norman Mackintosh had spent his childhood. In the Hamers' time it was a large, homely place, comfortable and welcoming rather than luxurious, set on a big block of about 3,000 square metres, or three-quarters of an acre. Dick loved gardening, and was an enthusiastic home-improver. His daughter Sarah remembers:

> Gardening was a lifelong passion. He planted an orchard and vege gardens. He made a rose bed and curved paths. It was a nice garden, built from scratch. I can remember a horse grazing out the back. There was a big old river red gum in the back left corner, where the boys had their swings and cubby house.
>
> He was one for projects. He basically dug out the swimming pool himself, with just a shovel. Some friends from the regiment came and helped pour out the concrete. It always looked a bit home-made, but it was a great pool. Then came the tennis court. We played

> a lot as a family at weekends, and with friends and relatives who came to swim in the pool. Later, after Dad retired, the court was used almost every day by various weekly groups, including a group of Dad's men friends.[4]

But it was the swimming pool, or rather, their failure to fence it, that was the cause of a ghastly tragedy that haunted the family forever after. In December 1954, April gave birth to their fourth child, Daniel. He grew into a happy little blond-haired boy, adored by his parents and older siblings, full of curiosity and a sense of fun. It was a very busy time in Dick's life — the swimming pool had been finished, but was still unfenced. April remembered that awful morning just before Christmas 1958:

> Danny was on his trike. It was Saturday morning. Dick had gone into the office. Christopher came running up to me and said: 'Danny's in the pool, Mum!' I came running down and brought him out. I sent Chris next door to get Jenny, who was a nurse. She came and did artificial resuscitation. We took him to Box Hill Hospital. They brought him around in a sense, but his eyes were closed, and he wasn't conscious … He was a wonderful little boy, full of joie de vivre, an absolute charmer.[5]

Dick Hamer was not an introspective man. His way of dealing with bad news was to put it behind him and forget about it. But Danny was impossible to forget. He was only four years old. Chris remembers his parents sobbing in their bedroom. Julia and Sarah remember their father pacing up and down the front lawn, racked with the pain of losing his son, feeling responsible for it, trying to think how it could have been avoided. Eventually, he reverted to his usual way of coping: he did not talk about Danny any more. 'My memory is that we children all grieved alone, and intensely,' Julia says. April was pregnant at the time. A few months later, their youngest child, Alastair, was born. Dick moved on.

One of the reasons Dick had not fenced the pool was that he now had two jobs. In November 1956, his long quest to win preselection had finally paid off: from a field of 17 contenders, he was endorsed as the Liberal candidate for the Legislative Council seat of East Yarra. It was the same blue-ribbon seat in which his uncle George Swinburne had defeated the young Robert Menzies in 1928. The barrister who succeeded Menzies in the seat, Clifden Eager, became president of the Legislative Council in 1943. Gradually, he drifted away from the party, refused to vote in the chamber, and won re-election in 1952 as an independent Liberal. In 1958, when the next election was due, he would be 75. The Bolte government was in its first term, and winning widespread support. The time was ripe for the Liberals to reclaim the seat, and for Hamer to resume where his uncle had left off in 1928. At the election on 31 May 1958, he won the seat in a landslide. His political career had begun.

Part II

The Bolte Years

CHAPTER SEVEN

Melbourne in the 1950s

Melbourne in the 1950s was a booming city of prosperity and poverty, challenges and complacency, change and resistance to change, liberal thinking and hostility to ideas that challenged the old thinking. To the young, society's rules seemed to be laid out like tram tracks. They had to stay at school till they were 15, then most of them left to find jobs. Many of those jobs were in factories: between 1931 and 1974, manufacturing employment in Victoria soared from 126,000 to 470,000. But they didn't leave home until they got married, which was a good reason to get married young. (Another was that sex before marriage was definitely against the rules.) Once they were married, men worked for pay, while women did the housework and raised the children. Men had short hair, and wore white shirts and grey-flannel trousers, often with hats. Women wore sensible floral dresses, often with hats. Shops closed at 5.30 p.m. on weekdays, and the pubs closed half an hour later. In Hamer's area, there were no pubs at all: when he became an MP in 1958, half the councils in his electorate were 'dry', with no pubs allowed in respectable suburbs such as Camberwell and Box Hill. Most people worked on Saturday mornings, but then the shops closed at 12.30 p.m., and Saturday afternoon was for sport. The shops were closed all day Sunday, apart from the odd milk bar or service station. There was no sport on Sunday. Nothing happened in Melbourne on Sunday, except for church services and family lunches. Nothing happened on Anzac Day, except the march in the morning and the boozy reunions afterwards.

But that social order was being challenged by new, rebellious elements. To the young, Elvis Presley, his hips swaying provocatively, brought sex out of the bedroom into the public gaze. In the newspapers and on the ABC, intellectuals — 'pseudo-intellectuals', as those in power called them — challenged accepted policies, values, and fashions on one issue after another. Society valued professionals such as doctors, nurses, and teachers, but often resented hearing clever people with new ideas challenge its traditional values. Australians had been brought up to submit to authority, and to accept what they were given. Only a minority aimed at achieving best practice in their field. The mainstream culture varied from a breezy 'She'll be right' acceptance of whatever, to a pervasive authoritarianism that settled arguments with a threatening 'Do what you're told.' Henry Bolte and Dick Hamer were on opposite sides of a generational fault line: Bolte, like many of his generation, often relied on intimidation to get his way. Hamer never bullied those under him, but relied on argument and example to win their support; sometimes that was not enough.

The social order was also being challenged more subtly by the impact of rising living standards. Before the war, half of Melbourne's population lived in rented homes. After the war, more and more people owned their own homes. Bolte, Rylah, and Menzies were all strong advocates of home ownership, and introduced schemes to help young people share in it. They would have been sorely puzzled by today's public policy, in which other taxpayers subsidise landlords through tax breaks for negative gearing.

By the end of the 1950s, most households owned their own car, and a growing number had two. For young men, owning a car became an important source of independence, even if they still lived with their parents. Having more money opened up more choices; and as choices grew, social conformity started to fragment. Pressures increased for more flexibility in the rules, whether set by government or by society. The new fault line between the generations widened dramatically when government rules invaded the freedom of the young. The Menzies government decided to conscript young Australian men for military service, then sent them to fight and risk death in a war in Vietnam. This led to a bitter generational divide that was to end the Liberal Party's ascendancy over Australian politics. Bolte was on the old side of that divide; Hamer showed a remarkable ability to hurdle it.

Melbourne's ethnic mix was also being transformed, changing the city's culture in ways that none could have foreseen. For a century, Melbourne, like the rest of Australia, had been a limited melting pot, where people of English, Irish, and Scots ancestries combined to create a surprisingly harmonious society. As late as 1947, the first post-war census found that 98 per cent of Victoria's population had been born in Australia, New Zealand, or the British Isles. Of the state's 2 million people, fewer than 40,000 — less than 2 per cent — had been born anywhere else. Yet by 1971, a generation later, almost 500,000 Victorians, or one in seven, had arrived there from the rest of the world. And by 2011, the census figures imply that as many as 1.25 million Victorians had been born outside the Anglo heartland — almost one in four of the state's people.

With immigration came migrant languages and cultures, which their new host country often found puzzling. Italian, Greek, and Yugoslav men were used to villages where taverns would stay open late and serve coffee, wine, beer, or spirits. Yet here the bars had to close at 6.00 p.m., and after that the only places allowed to serve alcohol were formal restaurants. Australians in the mid-1950s still ate an English cuisine of meat and three vegetables. The newcomers ate pasta, spiced meats, salamis, and a whole range of other foods that traditional Australians found exotic at best, and suspiciously smelly at worst. Even Hamer, as cosmopolitan as any Anglo–Australian of his time, wrote in his diary in 1939 of his first taste of 'a delightful dish called *Wiener Schnitzel*'. Anglo–Celtic Australians drank tea; the new European Australians drank coffee. The Anglos drank beer and whisky (or 'Scotch'); the Europeans drank wine. The Anglo society venerated the royal family, and Australia's British heritage. To most of the newcomers, these were curiosities.

The eventual triumph of the European and Asian migrant cultures over the established Anglo order, above all in food and drink, is one of the most remarkable stories in Australian history. In a sense, the old society assimilated into the new, rather than vice versa. But that story is outside the scope of this book, except to note that it grew as it rolled on, like a giant snowball, gathering momentum and weight as it went. It became increasingly important in the way Victoria defined itself, and added to the elements that divided the progressive, cosmopolitan liberals, such as Hamer, from the Anglo traditionalist conservatives, such as Bolte and the old guard. Despite his German heritage, Bolte was never at home with migrant cultures, especially Asian ones; he supported a White Australia to the bitter end. In his last year of life, he told Tom Prior: 'If there are any posthumous enquiries about my attitudes to immigration, refer them to Bruce Ruxton [the state RSL president, and an outspoken opponent of Asian immigration]. His ideas and attitudes on immigration, and most things, reflect mine pretty well!'[1]

Mass migration also made Melbourne very different in another way. The size of the city expanded rapidly, and its services failed to keep up. In the 25 years to 1946, Melbourne added 389,000 people. In the 25 years after 1946, it added 1.325 million people. In 25 years, it more than doubled to a city of 2.5 million people. The vast bulk of that growth was at the city fringes, and often the houses went up before government services got there. Country towns like Broadmeadows, Ringwood, Dandenong, and Frankston became the new outer suburbs of Melbourne. Thousands of hectares of orchards, market gardens, and grazing pastures were subdivided into suburban blocks. The old Melbourne of the inner and middle suburbs was serviced by trains and trams almost 20 hours a day, seven days a week. The new outer suburbs mostly had to rely on buses that shut down at nights and weekends. For their residents, cars became a necessity. The sewerage system, as well, failed to match the expansion of the suburbs. By 1972, Melbourne had almost 100,000 unsewered homes, and their wastes permeated down into its creeks, the Yarra, and the Bay.

The Bolte government gave priority to meeting the demand for new schools, especially high schools. Public hospitals were looked after, too, but they were all within a few kilometres of the city. Less obvious infrastructure needs went unmet. Level crossings suitable for rural areas remained in place as the farms and orchards turned into suburbs. Until the 1970s, there was still no bridge over the Yarra to the western suburbs, no underground railway, and no plans to get the city fully sewered. Frustrations over the state of Australia's cities were a key factor in the Whitlam government's election in 1972, on a platform of federal grants to fix the cities' problems.

Melbourne's problems were reflected in the smaller cities, especially Geelong. Between 1901 and 1947, it had grown steadily, but between 1947 and 1971, its population trebled to more than 100,000. The Latrobe Valley and Albury-Wodonga also trebled in size. Even Ballarat and Bendigo, whose populations had stagnated for decades, now grew by 50 per cent in a generation. Migrants clustered in Melbourne, but there was also a steady exodus to the larger towns from the land, from rural villages and small towns, as mechanisation raised rural labour productivity, requiring fewer workers, while cars enabled country people to shop and get their services in bigger centres. The big towns grew bigger; the small towns grew smaller.

By the 1960s, another change was brewing: Victorians began to retire to the coast. Mostly they settled on the Mornington or Bellarine peninsulas, but also in places with a charm of their own, such as historic Port Fairy, Lorne, the Gippsland Lakes, and Murray River towns such as Echuca. In the 25 years to 1971, what was then called 'country Victoria', including its cities, added almost a quarter of a million people, mostly in Geelong and the Latrobe Valley, but creating growth and prosperity almost everywhere — except on the land.

Immigration had another powerfully positive effect on Victoria. It lifted the state out of a long period of relative decline.

A hundred years earlier, the first gold rush had made Victoria the most important of the colonies. By 1859, the state's population hit half a million, and almost half of all Australians lived in Victoria.

Melbourne had overtaken Sydney to become Australia's biggest city, with Ballarat and Bendigo third and fourth. But the people were there because of gold, and as Victoria ran out of easily mined gold, the miners moved to other states where new deposits were discovered. Physically, Victoria was much smaller than the other mainland states; by the end of the 1850s, just 25 years after the first white settlers had arrived, most of its land had been claimed by squatters. A third of the state remained forest (and, mostly, still is). For the next generation, one of the key issues of Victorian politics was the campaign by radical politicians and *The Age* to break up the squatters' vast holdings and to provide small farms for ordinary people. To some extent they succeeded, but many of the new farms proved too small to be viable.

The 1880s became the decade of 'marvellous Melbourne', when Victorians became sucked in by the euphoria of a mighty land boom. They built with grandeur, but with excess. They borrowed too much, then saw their wealth collapse in the bust, and a third of the banks collapsed with it. Then the rains also failed, for almost a decade. Desperate people out of work left to find jobs elsewhere. In the 1890s, most of Australia had a recession, but Victoria had a Depression. The devastation of that boom and bust held Victoria back for the next 50 years. Among other things, the excessive borrowing by Victorian governments in the 1880s created a legacy of excessive fiscal caution in the next half-century.

By 1901, when Australia became one nation, Melbourne had 502,000 people, and Sydney, 497,000. Within a year, Sydney had regained the lead, and by the 1933 census it had almost 250,000 more inhabitants than its younger rival. Melbourne grew into the biggest manufacturing centre in Australia. It remained the headquarters of the big mining companies, was seen as the financial centre of Australia, and boasted a reasonable diversity of other firms. It also remained the home of much of the federal public service until the 1950s, when Menzies summoned them to Canberra.

Melbourne was, above all, the home of the Liberal Party and its precursors. From 1923 to 1985, the federal Liberals were almost always led by Victorians: S.M. Bruce (1923–29), Sir John Latham

(1929–31), Menzies (1939–41 and 1943–66), Harold Holt (1966–67), Sir John Gorton (1968–71), Sir Bill Snedden (1972–75), Malcolm Fraser (1975–1983), and Andrew Peacock (1983–85). Sydney interrupted this only twice, with the two Billys: Billy Hughes in his seventies (1941–43), and Sir William McMahon (1971–72). In 1961 and 1969, the Liberal Party's grip on Victoria kept it in government when the rest of Australia voted for Labor.

But while Melbourne still was seen by the public as the commercial capital of Australia, in reality Sydney gradually became the capital of finance, and of the new service industries: the media and communications, aviation and transport, wholesale trade and distribution, and, ultimately, retail chains. It had a bigger hinterland to supply and be supplied by; it had good coal to power its generators; and it became the city where foreign investors put their Australian offices. Between 1901 and 1946, Sydney's population trebled to almost 1.5 million. The population of the rest of New South Wales grew by 600,000 in that time, while the population of the rest of Victoria grew by barely 140,000. By 1946, New South Wales had almost 3 million people; Victoria, just over 2 million. In relative terms, Victoria had shrunk from having roughly half of Australia's population in 1860 to a third in 1900, and to roughly a quarter by 1950.

Why? The first reason is that the boom of the 1880s gave way to a long, painful hangover. The bust of the 1890s left the Victorian government, local governments, and many of the state's businesses and families with far less wealth and far more debt. Retrenchment, cutting back, making do with less became the order of the day. In his *History of Victoria*, Geoffrey Blainey wrote: 'It was as if, after the debacle of 1893 [when banks collapsed], everyone was forced to be the auditor and the accountant, the careful counter of farthings.' This became embodied in the Kyabram Reform Movement of 1901–03, sparking the first of successive waves of cuts in government spending, which eventually led to Victoria providing fewer government services than any other state. As always, the cuts fell hardest on spending for new infrastructure. Expansion of the rail and tram networks virtually halted for half a century. New schools were not built. Old trains and trams rattled on long past their use-by date. Governments leant towards meeting the desire of current voters for low taxes, rather than investing in structures and people to generate rising productivity in the future.

A second reason for Victoria's diminishing clout was that it was a relatively small state with limited mineral resources, once the easily mined gold ran out. Blainey points out that in 1901, Victoria still had 27,000 miners, and they supported 'an elaborate edifice of [other] jobs … in districts where no alternative jobs were offering'. By 1929, fewer than 1,000 gold miners were left in the state, and that edifice of jobs had crumbled. The State Electricity Commission under Monash began generating electricity from brown coal by 1924, but it took until the 1950s for power from brown coal to became as cheap as power in New South Wales. The number of farms peaked in the early 1920s through soldier-settlement schemes, then steadily declined.

And part of Victoria's decline was caused by bad government. Let us explore how that happened.

CHAPTER EIGHT

Politics before Bolte

Victorian politics between 1920 and 1955 was an unusual game. First, it was played between three teams, not two. At federal level, and in other states, the Country Party was either permanently aligned with the Liberal Party (under its different names: the Nationalist party from 1917 to 1931, and the United Australia Party from 1931 to 1945), or had merged into it. In Victoria, by contrast, the Country Party as often as not was a rival to the Liberal Party, rather than its ally. For almost a decade, the ruling alliance in the state was between the Country Party and Labor.

Second, while the Country Party was the smallest of the three parties, it was the party most often in power. Between 1920 and 1955, Country Party premiers — usually Sir Albert Dunstan — ruled Victoria for 15-and-a-half years, Labor for eight years and nine months, and the Liberals for ten years and nine months, including two short-lived governments under Liberal renegades. For a decade, there was no minister from Melbourne in Victoria's cabinet.

Third, Victorian governments were short-lived. In 32 years, Victoria had 22 governments. Fortunately, the state bureaucracy was set up in a way that gave much of the real power to autonomous semi-government authorities run by experts. But when Dunstan was premier, they were frequently overridden.

Fourth, Labor rarely held power. While the Labor movement began in Victoria at the same time as in other states, it had far less success. The first Labor caucus was formed in 1892; but over the next

90 years, Labor spent 81 years in opposition, and less than nine in government. In New South Wales, Queensland, and Tasmania, Labor became the normal party of government; in Victoria, it became the normal party of opposition. Its terms in government were few and brief: a fortnight in 1913, four months in 1924, four years between 1927 and 1932, and four-and-a-half between 1945 and 1955. And each of its two longer spells in government ended with a party split.

Fifth, the government formed in the Legislative Assembly had to share power with the Legislative Council, which was elected on a restricted franchise. Four times, the council forced governments out of office by blocking supply. The council had been set up to protect property interests; not until 1952 was every citizen given the right to vote for it. Even those who were entitled to vote rarely did so; voting was not compulsory, and until 1946, councillors were usually elected unopposed. Seats were often handed down within families. A remarkable example was the Clarke family, for years Victoria's wealthiest landowners: six men of the Clarke family, spanning four generations, spent 118 years between them in the council between 1856 and 1976. Until 1952, the council was always dominated by conservatives, and always acted as a brake on reform and on projects involving government spending.

Finally, most of these unusual features stemmed from the most enduring, divisive issue of Victorian politics: votes in the country had twice the weight of votes in Melbourne. In theory, democracy allows all citizens an equal right to elect their rulers: we call it 'one vote, one value'. But in Victoria, that principle was not accepted by the conservative parties until the 1980s. In the period before 1952, the party that would rule Victoria was often decided by a system that distorted voting power in favour of country voters; and the Country Party and rural Liberal MPs were determined to keep it that way. Unequal voting power meant that the Country Party and rural Liberals were over-represented in parliament, and Labor and urban Liberals were under-represented. Between 1908 and 1952, Labor won a majority of seats in Melbourne at 14 out of 17 state elections; yet only four of these led to a Labor government. It was the country vote that mattered; and there, Labor was weak. Henry Bolte strongly supported weighting votes to favour the country and, in turn, the number of rural MPs in the Liberal Party room played a key part in his rise to become Liberal leader. Hamer, by contrast, was an urban Liberal who believed in 'one vote, one value', and while as premier he could not carry the party all the way with him on that, he significantly reduced the disparity in voting power.

In the 19th century, 'one vote, one value' was accepted as the basis for drawing up electorates in the assembly. But in 1902–03, the Legislative Council forced the radical Tory premier, William Irvine, to allocate seats so that 70 votes in the country were worth 100 votes in Melbourne. Then Melbourne grew, and the country stagnated. In 1926, the conservative parties agreed on a redistribution in which 47 votes in the country would be worth 100 in Melbourne. In 1944, they combined again to design a redistribution with a ratio of 57:100. It was only in 1952, when a tide of voter indignation and a split in the Liberal Party gave Labor leader John Cain senior a clear majority, that the imbalance was reduced to tolerable levels. And it wasn't until the 1980s that the next Labor government, led by John Cain junior, combined with the Country Party's heir, the National Party, led by Peter Ross-Edwards, to finally return Victoria to 'one vote, one value'.

Shut out of power by the electoral system, and under the thumb of influential gaming, racing, and boxing boss John Wren, Labor chose to team up with the Country Party to keep its main enemy, the Liberals, out of power. In 1935, when an election left all three parties with roughly equal numbers of seats — despite very unequal votes — Labor offered cross-bench support to a Country Party government under the master manipulator, Sir Albert Dunstan, in return for a reform package. Labor's support lasted seven years, but its only gains were to set up the Housing Commission, the Slum Abolition Board, and the Fair Rents Court. There was little reform, virtually no building for the future — between 1931 and 1953, Victoria built just two new high schools — and no electoral redistribution. A round, shrewd, cynical man with a 'curious frog-like mouth', Dunstan was feared rather than loved, even on his own side. His priority was cutting taxes, which meant cutting spending. Writing in 1960, his biographer J.B. Paul summed up:

> Dunstan left an indelible mark on the State Treasury: to this day, succeeding governments have tried to regain the lost ground in public enterprise and social services that is his outstanding monument of ten years' office.[1]

Dunstan's sometime rival, sometime partner, Liberal leader Tom Hollway, endorsed that view. While Dunstan won popularity by cutting income tax to very low levels, Hollway wrote in his autobiography, to do it he 'starved' public services of funds. 'Education languished, rolling stock and equipment ran down, and … a sort of peaceful apathy descended on the land … After he was dislodged, the State had an enormous backlog in school buildings, railway maintenance and all manner of things.' The problem became almost permanent in 1942 when the federal government seized exclusive power to levy income tax, and, for the next 50 years, compensated the states using a formula based on how much they had raised between 1939 and 1941. Dunstan's leadership cost Victoria a fortune in federal grants over the decades.

Yet Labor supported him until, in 1942, he started attacking the federal Labor government, whereupon Cain pulled the plug. The Liberals, led by the urbane, ambitious Hollway, quickly replaced Labor as Dunstan's support team. But in 1943, Hollway and Cain negotiated a secret deal to dump Dunstan and to allow a Liberal government to take over, with Labor support, to carry out a fair redistribution. Alas, the governor spoiled the plot: when Dunstan fell, he commissioned Cain, the then opposition leader, rather than Hollway, to form a government. Labor was ready to support a Liberal government, but the Liberals could never support a Labor one: Cain's government lasted just four days. Hollway made peace with Dunstan, and became his deputy in a coalition government that pledged to carry out a redistribution. At last, Victoria had a redistribution, but not one that satisfied those demanding it. In 1945, Cain and Hollway tried again, but again, the governor frustrated them. When five Liberal rebels crossed the floor to bring down the Dunstan government, the governor commissioned the rebels' leader, Ian Macfarlan, to form a caretaker government and hold an election (just as Major Dick Hamer handed in his commission to resume civilian life).

As in Britain a few months earlier, Victorian voters turned to Labor. They gave it 31 of the 65 seats, the best any party had done for a generation, and it formed a minority government backed by three independents. Cain — a solid, tough, honest, pipe-smoking man — was respected by the public and his opponents. But his government was beset with problems. Communist-led unions caused electricity blackouts and public-transport stoppages. The Upper House repeatedly blocked government legislation. Within the ALP and the union movement, a dangerous gulf was growing between communist sympathisers and the anti-communist 'Movement' led by Catholic activist B.A. Santamaria.

And then prime minister Ben Chifley decided to nationalise the banks.

Amid a huge wave of opposition to bank nationalisation, the Legislative Council decided to block supply to force an election. Its action outraged those who cared for democratic principles, but, as was to happen in 1975, the mainstream of voters had other concerns: not just bank nationalisation, but the disruption of their daily lives by continual strikes and blackouts. Labor lost in a landslide, and Hollway led his Liberals into a coalition government, this time as premier, with the Country Party now the junior partner. Dunstan had stepped down as Country Party leader; but he became minister for health, and schemed behind the scenes to return to power. After a year of being undermined by Dunstan, Hollway told Country Party MPs that he'd had enough: they must choose between them. By a vote of just 15–14, they backed Dunstan. Hollway then terminated the coalition and formed a minority Liberal government.

It was the beginning of the end for the Country Party's dominance. In 1948, the Liberals proposed a merger of the two parties, but were spurned. Now they decided to invade the Country Party's turf. They renamed themselves 'the Liberal and Country Party', solely in Victoria, and invited Country Party MPs to join them; six MPs crossed sides, as did hundreds of Country Party members. Liberal Party officials then put forward a plan to divide every federal electorate into two state electorates. The bias towards rural electorates was far milder at federal level than in state politics: the 'two for one' plan would have ended the Country Party's dominance. Its state leaders were furious, but with a landmark federal election looming, they were told to bide their time.

In December 1949, Menzies led the federal coalition to victory, beginning an uninterrupted 23-year reign for the coalition parties in Canberra. In Victoria, warfare then resumed between the two partners. The 1950 election saw almost all seats contested — a rare event — and the once-dominant Country Party was reduced to just 13 seats and 10.6 per cent of the vote. The western half of the state, which it had controlled for decades, became Liberal territory: the Country Party's representation there was cut from ten seats to just three. It would never win back that lost ground.

Yet, once again, the Country Party emerged as the government. After being turfed out in 1947, Labor decided to make reform of the Legislative Council its top priority. It offered to support a Country Party government under Shepparton MP Jack McDonald if it signed up to 15 policy commitments. These included giving everyone a vote for the Legislative Council, nationalising the gas industry, creating a Greater Melbourne Council, and carrying out a new redistribution. For McDonald, the last Scottish migrant to become premier of Victoria, it was an opportunity to implement his dream of greatly expanding the small Lake Eildon to increase irrigation in the Goulburn Valley. Reform of the council was achieved in time for the council election due in 1952, and it came at the best possible time for Labor. The Korean War boom had pushed inflation over 20 per cent, shattering the Menzies government's election pledge to 'put value back into the pound'. The voters took it out on the state Liberals: they lost nine of their ten seats in the council, Labor won 11 of the 12 seats it stood in, and, for the first time since the modern parties had taken shape in 1909, the conservatives no longer controlled the chamber.

The Liberals were now deeply divided. Hollway came from Ballarat, but he was essentially a progressive urban Liberal: like Hamer, he was educated at Trinity College and the Melbourne University law school, and worked as a lawyer before being elected to parliament. He wanted to end the Country Party's control of Victorian politics, and turn it into the Liberals' junior partner, as it was at federal level. He proposed a deal with Labor to adopt the 'two for one' plan drawn up by the Liberal secretariat. But rural Liberals and conservative powerbroker Sir Arthur Warner had other priorities: to them, the gerrymander was essential to keep Labor out of office. The story of the machinations within the party is well told in Katharine West's 1960s classic, *Power in the Liberal Party*. In October 1951, Warner and the rural Liberals dumped Hollway as party leader. To replace him, they installed a young, intense, urban conservative, Les Norman. Another urban Liberal, Arthur Rylah, won the ballot to become his deputy. But the rural Liberals insisted that one of the two leaders must come from the country. Rylah was prevailed on to stand down, there was a second contest for the deputy's job, and Henry Bolte won it.

Norman and Bolte now pledged to block the two-for-one scheme that their party had put forward. Hollway, from the backbench, negotiated secretly with Cain to introduce it. After Labor's sweeping victory in the Legislative Council poll, Cain moved in for the kill. He withdrew Labor's support from the Country Party government. The Liberals crossed sides to shore it up, but Hollway and seven other Liberal MPs rebelled, joining Labor to move a no-confidence motion in the assembly — and then, when that failed, to block supply in the council. This time, a new governor, Sir Dallas Brooks, picked the right man, and commissioned Hollway to form a new government. But while Hollway had assumed that the Liberals would line up behind him, instead they expelled him from the party. Another election followed: Hollway fielded his own team, stood against Norman, and defeated him. But with the Liberals divided, Labor won an absolute majority. It was the first majority government that Victoria had seen since 1917. Within a year, the gerrymander was gone, at least in the extreme form of the previous 50 years. The Country Party never led another government.

Cain was then 70, although he admitted only to being 65. His victory might have been the start of a Labor era. The Liberals were left as a demoralised rump, with just 11 seats in the assembly. With Norman defeated, they elected Hollway's former deputy, Trevor Oldham, as their new leader. Like Hamer, Oldham was a former solicitor, and an urban Liberal who had been Hollway's deputy in his crusade for electoral reform; the deputy premier in Hollway's government, he wrote the Essential Services Act, which limited the right to strike in key state industries. But after just six months as Liberal leader, Oldham was killed in a plane crash on his way to London for the coronation of Queen Elizabeth II. Meredith farmer Henry Bolte became the party's fourth leader in two years; few thought he would last long. Arthur Rylah was elected as his deputy.

But then events on Labor's side took a dramatic turn. The successful anti-communist 'Movement' led by Catholic activist B.A. Santamaria in the unions and the ALP had begun targeting even Labor moderates. It withdrew council preselection from Victorian ALP secretary Pat Kennelly, Cain's closest ally. In late 1954, Labor's federal leader, Dr H.V. Evatt, a volcano of ambition, energy, brilliance, paranoia, and poor judgement, moved to head off critics of his own leadership by launching a campaign against Santamaria and the Movement. The spiritual leader of the Movement was the veteran Catholic Archbishop of Melbourne, Daniel Mannix, and Victoria was its home. Soon, the Victorian ALP was breaking apart. Cain was the only person who might have been able to hold it together; but he had his own scores to settle with the Movement, and decided to stand back and let the boys fight it out. It was a fatal error of judgement. Soon, trust was gone, restraint was gone, and both sides poured oil on the flames. By the time they had fought it out, the Labor Party had split in two. Cain's government collapsed, defeated on the floor of the assembly after ten of its MPs crossed the floor to vote for a motion of no confidence moved by Bolte. After just two-and-a-half years in office, Cain was forced to a new election facing the Liberals, the Country Party, and now a third of his old team, who formed a rival party (ultimately called the Democratic Labor Party, or DLP), and directed their preferences to the Liberals. At the election on 28 May 1955, mainly because of the DLP, Labor was trounced in a two-party swing of 15 per cent. It was the largest electoral swing that Victoria has ever seen. Henry Bolte became the new premier. The Bolte–Rylah era had begun.

CHAPTER NINE

Henry Bolte

Sir Henry Bolte became the longest-serving premier in Victoria's history. When he took office in June 1955, the state had just 2.5 million people. When he retired in August 1972, its population had grown by almost half, and its economy had more than doubled in size. Bolte and his government were re-elected comfortably five times. In place of the turmoil of the previous 35 years, he brought stability under an impressively united Liberal government. For 17 years — the fourth-longest reign of any premier in Australian history — he ran the state in tandem with his long-time deputy and right-hand man, Sir Arthur Rylah. Bolte was a populist and a pragmatist, an instinctive conservative, a sound financial manager — and a real character, with a larrikin sense of humour that Victorians today remember better than any of his achievements. He was cocky and opinionated, bald, short, and heavily overweight, a chain smoker, a racing man who loved to drink and yarn and bet on the horses, and he had a flamboyant bush wit that was earthy, cheeky, and irreverent towards authority and anything intellectual. In many ways, Bolte was an archetypal Australian male of his time, just less inhibited.

His wit could be razor-sharp. As a young reporter, I pestered him one morning to respond to a speech by prominent lawyer Frank Galbally criticising prison conditions at Pentridge. Bolte couldn't have cared less, and kept trying to brush me off. I persisted. Finally, he fixed his eyes on me and said: 'Listen, son, Galbally's got a vested interest. Doctors bury their mistakes. We have to put his up at Pentridge.'

His sense of humour was one of his assets, but when he turned it against ordinary people, it stung. Much of the opposition he encountered in his last years was exacerbated by his scathing quips. When a teachers' union threatened to sit on the doorstep of his farm to push its case for a pay rise, Bolte shot back: 'I don't have a doorstep low enough for them to sit on.' His putdowns of protestors and strikers become legendary: he ridiculed one group by saying 'They can march up and down till they're bloody well footsore', and another, 'They can strike till they're black in the face.' By the end, his constant derision of those who disagreed with him started to wear on Victorians. His time was up, and he knew when to let go.

We can't understand the Hamer era without understanding the Bolte era. And as his time recedes from us, the real Bolte keeps getting lost in simplistic caricatures. He was not a buffoon, nor a right-wing ideologue, nor a domineering Jeff Kennett who crushed anyone who got in his way. Bolte was, above all, a political pragmatist who believed in economic development, sound finances, and the social values he had been raised in. He was an instinctive conservative, but not a doctrinaire one. He was the first to admit that he was lucky in his timing, and lucky in the opposition he faced. But his political success was a triumph of personality, of self-discipline, and of his ability to set priorities, to inspire respect and loyalty, and to accept values and views foreign to his own. There is much that others can learn from him.

The essence of Bolte was his strong competitive streak, which he attributed to having grown up as a German–Australian amid the fierce anti-German sentiment of World War I. His paternal grandparents, George and Carolyn Bolte, had migrated from Germany in the 1850s. His father, Harry, was the youngest of 12 children. Harry became a gold miner, and struck enough gold to buy a hotel in Skipton, where he married the only daughter of the other publican, Bill Warren. Henry Bolte was born in 1908, the elder of their two sons, and spent the war at Skipton state school. 'I think I felt different from the other [kids],' he told Mel Pratt in 1976. 'It was a fear [of being ostracised]. That possibly motivated me to try to be ahead of everyone else, in sport and even academically — so that it wouldn't be said that you were a German who was second grade.' His father was 'a pretty hard man … [who] ruled with a strap'. But that was offset by indulgent grandparents: Grandpa Warren owned the first motor car in Skipton, and did what he could to ensure that his eldest grandson got what he wanted. A photo of the Skipton school football team shows Bolte sitting in the centre, proudly holding the ball; after all, it was his ball, bought for him by Grandpa. Bolte told Tom Prior in interviews just before his death that his grandparents had 'a huge influence' on his values. Among other things, he said, he inherited their hostility to Labor: 'Grandpa Warren was so keen on politics and personal choice, it probably is fair to say he made me a Liberal.'

Sport was his passion, but, he told Pratt, 'I did also apply myself to study, provided it didn't interfere with sport.' It's interesting to note that all three Liberal premiers between 1955 and 1982 won scholarships to private schools: Hamer won one to Geelong Grammar; Lindsay Thompson was awarded one to keep him at Caulfield Grammar after their solicitor stole the family's money; and, in 1921, the young Henry Bolte won a scholarship to Ballarat Grammar. At boarding school, he mixed with the sons of the landed gentry of the Western District, where his sporting ability and intense personality offset any sense of social inferiority. Cricket, footy, golf, and racing became his passport to making friends with men from prominent Western District families: Rutherford Guthrie, Chester Manifold, Bob Molesworth, Geoffrey Street, and Claude Austin. 'Playing cricket with those blokes [who] had a much better start in life than I did, you always felt you were their equal,' he said. 'I was a bit of an extrovert.' At 15, he was the youngest player in the first XI; one of his teammates was Tom Hollway, two years older, the dux of the school, and later the premier who gave Bolte his first ministry. Ballarat Grammar, Bolte told Prior, 'gave me confidence'. Did Henry Bolte really ever lack confidence? He certainly was never short of it again.

Yet Bolte left school at the age of 16. He was always good at maths, but study had become boring. He passed an exam to get a job as a bank teller, but then turned it down: it wasn't his thing. His mother started a drapery store in Skipton, with Henry as her offsider, but that wasn't his thing either. His father bought some small farms, and working on farms became Henry's thing. He played cricket in the Skipton XI, football in the Skipton XVIII, was secretary of the Racing Club, president of the Young People's Association, acted in local theatre productions, played golf, shot ducks, and went to all the local dances — particularly if his young neighbour Jill Elder was going. He became active in the Presbyterian church, attracted by its dynamic minister, Alexander Houston, later head of the church in Victoria. 'He had a tremendous influence on my life,' Bolte recalled later. 'He was the first to insist that you got up on your feet and made a speech.' That helped him when, in 1931, the young Nationalist MLA Robert Menzies, then 36, addressed a rally in Skipton; Henry Bolte, 23, seconded the vote of thanks. He stood out for his unusual energy, and his unusual willingness to be the one who did things. He had become a natural leader; his innate self-confidence made him willing to back his own judgement. He was 26 when, in 1934, Grandma Warren lent him £5,000 to buy a badly rundown farm: 'Kialla', 50 miles away at Bamganie, near Meredith. Bolte was now a farmer, and a farmer needs a wife, so he and Jill got married and headed off for a new life.

'Kialla' was a terrible bit of property, which was exactly what Bolte was looking for:

> I was really keen. It was 1,100 acres running 600 sheep … 600 sheep and 60,000 rabbits … I felt that with a measure of discipline and a bit of work, and putting back some of the money you made, you could get it up to 3,000–4,000 sheep … I led the way in this district sowing rye and clover, planted 14,000 trees as windbreaks, and fixing up the waterways. I made a bad farm into a good farm, and it is fair to say that my success as a farmer had a lot to do with my credibility as a politician.[1]

Bolte had spotted an opportunity. He was lucky to have access to money, but he then put in the work to make it happen. He and

Jill lived cheaply, stewed a lot of rabbits, and did without electricity, investing instead to put in a septic tank, and a windmill to pump the water. Bolte told Tom Prior that the farm got electricity only after he became premier. 'Their house was built in bits and pieces,' their friend and neighbour Sheila Molesworth told Prior. 'Jill put up with a lot for Henry.' It was a happy marriage, although never blessed with children. Once again, Bolte threw himself into community life. He became head of the bush fire brigade, played football for Meredith up to the time he became an MP, and played in its cricket team even as premier, well into his fifties.

The only time that Bolte could not get things to work his way was in the war. He was twice rejected for service: first, because farming was seen as an essential occupation, and then because he had flat feet. Finally, he was accepted, but was never sent overseas, or given a commission. Instead, he became an artillery instructor at Puckapunyal, which at least meant he could get back to Jill and the farm at weekends. His earthy, cheeky style did not go down well with his superiors; the army refused to send him to the front, citing his flat feet, and meanwhile the rabbits were taking back his farm. Was his German ancestry also held against him? Whatever the reason, in 1943, after two frustrating years, he quit the army and returned to 'Kialla'.

That decision played a crucial part in his future. It meant he was back in the groove of life in Meredith in 1944 when Menzies pulled the disparate elements of conservatives together to found the Liberal Party. Bolte joined up and became the Meredith branch president. (Tom Austin, later a minister in the Hamer government, was secretary.) A year later, the state parliamentary party MPs split in two over the proposed redistribution, and the MLA for Hampden, Ronald Cumming, joined the Macfarlan breakaways. An election was called — so suddenly that the local Liberals had to find a new candidate. Nominations closed on a Monday, and on the Saturday afternoon, they met at the Buninyong pub. All their proposed candidates had turned them down, mostly because they were friends of Cumming. So Bolte offered to stand himself, and became the Liberal candidate.

But 1945 was Labor's year, and Hampden became one of its gains. Bolte fell 600 votes short of winning the seat.

Bolte had tasted politics, and was hooked. He went to Melbourne to attend the Liberal state council. At Tom Hollway's suggestion, he briefly took elocution lessons. He organised local farmers to send food to Britain. In 1947, he stood again for Hampden, and won a tight preselection contest. This time it was the Liberals' year, and he won the seat easily. His old schoolmate Hollway was now premier, leading a coalition government with the Country Party. But when the Country Party rejected his ultimatum to dump Sir Albert Dunstan from the ministry, Hollway sacked all his Country Party ministers and replaced them with Liberals. Henry Bolte, after barely a year in parliament, became minister for water supply.

Bolte had a knack of being in the right place at the right time. He made a modest success of his job, and acquired rising influence. In the parliamentary chamber, he was unafraid and quick with a quip. He was soon at the forefront of rural Liberal MPs, and in 1951, when Hollway, then opposition leader, backed the Liberal secretariat's 'two for one' plan for a redistribution to create two state seats to each federal seat, Bolte led the opposition to it. When Hollway was dumped as leader in favour of Les Norman, Bolte stood for the deputy leadership, lost to Rylah, but was then given the job anyway, because the party decided that one of its two leaders should be from the country. Then the 1952 Labor landslide cost Norman his seat. Bolte held on in Hampden by just 72 votes, the closest result of that election. Had another 37 voters changed sides, he would have lost, and Rylah would probably have become premier in 1955, with Bolte as one of his ministers.

The next Liberal leader, Trevor Oldham, died when his plane crashed on his way to the coronation of Queen Elizabeth in 1953. By then, Bolte had the support of the party's powerbroker, Sir Arthur Warner, so this time he defeated Rylah to become opposition leader. When he finally won power in 1955, the Liberals won Bendigo by 12 votes and Prahran by 14, giving him a slender 34–32 majority. Had they lost either seat, he would have led a minority government, or would have had to form a coalition government with the Country Party. Victorian politics might have been very different, and more unstable. He won because the Labor Party split, and remained split. Labor's smaller part, the Democratic Labor Party, attached itself politically to the Liberals, whose wealthy backers paid the DLP's election bills in return for its preferences. John Cain senior died in 1957, and Labor was left with weak leadership, poor parliamentary representation, and an organisation with no real interest in winning office. Bolte was not born to rule. He was an unlikely leader who got lucky, and made the most of it.

The Bolte cabinet had few standouts. Bolte and Rylah chose the first cabinet, and picked more or less everyone who had survived the wipeout of 1952 that had left the Liberals with just 11 MPs in the assembly. All of them were in normally safe seats, and most were getting on in years. Bolte and Rylah were the two youngest, then 47 and 45 respectively. Half the ministry was from the country, and ten of the 14 ministers were former army officers, from either World War I or II. The only ex-serviceman to have come from the ranks was Bolte himself. He told his ministers at the outset that he didn't want to see them in the newspapers, and, by and large, he didn't. His cabinet members remained largely unknown to the public throughout his 17 years in office. There were able men among them: Warner had come from nowhere to establish an empire in manufacturing and the media; even his opponent Jack Galbally described him as 'one of the most gifted men who have ever entered Victorian politics'. John Bloomfield, who became minister for education, had been Oldham's legal partner before he inherited his seat. Sir George Reid and Sir Gilbert Chandler had long ministerial careers without putting a foot wrong. Lindsay Thompson, who joined the cabinet in 1958 when just 34, proved a highly competent performer, as did Hamer. But over the years there were plenty of also-rans who got into cabinet by acquiring seniority and being ex-servicemen. While there was a slow turnover of ministers, it was not until 1970 that anyone without an RSL badge was promoted to cabinet. Murray Byrne, who finally broke into cabinet in 1970, recalls finding it a huge disadvantage in the party room to have been too young in the 1940s to go to war.

The great strength of the cabinet was Rylah. Born in 1909, seven years before Hamer, his CV was remarkably similar to Hamer's. His father was a solicitor in the family firm, which became Rylah & Rylah. Arthur grew up in Kew, went to Trinity Grammar, studied law at Melbourne University, and lived in Trinity College. He, too, followed his father into the firm, served in the civilian militia, married, and served as an officer throughout World War II, mostly in New Guinea and the Northern Territory. In 1949, he defeated Hamer, among others, to win preselection for Kew. Only Warner's preference for Bolte and the solidarity of rural MPs prevented him from becoming party leader and, ultimately, premier. But in personality he was very different from both Hamer and Bolte. Rylah was an intense man who lived life to the full, and had an explosive temper. Throughout his time in government, he was deputy premier and chief secretary — a huge portfolio covering 27 agencies, including the police, and, alphabetically and literally, everything from Aborigines to the Zoo. For most of that time he was also attorney-general, and began by undertaking the consolidation of Victoria's statutes for the first time in 30 years. Older readers will remember him for banning Mary McCarthy's novel *The Group* because, he said, 'I wouldn't want my teenage daughter to read it.' But we forget that he set up a social-welfare branch in the chief secretary's department, that he made Victoria a leader in corporate law reform, and that he kept the state running with a capacity for work that became legendary. Bolte never took work home with him, and insisted that all submissions be no more than a page or two. 'I never saw him carry a briefcase,' wrote Vernon Wilcox, one of his ministers. Rylah, by contrast, would take home a bag bulging with papers, and the next morning would put them in his out-tray — all read, decisions made, and signed off. He was a speed reader; but he also lived life fast. Bolte's press secretary, Ted Barbor, wrote of Rylah: 'His life was divided into split seconds.'

A partnership between two men so different might well have ended with them falling out, and with Rylah mounting a leadership challenge. Instead, they developed an extraordinarily harmonious and effective partnership, which ended only with Rylah collapsing at his desk in March 1971 from a stroke. It was a partnership based on mutual respect and solidarity. They would consult each other before making any significant decision. They would meet each morning to monitor events and plan their tactics for cabinet, the party room, the press, and the public. It helped that, on most issues, they saw eye to eye, and both were racing men; Rylah used to arrange his country trips to coincide with local race meetings. Hamer once recalled:

> They sat together in cabinet, consuming endless Turf cigarettes and sharing a common passion for horse racing. Sometimes Henry would appear in cabinet with a portable radio, and from time to time, cabinet business would be suspended for a race description.

Bolte had less in common with his federal leader, Sir Robert Menzies, prime minister from 1949 to 1966, and yet they treated each other with wary but genuine respect. Menzies was highly educated, from the cream of the Victorian bar, and had an erudite wit and languid upper-class voice. He once told Bolte: 'Henry, you are an enigma to me. I have my way of doing things, you have yours, and it is entirely different to mine, but we end up with the same result.' After Bolte's retirement, Menzies wrote that he had often puzzled over why Bolte had been so successful, and kept coming up with the same answer:

> He was himself an average man, with an uncommon faculty for communicating to average men; not from a lofty position, but from one of equality with them … I always thought that Henry would have made a good criminal advocate. He would make the jury feel that he was just the same sort of person as they were, and thereby gain a great deal of influence with them … [But] he needed, and had, qualities which went far above the average … a quality of imagination and a capacity for being interested in distant prospects … [particularly] attracting industrial investment to this state.[2]

Five characteristics stand out in Bolte's political life. First, he was a political pragmatist, not an ideologue. There were reforms under Bolte's government, particularly of drinking hours and shop-trading hours, but the main driving force behind them was Rylah. Even there, they were cautious. In 1956, they held a referendum to end the infamous 'six o'clock swill' by extending hotel closing hours from 6.00 p.m. to 10.00 p.m.; but it lost overwhelmingly, and it took another ten years before they dared to do it. They nibbled away at the extraordinary restrictions on shop-trading hours and sport on Sundays, but mostly at the margin. Bolte was a creative treasurer, and pushed hard and often for reform of Commonwealth–state financial relations, but Menzies refused to open up that hornet's nest. Those issues aside, Bolte's government tended to let sleeping dogs lie. If a measure proved controversial, unless he had an overriding reason to do it, Bolte's response was to drop it. An example, which became very costly to Victoria, was his failure to reform the state's railways. Cain had begun to phase out uneconomic railway services; but that largely halted after Bolte took over, and did not resume until Hamer took power. Passenger numbers on some lines dwindled to ridiculously low levels; yet, until the mid-1970s, small towns such as Maryborough and Echuca still had two different routes to service them. In an age of rising productivity elsewhere, the railways remained massively overstaffed. It was a colossal waste of money, which Bolte financed by freezing investment in the railways at roughly $16 million a year — throughout his 17 years as premier. He told journalists that in his priorities, 'politics trumps everything'.

A classic example was one of the most divisive issues of that time: a woman's right to abortion. Personally, Bolte was anti-abortion, but as the abortion debate intensified in the late 1960s, he stuck to the sidelines. Abortion was illegal in law, but tolerated in practice. That was partly because Homicide Squad members were being paid lucrative bribes; but even after they were exposed, and charged, the government took no action to shut down the abortionists. To do so would have divided the party, and cost Bolte support from the other side. A way out of the government's dilemma came out of the blue in

May 1969. In a Supreme Court case, Justice Clifford Menhennitt ruled that under common law, abortion was lawful if the doctor believed it was necessary 'to preserve the woman from a serious danger to her life or her physical or mental health'. The Menhennitt ruling became the charter that effectively legalised abortion in Victoria. The Bolte government did not appeal against the ruling, or propose legislation to overturn it. Whatever his private views, Bolte was quietly relieved that a judge had neutralised this most emotive of issues.

Second, power was his obsession, yet he understood instinctively that he had to share it, and became expert at doing so. He was tough, he loved to win, and he had a range of ways to ensure he did; but he was also a good judge of when to back down. Former Hamer government minister Walter Jona put it nicely in his autobiography, *People, Parliament and Politics*:

> Henry Bolte was a born winner and a bad loser. He would seldom allow himself to become a loser in a party room debate, and if he thought this was likely to happen, he always had a strategy in place to counter it. I recall him on a number of occasions saying to the party: 'This matter will be going through, or I'll resign and you can get yourself a new leader.' This threat, of course, was never intended to become effective, but at times did serve as a bluff … If Henry could see a good likelihood of defeat, he would either have the matter deferred — sometimes indefinitely — or alternatively would introduce a new factor into the debate, that would provide him with a logical argument to support a better course of action, without the party having to reject his original proposal. This was a particular skill in a very shrewd leader who maintained party discipline, avoided member frustration, and throughout his years as Leader, never once faced or was likely to face a challenge.
>
> He handled party meetings in a masterly fashion, and, contrary to public perception, allowed members to be critical of government policy and permitted lengthy party room debates on controversial topics … Much of his success in the party room was due to the complementary role played by his deputy, Arthur Rylah. While

> Henry seldom read in full a detailed report even on a vital topic, Arthur Rylah would sit in his Parliament House office to a late hour studying every line of the numerous documents that passed over his desk. I never once saw Henry Bolte in the Parliamentary Library. He relied very heavily on personal briefings and two-page summaries of reports before going into the party room or into Parliament to make a lengthy statement or a speech on the subject ... Within the party room Arthur often manipulated the agenda, steered discussion and geared the strategy in order to bring about the desired result.[3]

Bolte and Rylah worked as a team. Bolte often acknowledged how much he relied on his workaholic deputy to get things done; it was really a Bolte–Rylah government. At times, they stood over opponents and bludgeoned their way through. But their usual approach was to consult, and listen to others' views before acting. If a measure struck resistance, they withdrew it to reconsider it, and often it disappeared from sight. Rylah in 1955 wanted to reintroduce late-night shopping to Melbourne, but dropped it after the party room said no. Bolte chose the first cabinet, but, later in that term, accepted a demand from the party room that, from then on, it would elect the cabinet, leaving him to choose just the final two ministers. There are many examples of Bolte and Rylah backing down after meeting opposition in the party room. Years later, after Jeff Kennett lost power in 1999, former deputy premier Bill Borthwick — who himself broke into cabinet against Bolte's wishes — wrote to *The Age* drawing a contrast between the way Bolte allowed the party room to operate as a check on his power, and the lack of such checks and balances under Kennett. The clear implication was that had Kennett allowed the party room the power it had in Bolte's time, his government would not have been over in just two terms.

Third, Bolte was lucky in his timing. To be the leader opposing Labor as it split apart in 1955, he said, was 'like winning Tatts'. And it stayed that way. 'I don't think I ever won an election,' he told his biographer Tom Prior in 1989. 'Labor lost them.' The Split left Labor in Victoria divided for 15 years. It replaced Catholic control of the party machine with control by left-wing unions that cared more about who ran the party than who ran Victoria. At state level, Labor's vote sank to average 37.4 per cent between 1955 and 1967. The Liberal vote under Bolte averaged 37.5 per cent, but it could count on support from the DLP (14.4 per cent) and, if necessary, the Country Party (8.3 per cent). It was only in the mid-1970s, after federal intervention had removed the old executive, that Labor in Victoria become serious about winning power. In Bolte's time, its MPs were mostly former union officials, given parliamentary seats as a reward for loyalty to the party's ruling clique. For years, the only really effective political opponent that Bolte faced was Labor's Upper House leader, Jack Galbally (whom he loathed). The press for most of his time as premier was docile, opposing him only when he wanted to hang someone.

Fourth, his government relied heavily on the expertise of its public servants. Power in Victoria had traditionally been decentralised to specialised agencies. Bolte and Rylah respected that, and made no attempt to change it. They did not hand out jobs for the boys; they expected senior public servants to know the issues and to give them objective, non-political advice. The culture of their government (and Cain's, and Menzies') was very different from the culture of government today, when so much power is entrusted to political staffers, and supporters are given key roles in the system. Chief Justice Sir Owen Dixon noted in his diary that after Bolte's election win in 1955, federal attorney-general Sir John Spicer 'sent an emissary to the state government to ask for a seat on the Supreme Court, and Rylah answered, "In such matters we keep our hands clean." '[4] Bolte and Rylah employed no political advisors, and very few staffers. Even Bolte's press secretary was a public servant. His first press secretary, Ted Barbor, served as press secretary to six premiers — Dunstan, Cain, Macfarlan, Hollway, McDonald, and Bolte — from three parties. Bolte's last press secretary, Syd Kelleway, who stayed on for most of Hamer's reign, had been the ABC's state political reporter. Bolte's main advisors, apart from Rylah, and in the early years, Warner, were his wife, Jill, and the secretary of the Treasury, Sir Ernest Coates.

But perhaps the most important thing about Bolte is that while he had the typical prejudices of a farmer of his time, he grew beyond them as premier. He took on board the priorities of people quite unlike himself, and delivered what they wanted. Bolte had left school at 16, loathed study, and constantly rubbished teachers and academics. He had no children of his own. Yet, as premier, he made it his top priority to build the schools that years of Country Party government had failed to build. In 17 years, the Bolte–Rylah government built twice as many high schools as all the governments in the 100 years before it. It more than doubled the number of technical schools in Victoria. It built two new universities. It dramatically cut student–staff ratios at all levels. The number of school students doubled; the number of university students more than quadrupled. Little of the growth in schools was due to federal funding — these were all state initiatives. Under Bolte, Victoria went from having the second-lowest spending per head on education to the second-highest. He understood that Victorian parents wanted their children to receive a better education than they had, and he made sure they got it. By the end of his time, 70 per cent of students stayed at school beyond the age of 15, and 38 per cent went through to year 12 (up from 9 per cent when he first took power). Under him, education went from 17 per cent of the state budget to 37 per cent. It was a remarkable redirection of the government's role — the more remarkable because its main author had no personal affinity with it.

Similarly, Bolte had no interest in the arts, libraries, or museums. Yet he was the premier who built the National Gallery in St Kilda Road. The land had been reserved by Dunstan; the legislation to build the gallery was passed by Cain; but the project had been in limbo for years until Bolte made it his job to get it built. On transport, he had long held out against building a bridge over the Lower Yarra to the western suburbs (no Liberal voters out there), and against building an underground railway (he went everywhere by car). But eventually he was persuaded to do both — partly by Hamer, but partly by accepting that voters wanted them. As Bolte himself put it:

> You have to be an average fellow yourself to understand average people. To represent people properly, you have to understand people's interests, their ambitions, their likes and dislikes. That's why I was always in favour of holding public inquiries if we were planning anything that would bring major changes to established Victorian lifestyles. We held an exhaustive inquiry into off-course betting before we established the TAB, and had a similar inquiry before extending drinking hours and abolishing the notorious '6 o'clock swill' … I was going to have a (hotel) room tax once, but bloody hell! I soon gave up that idea. Public opinion was overwhelmingly against it.
>
> I learned politics as I went along. I'll admit I didn't have much idea before I got in, except that I had resolved to try to improve things. That was the era immediately after the war, and people were sick of being regimented and governed by regulations. They were sick of restraints, of being told what to do and where to go, and of the loss of choice, of personal freedom. A man who came out of that era knew what he was in Parliament for, all right. He had purpose; he wanted to do things. It is different now [1989].[c]

An unusual example of the way the Bolte government worked was the one issue on which it led the world: making it compulsory for motorists to wear seat belts. Federal legislation in the 1960s required new cars to have seat belts fitted, but motorists were free to choose whether or not they wore them. Peter Joubert, reader in mechanical engineering at the University of Melbourne and a resourceful advocate, launched a campaign for a new law to make it compulsory to wear seat belts in cars where they were fitted. The Parliamentary Road Safety Committee, chaired by Walter Jona, was persuaded: in 1969, it published an all-party report urging the government to legislate to make wearing seats belts compulsory. Bolte and Rylah were dead against it. When Rylah received the report, he told Jona that the government had 'absolutely no intention' of implementing it.

But slowly the two rulers found themselves encircled by an army of common sense. In 1969, Victoria's road toll had soared to 1,034:

something dramatic had to be done. Walter Jona, Brian Dixon (who succeeded him as committee chairman), and others persuaded Liberal MPs that, to reduce the waste of lives, wearing seat belts had to be made compulsory. More surprisingly, perhaps, deputy opposition leader Frank Wilkes persuaded Labor MPs to back it, reversing Labor's traditional priority of putting personal freedom above road safety. The Country Party's Upper House leader, Sir Percy Byrnes, persuaded his colleagues. *The Age*, *The Herald*, and *The Sun* campaigned hard for a change. No campaign was more effective than that of the editor of *The Sun*, Harry Gordon, who called his campaign simply '1034'. He put the issue on his front page day after day, assigned his best writers and photographers to work on it, and the series of powerful articles and photos started to sway politicians' minds. The Australian Medical Association had long argued for reform, and now it was joined by the Royal Australian College of Surgeons, who waged a very telling campaign. The government was under severe pressure from all sides. The party room demanded action. Rylah gave in first, and Bolte followed. Victoria became the first government in the world to order its people to wear seat belts. In the next ten years, Victoria's road toll shrank by 38 per cent, while the road toll in the rest of Australia fell only 4 per cent. Forty years later, wearing seat belts has become compulsory in most of the world. Brian Dixon, interviewed for this book, cited one expert estimate that, worldwide, seat belts have now saved 1.5 million lives. Yet one person who was never convinced was Henry Bolte. In 1984, when Bolte was pulled out of his wrecked car after 'having a few drinks that afternoon', police found that the premier who had made wearing seat belts compulsory was not wearing his seat belt.[6]

Where Bolte was most unlike Hamer was in the skilful way he used his power as premier to enforce party discipline. He was a master at keeping control of his troops, and had a range of ways of doing so. Interviewed by Mel Pratt soon after Malcolm Fraser had led the federal coalition back into power at the 1975 election, Bolte revealed that:

> I told Malcolm on election night: get every new member into your office one to one in the next two weeks. Tell them what's expected of them. Tell them their rights. And tell them their responsibilities, even how they should dress.[7]

Nothing mattered more to Bolte than loyalty. MPs who gave it to him could count on his loyalty in return. Those who crossed him did so at their peril. In his interview with Pratt, Bolte said that once he became suspicious of someone, he never trusted them again. Some of the ablest Liberal MPs elected to parliament never made it past the backbench due to Bolte's opposition. In choosing new blood for the cabinet — as the party room usually re-elected the same old team, the new ministers were usually Bolte's picks — he rewarded loyalty above talent. As Bolte grew older, he became more inclined to see policy disputes as challenges to his authority. He claimed to hold no grudges, but he certainly did. To take one example among many: Barry Jones, in his autobiography, *A Thinking Reed*, recounts that during the debate over the Ryan hanging, he was teaching at Dandenong High School while working for the Anti-Hanging Committee after hours. One day, Bolte rang him in the school staff room and threatened to sack him, telling him: 'If you don't shut up, you're finished.' But Barry Jones had many other career options. He resigned from teaching, became an academic, and eventually was elected as a state and federal Labor MP, federal science minister, and ALP national president.

Yet there was a crucial distinction that set Bolte apart from other leaders of authoritarian bent: Bolte demanded loyalty, but he did not demand that everyone think like him. If you had a better idea, he was happy to hear it. Hamer's rise showed that you could disagree with Bolte without getting him offside. Glyn Jenkins, MLC for Geelong and later minister for water supply, recounted that during parliamentary sessions, Liberal MPs could raise issues with Bolte in one of two places: the parliamentary billiards room, or the members' bar:

> Henry used to go to the pool room at night, and after the adjournment, he was always in the bar. As soon as the bell rang, Henry would go to the bar and stay there for half an hour to an hour or so. He'd chat with people, he'd be sitting at the big table. So if you wanted to speak to him, you could engineer it. People would approach him and put the hard word on him about something. If you put your case well, he'd show interest, but you'd have to wait to see what happened. If it was a good idea, he'd get back to you.[8]

Murray Byrne recalled that Bolte preferred to hear from MPs orally, not to read their submissions. Anything you gave him had to be on one page. All he needed to know, Bolte would say, were three things: What will this cost? What will happen if we do it? And what will happen if we don't do it? It was a simple approach, but it worked.

Under Bolte's government, Victoria gained the stability it had lacked in the previous 30 years. He delivered economic development; he put state finances on a steady path; he invested in infrastructure while reducing debt; and he travelled overseas frequently to attract new factories to Victoria. His biggest obstacle as premier was the fact that successive High Courts and federal governments had sharply limited the states' power to tax, and hence to invest. Ideological slogans like 'no new taxes' had no appeal to Bolte. As he told his second biographer, Barry Muir:

> My policy was always that development should never stop. If we did not get enough for developing the state from Canberra, we had to raise it ourselves. That is why I never hesitated to raise taxes, or look for new taxes. No one could ever accuse me of not doing it in an election budget: I did it twice.[9]

Bolte introduced new taxes almost every year. He and his Treasury heads, Sir Arthur Smithers and Sir Ernest Coates, were as innovative a team as any state has ever seen in finding new ways to raise revenue. They needed to be, because the state had far many more needs than it had money to tackle them. Victoria was growing rapidly, it had a huge backlog of unbuilt infrastructure, and it was always given less than an equal share of federal tax reimbursements. In 1942, the federal government took over the states' income taxes as an emergency wartime measure; but then after the war, refused to give them back. The states went to the High Court, but, as always, it ruled in favour of Canberra. The federal government now had a monopoly of income taxes, and the states had nothing to replace them with. In two steps, the Labor government and the High Court dramatically reshaped Australian federalism, and the Menzies government consolidated the change. The states, which provided the vast majority of government services to citizens, no longer had the financial means to do their job. The Commonwealth, by contrast, had far more revenue than it needed. State governments became beggars dependent on Commonwealth grants.

Bolte tried every way he could to get back the states' lost income-tax powers. In his first budget, he raised the battle standard, declaring: 'Uniform [income] taxation must go. The government pledges itself to take all possible steps to that end.' He challenged it again in the High Court, and again, the states effectively lost. (Technically, they won: the court ruled that they could impose a state income tax, but it also ruled that the Commonwealth could cut off section 96 grants to any state that did so.) In the 1964 budget, Bolte imposed a state income-tax surcharge, but backed off after Menzies refused to collect it, and the Liberals lost a by-election. In 1966, going into an election, he imposed a 3 per cent tax on all gas and electricity bills. In 1967, he put a stamp duty on all receipts, including wages; the Commonwealth took it to the High Court, which overruled it. Bolte's next move was to put a 10 per cent tax on accommodation, but that too was buried after the Liberals lost the next by-election. He went to the brink of breaking party loyalty to publicly shame the Menzies government and its successors to try to get Victoria a better deal, including repeated litigation. If all his initiatives failed, it was because by the 1950s, centralism had become a central philosophy of the federal government and the High Court.

State debt levels under Bolte were far higher than at any time in recent decades — far higher, for example, than under the Labor government in the 1980s. Even so, Victoria's needs far exceeded the government's ability to meet them. Bolte focussed on building schools, yet even there was criticised for not doing enough. He froze investment in rail. He put off building an underground railway until he felt in danger of defeat. And as Melbourne expanded into the surrounding countryside, Bolte left rural level crossings in place on what became main suburban roads, leaving them for some future government to fix. By 1962, there were more than 200 level crossings in Melbourne, yet the government was building only one overpass a year. And yet, for all that, the years of Bolte's rule were a boom period for the Victorian economy.

Much of the boom was due to two nation-building initiatives by Victorian ministers in the federal parliament. In 1947, Labor's Arthur Calwell, as immigration minister in the Chifley government, pushed through a plan to attract large-scale immigration from continental Europe. Australia in 1947 was essentially an Anglo–Celtic country. Immigration from the continent was never popular with the mainstream of Australian voters, but it proved to be one of the best decisions any Australian government has made. Menzies, Bolte, and Hamer all had genuine respect for Calwell, who was a more complex man than the caricature of him we remember. Victoria attracted a disproportionate share of the new migrants. Melbourne became the largest city for the two largest ethnic communities, the Italians and the Greeks, as well as for the Dutch, Maltese, and other groups. The arrival of migrants sharply accelerated the state's growth rate. Between 1871 and 1947, in almost every year, Victoria's population grew more slowly than that of other states. From 1948 to 1964, it almost invariably outpaced the nation's growth.

Bolte had never been out of Australia before he became premier. But in 1956, he decided to head a business delegation to Europe to attract new investment in factories in the state. His great ally in that was the long-time federal Country Party leader and deputy prime minister, Sir John McEwen. As trade minister, McEwen had more economic clout in cabinet than the treasurer. He kept tariff protection high enough to make manufacturing in Australia viable, and established export programs to encourage it into global markets. Bolte travelled overseas repeatedly to attract investment, with great success. Victoria became the nation's manufacturing powerhouse, even as Sydney became the centre of its service industries.

Bolte was a hardliner on social issues. He grew up under the tough country code: you take responsibility for what happens to you in life, and there are no excuses. That was one issue on which he and Rylah disagreed: Rylah introduced and expanded social-welfare programs, whereas Bolte's instinct was to blame people for their own troubles. In 1958, against Bolte's vehement opposition, Rylah and most of the urban Liberals crossed the floor on a conscience vote to support Galbally's private member's bill to outlaw the shooting of live birds released from traps. As attorney-general, Rylah abolished flogging, and routinely recommended that cabinet should commute the death sentences given to murderers. Bolte in retirement said he would have liked to have imposed the death penalty in a number of cases that came before him. Mike Richards, in his impressively researched study, *The Hanged Man: the life and death of Ronald Ryan*, reports that before the Ryan case, Rylah proposed commutation in every case except one: Robert Peter Tait, a mentally deranged man who, in 1961, sadistically murdered an elderly lady in a Hawthorn vicarage. Bolte and the cabinet agreed that Tait should be hanged, and were prevented from doing so only when opponents, headed by David Scott of the Brotherhood of St Laurence, won a High Court injunction on the grounds of Tait's insanity. (Bolte and Chief Justice Sir Owen Dixon had little time for each other. Bolte was scathing in his criticisms of the court's centralist bias; while after an argument with Bolte one night at a Government House dinner, an exasperated Dixon dismissed the premier in his diary as: 'very lacking in knowledge of the machinery of govt: mind energetic but stupid & uninformed'.)[10]

Defeat in the Tait case only made Bolte more determined to win the next time. In December 1965, prison escapees Ronald Ryan and Peter Walker shot and killed a prison warder while escaping from

Pentridge. Ryan was found guilty of the murder, and was sentenced to death. Rylah was conscious of his responsibility to 'protect the protectors': prison warders came under his ministry. Richards reports that, for all his reservations about hanging, Rylah told his cabinet colleagues, 'If capital punishment was ever justified, the Ryan case falls into this category.' Only three cabinet members argued against the hanging: Hamer, Bloomfield, and the most junior minister, Jim Manson. Hamer felt so strongly against the hanging that he broke his family holidays and drove the 300 kilometres from Metung to take part in the final cabinet vote. Yet Richards' account reports Hamer recording his opposition at that meeting in a restrained, low-key manner. Publicly, he never gave any hint that he had opposed the decision.

Bolte was adamant that, this time, the death sentence would be carried out. In 1962, the Tait case had sparked the first student demonstrations against his government, and for the first time he found himself opposed by *The Herald*. In 1966–67, the opposition to the Ryan hanging was even more intense. All three Melbourne newspapers campaigned against it, there were frequent demonstrations outside Parliament House and Pentridge, and opponents tried every legal avenue they could. There were threats to Bolte's life: at one point, he had police sleeping in his Queens Road apartment. But the opinion polls showed most Victorians were behind him, and Bolte held firm. To him, the issue was: who was running the state — the government or the mob? When football legend and new Liberal MP Brian Dixon spoke out publicly against the hanging, Bolte savaged him so mercilessly in the party room that Dixon was reduced to tears: a highly energetic and able man, he became a minister only after Bolte retired. Ryan, a career criminal who met his fate with dignity, was hung on 3 February 1967. Three months later, despite a 2 per cent swing to Labor, the Bolte government was comfortably re-elected.

But the tide was turning. The 1964 election had been the Bolte government's high-water mark. Federally, the 1966 election was the Liberal Party's high-water mark. A new era in Australian politics was about to emerge.

CHAPTER TEN

Hamer enters politics

Dick Hamer began his political career as a part-time MP in a part-time chamber. The red-velvet chamber of the Legislative Council is the most beautiful part of Parliament House: it is smaller than the assembly chamber, and its debates tended to be more genteel and collegial. Until 1952, it was the last relic of the class-based society of old. Victoria's upper house had been set up in the 1850s as a colonial version of the House of Lords, giving propertied interests a brake on impetuous populists in the democratic Lower House. For almost 100 years, its franchise was effectively restricted to property owners; even in 1950, fewer than half the voters on the assembly rolls could vote for the council. It was a chamber of elderly, well-off, conservative men, who saw their parliamentary job as part-time, and often used their power there to block reforms. It took 19 private members' bills to get Victoria's women the right to vote. It took until 1979 for a woman to be elected as a member of the Upper House.

Members in the Lower House served three-year terms; members of the Upper House stayed for six years, and, until the late 1940s, most seats were uncontested. The rural bias was even more extreme than in the assembly; when Hamer became premier in 1972, almost half the seats in the council were still from country areas, although more than two-thirds of the voters lived in Melbourne. It was only in 1952 that ordinary Victorians were first allowed to vote for the council — and for the first time, Labor won a majority of seats contested. The council usually met after 4.00 p.m., to allow its members to pursue their careers by day before coming to parliament in the evening. Its half-yearly sessions were brief, often fewer than 20 sitting days. It was an arrangement that suited the young city solicitor. Hamer remained a full-time solicitor until joining the ministry, and remained a partner of Smith and Emmerton even as premier. He also became a director of public companies such as Nylex, and served as honorary legal advisor on the boards of the Royal Children's Hospital, the Swinburne Institute of Technology, and other non-profit organisations. A seat in the Legislative Council was a low-key start to his political career.

Murray Byrne, who entered the council on the same day, recalled that the average age of members seemed to be about 65. He was exaggerating, but only a few years earlier it had been almost literally true. In 1952, of its 33 members, 21 were over 60; nine were over 70; and the eldest, Sir William Angliss, was 87. The next six years, however, saw a rapid turnover, with two-thirds of its members replaced by death, retirement, or defeat. The new council that met in July 1958 mostly comprised men in their fifties or late forties. They included Bolte's mentor, Sir Arthur Warner, then 58: a dynamic manufacturer and media magnate turned politician, he was government leader in the chamber, and minister for transport. Warner, who owned Channel 9 in Melbourne, was to get himself into trouble a year later, when the railways removed the drinking fountain from Ringwood station and replaced it with a soft-drink vending machine supplied by a company owned by the minister. No minister would survive that now, but Warner did. His deputy, 'Gib' (later Sir Gilbert) Chandler, 54, was a genial horticulturalist from the Dandenongs, who had inherited his seat from his father in 1935; between them, Chandler father and son held the seat from 1919 to 1973. 'Gib' was minister for agriculture for 18 years in the Bolte and Hamer governments, eternally reasonable, liked and trusted by everyone, but the kind of minister who leaves few footprints.

Two younger members became important to Hamer. The rising star of the Liberal side was Lindsay Thompson. Small and slight of build, Thompson was then 35, good-looking, a natural mixer whom everyone found pleasant to deal with. He was bright, hard-working, with an endless store of self-deprecatory anecdotes, and a quick eye for an opportunity. His father, Arthur Thompson, had died young; he had been a teacher, yet stood for the Nationalists in 1919 in the Labor seat of Maribyrnong, losing narrowly. Teachers standing as conservative candidates are a rare breed, but his only child was to do the same. Doted on by his widowed mother and grandmother, Lindsay was sent to Caulfield Grammar, where he was school captain in 1941, and captain of cricket and debating. He then went off to war — as a private — until contracting malaria in Papua New Guinea. Like many Liberals of his generation, his first political involvement was to oppose Labor's failed '14 powers' referendum in 1944 seeking a wide expansion of Commonwealth powers. After the war, he went to the University of Melbourne to do an honours degree in history and politics, and became active in student politics. These were unusual times, and his fellow Liberal students included future state ministers Alan Hunt, Murray Byrne, and Jim Ramsay, and future federal politicians Ivor Greenwood and Alan Missen. Among other roles, Thompson ended up as joint sports editor of the university student newspaper, *Farrago*, with Geoffrey Blainey, later to become one of Australia's most engaging and original historians.

Like Hamer, Thompson was hungry to win Liberal preselection. As a young teacher at Melbourne High School, he put up his hand in vain for four assembly seats in 1953–54, before getting the nod in January 1955 for a by-election in the safe Upper House seat of Higinbotham. His timing was perfect. It meant that Thompson joined the tiny opposition party room, which five months later would provide all the ministers in the new government. Since Thompson was a teacher, Bolte told him to draft the Liberals' education policy. He almost made it into cabinet in June 1955 on the strength of it, but was told to wait. He didn't have to wait long: in January 1956, he was elected secretary to the cabinet, and two years later, Thompson was elected to the ministry. From then on, he was seen as a future premier. He and Hamer became friends who knew they were also rivals. Thompson had a head start: he had spent nine years in various portfolios, making a good name for himself, before Bolte chose him in 1967 to become education minister.

It was the most important job in the ministry after the premier and chief secretary, but his promotion was probably fatal to Thompson's chances of becoming Bolte's successor. High school student numbers were growing rapidly, straining the state budget, and Bolte tried to save money by squeezing teachers' salaries. Thompson found himself the meat in the sandwich between a leader only too happy to get into a fight with the teachers, and the Victorian Secondary Teachers' Association, which was just as happy to get into a fight with him. Thompson, ever-reasonable, was in no man's land, at times making concessions to the teachers that Bolte would then overrule. In 1969, with Bolte overseas, Thompson moved to sew up preselection for the assembly seat of Malvern, against Bolte's wishes. It put him in line to be the next premier, but strengthened Bolte's determination to see that it would be someone else.

The dominant figure on the other side of the Legislative Council chamber was Labor leader Jack Galbally. A silver-haired barrister, Galbally was the most impressive figure in Labor's ranks during the Bolte era. His father had been a drapery salesman, and the Galballys were a large working-class family who kept supplying Collingwood Football Club and the legal profession with new recruits. Jack was one of the few working-class students in the 1920s to go to university, financing his studies with a scholarship and part-time work. He played two seasons with Collingwood, as did his younger brother Frank, who became an even more successful courtroom advocate. In 1949, Jack stood as Labor candidate for Melbourne North, and defeated the veteran secretary of the Victorian Football League, 'Like' McBrien, a Liberal-leaning independent. At 38, Galbally was the youngest member of the chamber. In 1951, he introduced the first of many private member's bills, persuading parliament to amend the law so that victims of accidents caused in part by their own negligence could receive partial damages. A year later, Galbally became a minister in the Cain government, eventually as minister for labour and industry.

Then came the Split. As a prominent Catholic and Labor moderate, Galbally, like Arthur Calwell, was torn in two. But he admired John Cain senior, and despised the breakaways' leader, Bill Barry, a key figure in the John Wren machine, who was named in a corruption scandal in the 1940s. In an interview on his retirement in 1979, Galbally told me that one night in April 1955, Archbishop Mannix sent a Monsignor to his home, directing him to join the Coleman–Barry group. Galbally refused, telling the Monsignor: 'Would you ask the Archbishop: is he aware that the leader of his party, Barry, is a crook?' The next night, the Monsignor returned and told him: 'The Archbishop feels that if that is your view, then you should retire from politics.' Galbally ignored the direction, and stayed in the ALP; but for years afterwards, he, like Calwell, was snubbed by Melbourne's Catholic hierarchy. Of the five Catholics in the Cain ministry, he was the only one to stay in the party. But it had become a very different party, and his prospects of returning to a ministry, let alone leading one, became remote.

So Galbally settled for the role of a part-time MP, holding forth in the courts by day and the Legislative Council by night. He was without doubt the best speaker in the parliament, employing gentle but biting humour, a theatrical delivery, a versatile command of the language, a good memory for quotations, and a humanity that endeared him to friend and foe alike. He became the most persistent presenter of private member's bills that the parliament has seen. He persuaded the Liberals to outlaw trap-shooting of birds, despite Bolte's opposition. Year after year, he presented bills to abolish capital punishment, to abolish flogging, to abolish the crime of vagrancy, to set up an independent electoral commission, to protect parklands, and to give equal pay to women.

In Hamer's early years, Galbally formed a formidable duo with William Slater, founder of the law firm Slater and Gordon, and attorney-general in every Labor government from 1924 to 1955. Slater had entered the Legislative Assembly in 1917, and spent most of his life as a full-time solicitor and part-time MP. After having lost his seat of Dundas in the 1947 election, he had won the Legislative Council seat of Doutta Galla in 1949. By 1958 he was almost 70, a widely respected Labor moderate; he had been a colleague of Hubert Hamer at the Law Institute, and of George Swinburne in the Legislative Council, and he took an avuncular interest in Dick Hamer. The Liberals had few lawyers then, so Hamer was frequently called on to speak against Galbally and Slater when they moved private members' bills or urgency motions.

Hamer and Thompson were two of the youngest members. Two others who enter our story at this point were the two Liberals from Ballarat province. The first, Vance 'Pat' Dickie, then 39, was an energetic conservative from Bacchus Marsh, who ran his family's dairy company, and was on virtually every committee in town, including two terms as Bacchus Marsh shire president. Four years later, Dickie would be Hamer's main rival when a ministerial vacancy opened up in the council. In the 1970s, as a right-wing opponent in the ministry, he became one of the banes of Hamer's life; his performance as minister for housing was to cost Hamer dearly.

His colleague, Murray Byrne, was a renegade with an endless store of energy. At 29, he was the youngest member ever elected to an Upper House in Australia. Byrne was a Catholic in a Protestant party: a rebel who had broken from his tribe as a teenager to join the Liberals. We forget now how tribal Australian politics used to be. If you were Catholic, you were Labor; if you were an affluent Protestant, like Hamer, you were Liberal. Of 50 ministers in the Liberal governments between 1955 and 1982, only three were Catholics. The first, Sir George Reid, converted to Catholicism after joining the ministry. The second, Tom Darcy, was a popular war hero and former president of the Victorian Farmers' Federation, who was given a term in cabinet before retiring. The third was Byrne. In the final six years of the Hamer–Thompson governments, there was no Catholic in the ministry, and few on the backbench.

The Split in 1955 broke the historic bond between Irish Australians and Labor, but Murray Byrne's own split occurred a decade earlier. The Byrnes had been lawyers in Ballarat for decades. Byrne, Jones and Torney became the city's biggest law firm, and the family extended its interests to finance. They, too, were well-off; but, being Catholics, they were Labor until, in 1944, young Murray took exception to his teachers at St Patrick's College proselytising for Labor's referendum to expand Commonwealth powers:

> Our school was very Labor. I wrote an essay opposing the referendum, and the teacher marked it down. So I went to a Liberal Party meeting. In '45, Bolte stood for Hampden and lost. I worked for him in his campaign. Later I formed the Young Liberals here in Ballarat, then I became the youngest member of the state executive, and in '58 the youngest member of parliament.[1]

Byrne was as untypical of the Liberal Party as he was of Irish Australia. In the 1950s and 1960s, he was one of the first generation of Australians to travel to Asia often, and understand it. He was one of the first Liberals to see the perils of joining a losing war in Vietnam, to foresee the potential scale of Asia's growth, and to see the importance of Australia developing close economic ties with it. His outspokenness kept getting him into trouble; his energy and charm kept getting him out of it:

> People were trying to expel me from the party pretty regularly, for all sorts of things: opposing the White Australia policy, for example, publicly opposing capital punishment, attitudes to China. In early '73, I was the first Liberal minister to go to China after Whitlam recognised it. There was a lot of opposition: Joh [Bjelke-Petersen, Premier of Queensland] said I should be thrown out of the party. But Hamer stood by me, saying we shouldn't be left waiting at the post.

And they weren't. In 1977, Hamer signed the first of a series of agreements establishing a sister-state relationship between Victoria and the big coastal province of Jiangsu, which has become the largest recipient of foreign investment in China, its richest province, and home to booming cities such as Nanjing, Suzhou, and Wuxi. Bjelke-Petersen built his career on trying to resist the waves of change; Byrne built his on trying to surf them. His early retirement from politics in

1976 after a bad car accident was a serious loss to his old friend and leader.

Hamer had been sent into East Yarra to win back control of the Upper House for the Liberals. Sir Clifden Eager, the incumbent, was Liberal leader in the council in the 1930s; but after being elected president of the council, he ended all contact with the party, and never voted on legislation. In effect, as Hamer pointed out, that cost the Liberals a seat in the chamber. 'It's easy to do that in a house of 650 members [the House of Commons]. It's different in a house of 34 members,' he said. 'It could mean the government was in a minority.' In 1952, Eager, running as an independent Liberal, easily repelled a challenge from future Liberal senator George Hannan. But by 1958 he was 75, and seeking another six-year term; the tide was now with the Liberals, and Hamer was an attractive candidate. He won the seat in a landslide, with a 22 per cent swing, and held it comfortably until moving to the assembly in 1971.

But the coalition failed to win control of the chamber. It won just eight of the 17 seats contested, leaving it with 17 of the 34 seats in the chamber, while Labor had nine and the Country Party eight. Bolte tried to persuade 70-year-old Country Party MP Dudley Walters to become president, without success. Sir Gordon McArthur had to resign as health minister to become president, leaving the government in a minority of one on the floor. The numbers were like that for most of Hamer's time in the council. In 1964 and 1967, the Liberals briefly won control of the chamber at elections, only to lose it again within months at by-elections. That meant the council could, and did, act as a check on the Bolte government whenever Labor and the Country Party saw eye to eye. Sometimes they combined to block bad ideas, such as building a licensed restaurant in the Botanic Gardens, or opening up the Little Desert to farming. More often, they used it to block sensible ideas. Breathalyser tests, probationary driving licences, on-the-spot traffic fines, the TAB, extended trading hours for butchers, fresh bread at weekends, lifting rent controls, allowing sport on Anzac Day: all these reforms were blocked for years by Labor and the Country Party before finally becoming law.

It is ironic that the council held that power only because its rural gerrymander was so extreme that city seats such as East Yarra and Melbourne North had two-and-a-half times as many voters as the Country Party's seats along the Murray. At election after election, the Country Party won less than a tenth of the vote, but almost a quarter of the seats. At least it gave the council relevance.

Hamer and Byrne were the only lawyers on the Liberal side of the chamber until Alan Hunt joined them in 1961. For part-timers, they were kept busy: in his first year, Hamer spoke on reforms to the Companies Act, the Local Government Act, the Gaming Law, and the Hire Purchase Bill, on which he sharply took issue with Labor's support for controls on interest rates. He also served as a member of the Statute Law Revision Committee, one of the few avenues for law reform. Like most Liberals in the council, he voted for Galbally's bill to outlaw the live trap-shooting of birds, which became law over Bolte's opposition. A year later, he moved the address-in-reply to the governor's annual speech outlining the government's program. Given the freedom to outline his own policy, in effect, he focussed on three issues:

- The challenges of meeting infrastructure needs at a time of rapid population growth.
- The urgent need to reform Commonwealth–state financial relations to give the states sources of revenue adequate to meet their responsibilities.
- The need for annual grants from the state to subsidise theatre, opera, and ballet productions in Victoria.

All three issues became key themes throughout his political career. Very few politicians were thinking deeply about the arts in 1959. Not many (apart from Bolte) understood the importance of fundamental reform of the federal compact. Hamer was ahead of his time. Being a backbench member of the Upper House in those days carried a whiff of independence, and Hamer used his speeches to raise issues that were not on the Bolte government's agenda, and occasionally to oppose some things that were. His annual speeches on the address-in-reply became miniature policy speeches. In 1960, he argued that the need for a third university had become 'absolutely urgent', and suggested that it be formed from existing tertiary institutions in the provincial cities, such as the Ballarat School of Mines and the Gordon Institute in Geelong. In fact, the third university was built in Melbourne as LaTrobe University; but later as premier, Hamer successfully insisted that the state's fourth university, Deakin, be based in Geelong. In 1961, he devoted his entire speech to the imbalance in Commonwealth and state financial powers, urging a Commonwealth–state convention to review the Constitution; he eventually achieved this, in 1973, but Canberra would not give up power. In other speeches as a backbencher, Hamer warned against alienation of public parkland, and urged stronger measures to combat the rising road toll — measures that Labor and the Country Party kept rejecting.

Two issues loomed large on the agenda of the lawyer-politician: corporate crooks and booming land prices. As legal GPs, Smith and Emmerton dealt constantly with clients who had been ripped off by swindlers finding ways around the laws. Hamer rarely used parliamentary protection to name the offenders, but spoke out on what he called the 'running battle' between the parliament and corporate 'twisters', and urged that loopholes be closed and penalties toughened. Booming land prices were a big problem for young home buyers; as a solicitor, Hamer had seen too many clients get out of their depth financially, ending up in serious trouble. But when Galbally proposed that the government buy up outer-suburban land and develop housing estates itself, Hamer ridiculed the idea:

> His solution is a typically socialist one, and places the whole burden of providing houses for the people of Melbourne on the Government … The cost would be astronomical … and I doubt whether it would be able to solve the problem … One of the main difficulties is that people who attend a land auction fall over themselves to pay the price asked. They do not have to pay but they do … The 'boom' mentality is based on psychological factors, and the best approach towards

> pricking the bubble, or gently subsiding it, is to direct attention, as the Minister for Housing has done, to the fact that many people are paying too much for their land … I think that is the best approach to what is fundamentally a psychological problem.[2]

If only it were! As premier 13 years later, Hamer ultimately accepted Whitlam's demand that a government commission buy up the land around Albury-Wodonga and develop its housing estates; but that example only bore out his 1960 warning that 'the cost would be astronomical'. In 1973, Hamer's housing minister, 'Pat' Dickie, bought up large areas of land at Melton, Sunbury, and Pakenham to develop for welfare housing; the cost there, too, was astronomical, because Dickie paid urban prices for rural land. Half a century on, Australian governments have yet to find a solution to one of the most pressing problems facing younger Australians who want a home of their own and cannot afford it.

Few issues focussed more attention on the council than Galbally's annual private member's bills to abolish capital punishment. In October 1959, Hamer led the Liberals' response; at that stage, he was in favour of keeping the death penalty:

> One should not advance too far ahead of public opinion in this matter … If in any one case there is evidence, or if we believe, that this maximum penalty can prevent the murder of innocent people, then we are not justified in abolishing it.[3]

In 1962, the debate took place under the shadow of the Tait case, then being fought out in the courts. The exchanges were sharper on both sides, and Hamer's defence of capital punishment grew more strident:

> The death penalty is a deterrent, which is accepted as being a deterrent by the people who ought to know … Is it not our duty not to expose innocent lives to danger? If it comes to the choice between the death penalty in extreme cases, or running the risk of subjecting

> an innocent life to that sort of danger, I choose to retain the death penalty ... This Bill is simply a sledge hammer which does away with the death penalty absolutely and finally, and should not be allowed to pass.[4]

There was another reason for Hamer's tougher stand; he had been promoted to cabinet. Early in 1962, Sir Arthur Warner, the kingmaker behind Bolte's rise to the top, and his initial guide to the business world, suffered two heart attacks. Warner stayed in cabinet for another seven months, until it had dealt with the Tait case. He was a fervent opponent of capital punishment; Mike Richards records that Warner once told Barry Jones: 'There will be no hangings in Victoria so long as I am a member of cabinet.' But by 1962, Bolte had long outgrown his dependence on Warner; he would no longer bend to his one-time mentor. On 6 August, cabinet decided to hang Tait. Two weeks later, Warner announced he would retire from cabinet for health reasons. The health reasons were genuine, but the timing appeared pointed. His replacement had to come from the Legislative Council: Pat Dickie had seniority on his side, but Hamer was the standout of the large crop of new Liberal MLCs elected in 1958. The party room chose Hamer, and Bolte appointed him to serve his apprenticeship as minister for immigration, and minister assisting Rylah in his roles as chief secretary and attorney-general. His promotion evoked warm congratulations from Galbally, glad to see 'that another lawyer's talents have been recognised ... It was no surprise to us when his colleagues saw fit to raise him to his new status.'

Hamer's new portfolio sounded grander than it was. Immigration was essentially a federal responsibility. At state level, Hamer recalled later, his entire department had 20 people. But under an inter-governmental agreement, the states handled immigration from the UK, where they all had offices in London, while the Commonwealth looked after immigration from everywhere else. In those days, migrants to Australia were subsidised by government; they paid just ten pounds for their passage by ship to Australia. As minister, Hamer went down to Station Pier to meet the new shiploads of migrants arriving; twice he got in early, met the ship at Fremantle, and travelled on it to Melbourne, meeting new migrants 'to find out what had driven them to emigrate, and what they were expecting to find in Australia'. He handled difficult cases requiring ministerial decisions. One involved a family with ten children who had already emigrated from Birmingham on a ten-pound passage, returned home after staying the two years required, emigrated again on a ten-pound passage, and then the wife and five children stowed away in a bid to return home, but were discovered and put off the ship in Adelaide. Even Hamer, soft touch as he was, refused to make taxpayers pay for them to return to Melbourne a third time.

His real apprenticeship was working under Rylah, whom he admired. Rylah alone generated about a quarter of the legislation going through parliament, and Hamer had to handle all his bills in the Upper House. Rylah also delegated control of some less controversial areas to him, and Hamer filled in whenever the boss went on holiday. Among other things, he returned to Darwin for the first time since the war, for a meeting of Commonwealth and state ministers for Aboriginal affairs, which opened his eyes to the problems blocking assimilation of Aboriginal Australians into the white community. But for his first two years as a minister, his role was minor. Most of Bolte's original cabinet were still there, getting older, in the key portfolios. Hamer and Thompson were the only ministers younger than 50.

Promotion to cabinet forced more changes in his life. In the 1950s, Hamer had been a commuter, walking to Canterbury station every morning, catching the train into town, and getting home again in time for the family dinner. When he was elected to parliament, he crammed his work at Smith and Emmerton into fewer hours during sitting weeks, spending most of the day at his office, and then the evenings and nights at Parliament House. But to fit in both jobs, he eventually made the painful decision to hand back his commission as commander of the Victorian Scottish Regiment, in favour of his brother-in-law Fin Patrick. On 30 June 1960, Hamer retired with the honorary rank of lieutenant-colonel, ending 22 years of military service. In 1959, April had given birth to their youngest child, Alastair, and Dick was needed at home. He had added to his own workload by accepting several directorships, and joining boards and committees of management in the non-profit sector. While he remained a partner of Smith and Emmerton throughout his political career, he had to hand over the running of the firm. His ministerial apprenticeship would last only until the next election, in 1964. A much bigger job was waiting for him.

CHAPTER ELEVEN

Planning Melbourne

In 1964, Dick Hamer became the first minister to take responsibility for planning Melbourne's future. Before he was appointed minister for local government, no one in Spring Street saw it as their job to take charge of the city's planning. If something big came up, like the 1956 Olympic Games, the premier ran the show. Otherwise, local councils were left to muddle along on their own.

Traditionally, the minister's brief was to handle any issues to do with Victoria's 210 local governments — all of them creations of the state, and extremely varied. The city of Camberwell, Hamer's local council, had 100,000 residents; the shire of Pyalong, in the middle of Victoria, had five hundred. Shires like Mildura and Orbost each served areas as large as Lebanon, while some councils in Melbourne and Geelong were so small you could cross them in two minutes. Local government took up a lot of Hamer's time — a time he recalled as:

> frantic with centenary celebrations, new municipal offices, new local histories, and deep questionings as to what the next 100 years would bring ... For a century, [local government] had been providing principally services to property; now suddenly it was facing demands for community services of all kinds, from playing fields and parkland to swimming pools and indoor sports centres, from kindergartens to senior citizens clubs, from health services to town planning, from libraries, performing arts centres, and art galleries to social welfare.

> In short, it found itself serving people as well as property, but still depending for its revenue on ever-rising rates on property.[1]

Hamer encouraged these new demands, which he saw as bringing government closer to the people. But it was only when he himself became premier and treasurer that he could do anything to help councils pay for them, by setting up a system of state grants to councils, and subsidies for them to construct libraries, arts galleries, and theatres. He had a range of interests in this area, such as encouraging women to stand for councils, but it proved to be the smaller part of his portfolio. Local government produced no big scandals in his six-and-a-half years as minister. His big issue should have been to force councils formed in the horse-and-buggy era to amalgamate to form less costly units, but he and Bolte were politically far too pragmatic to allow that. When Melbourne City Council's town clerk Frank Rogan launched a bid to take over four neighbouring councils, he was overwhelmed by opposition. Hamer's approach was to encourage councils in the main regional centres — Geelong, Ballarat, Bendigo, and the Latrobe Valley — to form regional planning authorities, to create a wider sense of purpose and bring in more skills. But that, too, got virtually nowhere, as we shall see.

The bigger part of his portfolio was planning. And one can only regret that he did not arrive in the job some years sooner.

In Melbourne's early years, surveyor Robert Hoddle and superintendent Charles LaTrobe designed their small village as though it were a city of a million people. Every generation of Melburnians since has lived in their debt. But little or nothing followed in their wake. Broad boulevards such as Royal Parade and Wellington Parade gave way to narrow streets such as Sydney Road and Bridge Road. As Melbourne grew rapidly, people could build more or less what they liked, where they liked, without thought for the consequences. Factories went up side by side with homes. The new suburban roads were barely wide enough to carry the traffic they bore then, let alone have room for future expansion. The central city was surrounded by parkland, but little of it was being created in the new suburbs.

Town planning in Melbourne was initiated not by the state, but by a grass-roots movement. In 1914, the indefatigable social reformer Sir James Barrett and his friends set up the Victorian Town Planning and Parks Association to prod governments into action on both fronts. In 1920, the association's president, alderman Frank Stapley, an architect serving on the Melbourne City Council, dragged other councils and a reluctant state government into commissioning a team led by him to draw up a town plan. His Metropolitan Town Planning Commission was run and financed essentially by local councils; the state government was a half-hearted participant.

The commission delivered its report in 1930, and then disbanded. Yet its plan was, in Hamer's words, 'a remarkable and far-sighted document'. It brought together the old tradition of civic pride, with its concern for the appearance of the city, with a modern concern for efficiency in transport systems and use of space. It envisaged Melbourne growing as a city of scenic boulevards and roundabouts, a vast, medium-rise city centre spreading from Carlton to South Melbourne (with a 13-storey height limit, as then applied), parks along the creek valleys, and excellent public transport, including an underground rail loop and a new railway to Doncaster. From today's perspective, it was visionary. But as the Great Depression crashed down on Victoria in 1930, the report was received with ridicule and left to die. A few ideas were taken up as 'susso' make-work projects during the Depression years: building the Yarra Boulevard, the Swan Street bridge, and Brunton Avenue, and converting the old rail bridge over the Yarra at Fairfield into a road bridge. But it was not until 1944 that the state government set up the Town and Country Planning Board and passed its first planning legislation, and not until 1949 that it commissioned the Melbourne and Metropolitan Board of Works (MMBW) to draw up a planning scheme for the city.

The board's report, issued in 1954, was American-inspired and modernistic. It had no time for Melbourne's 19th-century architectural heritage, proposing instead to raze the inner suburbs and demolish their terrace houses — 'third class' housing, in its view — to replace them with hygienic blocks of 1950s flats. But it also envisaged new parks, roads, and rail links to serve the expanding outer suburbs, and envisaged Melbourne developing five key district centres in Footscray, Preston, Box Hill, Moorabbin, and Dandenong, as mini-CBDs located closer to where people lived.

Ten years on, its planning scheme was still awaiting adoption when Hamer became minister for local government in July 1964. The projects that had emerged were built because some powerful agency wanted them: the Housing Commission demolished inner-suburban terrace houses to build high-rise towers, and the board itself started building freeways and widening old roads and junctions. But as the city's population swelled by more than 500,000 a decade, no one in government was taking responsibility for co-ordinating that growth, or for turning plans into policies. The previous minister, Murray Porter, ran the portfolio for six years aiming to keep out of trouble.

Melbourne was following American trends, from a distance. Its first drive-in opened off Burwood Road in 1954. Its first parking meters went up in Bourke Street in 1956, the same year that television arrived in time for the Melbourne Olympics. A year later, its first boom gates were installed at Tooronga Road. The ICI building became the city's first modern skyscraper, busting the old 13-storey limit, and new architecture such as Kevin Borland's 1956 Olympic Pool, Barry Patten's Myer Music Bowl, and Frederick Romberg's Stanhill flats in Queens Road gave the city a new aesthetic range.

The biggest change was that Melbourne's people now owned cars. Historian Graeme Davison recounts that in 1951, only one in three households had a car. A decade later, that had become two in three, and by 1976, the city had more than five times as many cars as it had had 25 years earlier. Even in 1960, the official map shows Melbourne's suburbs extended out like fingers along the railway lines, with vast rural areas of farms and orchards between them. But as the city's population doubled, and those farms and orchards were converted to suburbs, the public-transport network did not grow to meet the new needs. Where people had once sought work in their own suburb or a neighbouring one, more and more Melburnians were living in one part of the city, working in another, and using their car to get between them. Public transport no longer met their needs.

Traffic congestion became a daily experience for many. The trains, trams, and buses slowly emptied. The total number of passenger trips on public transport shrank from 630 million in 1945 to 411 million by 1965; it would sink to 280 million by 1980. The Bolte government inherited a huge backlog of infrastructure needs, and tackled some of them. The King Street bridge was constructed, collapsed, and was rebuilt. The first stage of the South-Eastern Freeway (now CityLink) was opened between Richmond and Burnley. A new airport was developed at Tullamarine, and a new freeway — but no train line — built to meet it. But Hamer was about to take charge of a city that ran way behind the state of the art in almost every aspect of planning. He recalled later:

> I found the whole town planning field in something of a ferment. Communities throughout Victoria were busily trying to draw up town planning schemes, interim development orders abounded, and there was an almighty shortage of trained town planners. These difficulties led to some highly undesirable situations, particularly in the time taken — ten years in the case of metropolitan Melbourne — for a planning scheme to come into full approval.[2]

His first concern was that so many appeals ended up on his own desk:

> Following the British example, all appeals went to the minister. The cases were heard by four delegates [officials], sitting in pairs, who then reported in writing to the minister with their recommendation. I found myself deciding an average of 35 appeals a week, without ever seeing the parties; I used to spend my weekends inspecting the subject land in and around Melbourne, yet I could not always inspect the land involved in country appeals … It was highly undesirable to have the determination of so many complex and important issues in the hands of a minister, especially through such defective procedures.

His solution was to remove himself from the process. Instead of the delegates reporting to him, they became the decision-makers. Hamer set up the Town Planning Appeals Tribunal, where he hoped parties could obtain 'a cheap and speedy decision'. The legislation, he said later, was 'intended to ensure that the appeals tribunal should act informally' with the appeals heard by a lay tribunal, not a court of law, 'so as to avoid delays, expense and pettifogging obstruction, and ensure swift decisions on the merits of the case'.

Of course, it did not work out that way. As always, the lawyers won. Gradually, they colonised the tribunal, turning it into another court of law, with all the legalism, delays, and costs that Hamer had hoped to avoid. In retirement 20 years later, Hamer was scathing about the way 'some tribunals have allowed themselves to be bamboozled by highly paid counsel, have allowed the most scandalous and intimidating cross-examination of objectors, and have permitted the escalation of costs in a way not in any sense contemplated by the parliament'. He cited the 1982 case in which prominent footballer Doug Wade was allowed to build an illegal extension to his house in Parkville, while two neighbours who objected lost their homes to pay the legal bills. In 1986, he proposed that lawyers be banned from appearing at the tribunal hearings, except when needed to debate specific legal points. The tribunal has since been absorbed into the Victorian Civil Appeals Tribunal, but it remains dominated by lawyers.

The scope of planning in 1964 was relatively simple. As Hamer recalled later:

> Nobody had yet set out to protect the environment, the EPA did not exist, nobody was saving historic buildings, or regulating urban renewal, or protecting coastlines or scenic areas or mineral resources, or regulating outdoor advertising … Both building regulations and provisions on subdivisions were relatively primitive.

It became his task to make this less so. The 1960s was a decade of ferment among planners in the US and Europe, leading to new concepts of what cities should be, and what role government should play in shaping them. The ferment did not reach Bolte and Rylah, but it did reach Hamer. By 1968, the MMBW's planning scheme had finally become law, and the new tribunals were operating. A State Planning Council had been set up, at his urging, where the government and its various semi-autonomous authorities could co-ordinate their plans and discuss and make decisions on issues of mutual concern. Hamer had been put in charge of finding solutions to disputes over the routes of freeways; his youngest son, Alastair, recalls Saturday mornings when Dad would drive out to the works site of the South-Eastern or Tullamarine freeways to check on progress. But, most importantly, he had decided where the city should grow.

The idea of 'green wedges' was not new: that was how the city had developed between 1850 and 1950, with suburbs springing up along the railway lines, and farms and orchards between them. But the population boom of the 1950s and 1960s replaced the green wedges with suburbs, creating a different pattern of growth that was dubbed 'urban sprawl'. Prompted by Board of Works chairman Alan Croxford and his planning team, Hamer now proposed to restore Melbourne's former pattern of growth, by allowing urban development only in eight broad 'corridors' along the railway lines: towards Werribee, Melton, Sunbury, up the Hume Highway, the Plenty River, and to Lilydale, Pakenham, and Frankston. The areas between them would be zoned permanently for non-urban uses, mostly farming and parkland. In a ministerial statement to parliament in 1967, Hamer justified the strategy on grounds of both aesthetics and transport efficiency:

> Such development allows for the retention between the corridors of substantial wedges of open country which can be used for recreation or parkland, or simply retained as rural land. This places the 'green and pleasant land' within much more easy reach of the city dweller, and breaks up the residential pattern. Here again, nature comes to the aid of Melbourne in the shape of a system of radiating river valleys, particularly the Yarra, which can and must be preserved.[3]

His argument on transport efficiency was well put a year later in a forward-looking speech, 'Melbourne — 2000 A.D.', to a building-industry congress. Hamer argued that the government was planning for a Melbourne of 5 million people, which on trends at the time, he said, could come as early as 2000. He drew the lesson from New York's growth that even when congestion reached extreme levels, office development and job growth would tend to concentrate in the city's inner core. He went on:

> It is this continued growth at the very core of modern cities, and the absolute impossibility of providing road space and parking for more than a fraction of the private cars of commuters, which makes this fast and frequent public transport essential ... We are fortunate to have nine radiating rail lines from central Melbourne, with main roads closely associated with them.

The green-wedges strategy was one of a raft of changes that came together. Hamer also set a goal of redeveloping the inner suburbs to increase their population by 500,000, although he never spelt out how this would be done. He doubled the metropolitan planning area to a radius of roughly 50 kilometres from the city. He set up an inquiry into whether satellite cities should be developed at Melton, Sunbury, and Whittlesea. He declared that the government would accelerate the provision of services to the outer western suburbs to offset the city's tendency to grow to the east. And he pledged to establish a series of regional planning authorities for sensitive tourist areas, such as the Dandenongs and the Mornington Peninsula/Western Port, and Victoria's main regional cities, essentially to sidestep the parochialism of local councils and encourage broader thinking in planning.

The green-wedges policy was one of the most lasting changes that Hamer made to Melbourne, and one whose major impact still lies ahead, as it will shape the city's growth for a long time yet. But almost half a century after it was announced, it has been only a mixed success, due to the collision (or collusion) of politics and money. The strategy divides outer fringe land into two classes: land for urban development, and land to be zoned permanently rural (or non-urban). But, as we all know, urban-zoned land becomes valuable, while rural-zoned land remains cheap. Like moths to a flame, developers flock to the arbitrage opportunity of buying rural land cheap and then selling it as expensive urban land. All they had to do was to get someone in government to rezone it for them. This became one of the problems that brought down Hamer as premier. And since then, as Professor Michael Buxton has documented, governments of both sides have proved willing to shift the boundaries between urban and rural land for favoured developers, who turn out to be donors to their party. Hamer himself was the least corrupt of politicians. He recounted being bewildered once when a developer tried to give him a brown paper bag full of cash. Years later, party officials despaired that the premier would take no part in their thankless job of fundraising. Not all Victorian governments since have put in place such firm Chinese walls.

In a city of 5 million people, moreover, the strategy could work only if governments put a much higher priority on investment in expanding the rail network. The network has improved — above all because the Hamer government built the underground rail loop, the Bracks government upgraded regional rail services, and the Brumby government began building the new western suburbs line, and the Liberals have continued it. But Victorian governments since the Kennett era have become too debt-averse to allow rail infrastructure to keep pace with population growth, let alone make up the backlog of the lost decades.

Every government, including Hamer's own, has nibbled at the edges of his 'green wedges'. It is a fine balancing act to make sensible adjustments without undermining the certainty that planning is meant to provide. Dennis Simsion, who joined the Board of Works in 1968 as director of parks and then became its planning chief, warns that the more nibbling is allowed, the more the whole concept is undermined:

> Once you start that sort of thing, it will be very hard to control. There will be pressure from the development fraternity to say 'Why can't we go there?' Bearing in mind the times, it's amazing that we've been able to hold on to as much as we have.[4]

In August 2011, Lady April Hamer, then 90, entered public debate to warn the Baillieu government to think again about its plans to take 6,000 hectares out of the green wedges and then stage regular reviews at which developers could bid for the land they wanted. In a letter to *The Age*, Lady Hamer confessed that she was attached to her husband's ideals, and that as her arguments were not about money, 'perhaps they have little weight today'. But she noted that Dick's ideas on planning emphasised restraining development to allow families better choices and a better environment. She added:

> We should bear in mind that any encroachment into our green spaces is irreversible. Speculators, of course, will disagree, but remaining faithful to the original intention of the green wedges would give us all a more disciplined, sustainable and welcoming city for future generations.[5]

A second legacy that Hamer left to Melbourne was a network of regional parks. LaTrobe and others had bequeathed Melbourne a wealth of inner-city parkland, and Guilfoyle's sweeping, romantic vision had made the Botanic Gardens one of the most beautiful places in any city in the world. But a century later, that legacy remained largely confined to the inner suburbs; with some exceptions, the new parks added further out were smaller, and allocated to sporting clubs. Hamer and Croxford set out to give Melbourne a new generation of big urban parks, this time in the outer suburbs, dominated by the natural environment, and located primarily along the city's rivers and creeks. Croxford hired Dennis Simsion from Auckland to turn the concept into reality. While the board ran the parks program, Simsion recalls that Hamer's role was crucial, not merely as its political sponsor, but as its inspiration:

> Because of all the work we did [on regional parks] in Auckland, Hamer was pushing us all the time [to do the same in Melbourne]. We [the MMBW] would never have done it on our own. The MMBW was a works authority; the co-ordination this required was something new. It was as much at Hamer's prodding as anything that we became very strong on open space.

Ultimately, the board came up with a 30-year plan to develop six new parks, covering 5,000 hectares, in the outer suburbs. They included the Point Cook coastal reserve in the south-west, Brimbank Park on the Maribyrnong in the north-west, the Yarra Valley park in the north-east, the Dandenong Valley park and Lysterfield Park to the east, and Braeside Park to the south. As places for people to picnic, bushwalk, kick a footy, or generally unwind, they have become part of the fabric of their suburbs.

It was a sign of Hamer's growing influence that Bolte made him deputy chairman of the group preparing Melbourne's transport-strategy plan. It gave him the right forum to push for one of his obsessions: getting Melbourne an underground railway. In his 1968 speech on the future of Melbourne, he declared:

> A modern city of any size will depend increasingly on fast, frequent, reliable and comfortable (in that order) public transport … Among the 36 cities I visited (on a recent trip), every city which already had an underground was extending it, or planning to do so. Those who have no underground are either planning one, or have already begun to construct it.[6]

This was a tough fight to take on against a premier as cynical about rail as Bolte. As mentioned earlier, Bolte had frozen the railways' capital works budget at the nominal level he had inherited from Cain in 1955, and did nothing to try to improve their efficiency. Sir Arthur Warner as transport minister had fought hard to win cabinet approval for an underground railway back in 1959. The announcement was made, the map published, the legislation passed through parliament

— but the premier-treasurer refused to finance it. Given the severe financial constraints that Victoria faced, Bolte believed that building more public transport was pouring money down a sink. He would allow ministers to put up legislation for new rail lines, but he would not provide the money to build them. When Warner's successor, Ray Meagher, introduced a bill in 1965 to build a rail link to Tullamarine airport, Meagher was quite explicit that its primary aim was to allow the railways to buy the land, and that in fact no rail link would be built for years. He was right: almost 50 years later, there is still no rail link. The one being planned now is on a quite different route from the one in the 1965 bill — which, in any case, Bolte scrapped after Labor insisted that alternative routes be considered. Bolte finally endorsed the underground railway only after losing the Dandenong by-election, and then left it for Hamer as premier to get it built.

Hamer followed the trends of his time, and moved quickly to head off problems. When neighbours began complaining about having blocks of flats built virtually to their fenceline, he gave councils the power to designate areas where flats would not be allowed — but also required them to zone areas where flats could go up. To head off ribbon development along the coastline, he ordered councils not to allow new subdivisions outside the prescribed areas of coastal resorts. He commissioned the Town and Country Planning Board to publish statements of planning policy to cover Western Port, the Mornington Peninsula, the Dandenong Ranges, and the Yarra Valley, to tell developers that by and large, they were off limits, and would be preserved as recreation areas for the future people of Melbourne.

Hamer as minister made a strong impression in the Liberal Party; his future became one of the things that Liberals talked about. On 27 March 1965, Peter Howson had a long talk with Sir Robert Menzies late at night after the House of Representatives rose, and recorded in his diary his conclusion that 'the PM will back Dick Hamer, and not John Gorton, for Kooyong when [he] retires'. In January 1966, Hamer received a call from Menzies, summoning him to his suite at the Windsor Hotel, the prime minister's home in Melbourne. As Hamer told it later, the PM had called him to 'inform me that he was intending to retire from parliament, and that I was to take over his federal seat of Kooyong. He was greatly astonished when I informed him that I would prefer to stay where I was.'

Menzies' offer was a generous one: he was offering to help Hamer make the same transition from state to federal politics that he himself had made in 1934, when he replaced Sir John Latham as both MHR for Kooyong and attorney-general. Menzies had worked with Hubert Hamer for years as barrister and solicitor, and admired the abilities of his rising son. But there were important differences between them. Hamer had chosen to make his career in state politics, in large part because it offered a better work/family balance than federal politics. He lacked Menzies' ambition to climb to the very top of the tree. Menzies had left Victoria as deputy premier, and had arrived in Canberra as attorney-general and a leading contender to be the next prime minister. Hamer was merely a promising state minister: had he gone to Canberra, he would probably have had to start again on the backbench, with no certainty of gaining a ministry. The Liberals used an informal system of state quotas to allocate ministries, and Victoria's list was already crowded with contenders. He had a job he loved, which allowed him to spend time with his family. Why move? He chose to pass up the offer. Instead, the seat was claimed by the party's 26-year-old state president, Andrew Peacock.

Ironically, by this stage, the Hamer family nest was starting to empty. Chris, his eldest son, had outdone all of his illustrious family academically, winning the BHP Science Prize as Victoria's top school student of 1961. He followed his father to Trinity College, then went overseas, taking out a Ph.D. in theoretical physics from the California Institute of Technology. Julia and Sarah both went to the University of Melbourne, completing arts degrees, and moving out of home, and eventually overseas. Soon only Alastair was left at home, to be brought up, in his own words, 'mostly as a single child'.

Several issues in 1968–69 illustrate Hamer's growing clout. Bolte had been growing increasingly restive over the independence of the ebullient Croxford and his commissioners: when Bolte tried to blame the Board of Works for forcing Melburnians to water their gardens by bucket in the drought of 1967–68, Croxford immediately blamed the government for not having allowed the board to build more dams. Some would say that Melbourne was just too small for the egos of Bolte and Croxford to fit into one city. In early 1968, Bolte publicly appointed a party committee to inquire into whether the board should be sacked and replaced with appointed commissioners. Hamer intervened behind the scenes to persuade Bolte and the MPs that the board's independence was really an asset to the government, because it allowed Spring Street to distance itself from unpopular decisions. Bolte and the party committee eventually agreed that he was right: legislation was passed to make the board 'subject to the Minister', but its commissioners remained independent. Ironically, under pressure late in his political career, Hamer made exactly the change that Bolte had advocated. By the time he, the Cain government, and the Kennett government were finished with it, the board that under Croxford seemed to be the second government of Melbourne had lost all its commissioners and most of its powers, and had been reborn simply as Melbourne Water.

Hamer's prestige was rising in all quarters. In March 1969, the Town and Country Planning Association, the lobby of planning enthusiasts, awarded him its highest honour, the Barrett medal, for his performance as minister. Two years later, the land developers' lobby, the Urban Development Institute, did the same. His growing clout freed him to take bolder actions that revealed his liberal views. On 3 April 1969, as the Vietnam War increasingly polarised Australians, federal Labor MP and anti-war campaigner Jim Cairns handed out leaflets outside the Melbourne Town Hall urging 20-year-olds not to register for potential military service. Cairns and 12 others were then arrested by Melbourne City Council by-law officers, under an MCC by-law prohibiting Victorians from handing out leaflets on city streets. Four days later, Hamer stunned his colleagues by intervening publicly on Cairns' side, telling the council to repeal the by-law, which he called a ban on free speech. Two days later, the council meekly scrapped the by-law and dropped all charges.

The voting age was another issue on which Hamer used his growing clout. At the time, 20-year-olds could pay tax and be conscripted and sent to fight in Vietnam, yet they could not vote in elections. The Liberals, fearing that the youth vote would go against them, insisted that the voting age stay at 21. Labor, for the opposite reasons, pledged to cut it to 18. Bolte was adamant that he would not reduce the voting age for state elections, so it was startling when Hamer announced that 18-to-20 year-olds would be allowed to vote in local elections. The minister for local government had a different view from his boss, and had persuaded him to take a step towards a reform that most saw as inevitable.

In his last months as minister, Hamer tried to initiate a surprising new direction. He wrote to the Melbourne City Council urging it to establish its own planning department, to develop a three-dimensional plan of the way it wanted Melbourne to look — putting the issue of building height centre stage — and, moreover, to draw up a master plan to make Melbourne 'a colourful living city, functioning 24 hours a day'. In the Melbourne of 1970, when the CBD had no residents, and the shops shut at 5.30 each night, and at lunchtime on Saturday for the weekend, the idea of the city functioning 24 hours a day was so startling to the council that it still had not replied when Hamer left the portfolio some months later. But late-night trading once a week was soon legalised. As premier, Hamer would allow the weekend trading restrictions to be violated repeatedly, and he became a fervent advocate for a casino in the city (while firmly ruling out poker machines). As premier, his only significant reform was to allow weekend trading in defined 'tourist areas' — potentially including the CBD — but he was part of a new mindset that put the focus on expanding opening hours, rather than insisting that everything close at weekends and evenings. It was left to the Kennett government, however, to make this idea a reality.

None of these issues mattered as much as Hamer's win over Ray Meagher over the future of the inner suburbs. The Housing Commission of Victoria had been set up in 1937, by the Country

Party at Labor's urging, to clear the slums and build new rental housing for the workers and the needy. At first, it focussed on building houses, maisonettes, and three-storey walk-up units. But in 1962, it opened its first high-rise tower, Emerald Hill Court, in South Melbourne. Over the next decade, it went on to build 41 high-rise towers in Melbourne's inner suburbs, demolishing almost 4,000 old houses, including historic terrace rows, to build 7,000 new units in the towers. It was a dramatic change to inner Melbourne, and had it continued, most of the city's distinctive terrace housing would have been demolished. Hamer himself, after all, set a goal in 1967 of expanding the population of inner Melbourne by 500,000; the Housing Commission was on the job. But the commission started building high rises just when young professionals started moving into the inner suburbs to renovate the very homes that the commission called slums. Carlton became the key battleground, and in March 1969, residents formed the Carlton Association to defend their turf. Privately, Hamer sided with them. Meagher, as minister for housing, sided with the commission. Both ministers won cabinet approval for incompatible bills — Hamer seeking to establish the Board of Works as an urban-renewal authority for Melbourne; Meagher seeking to have the commission fill that role in the areas it wanted. The ministers kept their fight behind the scenes, but Croxford went public: there was no room, he said, for two urban-renewal authorities. Labor and the Country Party combined to block Meagher's bill in the council, and time proved to be on Hamer's side. By 1970, the Housing Commission's high-rise projects were halted, and when Hamer became premier, abandoned. Stopping the inner-suburban demolitions was one of his most important contributions to Melbourne.

In two areas, however, Hamer made no headway until he became premier himself: decentralisation, and protecting historic buildings from redevelopment. While Bolte was no ideologue, he had a firm view that companies and families alike should look after themselves; he refused to offer tax breaks to try to shift growth from Melbourne to regional cities. Nor did he have any interest in saving the past:

his attitude to the demolition of historic city landmarks was a shrug of the shoulders and a throwaway 'you can't stop progress'. Ending that destruction would have to wait for a new leader with a different concept of progress.

CHAPTER TWELVE

The succession

In January 1967, Gough Whitlam replaced Arthur Calwell as Labor's federal leader. Immediately, Labor acquired a more articulate, dynamic, and youthful image. As the casualties from the war in Vietnam climbed, without clear evidence of military progress, and the television cameras brought the horrors of war every night to Australian homes, public opinion moved inexorably against Australia's participation in the war. The issue that was the Liberals' main strength in 1966 became its Achilles heel; the party lost Australia's young, and began to bleed support.

In Victoria, Clyde Holding became Labor leader after the 1967 election, replacing Clive Stoneham. Yet another lawyer who was schooled at Trinity Grammar, Holding, then 36, in many ways resembled Bolte rather than Rylah or Hamer. He, too, was a brilliant larrikin, quick thinking, but often lazy. Unlike his opponents, he seemed to have a chip on his shoulder, a personal cloud of melancholy that hampered his effectiveness. But he was a skilful lawyer who had co-founded the firm of Holding and Redlich, and excelled on the floor of the House. He carried a burning sense of social injustice, and being younger and better educated, lapped up the new issues that Bolte could never understand: the environment, inequality, urban planning, and the arts. He was still saddled with a Labor Party that worked against him as much as for him; but, for the first time since Cain died, Bolte had an opponent worthy of him.

And for the first time, he had to contend with an electoral tide running against the Liberals. The summer of 1967–68 saw a severe drought, and water supplies ran so low that households were forbidden to water lawns and limited to using buckets twice a week on their gardens. As noted above, Bolte tried to blame the Melbourne and Metropolitan Board of Works, the city's water authority, but its new chairman Alan Croxford gave the premier back as good as he got. He reminded Melburnians that the board in 1964 had proposed taking water for Melbourne from the Big River, north of the Great Divide, only to see Bolte reject the plan due to opposition from irrigators. Victoria was starting to talk back.

In early 1968, Bolte lost control of the Legislative Council when Western Province fell to the Country Party in a 7 per cent swing. The public learned of serious problems in the Public Works Department, as dissident Liberals, led by the chairman of the Public Accounts Committee, Alex Taylor, used the forums they controlled to push for reforms to raise the standard of government. Bolte backed a strange plan — on one account, inspired by his wife — to build a licensed restaurant in the middle of the Botanic Gardens. After much damaging publicity, it was vetoed by Labor and the Country Party in the Legislative Council. *The Age*, for long a loyal supporter, from 1966 came under the energetic, idealistic leadership of Graham Perkin as editor-in-chief and Ranald Macdonald as managing director, and started to put the government under persistent pressure. In particular, *The Age* campaigned vigorously against another strange plan — this time by the minister for lands, Sir William McDonald, to turn the dry, austere beauty of the Little Desert, west of Horsham, into sheep farms. There was widespread opposition to this, not least from the eternally sensible minister for agriculture, Sir Gilbert Chandler, and other ministers. Bolte stood by McDonald, an old friend, but at the cost of ignoring public opinion. In December 1969, all this combined to see the Liberals lose the seat of Dandenong in a by-election, with a big swing to Labor.

In the version of events he recounted later, Bolte said he had not intended to contest the 1970 election. In his head, he had worked out his ideal succession plan, in which he would retire in 1969. But he struck a hitch: his intended successor did not want the job. The man he had planned to hand over to, he said, was his tireless, loyal deputy: Rylah. Bolte knew how lucky he had been to emerge as party leader in the 1950s after originally losing to Rylah in the contest for deputy leadership, and then to find himself blessed with a deputy who saw eye to eye with him, took on a huge workload, and gave him complete loyalty. He said later that he wanted to return that loyalty by giving Rylah his turn as premier. In early 1969, he told Rylah his plan:

> I offered to resign, to give him what I saw as his due, a term or so at the top. And he refused it, on the basis that he didn't think he was cut out to be the leader. Arthur confessed to me that he was a born 2-i-c: he was school vice-captain at Trinity Grammar, 2-i-c of his battery in the AIF, and then Deputy Premier.
>
> I'm a lazy cove, I still am. I can make decisions, but (some of them) take a hell of a long time to do. I could say to Arthur, 'You do it.' He was one of the broad-minded people of this world, and he had ethics. He owned racehorses, he gambled, he could drink with the best of us — and the worst of us — but Arthur was to me an ideal fellow. When we started out, Victoria was a conservative state, and there were no little shops open (at weekends and nights). If we were to be remembered for anything, it would be the promotion of home ownership, to establish a means for young people to get finance for housing. Arthur Rylah was one of the leaders in all this.[1]

But by early 1969, Rylah was a man under pressure. Punters rarely end up as winners, and he had separated from his wife. To repair his finances, he accepted a side job as a director of Avis Rent-a-Car. The news was greeted with such outrage that he was forced to back down. Holding ridiculed the 'Rent-a-Minister government', depicting ministers 'walking up and down Bourke Street with a sign on their backs saying "Minister for Hire".' Then, in March 1969, Lady Rylah, a leading veterinarian, was found dead in her garden. She appeared to have suffered a brain haemorrhage, and was cremated, with no inquest held. But while the mainstream media remained silent on such matters, Rupert Murdoch's muckraking weekly *Truth* reported that Rylah had already left her for another woman. The chief secretary who wanted to protect Victorians from sexy novels was living with his secretary, Ruth Reiner, a 43-year-old divorcee, at Mount Macedon. The mainstream media ignored the story, but the word got around. Rylah would have known that if he ever had an ambition to succeed Bolte, it was now too late. The successor would be someone else.

The two leaders decided to fight one last election together, and then retire. Rylah would go first, allowing a year or so to groom his successor as deputy before he stepped up to the top job. First, Bolte took the long holiday in Europe that he and Jill had planned for their retirement. Victorians were used to their premier taking long winter holidays and overseas trips, but his three-month break in the winter of 1969 set a new record. It was during this break that Lindsay Thompson, ignoring Bolte's opposition, arranged his move to the Lower House to position himself for the succession. In a sign of changing times, the chairman of the party's social-welfare committee, Julian Doyle, launched an inquiry into poverty in Melbourne. Bolte was furious to learn of it, refused to allow the report to circulate outside the party room, and then ignored its recommendations. Doyle, one of the most impressive Liberal recruits at the 1967 election, quit politics after just four years. He later married Kate Baillieu, the journalist and sister of future premier Ted Baillieu.

But this version of Bolte's plans for the succession conflicts with what he told people at the time. A crucial source for Victorian Liberal politics in the 1960s and 1970s is the diary of Peter Howson, a former minister in the Menzies, Holt, and McMahon governments. Howson was a wealthy, English-bred, upper-crust conservative who was involved in Victorian Liberal politics from the 1950s to the 1980s. Each night he recorded the day's events on cassettes that his secretaries transcribed into diaries which ran into many thousands of pages. In the years when his career was in the ascendancy, Howson was ideologically in the mainstream of the party. For a federal MP, he had an unusual interest in state politics, and was one of Bolte's few allies in Canberra for his campaign to win back the states' lost revenue powers. But when John Gorton dumped him from the ministry in 1968, Howson became an embittered man; as Gorton drifted to the left, Howson drifted to the right. He devoted himself to bringing down Gorton as prime minister, with ultimate success; he then rejoined the ministry under McMahon, but lost his seat in Whitlam's 1972 victory. He then failed in numerous attempts to regain it, and/or win key party positions. In 1973 and 1976, he was the right's (losing) candidate for the post of Victorian Liberal president. Howson's diaries are naturally self-serving, but they are invaluable as a record of the events of his time.

On 1 May 1968, at a Government House reception, Howson has a talk with Bolte, and afterwards confides to his diary: 'It's quite clear that he's hoping that Dick Hamer will transfer to the Lower House, and take over from him in a couple of years' time.'

Early in 1969, Howson and Bolte meet again at a Government House reception, and Bolte tries to persuade the disaffected federal MP to move to state politics by taking over the blue-ribbon seat of Malvern — the same seat that Lindsay Thompson had his eye on. The next night, Howson attends a dinner in honour of the governor, Sir Rohan Delacombe, and privately asks the governor his view:

> He tells me that he believes (the succession) lies between Dick Hamer, Vernon Wilcox and Lindsay Thompson, but he would think at the moment that Hamer was an odds-on favourite. I told him about Henry's suggestion that I should move into the State House, and Sir Rohan said he would get some opinions as to whether this would be a wise step …

On Saturday afternoon, 3 May 1969, Howson drops by at Government House (as you do) to hear the results of Sir Rohan's soundings:

> We also discussed how long Henry was likely to be there himself, and it's pretty obvious that he won't be there for more than 3 years, and that, almost certainly, Dick Hamer will replace him. It was suggested

> that I might not have the same degree of friendship and support from Dick Hamer as I would from Henry Bolte. His Excellency also suggested that once Gorton left (as PM), I would probably be back in the (federal) Ministry.

His Excellency, known to friends as Jumbo, was a shrewd general who had been the British commanding officer in Berlin when the Wall went up in 1961. He was to be the last of the long line of British governors of Victoria, holding the job for 11 years, and winning widespread popularity. As governor, he had no political role, except in a crisis, but he had good political nous. Later in 1969, after a Christmas party for state MPs, Howson records continuing support for Hamer to come down to the Lower House to succeed Bolte. Whenever the possibility of Rylah taking over is mentioned in his diary, it is only to record that state MPs dismissed it.

Maybe Bolte had conflicting feelings about who should succeed him. Maybe he himself would have preferred Rylah, but recognised that Hamer was the man that the party wanted. What is clear is that, despite a widespread assumption that the leadership was his to confer, in reality it was not. In 1967, the party room had rejected his candidate and elected instead the independent-minded Sir Vernon Christie as the new Speaker, and had put the equally independent Bill Borthwick into the ministry. If the MPs whom Howson and Delacombe spoke to were representative, the party by 1969 would have rejected Rylah, had Bolte chosen him, and insisted on a new generation of leaders.

Whatever the reason, by 1969 Bolte had accepted that his successor would be Hamer. At around that time, Hamer began to be named by the media as the heir apparent, with a hint that he was Bolte's choice. And his imprint started to be seen, as longstanding policies were reversed on issue after issue.

In a sense, the transition from Bolte to Hamer began on Saturday 6 December 1969, when Labor claimed the seat of Dandenong in a swing of 10.7 per cent. Six weeks earlier, Labor had almost won the federal election with a swing of 6 per cent. The previous year, the government had lost the Western Province by-election (and control of the council) in a swing of 7 per cent. In 1969, state politics was dominated by issues that ran against the Liberals: the Little Desert scheme, Bolte's plan to put a licensed restaurant in the Botanic Gardens, his continuing war with the teaching unions, strikes in public services, and a mounting scandal over allegations that senior police were being paid protection money by doctors performing abortions. Liberal Party research found a growing sense in the suburban heartland that, after 14 years in power, Bolte had become arrogant. The electorate was not yet ready to dump him, but the vote in Dandenong — in those days, a middle-class outer suburb — was a sharp wake-up call, just five months from the state election.

On the following Monday, Bolte met with cabinet and offered to resign. Naturally, the offer was rejected. Instead, he and the government changed course. The normally outspoken premier became mild and temperate in his comments. The Botanic Gardens restaurant had already been thrown out by the Legislative Council; now the Little Desert scheme, too, was jettisoned. In the next six months, Bolte finally committed to build the underground rail loop, after having blocked it for more than a decade. He promised to set up an Environment Protection Authority to control pollution, a Land Conservation Council to decide the best use of Crown lands, and a huge expansion of Victoria's national parks. Cabinet rejected a plan by Mobil to run an oil pipeline across Port Phillip Bay. It rejected a plan by the Board of Works to pump treated sewage into the bay, instead ordering the board to build a long pipeline to dump it in the ocean beyond Cape Schanck.

Yet, at the same time, Bolte also pledged to guard Victoria against 'pollution of the mind'. The DLP had sat out the Dandenong by-election to remind the Liberals how crucial they were, and Bolte got the message. As the election drew near, he arranged for DLP leaders to meet with Sir Ian Potter, the prominent stockbroker and Liberal fundraiser, who would ensure finance for their campaign. He also agreed to double state aid to church-run schools, which was the DLP's main issue in state politics.[2]

It was the shrewdest decision of the campaign. In 1969, the federal council of the Labor Party had ended the party's opposition to state aid to church schools, but the Victorian ALP executive delegates voted against the change. Clyde Holding himself voted for it, and now he pledged to match the Liberals' spending on state aid, but, unlike the Liberals, to distribute it on a needs basis. Holding was also negotiating with Country Party leader George Moss for a preference swap. There was talk — how serious, it is hard to know — that the ALP and the Country Party might yet again do a deal to provide an alternative government. But to the hard-left Victorian ALP executive, state aid to church schools and an alliance with the Country Party were both anathema. In the last two weeks of the campaign, the ALP executive become Bolte's greatest ally, staging two interventions that sabotaged Holding's campaign and ensured that the Liberals would return to power.

Labor had no hope of winning an outright majority. Holding's goal was to deprive the Liberals of their majority, forcing them to either seek a coalition with the Country Party, or attempt a minority government, or even open the way for Labor to make some deal with the Country Party. But a fortnight before the election, the ALP executive passed a motion 'reiterating' that Labor in government would phase out state aid, which by then subsidised the school fees of hundreds of thousands of students. The implications for the children's parents were obvious: a Labor government would make them worse off. To the electorate as a whole, it sent a clear message: Labor was a house divided, whereas the Liberals were united behind Bolte. Then, as Holding, Whitlam, and Galbally kept insisting that Labor's federal policy on state aid was binding on the Victorian party, the state executive blocked a preference deal with the Country Party, and allocated Labor preferences in most country seats to the Liberals. That decision cost the Country Party two of its 12 seats in the assembly, while the backlash from its own voters cost them another two, and gave the Liberals a lasting majority in the Legislative Council.

The Victorian ALP executive had delivered Bolte from danger. He was returned for a sixth term in office, with only minor losses. Labor gained four seats from the Liberals, and one from the Country Party. But the Liberals took three seats from the Country Party to emerge with a net loss of just one seat. It was an astonishing result, given that the two-party swing to Labor was estimated to be 4.2 per cent. Even with the state executive sabotaging its campaign, Labor won its highest vote since 1952, and easily outpolled the Liberals. Labor won 41.4 per cent of the vote, the Liberals 36.7 per cent, the Country Party a sharply reduced 6.4 per cent, and the DLP 13.3 per cent. Only preferences from the DLP — and Labor — kept the Liberals' majority intact. Had Labor given its preferences to the Country Party, and won an extra 1 per cent of the vote itself — which, arguably, was what the executive's intervention cost it — the Liberals would have lost another six seats, and been left with just 36 of the 73 seats, and three choices: seek a coalition with the Country Party, try to govern as a minority, or see the other 37 combine to form a government. All three would have been unthinkable to Bolte, and would have led to a new period of instability in Victorian politics. What it would have implied for the succession is anyone's guess.

But this time the ALP executive had gone too far: retribution was coming. In 1969, Victoria alone had kept the coalition in power at federal level. Now that federal Labor had the scent of power, it was not going to let Victoria stop it from getting there. On 15 June, the state executive took a further step over the brink, suspending Galbally for a year for publicly rejecting its policy to end state aid. Galbally then appealed to the federal executive, which not only upheld his appeal, but dissolved the Victorian ALP branch, dismissed its office-bearers, and reconstructed it to ensure that it would never again be run by a single faction. By 1972, Victoria was no longer a barrier to Labor winning power in Canberra. Transforming the Victorian party into a serious contender for office took longer than reforming its structure. But by the late 1970s, for the first time in a generation, Labor under Bob Hogg as state secretary had an organisation able to match it with the Liberals, and committed unequivocally to winning power.

When Thompson left for the assembly at the 1970 election, Hamer became the Liberals' new deputy leader in the Legislative

Council. The government's legislative program was particularly busy. The tactics that Holding employed — frequent points of order, constant debates on procedural matters, daily urgency motions on minor issues — made parliamentary sittings more drawn-out than ever. Between 1937 and 1955, parliamentary debates on average took up about 3,000 pages of *Hansard* a year. From 1955 to 1970, that rose to 3,900 pages a year. But in 1970–71 and 1971–72, an average year of debates consumed 5,750 pages of *Hansard*, and when we got to the Hamer government, parliamentary debates had proliferated to average more than 6,500 pages a year. Alas, the quantity of debate doubled, but not the quality.

Ministers in the council spent much of their time dealing with issues on behalf of their colleagues in the assembly. Hamer had been Rylah's voice in the council, shepherding through the bills he introduced as chief secretary and attorney-general. But in 1970, after his period as deputy chairman of the Metropolitan Transportation Committee, Hamer shifted to representing the minister for transport, making him increasingly the minister for Melbourne. It was with a sense of history that, on 19 November 1970, he introduced in the council legislation to build the Underground Rail Loop. It was, he said, a project that had been discussed for 40 years, and was 'both logical and necessary'.

In February 1971, Rylah announced that he would retire in March; but before he could clear out his desk, he was felled by a stroke. Hamer nominated for preselection to succeed him in Kew, allowing him to move down to the assembly. In an interview with a young Michelle Grattan from *The Age*, he ruminated on political life:

> Politics is a form of public service, and it gets you in. You get interested in things that are happening, and you find yourself anxious to learn more about them. Every effective Member of Parliament is a pragmatist — but I think you have to have a philosophical background. Mine comes from my studies of ancient Greek government, where everybody had a right to speak their piece and be listened to.[3]

His sole opponent for preselection was pressured to withdraw, and the subsequent by-election saw a 7 per cent swing *to* Hamer — an unusual result at a by-election. He was still little known by the public; yet in the party room, he was now seen as the hope of the side. How had he gained this ascendancy?

First, the field of potential leaders was small. Since Bolte did not tolerate critics, some of the most able Liberal MPs never made it into his cabinet: Sir Vernon Christie and Alex Taylor were obvious examples. In 1971, most senior members of cabinet were either political lightweights, or nearing retirement, or both. Five candidates contested the deputy leadership ballot. Of these, Vernon Wilcox was discarded immediately. Bill Borthwick had real leadership potential — perhaps more than any of them — but he was relatively junior, and his natural support base was similar to Hamer's. Many thought he was running to stake his claim to become Hamer's eventual deputy.

The three main contenders were Hamer, Thompson, and Ray Meagher. The closest to Bolte ideologically was Meagher. A burly, bald, soldierly conservative who had grown up in the northern suburbs and worked as a council clerk, Meagher had gone off to war, been wounded in Syria, sent to Java, taken prisoner by the Japanese, and sent off to the Burma Railway. There, as a major and a leader of the Australian prisoners, he became one of the heroes of the POW camps, displaying what his official citation called 'outstanding personal courage' in standing up for his men, often submitting himself to the cruelty of their captors rather than allow his troops to be subjected to it. After the war, Meagher bought a newsagency and milk bar in rapidly growing Beaumaris, joined the Liberal Party, and was made chairman of the Aborigines Welfare Board — essentially to administer the reserves to which Aboriginals were then confined — before being elected in the wave of new Liberal MPs in 1955. He was the first in that group to be elected to cabinet, and served long stints in the transport and housing portfolios. Like Bolte, he was an instinctive conservative, but Bolte's overbearing, bullying style rankled with him, and he didn't hide it. Bolte could not take personal criticism, so Meagher was consigned to his long list of people he didn't trust. Meagher was a man of integrity and competence, with what *The Age* columnist Claude Forell called 'surprising streaks of liberalism'; but he was at heart a conservative, out of sympathy with the new issues that the Liberals faced. And he was the same age as Bolte.

Thompson had seemed the most likely successor when he had made it to cabinet at the age of 34. He was ideologically in the centre of the party, able, and well liked. 'The conservatives always thought Lindsay was one of them,' one of his colleagues recalled. Yet in the Hamer government, he ended up as one of the liberals. Exactly why Bolte cooled on him as a successor is not clear; one assumes that their arguments over how to treat teachers was a central issue. Bolte's first biographer, Peter Blazey, wrote that Bolte suspected Thompson of following his own agenda. In retirement, Bolte underwent a *volte-face*, warming to Thompson as he cooled on Hamer. When Bolte finally agreed to step down as chairman of the MCG Trustees in 1987, he told premier John Cain it was on condition that Thompson succeeded him. Until Jeff Kennett broke it up in 1997, the MCG Trust was Victoria's House of Lords; most of its members were retired politicians, and had Bolte not insisted on Thompson, his successor might well have been Hamer. Bolte also chose Thompson in advance to deliver the eulogy at his state funeral. In a 1989 biography, he praised Thompson repeatedly while criticising or ignoring Hamer. Similarly, his 1976 oral-history interview with Mel Pratt contained nothing but criticism of Hamer, at a time when his successor was still riding high with the public. It is beyond doubt that in retirement, Bolte regretted that Hamer had been his successor. He told Tom Prior in 1989:

> The DLP kept me alive politically, and I kept the DLP alive. Dick Hamer didn't, and look where that left the Victorian Liberal Party! Poor old Lindsay Thompson was stranded in an unwinnable situation when Hamer got out. Lindsay was, and is, a good bloke, but he had no hope … It was unfortunate for Victoria, not just the Victorian Liberal Party, that Lindsay was not premier longer, and earlier … It was an election which was … lost before he got there. He didn't get a go [as premier] until it was all over bar the shouting.[4]

So why did Bolte back Hamer at the time? And why did the party room, a conservative group, see a liberal like Hamer as the best choice to lead the party forward?

Peter Blazey, who was not close to Bolte, put it down to loyalty; Hamer, he said, had given Bolte 'unstinted devotion'. Besides, Bolte's support for him was also 'an acknowledgment that Hamer was the intellectual giant of the cabinet. The premier respected men of a superior mind'. It is hard to take that seriously. Bolte was anti-intellectual, and felt uncomfortable with 'men of superior mind'. He certainly demanded loyalty, and Hamer from his army days had grasped the importance of giving it, but it is unlikely that he stood out from other Bolte ministers on that score.

Bolte's second biographer, Barry Muir, once worked for Bolte, and his book, a hagiography written in response to Blazey's more critical book, may be closer to Bolte's real views. 'For some years, Hamer had been gradually filling Rylah's shoes as state cabinet's "workhorse"', he wrote. Hamer stood out for his 'photographic memory' and extraordinarily cool head in the heat of political fire. That is probably closer to the truth. In 1969, Hamer was in his prime, and mentally very sharp. He had excellent political antennae. He could carry a big workload. He was reticent compared to other politicians, but had a pleasant personality which could make that work for him. Bolte was well aware that Hamer's views were to the left of his own. But after the 1969 federal election, the Dandenong by-election, the 1970 election, and the federal ALP's dramatic move to sack its Victorian executive, he also knew that the political tide had turned. He told journalists that if the Liberals were to stay in power, the next leader would have to be quite different from himself. And heading into the 1970 election, his views swung around on many issues to adopt those that Hamer was advocating: building the underground railway, setting up the Environment Protection Authority, the Land Conservation Council, and even a Ministry of Social Welfare. The Bolte era was ending. The Hamer era was dawning.

On 21 April 1971, the coronation took place: the party room elected Hamer as the new deputy leader, with a clear majority over

Meagher and Thompson combined. Bolte immediately appointed him chief secretary, and told Victorians: 'One of these days I look forward to seeing Mr Hamer as Premier.' The immense workload that Bolte had once deputed to Rylah now landed on Hamer's shoulders. The 1971 budget had his fingerprints all over it. Labor tried to score points over his diffidence in the assembly, but it meant nothing out in suburbia. The newspaper articles about Dick and April were invariably flattering, and readers got the sense that they were two genuinely nice people, and that Dick was a very competent and widely respected minister. While mud was thrown at him in the bearpit of the assembly, none of it stuck.

Hamer wasted little time in putting his own stamp on the job. While Bolte took a five-week break in Queensland in the winter of 1971, Hamer negotiated a deal with other premiers in the south-eastern states for a trial of daylight saving. As chief secretary, he started to dismantle Rylah's censorship regime, allowing the previously banned musical *Hair* to be staged in Melbourne with its full-frontal nudity. He began to reform the police in line with a report commissioned from former London police chief Colonel Sir Eric St. Johnson, advocating promotion on ability rather than seniority, more clerical assistance to get police back on the beat, and significant increases in pay and staffing. He overturned the century-old ban on women joining the elite administrative division of the Public Service. When federal police arrested a small group who were fasting on the steps of the GPO to raise money for the Freedom from Hunger campaign for refugees from Bangladesh, Hamer as acting premier sent a telegram to prime minister William McMahon demanding that charges be dropped, pointing out that the fasters had raised $20,000 for the refugees; McMahon quickly complied. Bolte was back in charge to welcome in late-night trading to Melbourne on 9 November 1971, but Hamer had established that he represented a new approach, and it was going down well.

The succession was never in serious doubt. Yet Bolte remained ambivalent. 'I don't think Dick was ever Bolte's favourite,' said Alan Hunt, who served under both. 'Henry Bolte never campaigned for me or lobbied,' Hamer told Christopher Sexton years later. Walter Jona recalled in his autobiography that, in June 1972, Bolte floated a surprising alternative to a group of backbenchers over lunch:

> Appearing to take a thought out of thin air, he said: 'What do you fellows think of Jim Balfour as my successor?' We were a little startled by this sudden suggestion of his obvious preference … Jim and Henry were very close personal friends who shared a similar outlook on most issues … Bolte then went on to present the virtues of a Balfour-Hamer leadership, thereby retaining country and metropolitan representation and enabling Dick Hamer to gain some experience in the Lower House as the Premier's deputy before being elevated at a later date.[5]

The three backbenchers were not impressed. Jona told Bolte that MPs would not vote for Balfour to become premier. Two months later, he was proved right: Balfour stood for deputy premier, and won only a handful of votes. With one exception, Balfour's former colleagues were incredulous when told of the conversation during interviews for this book. A shy, reticent man who at times trembled with fear when questioned by journalists, Balfour was an implausible candidate. It underlines the fact that Bolte's support for Hamer was ambivalent. He told journalists he did not campaign for any candidate, but left it to the party. Clearly, the idea that Bolte chose Hamer to be his successor is a myth. The Liberal Party chose Hamer.

In retirement, Bolte reverted to the simple conservatism of the values he grew up with. Some of the views he expressed in long interviews with Mel Pratt (1976) and Tom Prior (1989) were quite whacky. Twenty-three years after Australia had switched to decimal currency, Bolte told Prior in all seriousness that he had never forgiven Harold Holt for introducing it; metric measures, he said, were 'nonsense'. He blamed the 1989 Tiananmen Square massacre in Beijing on the student protestors, telling Prior: 'No government anywhere, no matter how good its intentions may or may not be, can allow students to dictate national policy.' He insisted that no

Australian should ever be appointed governor or governor-general. He blamed Hamer for the collapse of the DLP, yet the DLP collapsed in every state, because the electorate changed and it didn't. He told Pratt that Hamer should have been able to keep Victoria out of the 1975 recession, which no premier could have done. And, as mentioned earlier, he told Prior that on the issue of Asian immigration, he lined up with the unabashedly racist stance of Victorian RSL president Bruce Ruxton.

Once he stepped down as premier, Bolte no longer had to take account of other people's views and values. Within two years, he had become, behind the scenes, an unforgiving critic of the man he had endorsed publicly as his successor.

Part III

The Hamer Years: 1

CHAPTER THIRTEEN

Hamer the man

Bolte's round face and rotund body made him a cartoonist's dream. By contrast, his successor looked normal, even bland. At school he was one of the small fry — in the photo of Geelong Grammar prefects in 1934, Dick was the smallest — but he ended up as a man of middle height. His habit of walking everywhere kept him reasonably trim. Throughout his time as premier, his hair was mostly dark, with flashes of grey. His dress sense was erratic, but usually he wore grey suits with light-blue ties, his own fashion statement in the world of dark suits around him. His most unusual characteristic was his Mongolian eyes: long, narrow, benign. Every politician has a cartoonist who gets him best, and in *The Age*, Ron Tandberg's depictions of Hamer looking innocuous with eyes almost shut eventually became cartoons that defined their subject.

What Victorians saw in their new premier was a man who seemed youthful, fit, and vigorous. This premier loved to walk. Usually his driver would drop him off at about 8.00 a.m. in Melbourne's inner-city parkland — normally at the Fitzroy Gardens, a kilometre from his office, or, if he had more time to spare, in Punt Road, East Melbourne — and Hamer would walk to work, thinking as he went. He normally discouraged company on his morning walks, but invited it when he took another walk after lunch. Graeme Weideman, later a minister in the Thompson government, recalls one lunch with backbenchers ending with the premier leading them all on a very brisk walk around the Fitzroy Gardens. Hamer walked fast and often. His passion for walking was one reason he put so much money into Brian Dixon's 'Life. Be in it.' campaign to encourage people to get active.

In conversation, Hamer had a ready smile that melted opponents. Friend, foe, and electorate found him easy to like. Even under provocation, his courtesy was impregnable. He radiated a sense of goodwill and honesty that inspired trust. He was no orator — he loved the theatre and the creative arts, but his language was always that of a lawyer — yet he could work a crowd, and often enjoyed doing it. He always seemed to be on top of his subject; it was rare to come across a significant fact he did not know, or an argument he had not already thought of. Before the 1979 election, Tom Harley, later a leading corporate strategist, was one of a team of young Liberal activists who compiled a 16-page booklet on the government's achievements to be sent to voters: *More than Meets the Eye*. 'Dick then rewrote it,' Harley remembered. 'His grasp and recall of what had happened was remarkable.'

Hamer's days were packed, and, like Rylah, he worked late into the night. In 1978, *The Herald* published a diary of a day in his life. By 8.30 a.m., he is in his office overlooking the Treasury Gardens, being briefed on his day's itinerary, the issues in the morning papers, the phone calls received, and the files to read. The reporter, Jenny Brown, notes that while there are only four or five files sitting on the desk, 'underneath the desk are dozens more'. He then hits the phone, does half an hour of interviews for TV and radio, and gives a half-hour press conference — answering 40 questions on 14 topics, showing he was far more succinct than politicians are today. He meets the new Russian consul-general, a delegation seeking funding for the Victoria State Opera, a housewife, 'Mrs X', who had written to complain about waste in government projects, a deputation from the quarrying industry, an unnamed visitor about plans for a convention centre, the president of the Legislative Council, four Liberal MPs, and his women's advisor, Yolande Klempfner. In the middle of all this, he sits down for two-and-a-half hours with Treasury officials to plan the budget, breaking off at 1.45 p.m. for a sandwich and cup of tea. He makes more phone calls, dictates 20 replies to correspondents, discusses press releases and speeches, then heads out at 5.30 p.m. to launch Victoria's new tourism authority, where he stays to chat before going to a dinner to honour the visiting conductor of the Munich State Opera. Dozens of files go in the car with him, and after he leaves the dinner, they will cover the Hamer dining table until he goes to bed a bit after midnight.

Some of the letters he received make bizarre reading. My favourite is one he received in November 1973 from a boy from a Yugoslav family:

> Dear Sir
> I am the son of one of your friends, Mr Dragan ----. I have a great desire to study at Melbourne University.
>
> At present I attend ---- HS (Matriculation). I would be very grateful if you could assist me to obtain a place at Melbourne University.
>
> Since the beginning of time, man has existed only through co-operation and willingness to help others.
>
> PS My examination number is ----.
>
> Thank you for your valuable time.
>
> Yours truly,
>
> ------ ------

Hamer sent the boy a personal reply, expressing his willingness to help but explaining that he did not decide who went to university.[1]

Hamer was good at the socialising, the small talk. He loved flirting with pretty women he met at functions, but he also loved making trips to the country with April, usually on Fridays or at weekends. 'There were a lot of centenaries in local towns,' she recalled. 'He loved meeting new people, and hearing them tell their stories. And he loved telling stories himself.' Their daughter Sarah says Dick always came back from country trips with new enthusiasm for the job: 'He got a lot of reinforcement from going out to meet people.' Yet to others, these excursions used up time that would have been better spent meeting ministers and backbenchers to iron out problems, win support for policies, or work out compromises. There is something quaint in the *Bendigo Advertiser* account of a trip in 1978, when he was engulfed by the land deals scandal, to look at water issues in the Korong shire. The paper reported that at a civic dinner at the Wedderburn Motel that evening, the premier and the Wedderburn Old Timers' Orchestra entertained the guests by singing 'Look for the Silver Lining'.

He was good at all that. What he was not so good at were intimate relationships, and difficult conversations. Hamer had many friends, but few if any were allowed to get really close. He kept his thoughts to himself. Even at home, April recalled, 'we didn't talk about politics. He didn't discuss a lot with us.' His youngest son, Alastair, recalled 'papers spread out over the dining room table every night, files all over the place', but not conversations about the things on his father's mind: 'I couldn't talk to him, because he always had such a horrendous amount of papers to get through — but at least he was there.' Dick belonged to the World Record Club, and would read his files and draft correspondence to the backing of Beethoven, Mozart, Joan Sutherland, or Gilbert and Sullivan. Most nights he was home for dinner, but his main family time was at weekends — when they would play tennis together, work in the garden, or go to the footy. Every January there was an annual family holiday at Metung, in a plain fibro house with a big verandah overlooking the Gippsland Lakes. The house belonged to the Armit family, legal clients who farmed along the upper reaches of the Tambo. Holidays at Metung became a Hamer family institution, and an opportunity later for a busy premier to catch up with his new grandchildren.

The 1970s were a time when many families were riven by deep generation gaps between parents and children, but only once did that erupt in the Hamer home. His daughter Julia recalled:

> My father was tolerant and open-minded about many things. He tolerated without comment some of us voting for other parties. This was our perfect democratic right in his eyes … He only once lost his

> temper with me, when I pasted a poster advertising the [Vietnam] Moratorium marches on the front wall of the Monomeath Ave house. He roared at me that he had never shoved his political beliefs down my throat, and I should not shove mine down his. I was secretly impressed by this clarity in rage, and did as he told me. The incident was never referred to by him again.[2]

John Brenan, Sarah's future husband, recalled a night in the early 1970s when Dick came to pick her up from a Carlton party, and ended up sitting on the floor deep in conversation with the students: 'There was pot being smoked, but he was completely unfazed.' John and Sarah married in 1973, spent two years in England, then returned to pursue careers in teaching and publishing respectively. When they both joined the Labor Party in 1977, Sarah found that their problems were not with her father, but with the media (and her grandmother, who told her she was being disloyal):

> John and I joined the Labor Party in Hawthorn under the influence of Evan Walker. John became branch president. A journalist got a whiff of it and rang me. He implied that I had joined because of the land deals. It was the only time in my life that I lost my temper at someone. I slammed down the phone.[3]

The family member most affected by Dick's rise to the premiership was April. Until then she had settled for the role of a wife and mother, quietly doing her bit for the world: making clothes to send to overseas children, being secretary of the Canterbury women's branch of the Liberal Party, working for other charities. 'I was never really career-minded,' she told one newspaper. 'I would have been happy in Jane Austen's day, just pottering,' she told another. Now she found herself thrust unwillingly into the role of a public figure:

> Being premier didn't change him, he just became a lot busier. I was the one who had to make the adjustment, because I had to give speeches and make public appearances. I was just a hired key: I used

> to go and open things. I found that very difficult at first. I had to go out and talk to Liberal Party branches, churches and all that, all over the state … We did an enormous amount of travelling, and gave a lot of speeches.[4]

What grieved April most was that her new position made her unable to look after her widowed mother, who by then was in serious decline, and living alone in a granny flat in the Hamers' garden. A series of strokes took away her power of speech, and then even her ability to write legible notes. Alastair was the only child still living at home, and his parents were often away. It was during one of their absences in 1975 that April's mother died. A year later, April's sister, Anne, also died, from heart disease. Sarah remembers it as a very distressing time for April, who was torn between meeting her family's needs and meeting the expectations placed on her as the premier's wife. April had many interests of her own, and, unlike Dick, was instinctively artistic in her use of language. But whenever Dick suffered, she felt the pain, and she often felt a misfit in her role, the more so because Jill Bolte (or Dame Edith, as she became) had handled it so well. A feature in *Woman's Day* in 1979, 'The Forlorn First Lady', captures April in a rather depressed state. She describes herself as 'a dull and boring person … with an enormous inferiority complex'. She blamed this on having grown up with a 'tremendously talented and artistic' mother and sister, then marrying into 'this enormous, argumentative, strong and overwhelming Hamer family'. 'Life,' she tells the interviewer, 'is like a corduroy road — full of bumps.' The interviewer suggests helpfully that we always climb out of them. April retorts gloomily: 'Yes, but there is always another bump.'

Hamer himself did not feel the bumps. Many politicians pretend that they are impervious to criticism. Hamer genuinely was. 'He took criticism as part of the job,' Sarah recalls. 'He didn't mull over things, he put them behind him. He was a champion sleeper.' The bedrock of self-confidence that his mother instilled in him never deserted him in all the disappointments of his later years as premier. Bolte never forgave anyone who crossed him; Hamer always forgave them. This says a lot about his gentle nature and his ability to live out his values, but it also reflects a trait Tom Harley calls 'mildly egocentric'. To Dick, his confidence in his own judgement was what mattered; other people's approval was welcome, but not essential.

He was not much of a sports fan. Bolte and Rylah were regulars at the races, and Bolte followed every sport. Menzies became Australia's most famous cricket lover. Hamer played all sports when he was young; but as an adult, his only sporting interest was 'the footy': the Victorian Football League, then still a competition of 12 teams from Melbourne and Geelong. Dick grew up as a Melbourne fan, but his diaries show that by his twenties, he had lost interest. Later he regained his love of footy, and took young Sarah to watch the Melbourne games, before changing teams to support his local club, Hawthorn. Alastair remembers spending many Saturday afternoons at the Glenferrie Oval with his father. In later years, Dick used to sit with former club president and medico Sandy 'Doc' Ferguson, and Victoria's police chief Mick Miller: 'Dick, Doc, and Mick', as one wag called them.

The real hobby of the man who made Victoria 'the Garden State' was his own garden. Sarah recalled:

> It really was a quiet passion, something he did all his life — making pleasing curves for the rose beds, creating a ferny space and stone barbecue (hardly ever used) beside the house, building a rockery, tending fruit trees, and growing veges. Most weekends he would be out there for at least a couple of hours in his old army shorts and boots.

Who's Who for years listed his hobbies as 'golf, fishing, sailing, tennis'. But when a journalist asked in 1971 about them, April laughed. 'Dick hasn't played golf for ages,' she said. 'He's too busy. He hasn't fished for years. He'd sail if we had a boat, but we don't. He does play tennis when he can …'

Two questions about Dick Hamer might puzzle Australians of a later age. Why was he in the Liberal Party, when his values seem to be at odds with those of the Liberal Party of today? And why did a party room of mostly conservative MPs elect someone so liberal to be its leader?

Hamer was in the Liberal Party because it was his tribe. For most of its history, the Liberal Party was a broad church, open to affluent Protestants (and the odd Catholic) with a wide range of views. From the moment that Deakin's Protectionists merged with their traditional enemy, the Free Traders, to form the Liberal Party in 1909, it had to be a home to people of widely differing views. In the Liberal Party, the streams of progressive liberalism, social conservatism, and economic radicalism all had to find common cause. Hamer was in a long Liberal tradition of practical reformers with a strong social conscience. It was a tradition dating back to 19th-century British reformers, such as William Wilberforce, who led the fight to abolish slavery, the philosopher John Stuart Mill, and prime minister W.E. Gladstone. Hamer's political ancestors include Alfred Deakin, the liberal Victorian politician who put aside state politics to campaign for Federation, and ultimately became prime minister, founded the Liberal Party, and gave Australia its arbitration system, defence forces, old-age pensions, and tariff protection. Hamer greatly admired Victoria's first ruler, lieutenant-governor Charles Joseph LaTrobe, the sensitive, enlightened leader of the young colony who gave Melbourne its parks and gardens, and helped found key institutions such as its university and hospital. He had grown up admiring his uncle George Swinburne, who founded the technical college for working-class boys, and created the basis for Victoria's irrigation system by nationalising state rivers, and devising a system for managing and using them that was to last for 80 years.

The tradition of Deakinite liberalism has always been strong in Victoria. Hollway was in its mainstream; Harold Holt and John Gorton were influenced by it; and in Hamer's own time, his fellow liberal Liberals included Don Chipp, Andrew Peacock, Ian Macphee, Murray Byrne, Bill Borthwick, Alan Hunt, Haddon Storey, Brian

Dixon, and many others of like mind, in the parliament and the wider party. Today the radical right worships Menzies and disparages Deakin, yet Menzies, who grew up under Deakin as prime minister, personally had great admiration for him. Howson recorded in his diary that the night Menzies stepped down as prime minister, he told Howson and other colleagues over drinks that he thought Deakin was Australia's greatest prime minister, partly because he had set up the conciliation and arbitration system which brought the interests of labour and capital together. Menzies adopted Deakin's core policies virtually unchanged — and, as we have seen, he wanted Hamer to be his successor in Kooyong. He did lose faith later, however, telling Howson in January 1974 that Dick was 'far too much like Harold Holt, trying to be all things to all men'. Hamer, he said, needed 'more iron in his velvet glove'. In late 1976, Menzies told Howson he was 'disgusted with the way in which Hamer dithers'. At the 1976 election, he added, he had voted for another party (almost certainly the DLP).

Hamer's only alternative in the 1940s would have been to join the Labor Party — and Labor in the 1940s and 1950s belonged to a very different tribe. It was union dominated, working class, largely Irish, and Catholic — and still proclaimed socialism as its ultimate goal. Among Hamer's contemporaries, two upper-middle-class lawyers did join Labor and thrived in it — Gough Whitlam (an old boy of Canberra Grammar School) and Don Dunstan (an old boy of St Peter's, Adelaide) — but both were misfits in their own tribe. Hamer was always at home with his class, always comfortable in his own skin. He was never attracted to socialism as a goal, or to equality as an end. While his values and Labor's overlapped, Labor as a political party had no appeal for him. The Liberal tradition in those days tolerated a certain independence of thought among its MPs. Labor imposed conformity.

Like Bolte and Menzies, Hamer was no economic rationalist. Menzies initially sold off the Commonwealth Oil Refineries, but took no further interest in privatisation, maintaining a government airline, a telecommunications and postal monopoly, and many other enterprises. Bolte privatised nothing. All three were pragmatists, with an instinct to favour free-enterprise solutions, so long as they appeared likely to provide better outcomes. The Hamer government did sell off some government enterprises — some meat works and cool stores, and a factory producing pre-fabricated homes — but that was the work of ministers: Ian Smith in agriculture and Brian Dixon in housing. Hamer took on the party's economic conservatives to win protracted disputes on two issues: allowing the State Government Insurance Office to enter the field of general insurance, and the Gas and Fuel Corporation to start exploring for gas in the Otway Basin (in partnership with Beach Petroleum, but in opposition to the Esso-BHP partnership). Both moves were initiated by the state enterprises themselves, but Hamer backed them all the way against strong opposition, including from the Liberals' state council. It exemplified the pragmatism adopted by Liberal governments of his time. The Fraser government, too, privatised little in its seven years in power.

Hamer was less an originator of ideas than a selector choosing between competing ideas. As minister for local government, he immersed himself in the debates about planning policy. He read widely, travelled, consulted — but expected his officials to come up with policy options for him to choose from. The green-wedges policy of extending Melbourne out along the train lines was not his original concept, but he made it his policy, and won public acceptance for it. Alan Hunt, his minister for planning, argued that in politics, to be a visionary is not to dream up your own ideas, but to judge which ideas will serve the community best in the long term:

> Hamer was a long-term visionary: he picked up ideas and he developed them. The green-wedges policy originated with the board, but Hamer drove and developed it. He deserves to be recognised as the developer of the policy. Without his policy drive, Melbourne today would be a far different place, and a far less attractive place in which to live. It is something that distinguishes Melbourne from Sydney.[5]

As premier, he allowed ministers a free hand. When he was criticised for neither focussing more selectively on key issues, nor intervening when things started to go wrong, Hamer was unapologetic:

> You don't hire a dog and then bark yourself. You hand a job to a person you expect can do it, and leave it to him to carry out his responsibilities. Only very rarely do you step in and overrule him — and then mainly because his decision has ramifications outside his particular portfolio.[6]

But others saw this reluctance to intervene as reflecting his dislike of confrontation, and of the 'difficult conversations' required to close the gaps with those with different views. Robert Maclellan, a minister in the Hamer, Thompson, and Kennett governments, put it most pungently:

> He wasn't very good at building the other end [to bridge the gaps with others]. He was more comfortable opening a kindergarten or an arts festival. He tended to spend too much time doing what he enjoyed, or had empathy with, rather than cultivate the areas with which he was not comfortable … Dick stayed where he was welcome, and part of being premier is to go where you're not welcome.[7]

Maclellan was one of many ministers who was surprised to discover how much freedom he was given by his boss:

> As a minister, I would have talked to him for 20 minutes in a year … If Dick felt you were able to do the job, that was it. He had utter and complete reliance upon the people he trusted and felt to be competent. He was extraordinary in his sense of trust.

Haddon Storey, attorney-general from 1976 to 1982, had a similar experience.

> He let ministers do their own thing. If ministers couldn't correct the problem, then he'd step in … After I was appointed attorney-general, he had a long discussion with me about what I was to do. And after that, we didn't have a long discussion for three years. We had constant discussions about things, but short ones.[8]

Maclellan was on the right of the party, while Storey was one of Hamer's closest allies: political leanings had no bearing on his willingness to trust people. Several who had served under both Bolte and Hamer recalled that Bolte kept a closer watch on his ministers; they always had the sense that he was looking over their shoulder, and was quick to say no, whereas Hamer gave them free rein. 'Bolte knocked me down a few times,' Murray Byrne recalled. 'Hamer agreed with everything I was doing.' Alan Hunt, who was minister for local government under both, described the contrast:

> Bolte left things to his ministers unless there was some problem. If some minister was not performing, then Bolte would come down on him very hard. If a minister didn't get a vital decision of cabinet implemented, then he was in trouble. Bolte expected to be advised of anything important, and to have a say in the decisions. In practice, that meant anything important had to go to cabinet.
>
> Dick, on the other hand, wanted to know if everything was going all right — not whether anything was going wrong. He wanted to make sure that he was kept informed. But if he'd been more engaged, some of those (bad) planning decisions [between 1976 and 1978] would not have been made.

The contrast between the two leaders was more striking in the way they handled cabinet and the party room. Bolte always wanted to be in charge, and to run meetings crisply. Cabinet meetings under him began at 11.00 a.m. and ended at lunchtime — usually at 1.00 p.m., but often sooner, if he felt the real business was done. While he generally let the cabinet debate issues freely, there were plenty of times when he put his foot down. Murray Byrne recalled:

> One time he was trying to get something through, and when the time came for a vote, he was clearly going to lose. Bolte just got up out of his chair and said: 'Well gentlemen, I have given my word on this. If you don't support it, you won't have me here any more.'[9]

It was a frequent tactic of Bolte's, and it always worked. He applied similar tactics in the party room, where, as Alan Hunt recalled in a tribute to Bolte, 'Everyone was expected to put his case succinctly, and raise nothing that had been raised before — only new material — so that the party room could proceed to dispatch its business effectively and efficiently, with a minimal waste of time.' The other side of this efficiency, however, many MPs recalled, was the use of heavy-handed tactics by Bolte and Rylah to get the party room to do what they wanted. 'Arthur often manipulated the agenda, steered discussion and geared the strategy in order to help bring about the desired result,' Walter Jona wrote. They ganged up against dissidents, and, *in extremis*, Bolte's resignation threats always worked. The party-room revolt in 1967 that installed Vernon Christie as Speaker and Bill Borthwick in cabinet was essentially about fighting for democracy within the party.

As a soldier, Hamer had rebelled inwardly against generals issuing dictates without consultation. As an instinctive democrat, he believed strongly that everyone had something to offer, and that their views should be heard and considered. This was the philosophy he tried to put in place when he was running the cabinet and the party. It worked when he was able to command deference by virtue of his runaway election victories. But as his electoral authority eroded, moral authority alone would not allow him to keep debates succinct and focussed on the issue at hand. Bolte didn't care whose toes he trod on to get his way. Hamer was more reticent, and in later years, meetings frequently became heated, ran over time, and failed to reach the decisions they were intended to make.

Did Hamer allow ministers and MPs too much freedom of speech? His former colleagues, with some differences of emphasis, tend to agree that he did. Digby Crozier, who served in the Hamer and Thompson cabinets, says that while Bolte had insisted on keeping debates short, and reaching a decision, under Hamer, that discipline broke down:

> Dick, being a very civilised man, handled the cabinet with an extraordinary tolerance. Our meetings were seldom completed by lunchtime. Dick would let people go on in a pretty fulsome way. He was extraordinarily tolerant of some of the more vociferous members of cabinet. I often used to wish that Mr Hamer, LL.B., would make way for Colonel Hamer of the AIF, who might pull the meeting into gear.[10]

CHAPTER FOURTEEN

Hamer makes it happen

Dick Hamer took power as a new political wind swept across Australia. After 27 years in opposition, federal Labor under Gough Whitlam was cruising towards victory at the coming election. The Liberals' gamble in dumping John Gorton to make William McMahon prime minister had backfired. The Nixon administration's decisions to negotiate to withdraw from the Vietnam War and recognise communist rule in China had pulled the rug out from under the anti-communist crusade that the Liberals had followed for a generation. Whitlam had come to be seen as Labor's moderniser, the leader and symbol of its transformation from a party based on union allegiance to one drawing its leadership from middle-class activists, and its world view from a wide mix of sources. His policies were targeted at Australians living in the cities, pledging that Labor would fix urban and social problems by setting up expert commissions and putting Commonwealth money into fields that until then had been left to the states: new cities, urban transport, sewerage, and the environment. The Whitlam of 1972 exuded ability — as articulate as Menzies, but more modern. He appeared far more prime ministerial than McMahon. The political tide was turning.

New forces were also rising at grass-roots level. In August 1972, as Hamer took office, Melbourne University political scientist Jean Holmes, writing in the *Australian Journal of Politics and History*, described the new mood:

> Public opinion has come alive in Victoria, confronting the Government with criticism and demands. Sometimes it has been in the form of traditional strike action, sometimes there has been orthodox pressure group activity, often it has been expressed in the new direct action style, and there has even been an example of simple old-fashioned 'influence'. The Victorian electorate has not been as lively as this for some time, although there have been signs that something was stirring 'out there in Muggsville'.[1]

She cited a ten-day strike by LaTrobe Valley power workers to demand an extra week's leave; a black ban by the Trades Hall Council on Safeway stores to oppose late trading; strike threats by prison warders at Pentridge over pay and conditions; marches by secondary-school students on Parliament House; the unexplained disappearance of a Ship Painters and Dockers official during a union election; and Carlton residents burning an effigy of housing minister Ray Meagher in protest against Housing Commission plans to raze blocks of terrace houses. And over Bolte's opposition, the Liberal Party state council voted that 18-year-olds should be given the right to vote.

The lid of repression had been taken off, and a range of discontents were surfacing. For a generation after the war, Australians by and large had accepted that if things weren't right, you just put up with them. Now, in an age of global protest born out of the US civil rights movement and opposition to the Vietnam War, young people and community groups were demanding what they saw as their rights. Throughout the Western world, governing became more difficult. Resident groups formed to fight freeways and urban-redevelopment plans. Interest groups became more vocal in demanding more for schools, health care, public transport, and previously neglected issues such as mental health and services for the disabled. The union movement grew militant. Strikes became commonplace, ambit claims for wages and conditions more ambitious, even ludicrous — and in Victoria, the Builders Labourers Federation, under its thuggish Maoist boss, Norm Gallagher, banned work on projects it disapproved of, or by firms with whom it was in dispute. Social consensus was breaking down, yet consensus was what Hamer was offering. Blue-collar union militancy became an issue he could never control.

Initially, however, Hamer's arrival as premier brought peace. On 22 August 1972, the party room gave him an overwhelming victory over Ray Meagher to be Victoria's new leader. Lindsay Thompson was elected deputy premier by one vote over Bill Borthwick. Both were Hamer allies, and while most of the cabinet were not, Hamer put ministers he trusted into the portfolios that mattered most in redefining his government's new direction. Borthwick as minister for conservation had all environmental agencies brought under his new department. Alan Hunt retained the key portfolio of planning, while Hamer made Murray Byrne the minister for state development and decentralisation, with an ambitious agenda to redirect Victoria's growth into country towns.

The new premier enjoyed plenty of goodwill. The Melbourne media gave him a dream run. Sir Philip Jones, executive chairman of The Herald and Weekly Times, was a firm Liberal supporter. At *The Age*, editor-in-chief Graham Perkin and managing director Ranald Macdonald were ambivalent about the federal Liberals — *The Age* was the only metropolitan daily to endorse Whitlam in 1972 — but gave strong support to Hamer and his reformist style. And Victorians generally welcomed the arrival of a premier who, unlike his predecessor, was unfailingly polite, positive, reasonable, and progressive. 'The new premier is both the expression of Victoria's traditions, and the epitome of its modern aspirations,' Jean Holmes told fellow political scientists. Outside parliament, in those first months he faced virtually no opposition.

Hamer's task was to establish very quickly that he was different from Bolte and McMahon. Until then, like all Bolte's ministers, Hamer had lived in the shadow of his ebullient leader. Even when the spotlight fell on him, his natural reserve meant that viewers rarely got past the impression that he seemed to be a good man, reserved, but intelligent and highly competent. The party's fear of defeat gave him an extraordinary opportunity to put his personal stamp on it — and he took it. The ease of his leadership win, and the threat from Labor, saw conservative voices pushed to the sidelines. The party organisation was now directed by Leo Hawkins, a young, highly intelligent advertising executive who shared Hamer's liberal views. The state executive was dominated by Peter Hardie, a progressive businessman who had been close to Gorton, and in July 1973 would become the party's state president. Both wanted to rebuild the Liberal Party on a base of mass membership.

Hamer quickly set out a wide-ranging reform program, as if he were leading a new government. The phrase he used to define the change was 'the quality of life': his government would focus not just on economic growth, but on increasing the enjoyment we derive from it. He set up new ministries for conservation, planning, and the arts — the latter with himself as minister. He foreshadowed the appointment of an ombudsman to handle citizens' complaints against departments, and set up an Administrative Appeals Tribunal. A range of consumer-protection laws were introduced, including a Small Claims Tribunal to settle minor disputes. Compensation was introduced for victims of criminal assault. He pledged that 18-year-olds would be allowed to vote once the federal government agreed. He initiated a comprehensive rewrite of the state Liberal platform to reflect the party's new thinking.

Relics of the Bolte era were gradually swept away. Margarine was allowed to be sold freely without being coloured pink or labelled 'for cooking purposes only'. Daylight saving was made permanent in the summer months. Fluoride was finally added to Victorians' water supply. The government flagged new approaches to punishing offenders, such as periodic detention, weekend jail, and work release, aiming to provide better pathways to rehabilitation. And the fight against the road toll stepped up a gear, with police empowered to require blood samples from drivers in accidents. The message was that this was a new government, with new solutions.

The budget brought down on 12 September was Hamer's first. While Bolte had retired only three weeks earlier, he left it entirely for Hamer to prepare, and it was designed as an election budget. No taxes or charges were increased. 'Composite fees' in state schools — in effect, compulsory parent contributions for various expenses — were abolished. School spending was lifted to record levels, with 2,500 more teachers to be hired, including 900 recruited from Britain, the US, and Canada. Payroll-tax rebates were introduced for businesses located outside Melbourne. Foster mothers were given increased payments, and public servants received increased superannuation. The budget allocated funds to finally start work on the underground railway and the Dartmouth Dam — a huge storage on the Mitta Mitta River to guarantee water in dry years for irrigators and towns along the Murray. Subsidies to libraries were doubled, and a new fund set up to help finance tourist projects on historic themes. The Health Department set up a new branch to tackle alcoholism and drug dependency. Whatever Hamer's musings on the meaning of life, the meaning of his budget was to give Victorians the sense of new life in Spring Street.

Construction finally resumed on the West Gate Bridge, after the tragic collapse of a 112-metre span in 1970, which had killed 35 construction workers. Work on the Eastern Freeway began, the Mulgrave Freeway was advancing on Melbourne bit by bit, and the dramatic reshaping of St Kilda Junction, which Hamer initiated as minister for local government, was almost complete. His government now promised to build a new bridge over the Yarra, linked to a new road that would provide a western bypass of the city: these days we call it Wurundjeri Way. The Board of Works was building a 19-kilometre tunnel through the mountains to bring water from the Thomson River to the Upper Yarra Dam to boost Melbourne's water supplies. And in December 1972, Hamer unveiled detailed plans for the second stage of the Arts Centre: the theatre complex and the spire, which he told Victorians would cost $27 million. Showpiece projects such as these were given priority over more prosaic needs, such as renovating the city's 19th-century drainage system, or replacing level crossings on suburban roads.

For Labor, Hamer and his new policies created huge problems.

As future Labor minister Race Mathews put it, 'It felt like a change of government without a change of party.' The fact that many of Hamer's new policies were similar to Labor's own made them impossible to attack. Like many oppositions, Labor had to sit and watch as the government stole its most attractive policies and sold them to voters as its own. Steve Bracks and Kevin Rudd would later lead Labor oppositions to power by identifying two or three key issues, and establishing clear ownership of them, but Holding and his team lacked that discipline. Holding had the edge over Hamer in parliamentary debate: like Bolte, he was quick-witted, and could spot the holes in the other side's case and exploit them with ridicule. But in the spring session of 1972, Labor wasted much of its energy by trying to inflate trivial issues into scandals, only to see them die like bubbles in the air. Hamer and the public ignored them. The most prominent became dubbed 'the storm in a gluepot': Labor revealed that in the 1960s, when Hamer was a director of Yorkshire Chemicals, the company sold glue worth $1,780 to the Government Printer. The sales were trivial, and Labor conceded that Hamer had not even known of them. Holding liked to push such attacks because he was good at parliamentary theatrics, but he became identified with cheap smears. Labor lost the opportunity to seize the policy high ground, to identify key policy issues, and relate its solutions to voters' concerns. Its ill-discipline made it easier for the Liberals to take over that territory themselves.

The most memorable event in that session occurred far away, at a one-room country school. In the early afternoon of Friday 6 October 1972, two men, one armed with a gun, entered the schoolroom at Faraday, near Castlemaine, where 20-year-old Mary Gibbs was teaching a class of six children. At first, the little ones thought it was a joke; but Edwin Eastwood and Robert Boland were deadly serious. They planned to kidnap the children and demand $1 million ransom from the government — an idea they pinched from Clint Eastwood's new movie *Dirty Harry*. They forced the teacher and children into a panel van, drove their hostages deep into a forest near Lancefield, and rang *The Herald*, demanding to speak to Lindsay Thompson, the minister for education. They failed to get through, but *The Herald* passed on the message, and police confirmed that the teacher and children were missing. Thompson and Hamer drove to Russell Street police headquarters, conferred with assistant commissioner Mick Miller, and agreed to pay the ransom if necessary. The kidnappers rang again to demand that Thompson hand over the money outside the Woodend post office at 5.00 a.m. He drove there in an unmarked police car, with Mick Miller hiding on the floor of the back seat under a rug. A police photo of the frail Thompson standing alone and vulnerable in the darkened street with $1 million in a suitcase beside him was a profile in courage. But the kidnappers never came. While they were making the phone call, Mary Gibbs and the two oldest girls succeeded in kicking a hole in the back panel of the van. All seven of them managed to climb out and escape into the forest, where their teacher led the way until they found a group of rabbit shooters, who drove them to freedom. The drama overshadowed anything happening in Spring Street.

State politics was also drowned out by the federal election. After 23 years of coalition rule, Whitlam's campaign slogan — 'It's time' — caught the mood of Australia's big cities. In 1969, Labor had won a majority of votes and seats in the rest of Australia, but won just 11 of Victoria's 34 seats. This time, Victoria did not spoil the party. On 2 December, Whitlam swept to power with a comfortable majority. In Victoria, the Liberals won the state's four closest races, but Labor picked up four outer-suburban seats, and won a landslide swing in the booths. On first preferences, its vote in Victoria jumped 6 per cent; the Liberals lost 4 per cent, and the DLP 2.5 per cent. In two-party terms, Victoria recorded a 5.5 per cent swing to Labor, giving it an estimated 50.4 per cent of votes after preferences. It was the first time since 1954 that Labor had outpolled the coalition across Victoria. Excluding Hotham, where Don Chipp had created his own brand as a progressive Liberal while Labor ran a draft resister as its candidate, the average swing to Labor in Liberal seats in Melbourne was a stunning 7.8 per cent. On one estimate, the same swing on state boundaries would see Labor pick up 14 seats, giving it a serious chance of winning government. At best, the Liberals would be forced into coalition with the Country Party — a prospect they loathed, although their federal MPs found such coalitions quite agreeable.

Six months into Hamer's premiership, the polls showed the state Liberals still struggling. In February 1973, the Morgan Gallup Poll reported that the DLP vote had collapsed, but it was going everywhere except to the Liberals. Labor was not doing as well as it had at the federal election, but both it and the Country Party were doing well enough to force the Liberals into coalition or minority government. The polls in March were similar. But as the 19 May election date approached, positive signs began to emerge. A survey in Mitcham by the Liberals' pollster, George Camakaris, found many voters said they supported Whitlam at federal level, but Hamer at state level. In mid-April, Camakaris reported that the Liberals were making up ground, but still faced the possible loss of six metropolitan seats. Yet as the campaign went on, the Liberals' vote grew at Labor's expense. Liberal polling showed that voters rated Hamer well ahead of Holding on almost every count: he was seen as intelligent, stable, competent, strong, and generally concerned about ordinary people.

The election campaign only reinforced these perceptions. Holding created a new issue by seizing on public concern over rising inflation to promise state regulation of prices to keep it down. But his promise was more ambitious than it was carefully thought out; he was not able to convince Victorians how it would work. Hamer, by contrast, had been rolling out new policies for months; the Liberals now capitalised on both that momentum and his personal popularity with the audacious slogan 'Hamer makes it happen'. No campaign slogan had ever focussed so directly on the party leader, or succeeded so brilliantly.

Hamer's main campaign promise was to take an axe to the government's freeway plan — drawn up four years earlier by the Metropolitan Transportation Committee, of which he was deputy chairman. On 21 December 1972, he announced that existing freeways under construction would be completed, but that no new freeway would be commenced that would seriously disrupt a built-

Above: Muriel's wedding, 1915. Attendees at the marriage of Muriel Swinburne (Dick's cousin) to Russell Martin (later Mr Justice Martin, known to Dick as 'Uncle Justice') included Sarah Hamer (Dick's grandmother, third from the left in the front row) and Ethel Swinburne (Dick's aunt, seated to the right of the wedding couple). Nancy Hamer (Dick's mother) is standing at the right end of the middle row. In the back row, Hubert Hamer (Dick's father) is third from the left; and George Swinburne (Dick's uncle) is the tall figure at the far right. [HAMER FAMILY]

Below: Madonna col bambino. Nancy Hamer with baby Dick, summer of 1916–17 [HAMER FAMILY]

Above: Dick at Geelong Grammar School, c. 1934 [DR JIM GUEST]

Below: GGS prefects, 1934. Standing: Ross Cameron, Aurel Smith, G.L. Lindon, David Hay, Randall Deasey, Dick Hamer. Sitting: Sir James Darling (headmaster) and J.S. Leach (captain) [GEELONG GRAMMAR]

Above: April as a teenager around the time she first met Dick [HAMER FAMILY]

Right: Dick as a Trinity College footballer [HAMER FAMILY]

Above: Battalion O group officers at Tobruk, October 1941. From left to right: Capt. W.R. Tucker, Maj. F.A. Lidgertwood, Lieut. R.J. Hamer, Lieut.-Col. W.W. Crellin, Capt. J.D. Rice, Capt. A.I. Hare, Capt. B.J. Hemmings, and Capt. H.J. Williamson [BOB HARE]

Below: The future politician meets his future electorate: Lieutenant Hamer and some of his men in camp at Woodside, 1940 [HAMER FAMILY]

Right: Hamer's how-to-vote card 1958 [HAMER FAMILY]

Below: Dick and April on their honeymoon in Tasmania, 1944 [HAMER FAMILY]

Introducing the ONLY ENDORSED LIBERAL CANDIDATE

R. J. HAMER

for

EAST YARRA

LEGISLATIVE COUNCIL ELECTION

(Victorian Upper House)

21st JUNE, 1958

Above: Sir Henry Bolte, 1975 [FAIRFAX]

Below: Bolte's right-hand man: Sir Arthur Rylah [VICTORIAN PARLIAMENTARY LIBRARY AND INFORMATION SERVICE]

Above: The immigration minister meets young migrants on board the P&O liner *Stratheden* approaching Melbourne, 1963 [FAIRFAX]

Below: Friendly rivals: Lindsay Thompson and Dick Hamer at a Liberal Party state conference, March 1963 [FAIRFAX]

Above: Hamer makes it happen at Doncaster Primary School, May 1973 [FAIRFAX]

Below: Here's looking at you, kid: Bolte and Hamer in the tally room on election night, 20 May 1973 [FAIRFAX]

Above: Opposites collide: the only joint press conference that Dick Hamer and Joh Bjelke-Petersen ever held, January 1974 [FAIRFAX]

Below: Bolte and Hamer toast each other at the opening of Kryal Castle in Ballarat, November 1974 [HAMER FAMILY]

Above: Hamer announces the 1979 election date, setting off a three-month campaign [FAIRFAX]

Opposite: The premier of the Garden State cultivates his own garden, the day after the March 1976 election [FAIRFAX]

Below: An appreciative (and influential) audience at Hamer's 1979 election-campaign launch. From left: Mark Birrell, April Hamer, Bill Borthwick, Joan Thompson, and Tamie Fraser [FAIRFAX]

Below: The Hamer cabinet sworn in by the governor after the 1979 election. Back row: Glyn Jenkins, Alan Hunt, Robert Maclellan, Jim Balfour, Lou Lieberman, Digby Crozier, Jock Granter. Middle row: Brian Dixon, Jim Ramsay, Ian Smith, Lindsay Thompson, Alan Wood (slightly behind), Walter Jona, Vasey Houghton, Haddon Storey. Front row: Tom Austin, Sir Henry Winneke (the governor), Dick Hamer, Bill Borthwick, Norman Lacy. [FAIRFAX]

Above: Sue Calwell and the Melbourne she sought to promote, June 1979 [FAIRFAX]

Below: Federal Hotels' design for a casino, incorporating a glass pyramid. The building would have been an architectural gem if it had been proceeded with. [JOHN HADDAD]

Above: The future republican and the Queen [HAMER FAMILY]

Above: Ian Smith gatecrashes the press conference at which Hamer announces that he has sacked Smith from the ministry, 16 March 1981 [FAIRFAX]

Below: Hamer announces his retirement to the media, 29 May 1981 [FAIRFAX]

Right: Dick in retirement at Monomeath Avenue, 1986 [NEWS]

Below: Dick and April on Hamer's last day as premier, 1981 [HAMER FAMILY]

up area. Wilcox as transport minister and Hunt as minister for local government were assigned to perform the surgery, and they eliminated roughly half the freeways previously proposed. Among others, they removed the continuation of the F19 or Eastern Freeway through Fitzroy and Carlton, and the F12 freeway, which would have connected it to Sunshine: 40 years later, another Liberal government would resurrect them, in underground form, as the East West Link. They also scrapped the F1 through East Melbourne, intended as the eastern link of a city ring road; the southern part of the F2, a long north–south route that would have run from the Hume Highway to the South Gippsland Highway at Cranbourne; and two sections of the Outer Ring Road: the F7 through Eltham, and the F5 through the western suburbs. What was left was no longer a coherent freeway network. Sections of freeways were left dangling, leaving gaps that future governments, including Hamer's own, would have to fill in later. The South-Eastern Freeway did not connect with the Mulgrave Freeway. The Outer Ring Road was broken in two places. The Eastern Freeway would have connected only with the northbound F2, which itself was deleted a few years later. The cuts were really aimed at quietening opponents of particular freeway plans, but they also assured Victorians that Melbourne would not become another Los Angeles, and that the government would handle freeway issues reasonably.

The election result surpassed all expectations. In Melbourne just one seat changed hands — Greensborough — and it went *to* the Liberals, by just five votes. (The courts then ordered a rerun, which the Liberals won comfortably.) In the country, the government took three seats from Labor, and swapped two with the Country Party, gaining Swan Hill but just losing Gippsland South. In all, Hamer increased the Liberals' majority by four seats. In six months since the federal election, the Liberal vote had increased by a quarter, from 33.6 per cent to 42.3 per cent, while Labor's vote had shrunk from 47.3 per cent to 41.6 per cent. At his first election, Hamer had attracted a higher Liberal vote than Bolte had ever won. In two-party terms, the combined Liberal–Country Party vote was estimated to be

55.2 per cent, up from 49.6 per cent at the federal poll. It was the best result that the Liberal Party had achieved at any election since Harold Holt's landslide win in 1966.

It was a triumph not only for Hamer, but for Hawkins and the team he had assembled. They included the party's first full-time public relations officer, the livewire Noel Tennison, who had been an organiser for the National Civic Council, and former federal minister Peter Howson, who oversaw the PR campaign. The conservative Howson was only too willing to give Hamer a hand to shift the party to where the voters were moving. Tennison's memoir, *My Spin in PR*, recalls Howson, whisky in hand, berating him gently one evening: hadn't Noel realised that everything they were doing was aimed at 'converting Whitlamism into Hamerism'? Many of those who voted for Whitlam in December 1972 voted for Hamer in May 1973 because they saw them as sharing similar values. But over the next two years, the two lawyer-politicians born in Kew in July 1916 would go very different ways.

CHAPTER FIFTEEN

Living with Whitlam

Politics in Australia is often intense, but never has it experienced such sustained intensity as in the three years of the Whitlam government. Never has any government set out so ambitiously to remake Australia, or run up against so much opposition in the process. The Whitlam government became a watershed in Australia's history. Before it, in the long boom of the post-war years, Australia was essentially a land of white people, where men were fully employed in factories or on farms, and women were fully employed raising kids. It was prosperous; for a quarter of a century, its economy had averaged growth of almost 5 per cent a year, unemployment averaged less than 2 per cent, and inflation was mostly low. It was a land that, despite having taken more than a million non-British migrants, saw itself as British, followed the wishes of its 'great and powerful friends', took its culture from others, and expected the poor to get a job.

After Whitlam, Australia became another country, an adolescent nation that had left home to find a new identity. It no longer had full employment, rapid economic growth, or low inflation. Women were no longer necessarily at home; mothers were no longer necessarily married. Governments had grown big and deficit-prone, and supported millions of people. Yet the country had a new independence, and, in some areas, a new pride in itself. Not all these changes began with the Whitlam government, or were caused by it. But it was a government of change, in a world that was changing more rapidly than ever. It inspired intense partisanship on both sides in a way that Australians had not experienced since the battle over conscription in World War I.

In the three years that Whitlam was in power, the Vietnam War ended, and with it, the military confrontations of the Cold War. Throughout the Western world, the long economic boom came to a close. Oil became expensive, and mass unemployment arrived. Families broke up, and sexual and social taboos broke down. It was a time when men wore sideburns, bell bottoms, and wide lapels, and women wore short hair, jeans, and platform shoes. The Kingswood was in the driveway, and the first colour television set was in the lounge. Skyhooks was our favourite band, Abigail was getting hot and bothered at *Number 96*, Peter Weir was shooting *Picnic at Hanging Rock*, and Patrick White won the Nobel Prize for Literature.

The Whitlam government was as much a manifestation of social change as an instigator of it. But while the fashions of the time soon passed, the legacy of its policy changes has been enduring. To those who lived through that era, it seems amazing that so many reforms which provoked so much controversy at the time have since been adopted peacefully by the conservative side of politics. They include Aboriginal land rights, large-scale immigration from Asia, multiculturalism, Medibank (now called Medicare), equal pay for women, welfare benefits for single mothers, no-fault divorce, an Australian honours system, and extensive funding for the arts. Over 40 years later, it seems hard to believe the antagonism these changes met with at the time. In the bush, in particular, the Whitlam government became identified with Asian migrants, dole bludgers, single mothers, radical lesbians, and alien arty types. No act of government attracted more derision than the new National Gallery's decision to spend $1.1 million to buy Jackson Pollock's *Blue Poles*.

But the new thinking behind Whitlam's reforms, many of them long overdue, went hand in hand with a chaotic, dysfunctional style of government, a centralist approach to policy-making, and a blithe indifference to economic constraints. For all his towering dominance, Whitlam was bound by his caucus in ways that past and future prime ministers were not. Sometimes his announcement of a new government policy was overturned by his party room within days. One minister, the veteran minister for minerals and energy, Rex Connor, followed his own agenda without reference to cabinet, secretly commissioning a Pakistani trader, Tirath Khemlani, to negotiate a $4 billion loan from Arab governments so Connor could nationalise the mines of foreign-owned companies and 'buy back the farm'. Labour minister Clyde Cameron, a former secretary of the Australian Workers' Union, encouraged the Arbitration Commission to grant double-digit pay rises, regardless of their impact on a spiralling rate of inflation. Whitlam had no interest in economic policy, and little appetite for managing his team of wild horses, who consequently went their own way. To contain inflation, his government in July 1973 made a reckless decision to cut import tariffs immediately by 25 per cent: it certainly made imports cheaper, but also shut down hundreds of Australian factories. On the one hand, the government was ordering manufacturers to give big pay rises to their staff, while on the other it reduced their competitors' tariffs by 25 per cent. Manufacturing output plunged by 10 per cent in a year, and over the next five years almost 200,000 manufacturing workers were laid off. The share of GDP going to wages, which had averaged 55.3 per cent in the 1950s and 1960s, soared to 63.5 per cent in 1974–75, as profits slumped. The combination of wage-price inflation at home, poor policy decisions, and soaring oil prices abroad sent Australia into its worst recession for 40 years.

The Whitlam years brought a dramatic surge in the size of government. In just three years, government activity swelled from 22 per cent of Australia's output to 26 per cent. What was less understood, however, was that most of this new spending — more than 80 per cent of it — was actually carried out by the states and local councils, using Canberra's money. The amount that the federal government spent on its own activities rose just from 9 per cent of GDP to 9.8 per cent. State and local government spending, by contrast, rose from 13 per cent to 16.3 per cent. State governments in the Whitlam years were better resourced, and played a bigger part in Australians' lives, than they ever had before. What they lost was independence.

Menzies had treated state governments with benign neglect, blocking them from levying income tax, using the Loan Council to restrict their borrowings, and implicitly accepting the long-term implications of allowing the Commonwealth to dominate revenue raising. Whitlam's approach was openly coercive. He saw the states as an anachronism, and believed power should be split between Canberra and a new tier of regional authorities subservient to it. As early as his Chifley Memorial lecture at the University of Melbourne in 1957, he dismissed the states as being 'too large to deal with local matters, and too small and weak to deal with national ones'. State boundaries, he argued, were an anachronism, 'imposed on Australia a century ago from Westminster', and there was 'no economic reason for preserving them'. In the *Australian Quarterly* in 1971, he proposed 'a House of Representatives for international matters and nationwide matters, an assembly for the affairs of each of our dozen largest cities, and regional assemblies for the few score areas of rural and residential (areas) outside these cities'. His preferred two-tier system would have abolished the states, the Senate, and local councils. As prime minister, he was forced to negotiate with the states, but his preferred approach was to ignore them, or dictate to them.

An unintended ambiguity in the Constitution allowed him to do this. Section 51 limited the Commonwealth's responsibility to 35 areas, mostly dealing with international or border issues, interstate trade, and economic regulation. Education, health, and transport were among the crucial government services that the Constitution assigned solely to the states. But section 96 allowed the Commonwealth 'to grant financial assistance to any state on such terms and conditions as the Parliament thinks fit'. And the High Court has ruled consistently that section 96 allows the Commonwealth to get around section 51, and make grants to the states for any purpose, and under any conditions — including ordering the states not to levy income tax. As a result, from Chifley on, federal governments edged deeper into state areas of responsibility. By 1972, the Commonwealth had used section 96 to become the main source of public funding for highways, universities, and non-government schools, and had crept into funding programs for causes from tuberculosis to natural disasters, dams, and rural infrastructure. All were state responsibilities. Even before Whitlam, economists Russell Mathews and Robert Jay noted, such payments quadrupled in the 12 years to 1971–72; and increasingly, they came with strings attached. The states were getting more money, but losing control of their own areas of responsibility.

After 1972, what had been a river became a flood. From $708 million in 1971–72, section 96 grants to the states increased to $4.2 billion by 1975–76 — from 1.6 per cent of GDP to 5.5 per cent. Some of that was snipped off untied grants and state borrowings, which were still rationed by Canberra, as if the states were children who could not be trusted with money, but total federal grants to the states climbed in those four years from 7.1 to 10.3 per cent. It was a huge transfer of resources in a short space of time. But it came with strings attached, and a loss of sovereignty — and the Hamer cabinet was divided on how it should respond.

The Liberal leadership in Victoria had changed direction, but the cabinet had not. At the 1973 election, Gib Chandler and George Reid had accepted knighthoods and followed their old boss into retirement. But rather than allowing Hamer to renovate the cabinet, the party room re-elected all of Bolte's ministers. Hamer brought in Vasey Houghton, a Yarra Glen farmer and former local councillor, and Brian Dixon, a former star Melbourne wingman and economics teacher, as his two choices. Cabinet still had a core of Bolte-era conservatives who were not going to be told what to do by the Whitlam government — or, on many issues, by Hamer himself. They tolerated him taking the party into the middle ground when there was an election to win; but once the election was over, they stood up for their own values, which collided with his. The situation called for skills in people management that Hamer had yet to learn. How to respond to the Whitlam government's offers of tied aid became the key battleground between liberals and conservatives in Hamer's first full term.

Tackling urban problems was at the centre of Whitlam's agenda, and at the centre of disputes between the two governments. New federal money was welcome in Spring Street, but the strings attached to it were not. The Whitlam government offered more money to build rental housing, on condition that the states stopped allowing Housing Commission tenants to buy their homes (which reduced the rental stock). For the Liberals, encouraging public-housing tenants to become owners was a key plank of their housing policy; without it, many Liberals would not have supported state-funded housing at all. Rising land prices produced a similar conflict. Tom Uren, the federal minister for urban and regional development, wanted to set up a new land commission to buy broadacres in the outer suburbs, develop blocks on them with full services, and put them quickly on the market. As he saw it, private developers were hoarding land to keep up prices, so competition from government would break up their game and drive prices down. But the Liberals and the developers were closely linked, and key figures in the Hamer government strongly opposed any government intervention that they saw as threatening the viability of their supporters' business.

Decentralisation was a key policy priority for both governments. At the time, the Bureau of Statistics estimates showed that between 1966 and 1971, Melbourne had added more than 250,000 people, while regional Victoria shrunk in population. (The figures were significantly revised later.) Economist Max Neutze of the Australian National University published estimates of the soaring cost of congestion in Sydney and Melbourne, and his work had a big influence on the debate. But while Hamer and Murray Byrne adopted a policy of freeing country businesses from payroll tax, wherever they were based, Whitlam and Uren believed the solution was to develop 'growth centres': using government investment to kickstart rapid growth in towns seen as potential magnets that could offer people an alternative to Sydney and Melbourne. Their top priority was Albury-Wodonga, which Whitlam and Uren hoped to expand from fewer than 50,000 people to 300,000 by the turn of the century. Hamer was taken with the idea, and persuaded his more reluctant New South Wales counterpart, Sir Robert Askin, to sign up. Whitlam was happy to pay the bills to develop the twin city, so long as a government agency bought and developed all the land it would need. For the Liberals, that was a problem. Similarly, Whitlam and Uren were keen to develop Geelong as a second growth centre, but only if a government commission was set up to run it, and land prices were frozen so that speculators did not inflate the price of home sites. To Uren, that was the way the Menzies government had developed Canberra, so he saw no reason why Liberals in Victoria should object. But that was not how Liberal governments in Victoria worked. A number of Hamer's MPs dabbled in land speculation themselves; and in Geelong, Wodonga, and Melbourne's urban fringe, virtually all relied partly on private developers to finance their campaigns. (Even Alan Hunt had developer Peter Leake running his 1973 campaign, using funds contributed largely by developers. But Hunt was one of the few who disregarded such ties when he sat down to make decisions.)

Hamer had appointed as housing minister his old colleague Vance 'Pat' Dickie, a Liberal with a big L and a Conservative with a big C. Dickie was only too happy to take on the Whitlam government. He had an early victory when he successfully stared down his federal counterpart to win a housing deal that maintained the right of public-housing tenants to buy their homes. But he saw the federal plan for a land commission as invading the turf of his own Housing Commission, and decided to head it off by directing the Housing Commission to go out and buy land around Melbourne. The story of those land deals will be told in a later chapter, but we should note here that Dickie's goal was to pre-empt the plan for a land commission subject to federal direction.

The Albury-Wodonga agreement was signed early in 1973, when Hamer had a free hand. He and Byrne quickly endorsed the Whitlam government's plan to establish the Albury-Wodonga Development Corporation as the executive body to develop the river towns. They accepted Whitlam's insistence that the corporation should acquire all the land required for that growth. There was little local resistance: on the contrary, many battling farmers around Albury-Wodonga retired as wealthy men, thanks to selling their land to the corporation.

But when a similar deal was proposed for Geelong, landowners, rural councils, and Liberal MPs erupted in outrage. Hamer had long favoured diverting some of Melbourne's growth to Geelong: he had already declared Geelong a growth centre and set up a regional planning authority over the nine councils in the area. But far from favouring Geelong, his government's decentralisation incentives discriminated against it. While factories in other towns could receive 100 per cent rebates of their payroll tax and land tax, in Geelong they got just a 50 per cent rebate. State government policies would make little difference to Geelong's growth. The federal government mattered more, because it had deeper pockets and planned to focus its spending on just a handful of cities. (Uren's goal was to develop just four growth centres: Macarthur and Geelong as alternatives for growth in Sydney and Melbourne respectively, and Coffs Harbour and Albury-Wodonga as independent cities. Politics, however, blocked his way: only Albury-Wodonga took off, and it was then gutted by the Fraser government.)

Uren proposed building two satellite cities south and south-west of Geelong to accelerate the city's growth, potentially to 400,000 people by the year 2000. As in Canberra and Albury-Wodonga, one authority would be given full power to direct the city's growth — the Geelong Regional Planning Authority, later renamed the Geelong Regional Authority, and ultimately the Geelong Regional Commission. Hamer, Byrne, and Hunt agreed that all the land around Geelong would be designated for potential acquisition (with price controls), the authority/commission would have the power of compulsory acquisition, and what was then rural land would be bought at rural prices. But that blueprint cut across the interests of local Liberal powerbrokers — notably Geelong businessman Ernest (Ernie) McCann and his family, who owned a lot of rural land and expected to reap the benefits when it became urban. Uren's plan also shrank the roles and significance of the rural councils.

Geelong became bitterly divided. Councils in its inner and middle suburbs agreed with the goal of bringing more growth to Geelong, and agreed that a strong locally based commission should run the show. (Under the formula agreed by Uren, Hamer, Hunt, and Byrne, council representatives would form the majority of the commission.) But the councils on the rural fringe opposed the lot: they were against compulsory acquisitions, against the commission replacing them as planning authorities, and against it being able to buy rural land at rural prices. South Barwon MP Aurel Smith, who had been a prefect with Hamer at Geelong Grammar in 1934, led the opposition to him in Spring Street in 1974. Smith himself owned some land as a speculator, in partnership with Geelong builder and Liberal fundraiser John Taylor. The cabinet and the Liberal Party room were too divided to make a decision. When no agreement was reached by June 1974, the $3 million of federal money allocated for 1973–74 lapsed. Uren then fine-tuned the deal with Hamer, Hunt, and Byrne, proposed $10 million of funding for 1974–75, and quietly started paying the commission's wages and bills.

But Geelong's Liberal powerbrokers would not accept it. In November 1974, cabinet rejected the bill drawn up by Byrne and Hunt. Aurel Smith declared publicly: 'The proposed legislation runs counter to my ideas and beliefs in Liberalism, and unless it is changed, I will oppose it again. I will not have a bar of anything that looks like the clenched fist of socialism.' McCann publicly warned Geelong MLC Glyn Jenkins, who supported Hamer, that he might find an independent running against him unless he fell in line. Finally, the party agreed on a revised bill drawn up with the Geelong MPs that gutted the powers of the authority/commission. Hamer introduced the bill to the assembly in May 1975, but it had not been voted on by 30 June, so another $10 million of federal money was lost.

Geelong went into limbo. Uren would not accept the Geelong MPs' changes, while Hamer was powerless to overrule them. After 11 November, when governor-general Sir John Kerr dismissed the Whitlam government, and the succeeding general election, the new Fraser government flagged that spending on Geelong would be axed in its austerity drive. The Victorian Liberals hurriedly passed Hamer's bill, but too late. Machinations continued for another two years, including a bizarre episode in which Geelong MPs rewrote the legislation to require the commission to rezone land before purchasing it, so that all profit from rezoning went to the landowner. But it no longer mattered. The Fraser government threw out virtually the entire canvas of urban and regional programs on which Uren and his department had been working. Albury-Wodonga limped on with minimal funding, but Geelong was scrapped.

In hindsight, it might have made no difference to Geelong's future even had the Hamer government been able to unite on the issue. The Fraser government probably would have dropped the scheme anyway, and the state could not have run it alone. The Geelong Regional Commission under its dynamic chairman, Colin Atkins, remained an active force in the region until the Kennett government abolished it in 1993 and merged the councils to make one Greater Geelong council. The commission brought industries and job growth to Geelong, gave the region a planning scheme, had its ring road rerouted, and reshaped the CBD. But the Hamer government's handling of the issue had been a fiasco played out in full public gaze. Bolte would have sensed the opposition early, and either bowed to it, or stood over his opponents to tell the party it was his decision, and that they had better accept it. Hamer relied on the power of his arguments, but when they failed to persuade his colleagues, he would not use his clout to overrule them. The message to Victorians was that the premier was not in control of his government. And it opened the way for further backbench and cabinet rebellions which underlined that perception.

The Whitlam government's plan for a land council to develop cheap housing sites in the outer suburbs provoked a similar division in the Hamer cabinet. Australia in 1973–74 went through one of its biggest speculative land booms, which almost doubled prices for outer-suburban blocks in Melbourne. Hunt, as minister for planning, wanted more blocks developed and put on the market, and saw the federal government's plan as an opportunity to keep developers honest by injecting new competition into the market. He agreed with Uren to set up a land commission to buy and develop land in the outer suburbs. But Dickie, as minister for housing, insisted that any federal money should be given to the Housing Commission to develop the land it had bought already at Melton, Sunbury, and Pakenham. However, the questions raised in *The Age* about those land deals, and the high amounts paid despite the problems with the sites, made that politically implausible.

Dickie eventually backed down, accepting a compromise in return for Uren buying Emerald Hill, the blocks around South Melbourne Town Hall, as rental housing to be run by the Housing Commission. In 1975, cabinet set up an Urban Land Council, run out of the Housing Ministry. Hamer told parliament that its first blocks, in Thomastown, were sold on average for $12,000, 'at least $1,000 below the ruling price in the area'. Federal funding for the scheme ended when the Whitlam government fell, but the council by then owned a stockpile of land, was operating profitably, and more than recouped the money it spent. In 1979, Brian Dixon as housing minister restructured it as the Urban Land Authority — and, ironically, gave it all the Housing Commission's land to develop. The authority, with various changes of name, became a very successful player in Melbourne's housing market, developing low-cost estates such as Roxburgh Park, which helped to swing Melbourne's growth towards the north and west, as well as inner-urban sites such as the Port Melbourne gasworks and the Hawthorn tram depot. It was one fruit of Hamer–Whitlam co-operation that made a lasting difference.

And there was co-operation on many issues. The states peacefully handed over responsibility for tertiary education to Canberra from January 1974 — but not before Hamer finally triumphed in his long campaign to build a university outside Melbourne, with Canberra agreeing to build Victoria's fourth university, Deakin, in Geelong. Commonwealth funding for schools increased ten times over in the four years to 1975–76. Transport minister Ray Meagher had plenty of public stoushes with his federal counterpart, Charlie Jones, but neither allowed their differences to get in the way of Canberra investing heavily in Melbourne's by now antiquated public transport to build new tracks for express trains, construct new stations in outer suburbs, replace the old signal boxes with a centralised system, and buy new trains, trams, and buses. In all, federal grants to the states swelled massively, from $3.6 billion in 1972–73 to $8.6 billion in 1975–76. One never heard a premier complain that he was getting too much money.

The most damaging collision between the Whitlam and Hamer governments was over Medibank, the federal government's system for state-funded universal health care. It was one of Whitlam's most ambitious reforms, and, given the interest groups he was taking on, one of his most contentious. Only Queensland then provided free health care for all, a legacy of its almost unbroken period of Labor government between 1915 and 1957. In the rest of Australia, one in six people were not insured for medical and hospital bills. Working with Whitlam and his shadow ministers, Melbourne Institute health economists John Deeble and Dick Scotton proposed a universal-insurance scheme funded from taxes, to cover at least 85 per cent of hospital and medical bills. They envisaged a 1.35 per cent levy on incomes to pay for it, with doctors being paid at a sessional rate rather than under the expensive fee-for-service system. The complexities of the scheme and its politics are beyond the role of this book; but, clearly, it was a threat to the private health insurance funds, and to doctors' incomes, since the new Health Insurance Commission would become the dominant purchaser of their services. The coalition was the political partner of the private health funds and the doctors, so it blocked the scheme in the Senate. But after the Whitlam government was re-elected in the double-dissolution election of 1974, the scheme was passed at the historic joint sitting of both houses of parliament. The federal minister for social security, Bill Hayden, then set about negotiating with the states to introduce Medibank, as it was known, from 1 July 1975.

Given the sensitivity, complexity, and importance of the health portfolio at such a time, it seems strange that Hamer in 1973 entrusted it to Alan Scanlan, a brash young conservative with less than a year's ministerial experience. Scanlan and Hayden soon fell out. When Hayden wrote a formal letter to Scanlan setting out the broad proposal and inviting him to negotiate, the minister took six months to reply. He and Hayden did meet to discuss the plan, but made little progress, and Scanlan refused to authorise officials to negotiate. In March 1975, three months before the scheme was to be introduced, he introduced a bill to the assembly providing for the dismissal of any hospital executive or doctor who took a position on any Medibank advisory committee. Victoria raised concerns on a range of fronts. How much of pensioners' hospital bills would be covered? How would the federal government define the hospital costs covered by its 50:50 cost-sharing offer? Who would pay for psychiatric patients? Who would run the hospitals? These were good questions, but Hamer demanded 'ironclad guarantees' on these concerns, with little apparent sense of urgency. He had misread the politics. The era when doctors gave their services to hospitals on an honorary basis was ending. Wage growth was out of control, new medical technologies were expensive, and so the costs of treatment were soaring. In September 1973, his cabinet had lifted public-hospital fees by 33 per cent, and then by another 35 per cent ten months later. In his autobiography, Hayden conceded that he deliberately allowed the standoff with Liberal states to continue, knowing that he had to make budget cuts somewhere in his portfolio, and that a late start would reduce the cost of the scheme.

And it did. When Hayden warned in March that it was getting too late for Victoria to enter the scheme from 1 July, Hamer intervened to negotiate an agreement in principle. But then he handed the issue back to Scanlan, the standoff resumed, and in June the state began a $150,000 taxpayer-funded ad campaign to justify Victoria's opposition. Around the kitchen table, the ads had far less impact than the revelations that taxpayers were paying for them, that the state itself would lose $1 million for every week it stayed out of the scheme, and that Victorians would lose more than $10 million a month in benefits. On 17 June, *The Age* front page reported the cost of the standoff, and a scathing editorial blamed the Hamer government. (Critics on the right often accused Hamer of changing policies whenever he came under fire from *The Age*.) The next day, Hamer flew to Canberra, in Hayden's words, 'the quintessence of co-operation', to negotiate a deal, more or less on Canberra's terms. Victoria entered Medibank on 1 August, a month late. Scanlan's reputation suffered irreparable damage in the community, yet not in the party room, which re-elected him to cabinet the following year. The episode became widely quoted as showing how little control Hamer exercised over his ministers.

Overall, the Whitlam government helped Hamer to advance his reform agenda. He resented Whitlam's attitude, but got on well with him, as he got on well with everybody. During the 1974 federal election campaign, the Goulburn River flooded Seymour, and both Whitlam and opposition leader Bill Snedden separately asked Hamer to come with them to inspect the damage. Hamer chose to go with Whitlam; to him, the business of government was more important than party loyalty. He would denounce Whitlam fervently to the Liberal state council, but unlike Queensland premier Joh Bjelke-Petersen or Western Australia's Sir Charles Court, Hamer did not carry on a daily war of sniping and obstruction. He knew that federal grants were enabling him to do a lot of things he could not do otherwise. Money from Tom Uren helped Hamer to buy historic buildings and land for his metropolitan parks, and to reduce the backlog of unsewered homes (and hence improve water quality in rivers and at beaches). Whitlam government money not only improved Victoria's schools and hospitals, but introduced legal aid and community-health centres, paid for new kinds of welfare services, and increased funding for local government. It helped to generate support for Hamer among voters.

But the Whitlam government's programs assumed strong economic growth to pay for them. In 1973–74, around the world, oil prices doubled, and the long post-war boom ended. Australia went into recession, and the Commonwealth budget went into a deficit of unprecedented depth, at least on the measures used then. (On the more sophisticated budget bottom line used by the Bureau of Statistics since 1996, which separates investment from recurrent spending, Whitlam's 1974–75 budget, which increased spending by 46 per cent in nominal terms, and 20 per cent in real terms, actually ended up in surplus — because so much of its spending was on capital works and acquisitions.) On the measures used at the time, it seemed clear that the government was spending beyond its means, and that became one of the many reasons for Labor's defeat. The Fraser government gradually shut down many of the programs that Whitlam had started up — and imposed far worse cuts to the states' untied grants and loan allocations than anything they had complained about under Whitlam. All this would add to Hamer's problems in the second half of his years as premier. Between 1972 and 1975, for all the daily brawls between their ministers, Whitlam had helped Hamer to make it happen.

CHAPTER SIXTEEN

Australia's most popular premier

In July 1974, the Morgan Gallup Poll reported that Dick Hamer had become Australia's most popular premier. An extraordinary 76 per cent of Victorians polled approved of the way Hamer was handling his job as premier; just 17 per cent disapproved. Only South Australia's Don Dunstan even came close (67 per cent for; 21 per cent against). Less than half the Queenslanders asked approved of Joh Bjelke-Petersen's performance as premier, and even fewer New South Wales voters approved of their premier, Sir Robert Askin. It was a resounding pat on the back from his electorate. The report of the poll in *The Sun* became one of the few articles about himself that Hamer clipped and kept.

He was at the height of his political popularity, and power. As premier and treasurer, he had a free hand to decide where taxpayers' money would be spent. As party leader, he had the power to manipulate cabinet and the party room to get his way on the issues that mattered, although he was reluctant to use it. As Victoria's most popular politician, he had the power to influence community thinking on broader issues, including federal ones; but party loyalty was so fundamental for him that to step out of line with his federal colleagues went against the grain.

Instead, he used his power to bed in his first wave of reforms and to press ahead with new ones. In those early years, Hamer had a broad reform agenda. No state government, not even Dunstan's, was doing more across such a wide front to improve social and environmental outcomes. There was far less focus on economic outcomes. This was the great period of reforms in conservation and planning, in which Victoria was widely seen as leading the nation. It was a great age for the arts, as Victoria built new galleries and theatres, and broke new ground with sizeable subsidies to its main performing groups. But it was also a time of reforms to the police, to road-safety rules, to energy policy, consumer affairs, welfare services, and support for local government. Sir Henry Winneke, Victoria's chief justice and former solicitor-general, became the state's first Australian-born governor. For the first time, Victoria was given a written constitution, a fairer redistribution of electorates, and, in a sign of the optimism of the age, Hamer even directed that foundations be dug for the long-delayed North Wing of Parliament House — a wing designed in 1856, but never built. He planned to build it to house the new MPs introduced by his expansion of parliament, but as the Commonwealth slashed untied capital grants and loan allocations for the states — from 2.2 per cent of GDP in 1972–73 to 0.9 per cent by 1982–83 — any works that were not urgent priorities were put off. The North Wing remains unbuilt today.

Many of the reforms that Hamer and his ministers introduced were in the fields where he set up new ministries, especially in conservation and planning. The new emphasis on environmental values won Hamer broad electoral support, but at the cost of losing support from big business and from the right of his own party. Victoria was seen as having the most advanced environmental legislation in the nation, ahead of any Labor state. Today that might sound implausible; but in the early years of the conservation movement, many of the activists were Liberals, and the message of environmentalism was understood, if anything, better on the Liberal side of parliament than on the Labor side. In Bill Borthwick (Conservation) and Alan Hunt (Planning), Hamer had two outstanding ministers, progressive thinkers with quick minds, a subtle understanding of their political options in each situation, and plenty of courage and resourcefulness

— which, as ministers pioneering new policies that cut against vested interests, they needed to have. Labor's frontbench had no one with such an instinctive, intelligent empathy with long-term environmental thinking.

Bill Borthwick was one of the great characters and achievers of the Hamer government: very like Hamer in his outlook, very different from him in personality. Borthwick was born in 1924, into a farming family in the Mallee, on the edge of the Big Desert. They were hard years for Mallee farmers. As a boarder at Ballarat Grammar (like Bolte, on a scholarship) during the long drought of the 1930s, young Bill would look up at the sky, red with Mallee dust blowing west, and say, 'Well, there goes the farm!' A later Liberal premier, Denis Napthine, said that a tough upbringing in a remote area gave Borthwick a 'down-to-earth, commonsense approach to life … Bill learned a lot about how to get on with people and how to achieve the outcomes he sought'. The 1930s drought also left him with a strong sense of the importance of the environment. Borthwick grew into a shrewd, passionate, caring man, who loved life and partying, had a great intuitive understanding of people, and thought for the long term. He served in the war as a fighter pilot over Yugoslavia, and then came back and settled in the Dandenongs, where he worked in insurance, married and had a family, and became a driving force in local institutions — sports clubs, the CFA brigade, and the hospital board — before being elected to parliament in 1960 and to the ministry in 1967. His experience in the 1930s made him a passionate opponent of the plan to subdivide the Little Desert into farms. When the Dandenong by-election persuaded Bolte to finally change policies, Borthwick moved into the empty space by writing an environment policy for Bolte's 1970 policy speech. Thanks to Borthwick, Bolte promised to set up an expert body, the Land Conservation Council, to determine the future use of Crown lands, which still covered roughly a third of Victoria. He pledged to expand national parks and other reserves to take in at least 5 per cent of the state, representing all its key ecosystems. And an Environment Protection Authority would be set up to tackle pollution.

Hamer strongly endorsed all of this. And it was essentially the Hamer government that implemented this policy, developed it into new areas, and gave it a level of funding that it would never have received from Bolte. The new Ministry for Conservation began life in 1972–73 with a budget of $6.5 million; by 1978–79, that budget had swollen to $30 million. The EPA budget grew from $1.3 million to $6.2 million. The National Parks Service was given $1 million to spend for the first time in 1973–74; five years later, its budget was $5 million, its staff numbers had almost trebled, and annual park-visitor numbers had grown from 700,000 to 3.4 million. By then it was managing 775,000 hectares or 3 per cent of the state's landmass, in 52 parks — from the Hattah Lakes near Mildura to the Croajingolong National Park along the beaches of East Gippsland, and from the Alps to the Lower Glenelg National Park. They ranged from wilderness areas to popular holiday spots like Tidal River, and the Stieglitz Historic Park, set up to preserve a 19th-century gold-mining town. John Brookes, of the old Melbourne family that had established and run Australian Paper Manufacturers (APM) for almost a century, was recruited to become director of national parks. In stark contrast to subsequent Liberal governments, Brookes and Borthwick fought to keep out commercial development and uses that conflicted with conservation. The Tatra ski resort owned the lease at Mount Buffalo, but when the lessees demanded approval to build a 200-bed motel, artificial lake, and large car park, Borthwick and Hamer bought back the lease and put the park under the control of Brookes and his team.

Most of the new and extended parks were the outcome of the Land Conservation Council's systematic review of Victoria's public land. It was an unusual and remarkably transparent process in which the 12-member council arbitrated on the claims by various government agencies, interest groups, and industries for the use of public lands. It ended the Forests Commission's sole control of Victoria's vast forest area, and set up management plans that delineated some areas for lovers of the bush, and others for the timber industry. These were exciting times for the environment movement. The council was stacked in favour of conservationists, but Borthwick was unapologetic: to him, that was a necessary correction after more than a century of development when conservation values had counted for little. At the council's opening meeting in 1972, he urged its members to plan Victoria's land use 'as if it were to last 1,000 years'.

The Victorian Conservation Trust was another success story. Set up to buy land for conservation purpose, it quietly purchased (or accepted as donations) significant areas that would otherwise have been colonised by suburbia, and added them to parks. Every year, as treasurer, Hamer outlaid several million dollars to buy land or buildings of significance. He bought farms, forests, mansions, hotels, and islands to maintain the state's heritage. He bought dozens of historic buildings and properties to save them from the wreckers and preserve them for the future. In a decade when Queensland premier Sir Joh Bjelke-Petersen sent bulldozers in at midnight to knock down Brisbane's historic Bellevue Hotel, Hamer bought its Melbourne counterpart, the Windsor, and the Shamrock in Bendigo, so they could be renovated to remain the grand old hotels of their cities. The former Chirnside family mansion, Werribee Park, was bought to become an island of history, parkland, and wildlife in the outer-western suburbs. John and Sunday Reed's home, 'Heide', a centre for new artists such as Sidney Nolan in the 1940s, is now a celebrated art gallery and park. Churchill Island, just off Phillip Island, was bought as a wildlife refuge. Hamer bought back bushland for parks on the Mornington Peninsula and the Gippsland Lakes, farms in the Yarra Valley as working museums for schools and tourists, and small blocks in the Dandenongs to be restructured and resold as larger bush blocks. He was also generous with grants to the National Trust to help restore the sailing ship *Polly Woodside* and its collection of historic homes, as well as to councils and community groups to restore their local icons.

Tom Uren was a willing partner in much of this. Dennis Simsion, the Board of Works' chief planner, remembers taking Uren on a helicopter ride over Melbourne to look at some of the areas that the government was trying to buy back for parks to stop inappropriate development. 'Tom really took to it,' Simsion recalls. 'In no time, we had a hefty grant to help us buy land, and that then encouraged the state government to help out.' A classic example was in the Darebin Creek valley, where middle-class Ivanhoe met working-class Alphington. A small rundown park on the Ivanhoe side looked over the creek to a former quarry that had become the local tip, and, next to it, an unused weed-strewn wasteland. In 1973, the Board of Works began bulldozing the remaining trees, and Ivanhoe residents, led by Sue Course, formed a group of resourceful campaigners to try to create a park from the wasteland. Ellis Stones, the great landscape architect, lived nearby; he directed the first of many working bees to plant native trees and clear away weeds. Uren gave Northcote council the money to buy back the quarry, and, once the tip was full, it too began to be planted out. In 1977, Hamer offered the councils a 1:1 subsidy to buy back other key blocks, while Borthwick gave them a grant to eradicate the weeds. It was what Hamer loved to do: slipping small but useful amounts to councils and resident groups trying to create a park, or a welfare service, or a cultural event. Today, the Darebin Parklands is a 33-hectare haven of bushland and grassy lawns, with platypus in the creek, just 8 kilometres from the GPO. Helping projects like this to succeed was one of the things that kept Hamer going in his later years as premier. It was his escape from the trenches of political combat.

It was around this time, too, that the Melbourne Zoo experienced a dramatic makeover. For 100 years, it had been a place where humans walked around looking at animals enclosed in pits and small cages. Gradually, over the 1970s, Zoo chairman Alf Butcher and his team transformed it into a place where humans were enclosed in walkways, looking at animals enjoying something like their natural environment. Soil conservation had been a priority of Bolte's, but it was one for Borthwick, too. Major environmental studies were carried out on Port Phillip Bay, Western Port, and the Gippsland Lakes, to provide a knowledge base to guide future decisions. And the state brought in legislation requiring major projects to undergo an environmental assessment before they were given final approval.

The Environment Protection Authority had a more troubled history. Initially one of Hamer's marketing assets, it caused the government a lot of angst before it faded quietly from view. The Liberals' own sales pitch had raised community expectations: the EPA, they said, would be an 'independent watchdog' to guard our environment from polluters. But, in fact, it was made part of the public service, within the Ministry for Conservation. These were the early days of environmentalism; trained scientists were few, and hard to get. The EPA was perpetually short-staffed, yet it faced a mountain of work to set up its policies, standards, and way of operating. It had no freedom to hire or set its own budgets, and its director, Dr Alan Gilpin, fought to free himself from the control of the new director of conservation, Dr R.G. (Geoff) Downes. Both men were fine scientists, but neither had a doctorate in human relations. Their dispute, widely reported in the media, spiralled out of control. Borthwick tried to mediate, but without success. Eventually, Gilpin wrote to the minister, threatening to quit. Borthwick, by then fed up with what he saw as Gilpin's intransigence and refusal to compromise, seized on the opportunity, demanded that he set a departure date, and when Gilpin refused, sacked him.

This was an extraordinary event in the 1970s, when senior public servants had lifetime tenure. But voters didn't care. They were more alarmed when the EPA reported that Melbourne kept topping the World Health Organisation's safety limits for acceptable levels of pollution. In the early days, no one really knew what level of pollution was safe. The WHO, which set the global standards, chose to err on the side of caution, and set such stringent standards that in 1973 alone, Melbourne exceeded the WHO's smog pollution thresholds on 29 days. Every time the EPA went out to measure *E. coli* levels on Melbourne's beaches, some beaches would be way over the WHO's safety limit. People came to believe that if you went to Elwood beach, you might be swimming in diluted sewage. Opponents alleged that the government was muzzling its watchdog to prevent it reporting bad news.

But, over time, as car exhaust fumes became cleaner, and the EPA's rulings reduced pollution from factories, air pollution dropped. Over time, a scientific consensus developed that *E. coli* counts in seawater were too erratic to have any predictive value. And on both issues, the WHO's safety limits became seen by other scientists as too stringent to give a realistic guide to health hazards. Melbourne's skies and beaches gradually got cleaner, and pollution disappeared from the ranks of frontline issues.

Planning, however, never disappeared as a frontline issue. It is dealt with later in this book, but let us note here the Historic Buildings Act of 1973–74, which established a register of the state's most prized historic buildings. It was a turning point in Melbourne's history. In the Bolte era, developers had a free hand to knock down anything for redevelopment; in the 1960s and early 1970s, the Paris end of Collins Street was transformed into something else, and many of the great hotels and office blocks of the 19th century were demolished. Thanks to Alan Hunt's determination and resourcefulness, and the public advocacy of the National Trust and iconic *Sun* columnist Keith Dunstan, the Hamer government was able to put the cream of the state's historic buildings off limits. They could be redeveloped with the approval of the Historic Buildings Council, as the Rialto eventually was, but no longer could they be demolished. What began as the Historic Buildings Register in 1974 is now the Victorian Heritage Register, including several thousand buildings, structures, and other items, while thousands more are protected at municipal level. It has proved one of those lasting reforms that divides the past from the present.

For the premier, one test case was very close to home. Before the bill was passed, the Commercial Bank of Australasia, the biggest client of his law practice, decided to demolish its historic headquarters at 333 Collins Street, including its gorgeous Italianate banking chamber. For the National Trust, this was exactly what the law was meant to stop. Hamer was initially reluctant to intervene, but soon realised he had no choice. He persuaded the bank to have its plan reviewed by a committee of experts. The outcome was that the front of the building, including the banking chamber, was preserved and restored to its full glory, while the bank was allowed to build a new office tower behind it. It would be the first of many similar compromises.

Hamer's own passion, other than history, was for the arts. 'I regard it as the mark of a civilised society that it has an arts sector,' he told an interviewer in retirement. As soon as he became premier, he appointed himself minister for the arts — the first in Victoria — and set up a tiny ministry as his support team. Introducing the legislation for the ministry, he defined its goals as being to meet 'the wider community interest in the arts', to train young artists, and to stimulate the arts in 'the principal country centres'. Eric Westbrook, director of the National Gallery of Victoria, was persuaded to head the ministry. From a modest start, the department grew rapidly, taking over the museums and libraries, while Hamer sent money flowing its way. In its first year, 1972–73, it spent $9 million. Six years later, in Hamer's final year as treasurer and minister for the arts, it spent $48.5 million. Subsidies for municipal libraries were roughly 40 cents per head in Bolte's last budget, but grew to $3 per head by Hamer's last one. Hamer introduced a $50,000 annual grant to help the National Gallery of Victoria acquire new works; by his final budget, that had grown to $500,000 a year. And, of course, with each year, more and more money was pumped into the never-ending project of building the theatres and concert hall of the Arts Centre.

Within the arts, Hamer's own passion was for the performing arts, and his first budget lifted grants to performing groups from $600,000 a year to $1 million; in his first five years, they almost quadrupled to $2.2 million. A third of that went to three flagships: the Melbourne Theatre Company, the Victoria State Opera, and Ballet Victoria. A third was split between the Elizabethan Theatre Trust (itself a distributor of grants to performing arts bodies), the Arts Council of Victoria, the national opera and ballet companies, the Moomba festival, and the Melbourne City Council for its Entertainment in the Parks program. But another third of it was divided into mostly small grants to 187 performing groups or festivals all over the state: from the Colac City Band to the Melbourne Film Festival, the Berriwillock Arts and Crafts Group, the Astra Chamber Music Society, the

Yallourn Madrigal Singers, and the Pilgrim Puppet Theatre. Festivals flourished with government subsidies: the Castlemaine Arts Festival, founded in 1976 by Berek Segan, with support from Hamer and local MP Bill Ebery, became a particular favourite, which Dick and April attended almost every year for decades. Most arts policies concentrate on elite performers, but Hamer was determined to encourage participation by ordinary people. 'Arts policy should constantly seek to enlarge the number of people who are able to experience, or practise, the arts and crafts,' he wrote in retirement. All he asked was 'a firm dedication to excellence'.

It became a golden decade for all forms of the arts, all over the state. In 1978–79, the Grants Commission found that, relative to population, Victoria spent one-third more than the other states did on museums, and two-thirds more on art galleries. Hamer offered local councils a 2:1 state subsidy to build art galleries, or venues for the performing arts, which led to a surge of 1970s-era art galleries and theatres, such as the striking Benalla Art Gallery, the Geelong Performing Arts Centre, and the West Gippsland Performing Arts Centre. He bought the old Meat Market in North Melbourne, and had it redeveloped as a crafts centre. The Victorian Tapestry Workshop dates from this era, as does the Science Museum and the St Martin's Youth Arts Centre in South Yarra. The Flying Fruit Fly circus started up in Albury-Wodonga, the first of the new age of circuses in Australia. And, in the most visible of all the ministry's efforts to take the arts to the people, dozens of Melbourne trams were painted by different artists, adding a touch of surprise to the daily commute.

One of Hamer's priorities was to create a better environment for training elite artists. This ended up as the Victorian College of the Arts, which won a keenly contested battle to take over the old bluestone Defence Department headquarters on St Kilda Road. The college has since become an alma mater to a host of actors, filmmakers, artists, writers, musicians, ballet dancers, and stage designers, including Vince Colosimo and Sibylla Budd, Gillian Armstrong, Adam Elliot and Sarah Watt, Patricia Piccinini and Bill Henson, Hannie Rayson, and too many others to name. Opera Australia's star couple Cheryl

Barker and Peter Coleman-Wright met there as fellow students. When the college was under threat in 2009 from a misguided plan to merge it into the University of Melbourne, a survey found that one in nine musicians in Australia's professional orchestras were VCA graduates.

Hamer also gave priority to expanding social-welfare services, particularly in innovative ways. After he retired, I asked him which reform he was most proud of, expecting him to talk about planning, the environment, or the arts, and was surprised when he replied:

> The whole idea of domiciliary services has always appealed to me. People who have trouble being in the mainstream of the community, for all sorts of reasons, ought to be maintained in their own homes rather than stuck in institutions. Things like special schools, and day care for the elderly, have always given me great pleasure.

Compassion was one of Hamer's core instincts. Policy innovations in social welfare were as important to him as those in the environment, the arts, or planning. The Grants Commission's benchmarking found that in 1978–79, Victoria's spending on welfare relative to needs was 15 per cent above the national average, and 28 per cent higher for child welfare. In just seven years between Bolte's last budget and Hamer's last budget, it swelled from $22 million to $99 million, and — with one important exception — it soared in almost every field. Every budget seemed to offer a new pensioner concession: one year, it was a free return rail trip for a holiday anywhere in Victoria; another, it was taxpayers paying part of pensioners' municipal rates bills; then it was their MMBW (water and sewerage) bills, and so on. When Fraser cut federal government subsidies for councils' home-help services, Hamer stepped in to fill the gap from state funds. His government set up the first women's shelters, and introduced the first serious program to tackle the abuse of children.

These were the years when Australia found itself facing unprecedented problems with long-term unemployment, hard-core drug abuse, homelessness, marital breakdowns, and men dropping out of work. Between 1968 and 1978, the number of Australians unemployed more than quadrupled, from 94,000 to 409,000. Five years later, it would reach 697,000. The Fraser government delivered one of the great welfare reforms when it replaced tax rebates for dependent children with family-assistance benefits paid to the mother. But the voluntary welfare agencies and state and council welfare departments had never been busier. As treasurer, Hamer rose to the challenge.

The one area of social welfare on which Victoria deliberately spent less than other states was jails. Hamer gave strong support to a succession of ministers who wanted to reduce the number of people sent to jail, particularly to Pentridge, and instead impose alternative punishments that offered better prospects to rehabilitate offenders back into society. In 1973, Ian Smith introduced legislation to establish lower-security centres where offenders could be sentenced to periodic detention such as weekend jail, work-release schemes, and community service. The first centres opened in 1976, and after four years the government reported to parliament that only 16 per cent of attendees had reoffended. In 1981, Haddon Storey as attorney-general put through legislation allowing judges and magistrates to impose community-service orders as an alternative to imprisonment. These moves were not designed to save money, but to shift the focus to rehabilitation.

The government began to phase out Pentridge, the old bluestone castle in Coburg that had been the state's main prison for a century. A separate remand prison was built in the city for people awaiting trial. Ararat prison was expanded, and the notorious H block for high-security prisoners at Pentridge — described by prison chaplain Father John Brosnan as a place that turned bike thieves into murderers — was demolished. Alas, its replacement, Jika Jika, was even worse — 'an electronic zoo' in which inmates were monitored constantly, but had little contact with other humans. Warders and prisoners alike hated it, and when five inmates died in 1987 after setting fire to their cells, the Cain government closed it after just seven years of use.

The biggest beneficiary from Hamer's largesse as treasurer, however, was the education sector. For all his government's initiatives in new areas, most of its spending was in the three core areas of education, health, and transport. Throughout his time as premier, these remained the mainstream issues. As treasurer, Hamer kept pouring more money into education, even after school student numbers peaked in 1977 and then began to fall. Between 1972 and 1979, despite the Commonwealth taking over tertiary education, Victoria's spending on education almost trebled, from $424 million to $1,157 million. The number of teachers in government schools climbed from 37,800 to 53,550, despite only a small rise in the number of students. Hamer and Thompson, like their Liberal successors, gave top priority to increasing grants to independent schools, which rose more than sixfold in Hamer's seven years as treasurer. Funding them had become a priority for Liberal voters, and hence a priority for the Liberal government. Hamer and Thompson introduced the formula of paying independent schools 20 per cent of the cost of educating a child at government schools. Even in 1979, when Hamer had to impose a staff freeze across the public sector and make deep cuts to capital works, his government still found the money to begin increasing that number towards a new goal of 25 per cent.

The Grants Commission estimated that in 1978–79, Hamer's last year as treasurer, Victoria spent considerably more on education than other states, especially at secondary level. Relative to needs, Victoria's spending on secondary education was 19 per cent above the national average for government schools, and 16 per cent above for Catholic and independent schools. Even Thompson, once he had moved out of Education to the Treasury, wondered publicly why the government had increased the number of teachers by 4,000 between 1976 and 1979, when they had 12,000 fewer students to teach. In 1979, Australian governments had yet to develop a mania for testing students' ability to read, write, and count, so there were no interstate comparisons of the quality of education. But conservatives such as Vance Dickie publicly questioned whether the state's massive investment in education was delivering value for money.

The Hamer–Thompson policy to lift funding for independent schools was matched by a policy to give government schools more independence. By any measure, schools remained under the heavy thumb of the Education Department and its standard rules. But at the end of Hamer's term as treasurer, at the urging of Brian Dixon, almost 3 per cent of the total education budget was handed to school councils to spend on their own priorities. Schools were pushed into forming partnerships with their communities. Dixon also used his term as assistant minister to get school ovals and gymnasiums opened up after hours for community sport and after-school care. Migrant and adult education were also on Hamer's crowded priority list; by 1979, Victoria employed more specialist migrant teachers than all other states combined. But he also came up with a populist handout similar to the schoolkids' bonus that Labor introduced later: an 'education allowance', which was given to parents, not schools.

In the 1970s, Hamer's governments spent twice as much on education as on health. A generation later, the ratio would be very different. Yet while health costs to the budget had risen inexorably for decades, in the 1970s they grew at explosive rates. Part of that was the result of the gradual collapse of the honorary system, under which doctors traditionally worked for hospitals free of charge, and got their share when the patients were released from hospital and paid for consultations at the doctor's private practice. Part was due to the rising cost and spread of new medical technologies, as Victoria's hospitals became increasingly concerned with providing the best for their patients. Part of it was also due to an explosion of demand: the more patients survived illnesses that once would have killed them, the more hospital beds they occupied, at state expense. And part of it was because, over time, the government's role changed from subsidising hospitals run by charities to gradually absorbing them into the government sector. The rising cost of hospital care would have broken the state budget were it not for Whitlam's pledge to pay 50 per cent of the cost — a commitment that the Fraser government pledged to maintain, although with such creative reinterpretations that, over time, it became unrecognisable. The state's health budget trebled from $201 million to $599 million in Hamer's seven years as treasurer, mostly for hospitals, but also for rapidly expanding programs for community health and nursing homes, especially after the Fraser government cut its share of the community health bill from 90 per cent to 50 per cent. Once again, Victoria outspent the other states; the Grants Commission estimated its health spending in 1978–79, adjusted for relative costs and needs, was 12 per cent above the Australian average.

The Hamer government was the first to try to move a hospital from Melbourne's city centre to the suburbs. Hamer decided it should be the Queen Victoria Hospital, which his grandmother had helped to found, and which his mother had helped to run for decades before handing over the presidency to his sister-in-law, Margaret Hamer, wife of Alan. The plan was to move the hospital from its central site on Lonsdale Street, which it had occupied since the 1940s, out to Clayton, where it would become the nucleus of what is now the Monash Medical Centre. That did eventually happen, but not until 1987, almost 15 years after negotiations began. Margaret Hamer was as independent-minded as any of the Hamer women.

Kindergartens and infant-welfare services were also favoured in Hamer's budgets. During his time, the state took on the full cost of running kinders, and paid most of the salaries of councils' infant-welfare sisters. In 1976, despite budget shortfalls, he restored state-funded deliveries of free milk to kindergartens; he also paid the salaries of infant-welfare sisters and kindergarten teachers. Hamer was the first of many Victorian leaders to pledge that every child would have a year of free pre-school education. That, too, proved harder to deliver than it had been to promise, which has allowed governments to go on promising it.

Hamer tried to reform transport policy, and partially succeeded. Bolte had focussed on building roads and bridges — the South-Eastern and Tullamarine freeways, and the King Street and West Gate bridges — while keeping public transport going for a diminishing clientele, and trimming its services to keep costs and revenue in balance. As noted earlier, annual investment in the railways remained stuck at around $16 million a year throughout Bolte's long reign. Hamer was one of the first to realise that as Melbourne's population grew towards 5 million, public transport would become more important in future, not less so. From the 1960s on, he publicly advocated more investment in public transport, and especially the construction of an underground rail loop. Bolte had pledged in his 1970 policy speech to start work on the Underground, but only preliminary work had been done when Hamer took over. He planned to increase investment in public transport across the board, announcing plans to buy 100 new trams and 30 buses, on top of the 50 trains already on order, and to carry out a wide range of improvements to the network. But once the Fraser government made state infrastructure spending bear the brunt of its austerity measures, those plans had to be stretched out. In fact, in Hamer's time as premier, the loop soaked up most of the growth in state-funded spending on public-transport infrastructure, and the new rolling stock and track improvements were funded partly by the Commonwealth, under a deal signed with Whitlam but delivered mostly by the Fraser government.

His great achievement in public transport was to build the Underground. It was a scheme with many fathers — the legislation to build it had been passed in 1960, at Warner's behest, and after fobbing off three reports recommending that he build it, Bolte finally gave way and agreed to it in 1970. But Hamer as treasurer had to find the money to construct it and to give it priority over other demands on his scarce resources. It is worth noting that McMahon and Whitlam each refused to contribute Commonwealth money to the project — and that, at the time, many argued that it was the wrong priority. But it added 12 kilometres of tunnels and four heavily used stations to the rail network. Today one could not imagine how Melbourne would function without it. Hamer never seriously doubted that he had made the right choice. In an interview in 1982, he conceded that the demand projections on which it was based had proved optimistic, but argued that, in the long run, Melbourne would not regret having built it. Time has proved him right.

But as time went on, the ambition of Hamer's plans for public transport became disconnected from the meagre reality of what he was able to deliver. Acute cost escalations and the shortage of funds saw his policies swing around in circles. His 1976 election policy, written when Ray Meagher was transport minister, could have been a turning point for Melbourne public transport, marking the birth of the contemporary transport system. Among much else, Hamer and Meagher promised:

> The Government will establish a Metropolitan Transport Authority, to co-ordinate and manage the whole metropolitan public transport system. Our purpose is to see that Melbourne has totally integrated public transport, with a single uniform price ticket interchangeable between rail, tram and bus.

This pointed the way that Melbourne would go: to a unified transport system of trains, trams, and buses using a single ticketing system with a common price within wide zones. Initially, it ran into deep resistance from entrenched culture in the Victorian Railways and the Tramways Board. The jump to single-zone (or two-zone, or three-zone) pricing raised difficult issues. The single ticket was introduced initially as an option, and became the rule only under the Cain government of the 1980s. In every area of public transport, decision-making became crowded out by the need to tackle the explosion of operating deficits to levels that began to overwhelm the budget.

The old rules were clear. Under Bolte and his predecessors, trains, trams, and buses had to pay their way; if they didn't, services were cut to match the fall in revenue. But by 1970, in Melbourne and the country alike, cars and trucks had taken charge completely. Public transport had mostly lost the critical mass of passengers and freight needed to make its labour-intensive services profitable. The new suburbs had no train or tram lines; journeys between home and work were becoming more diverse, and the transport-rich inner suburbs were losing population as the migrant families moved out and fewer residents with higher incomes moved in. Through the Bolte era, passenger demand was kept up by the sheer size of the immigration intake. But in the early 1970s, the number of new migrants plunged by half, just as public transport's low-income workers were reaping big pay rises. Between 1971–72 (Bolte's last year) and 1980–81 (Hamer's last year) annual rail journeys shrank from 142 million to 88 million. The cost of running the public-transport network doubled in five years, but the revenues from it rose very little.

Bolte performed one financial rescue in the 1960s by taking the railways debt onto the state budget balance sheet. Even so, in his last year as premier, annual public-transport losses climbed to $31 million. Within six years, they had blown out to $188 million. Part of that was due to a failed marketing ploy in the 1973 budget, in which Hamer cut fares for outer-suburban commuters, hoping to win a positive response. There was one, but too small to matter: the problem was not that fares were too high, but that public transport could not provide most of the trips that residents in outer suburbs needed to make. By 1977–78, the budget's net spending on public transport, investment, and subsidies almost matched the spending on hospitals. At a critical time for the budget, this was a huge new burden to bear; for the first time since the Cain government of the early 1950s, the state started to take hard decisions to reduce rail losses.

In 1973, Hamer commissioned a former senior Commonwealth public servant, Sir Henry Bland, to report on solutions to the railways losses. Bland repeated the traditional view that public enterprises had to pay their way, and that public transport should be no exception. He recommended ending the railways' monopoly of rural freight and passenger services, and opening those markets up to competition. Gradually, this resulted in trains on minor routes being replaced by privately run buses working under contract to the government. In his last 15 years, Bolte closed passenger services on just eight country lines, mostly small ones. In the three years from late 1975 to late 1978, Hamer and transport minister Joe Rafferty shut down services on 17 lines, replacing them with buses. The core lines of the country network, however, remained. The railways centralised their freight operations at a few depots. Most country stations were abandoned and sold off, or remained in service as essentially unmanned stations.

Hamer was willing to compromise with his conservative colleagues when it came to the most vexed issue of 20th-century Victorian politics: electoral redistribution. He agreed to a redistribution of seats in both houses that maintained a bias towards country electorates, but reduced its extent. Under the new boundaries for the assembly, 89 country votes were given the same weight as 100 city votes. This was a long way from the 47:100 ratio that the coalition adopted in the 1920s, but it still allowed the Liberals an extra seat at Labor's expense. In 1979 that one-seat bias would prove crucial, allowing the Liberals to retain power alone, rather than being forced to share it with the National Party. The council was left in far more distorted shape, with 71 country votes given the same weight as 100 city votes. That, too, gave the Liberals a buffer that was to prove crucial later. In 1985 it stopped Labor winning control of the Legislative Council — and using it to bring in proportional representation for the Upper House. It would be another generation before the Liberal Party finally accepted that giving electorates unequal weight for partisan reasons had no place in democratic values. Hamer was ahead of his time.

The big issue on which he would not compromise was the abolition of capital punishment. In the 17 years of Bolte's rule, no issue had been more controversial than the decision to hang Ronald Ryan. Bolte had withstood so much criticism over his insistence on hanging Ryan that, politically, it almost came to define him. For Hamer then to set out to wipe the death penalty from the statute books, less than three years after Bolte's retirement, amounted to repudiating a central part of his old leader's legacy — and it was seen as such, especially by Bolte. In turn, Hamer's move to abolish the death penalty became one of the things that defined him.

It was an uncharacteristically bold move from such an instinctively cautious leader. While most other Australian jurisdictions had already abolished the death penalty, each time it was a Labor government that took the decision; no previous Liberal government had ever done so. Opinion polls showed consistent public support for keeping the death penalty, so Hamer's move was the opposite of focus-group-driven policy. The Liberal Party room was evenly divided on the issue, even after Hamer made his intentions clear. That he decided to risk some of his political capital to get this reform passed shows how much the issue had come to mean to him — and, one assumes, despite his public silence on the Ryan hanging, how deeply he disapproved of it.

Justice should have dictated that hanging be abolished as a result of the Liberals being given a free vote on Galbally's annual private member's bill. But it became clear that this would have less chance of winning Liberal support than a private member's bill moved by Hamer himself. So Hamer decided to make it his own bill, and ask all parties to allow a conscience vote. In reality, the deep division in the party room allowed him no choice — and he was fortunate that this was one of those issues that lent itself to a conscience vote. Initially, Hamer insisted on a free vote for all parties, but he backed down after Holding pointed out to him that it was longstanding Labor policy to end capital punishment; and, conversely, Peter Ross-Edwards, the Nationals' parliamentary leader, pointed out that it was his party's policy to keep it.

Opponents tried two amendments. Wimmera backbencher Jim McCabe, a Liberal, moved that the issue be sent to the people at a referendum. That amendment was lost 38–33 in the assembly, but 25 of the 45 Liberals present voted for it, including 20 of the party's 33 backbenchers. Ross-Edwards then moved an amendment to send the bill to a committee of legal experts, who would look at abolishing the death penalty for all cases of murder except those committed during a kidnapping or hijacking, or with 'exceptional cruelty or sadism'. His compromise offered Hamer an honourable way to back down to maintain party unity, but he declined that, too, and his supporters stood firm. Hamer did accept a third amendment from attorney-general Vernon Wilcox (an opponent of the bill), that if his bill passed, judges should lose the discretion to impose anything but a life sentence for murder. Among Liberals, only Brian Dixon and Athol Guy opposed this draconian rule, which was quickly abolished by the Cain government. Hamer's bill finally passed 37–31, with several Liberals swapping sides in the final vote to support it, including Robert Maclellan and health minister John Rossiter. A year later, Hamer gave Rossiter the widely desired post of agent-general in London; not a few wondered unkindly if his vote for the bill played any part in that.

The vote in the council was straightforward; over the years, Galbally had converted most of the Liberals to his cause. The council voted 20–13 for the bill; the Liberals voted 11–7 with their leader, and the only sour note was the ageing Galbally's pique that it was a Liberal bill, not his own, that would finally wipe capital punishment from the books.

A major reform had been achieved, but at a cost. In the assembly, almost half the votes for the bill came from Labor. On the Liberal side, the combined final tally in both houses was 30 votes for and 30 against. Cabinet voted 11–6 in favour of the premier's bill, but Liberal backbenchers voted 24–19 against. The cabinet opponents included Dickie, by then deputy government leader in the Upper House, Wilcox, Meagher, Smith, Scanlan, and Jock Granter, a genial Heathcote grazier who entered cabinet in 1973. On the backbench, the main division was between country MPs, who tended to vote as a bloc, and those from the city. Including pairs, country MPs were almost 3–1 against the legislation. Suburban and urban fringe MPs were almost 2–1 for it. In a sense, country MPs were voting for Bolte; city MPs, for Hamer.

One could not imagine Bolte allowing MPs a free vote, in which party divisions would be put on show. But Hamer felt that on an emotive issue like this, MPs should be free to make up their own minds. And, as usual, he made no attempt to lobby them. Barry Jones, secretary of the Anti-Hanging Committee since 1962, was a Labor frontbencher in 1975, and an articulate advocate of the bill. In his autobiography, *A Thinking Reed*, Jones tells that he kept asking Hamer how this or that Liberal would vote:

> His invariable answer was 'I have no idea'. When I asked: 'Have you talked with him?' the answer was 'No'. 'Do you propose to talk with him?' 'No' again.

To the public, the divisions in the party didn't matter. All three newspapers supported the bill, and all feted Hamer when it was passed. His victory helped to give him an image as a decisive leader. He was certainly on the side of history: while opinion polls continue to show that a majority of Australians want the death penalty in extreme cases, all jurisdictions have now abolished it. No government has ever tried to bring it back.

CHAPTER SEVENTEEN

The Liberals turn right

The year 1975 was not a good one for politicians of the centre. The Whitlam government's style and the coalition's obstruction divided Australia into two partisan sides. In New South Wales, Liberal premier Tom Lewis tore up the convention that senators who leave or die mid-term are replaced by another from the same party: when Lionel Murphy resigned as attorney-general to join the High Court, Lewis appointed the independent 72-year-old mayor of Albury, Cleaver Bunton, as his replacement. When Labor senator Bernie Milliner died suddenly in June, Queensland premier Joh Bjelke-Petersen went a step further by appointing as his replacement a 64-year-old French polisher, Albert Field, who promised never to vote with Labor. That gave the coalition a virtual majority in the Senate; and, in October, Fraser used it to block supply to the Whitlam government until an election was called. Whitlam held out, and the month-long standoff ended with the unprecedented dismissal of the government by the governor-general, Sir John Kerr. For much of 1975, conservative Australians indignant with Whitlam over one issue or many were joining Liberal branches. The conservative groundswell against Whitlam was creating a subtle but important transformation, moving the Liberal Party to the right — and away from Hamer.

It reversed the direction of the Victorian Liberal Party, which for a decade had been moving towards the political centre. In the 1960s, the rising force in the party was the Young Liberal movement, a new generation impatient with the status quo, and attracted to the new ideas that Bolte and Rylah opposed. In 1962, the Melbourne University Liberal Club publicly opposed cabinet's decision to hang the insane murderer Tait. By 1969 the club also opposed Australian troops fighting in Vietnam. Charles Hider, whose great-great-grandfather Graham Berry was a radical liberal premier in the 1870s, was the Young Liberals' state president for part of that time. 'In the early Sixties, the Young Libs had 3,000 to 4,000 members', Hider recalls. 'We always had 50 or 60 people at meetings.' Hider and others organised the network to increase its influence in party positions, preselections, and policy issues. Menzies did the same at the start of his political career, founding the Young Nationalists and using it to speed his rise in the party. (In 1939, the Young Nationalists were the political group that Hamer planned to join before the war got in his way.) In 1965, even Bolte used the Young Liberals as his forward attack troops to pave the way for state conference to drop its insistence on holding a referendum before extending drinking hours from 6.00 p.m. to 10.00 p.m. Andrew Peacock mobilised his troops to go from being state president of the Young Liberals to state president of the Liberal Party when he was just 26 — and then to win the contest for Menzies' seat after Hamer had turned it down.

In 1969, Hider moved a resolution at the Liberals' state council urging that abortion be decriminalised; it failed, but it exemplified how the party's new idealists were using all available levers to make it rethink old attitudes. In 1970, Hider won Lindsay Thompson's council seat when he moved down to the assembly. A year later, Haddon Storey and Athol Guy of The Seekers won seats at by-elections, and in 1973, Peter Block joined the council. All were Hamer allies. Most significant were the appointment of Leo Hawkins in 1971 as the Liberals' state secretary, and the election of Hamer in 1972 as premier and of Peter Hardie in 1973 as Liberal state president. It was the high-water mark for the progressives or 'small-l Liberals' in the party. By 1973 they were in control; the question was how they would use that control.

Unwisely, they chose to take on the Country Party — not at state level, where they had long been enemies, but at federal level, where the Country Party was a reliable coalition partner. Many, especially on the conservative side, saw that as the relationship the Liberals should aim for in state politics, too. But Hardie and Hawkins wanted to put the Country Party out of business. In July 1973, flush with confidence after Hamer's big victory, the Victorian state executive voted to end the longstanding agreement that gave the Country Party a safe seat in the Senate, instead offering its sitting senator Jim Webster the vulnerable third position on a joint ticket for the next half-Senate election. Two weeks later, Sir Robert Menzies intervened, using the opening of the party's new headquarters in Albert Road to sharply disagree with a decision seen as emblematic of the Victorian party's shift to the left. Speaking from a wheelchair, Menzies was polite in public, but blunt:

> I not only deplore (the decision), I think it may be a cardinal blunder … Two parties that have so much in common must not start quarrelling with each other. You don't quarrel with your allies. I, for one, propose to give my second vote to Jim Webster …
>
> Don't be misled into believing the marvellous state of affairs in Victoria — (*turning to Hamer*) thank you, Dick — is of universal application in Australia. And if you look at the position in Australia overall, as you indeed must, we must look forward to if and when we win an election in the Commonwealth — and to having a partnership with the Country Party. I suppose I can say without much vanity that I know as much about having governments in coalition with the Country Party as any man alive — and I'm practically alive — I am perfectly sure I am right in saying we mustn't quarrel with our inevitable partners in the federal parliament.[1]

In private, inside the new building bearing his name, Menzies tore strips off the state party's leaders. As he was leaving, he spotted Malcolm Fraser in the crowd, and called him over to his car for what became a long conversation. To onlookers, it appeared that the party's founder was subtly indicating support for the man then seen as the conservative alternative to the party's struggling federal leader, Bill Snedden.

The next day, however, the state council comfortably elected Hardie as state president over his conservative rival, former federal minister Peter Howson. The next month, it dumped veteran conservative George Hannan from its Senate ticket, replacing him with civil libertarian Alan Missen, a co-author of Hamer's progressive 1972 party platform. On 20 September, Howson records in his diary a chance meeting with Ray Meagher, who tells him: 'Some of them have forgotten where the dividing line is between the two parties.' It was typical of many conversations that helped to fuel a new mood of militancy on the right of the party as the Whitlam government got deeper into trouble. After the March 1974 state council, Howson notes that the council, 'having moved last year to the left, has begun to see the damage, and are [*sic*] moving back again'. But in July, when two right-wing candidates challenged Hardie, he won an emphatic victory, leading Howson to complain to his diary:

> I fear that some of our state members are so enamoured with Dick Hamer that they can't see some of the very real problems that are taking place in the party at the present time. They feel that so long as Hamer's there, they've got nothing to worry about, and that he will carry them through election after election.

Hamer was seen publicly as aligned with Hardie, his fellow progressive. Yet from Howson's account, he seems to have generally stayed aloof from party infighting, and at times sided with the conservatives. When Hardie moved for the Liberals to contest all seats at the next federal election — including Gippsland, held by Country Party frontbencher Peter Nixon — Hamer endorsed a counter-move by Snedden to allow the leader to negotiate which seats to contest. Snedden got his way.

But divisions in the party worsened after the coalition lost the 1974 snap federal election, called by Whitlam when Snedden pledged to use the Senate to block supply. The Liberals lost another two seats in Victoria to Labor — one of them, David Hamer's seat of Isaacs. Those on the right saw this as evidence that the premier should be more aggressive in opposing Whitlam, as Bolte would have been, and his counterparts Sir Joh Bjelke-Petersen (Queensland) and Sir Charles Court (Western Australia) were. Hamer tended to give Whitlam a bucketing at Liberal Party state council, and in election campaigns, but otherwise sought to minimise the criticism and maximise co-operation between the two governments.

Gradually, more Liberal insiders grew alienated from Hamer's mild-mannered approach, from Snedden's ineffective leadership, and from the focus by Hardie and Hawkins on taking on the Country Party. Australia's slide into recession and Hamer's impotence in the face of union bans on the Newport power station fuelled a sense that tougher leadership was needed, more like the old style. The balance of views in the party began to swing to the right. In October 1974, Howson records party pollster George Camakaris telling him (in Howson's words):

> The facets of [Hamer's] character, such as intelligence and [commitment to] quality of life issues such as conservation, were useful in winning the 1973 state election, because that was a time of affluence when these issues counted with the electorate. However, when the mood of the country has changed to a feeling of insecurity … those qualities of Dick Hamer are no longer so important. What are required are qualities of decisiveness with strength.

A mood of crisis was building. On 16 November, *The Age* reported that backbenchers were canvassing support for a cabinet reshuffle that would replace Lindsay Thompson as deputy premier with the more forthright Bill Borthwick, and bring new blood into the ministry. Noel Tennison, as the party's spokesman, was asked to comment on the story, but declined, since he knew of the moves — organised, he recounted later, by respected backbencher Geoff Hayes. When the article appeared on the eve of a special state conference,

Hamer hit the roof. Thompson was one of his closest friends, and he would fight any move to demote him. Hamer rounded on Tennison for letting the story get an airing. A few days later, Fraser launched his first challenge against Snedden for the federal leadership; he lost, but by a margin that would encourage him to try again.

At the same time, Hawkins submitted a proposal to the federal redistribution commissioners that could have almost wiped out the Country Party in Victoria, abolishing its seat of Wimmera, and making changes to the boundaries of its other seats that put most of them at risk of falling to the Liberals. The conservatives saw Hawkins as a left-liberal who did not belong in their party; his submission went well beyond his brief from the state executive, and his enemies seized on this to force his resignation. As Tennison tells it in his autobiography, *My Spin in PR*:

> He was summarily dismissed on 6 December 1974. Ten days later, Hamer let it happen, and I joined Leo in the tumbrel as Peg Pelchen [secretary of the women's division] sat knitting at the front door like Madame Defarge as the axe fell.

Nineteen seventy-five was a year of preselections. They were carried out in a mood of unprecedented conservative militancy, stirred up by opposition to the Whitlam government. They were to transform the Victorian Liberal Party, and slowly erode its dominance of state politics — and Hamer's dominance of the party.

Hamer's redistribution of state electorates had expanded the assembly from 73 to 81 seats, and the council from 36 to 44. Nine Liberals in safe seats decided to retire, including four ministers: state development minister Murray Byrne; transport minister Ray Meagher; attorney-general Vernon Wilcox; and health minister John Rossiter (who became agent-general in London). Veteran backbencher Sir Edgar Tanner, then president of the Australian Olympic Federation, announced his retirement minutes before nominations closed for his seat of Caulfield, so that his son Ted would be the only candidate; however, the party called foul, and reopened nominations.

It was a great year for those running on the right of the party. Two preselections exemplify the mood. One of the party's most impressive backbenchers in the upper house, Haddon Storey, QC, a friend and ally of the premier, nominated for the lower-house seat of Burwood, hoping that it would open the way for him to replace Wilcox as attorney-general. But among the field of 14 contesting Burwood was a brash, energetic 27-year-old, a former army officer with no political track record, who owned an advertising agency, called himself 'an outspoken conservative', and had strong ideas about how to campaign and how to govern. His name was Jeff Kennett. Kennett produced a glossy pamphlet on why he should be pre-selected for Burwood, and on where the Hamer government needed to be put right. He pledged that, if elected, he would stay in politics for just six years. Young Jeff personally lobbied every member of the preselection panel, presenting them with his pamphlet and arguing his case. No one had ever run a preselection campaign like this before, and no one would be allowed to do so ever again. For it worked. The vote ended up as a dead heat between Kennett and Storey. In these circumstances, the preselection chairman decided that both candidates should put their case afresh. Tony Parkinson's biography, *Jeff: the rise and fall of a political phenomenon*, quotes Kennett's clinching argument:

> I said, 'I respect Haddon Storey, he is a very good man, he has a lot to offer, and he is going to be a minister. But you people here today have the opportunity to pre-select two Members of Parliament. You can decide to retain Haddon Storey for the Upper House, and to introduce a younger member with different ideas, fresh ideas, for the Lower House. It gives you a wonderful opportunity.'

Kennett's quickness on his feet decided the contest; he won by six votes. He soon became a forceful presence in the Liberal Party.

Kennett's preselection campaign was a model of team play compared with Doug Jennings' campaign for Western Port. The wild younger son of housing developer Sir Albert (A.V.) Jennings, Doug's hot temper had led to him quitting the family firm to go farming in

Queensland, where he became a big fan of the combative style of Sir Joh Bjelke-Petersen. By the mid-1970s he was back in Melbourne, living in Balwyn, but with a stud farm at Flinders, from where he had become chairman of the Liberals' Flinders electorate committee, and had his eye on the new seat of Western Port. In May, Hamer launched an ambitious conservation plan for the Mornington Peninsula. It was drawn up by the Western Port Regional Planning Authority he had established, to implement goals he had set out as minister for local government, and using powers given to it by legislation sponsored by his successor in that role, Alan Hunt. The plan had many elements, but three stood out. It would ban subdivisions of fewer than 200 acres (80 hectares) around coastal villages such as Flinders. In the most sensitive parts of the peninsula, new houses would require planning permits that could specify the site, size, colour, materials, and 'general appearance' of the home. And in many areas, landholders would require a permit to fell trees on their land.

Planning restrictions such as these were well established in the national parks of Britain, where most land is privately owned and farmed by people who want to keep the countryside as it is. But for decades in the Mornington Peninsula, landowners had grown rich by subdividing their land for hobby farms or housing estates. They or their forebears had ripped out most of the native trees, and planted cypress and pines as windbreaks. (The great exception, Greens Bush, between Flinders and Main Ridge, was bought by Hamer to become the centrepiece of the Mornington Peninsula National Park.) And no one in Victoria had ever been told they would need a permit to chop down a tree on their land, or build their house in the style they liked.

But the issues were similar to those in other areas that the Hamer government wanted to preserve, in parts of the Dandenongs and the Yarra Valley: stop the spread of subdivisions and hobby farms, maintain the area as viable farmland, and keep it aesthetically attractive. At the launch of the plan in May 1975, the premier's support was unstinting:

> Here in the Mornington Peninsula we have one of the most important, sensitive, areas in the country. It's an area which we're either going to preserve now, or lose. We can't escape it — it's this generation that's going to ensure whether or not it will be preserved.
>
> I don't see that people should be upset by these controls. The controls give an assurance that the land will be preserved for the uses we need; after all, controls are only irksome to people who want to change the land in some way. They have to be seen in the light that the overall purpose is for it to be preserved … It's up to us all to support what the authority's done, what the planners had achieved, in keeping the Mornington Peninsula forever the way we want it to be.

It was a strong speech. Graeme Weideman, who won Frankston in 1976, says he never saw Hamer more impressive than when he met with local groups who opposed the plan, and set out to win them over. But the plan gave Jennings the enemy he needed. He and his supporters revived a dormant group, the Peninsula Rural Landholders' Association, to be the vehicle for their campaign against the plan and all associated with it: Hunt, Hamer, public works minister and Mornington MP Roberts Dunstan, and local MLC Roy Ward. On 8 June, the association's members voted 83–2 to endorse a statement drafted by Jennings that vowed to 'oppose the plan in every way possible', declaring that if it were implemented, 'it will be the catalyst for welfare state control of all land … [farmers would] require a permit to live normally'. Jennings' statements allowed no compromise:

> This so-called conservation plan is, we believe, the most destructive way-of-life legislation yet introduced in this country. This plan is not about conservation, it is about destroying every basic lifestyle and initiative in the community … This plan is so autocratic and so bad it is good in the sense that it has made thousands of people in all walks of life realise the type of dictatorial officials we are dealing with, and the insidious authoritarian controls being planned for other areas in Victoria.

> This is a matter on which there can be no half-measures — the issues have never been clearer — it affects our basic way of life and our freedom to live normally. There can only be one answer and that is NO, it is not acceptable at any price in this democratic country.

This was no civilised disagreement between party colleagues with different priorities. It was an emotive rant by a paranoid crusader deaf to arguments by any who disagreed with him. The platform on which Jennings sought Liberal preselection for Western Port was a call to arms against a Liberal government supposedly trying to impose totalitarian controls on its people.

The Liberal Party now faced an unprecedented dilemma. One suspects that Bolte and Rylah would have recognised danger immediately, and stood over the party to ensure that Jennings would not get preselection. Hamer was too reasonable and trusting for that. Alan Hunt waged the battle on the peninsula, telling a local meeting attended by Jennings and his supporters:

> The attack … isn't just an attack upon this plan. It's an attack on planning. It's the claim that every landowner has the right to do exactly what he wants at all times with his own land — and to hell with the rest of the community, and let the future fend for itself. That is an approach which no responsible citizen ought to accept for one moment. That is an approach which everyone who cares for the future ought to throw back in the teeth of those who claim it.

Hunt was perhaps the most formidable of Hamer's team: tough, smart, principled, and far-sighted, he was the ideal minister to be implementing the 'quality of life' reforms Hamer had introduced. The son of a teetotal, non-smoking Methodist parson, he had a free-thinking mind and an extravagant zest for life at odds with his upbringing. As a boy, he won a scholarship to Melbourne Grammar, and then a free place at the Melbourne University law school, where he became president of the Liberal Club, and secretary of the Australian Union of Students. In 1951, he was one of the handful of

Liberals who opposed Menzies' bid to ban the Communist Party as a breach of Liberal principles of free speech and free association. He settled in Mornington as a local solicitor, and in 1961 was elected to the Legislative Council. In 1963, he courageously exposed Sir Reginald Ansett's use of political influence to get the government to compulsorily acquire a widow's farm for its new Mount Eliza reservoir, after the experts had selected Ansett's land as the most suitable. Hunt was too shrewd to name Bolte as the agent of that influence, but Bolte was furious; despite Hunt's outstanding ability, he entered cabinet only when Hamer chose him to be his successor as minister for local government. A Liberal who had defied Menzies and Bolte on his way up was not going to be cowed by Jennings.

Hamer, as always, tried to find a compromise. Two days before the closing date for preselection nominations, cabinet approved new guidelines for the plan, including flexibility on subdivisions in cases of hardship or splitting land between family members, and no controls on painting or siting of houses, 'save in the most exceptional circumstances'. Jennings claimed victory, but cabinet's backdown was also designed to smooth the path for Robert Maclellan, whose old electorate had been divided between Berwick and Western Port, to stand for the seat against him. Maclellan was happy to settle for Berwick, but bowed to pressure from Hamer, Hunt, and others to stand for Western Port to keep Jennings out. The move failed: Jennings won a narrow victory. Maclellan then won preselection for Berwick, while Jennings went quiet until after the election, and then became the most disruptive force the Liberal Party room had ever seen.

Other preselections confirmed the trend against Hamer and his supporters. Brian Dixon, the livewire minister for youth, sport, and recreation who was trying to get Victorians off their couches with his 'Life. Be in It.' campaign, sought to move from his vulnerable seat of St Kilda to its safe neighbour Brighton, but was defeated by local solicitor Jeanette Patrick, daughter of former senator Marie Breen. Graham Nicol, who had entered the Legislative Council with Hamer in 1958, was dumped in favour of barrister James Guest, who became one of the first Liberal MPs to crusade for smaller government and effective parliamentary committees. And in Caulfield, the preselection went to Charles Francis, a 52-year-old barrister whose wife, Babette, was a prominent anti-feminist and strident campaigner against the liberalisation of sexual mores.

These preselection reverses for Hamer had no impact on the voters. An ANOP poll conducted for the Labor Party in November 1975 found that 67 per cent of Melbourne voters were satisfied with the Hamer government, and a stellar 72 per cent were satisfied with their premier.

On the weekend of 11–12 October 1975, at the Liberal Party's federal council meeting, Fraser told Hamer that he was thinking of using the Senate to block the federal budget, so as to force Whitlam to an election. Hamer's instincts were strongly against it, on political and constitutional grounds, and he told Fraser so. But he also told him that he would be publicly loyal to whatever decision Fraser took as federal leader. Three days later, Fraser announced that the coalition senators would block supply. Publicly, Hamer stayed silent, despite his deep concerns; but privately, as the crisis wore on, both he and April separately wrote personal letters to Fraser urging him, in Dick's words, 'to review the position calmly'. In a long letter, he went on:

> I want you to be Prime Minister of Australia as soon as possible, but in our present national difficulties, I want you to take office with a full head of public confidence and support, and without the active resentment or mistrust of a substantial section of the Australian electorate.[2]

It was a prescient warning. Many concluded — although Fraser denies it — that fear of fuelling that resentment was the reason his government later failed to take on the unions, despite the massive wave of strikes and industrial action that plagued Australia in the late 1970s.

Fraser was not persuaded by Hamer's plea, but he invited all the state leaders of the Liberals and Queensland premier Sir Joh Bjelke-

Petersen to a summit in Melbourne on 2 November to co-ordinate their planning and to keep them onside. The next day, at Hamer's suggestion, Fraser offered his one compromise: he would instruct coalition senators to pass the budget if Whitlam pledged to go to an election, with half the Senate, by 30 June 1976. Predictably, Whitlam rejected the offer. A week later, he was dismissed by the governor-general, Sir John Kerr, Fraser became prime minister, and an election was called for 13 December 1975.

Hamer kept his feelings to himself. He was frequently on the hustings for Fraser during the campaign. In Australia's greatest political crisis of his lifetime, he buried his own opposition to Fraser's strategy, and played the role of a good team player. But the country was left bitterly divided, and what Fraser had done went against all his instincts. Hamer's son-in-law John Brenan recalled going with him one night during the campaign to a Musica Viva concert; the audience was mostly middle-class Jewish music-lovers, with whom Hamer was among friends. But that night, backs turned as he approached; one man spat in his direction. 'Dick was very upset and angry,' Brenan said. 'As we sat down, he was muttering against Fraser: "The man has no idea what damage he's done." '

But Musica Viva's clientele was not typical of Australia. The election outcome was a landslide: Fraser swept to victory in the most one-sided federal result since 1931. The coalition won 91 of the 127 seats in the House, and 55.7 per cent of the vote after preferences. The swing against Whitlam and his deposed government was 7.4 per cent; in net terms, one in seven Labor voters crossed to the coalition, the biggest collapse in any party's support at any federal election since the war. Victoria mirrored the national result: the coalition won 24 of the state's 34 seats, taking back all the gains that Labor had made since 1969, including David Hamer's seat of Isaacs. With a clear Senate majority, no serious dissent or division within his party, and strong support from the media, Fraser had a blank cheque to reform Australia as he saw fit.

The 1976 state election was due in May, but Hamer decided to follow up Fraser's landslide victory quickly by holding it in March.

The election was virtually a non-event. A survey of four marginal electorates at the end of January by the Liberals' pollster, Quantum, found that 67 per cent of voters surveyed thought the Liberals were better equipped to govern Victoria; only 25 per cent preferred Labor. Hamer's own ratings were just as high as three years earlier, and well above Holding's on almost every count. He was seen as intelligent, stable, competent, strong, and trustworthy, so the Liberals seized on this for their slogan: 'Stay in good hands.' Nothing happened in the campaign to disturb those images. In fact, it seemed as though nothing happened at all. Neither side wanted to mention the long union ban that was blocking construction of the Newport power station. Both rolled out, more or less, the usual promises.

Three stood out. Hamer promised to build the vast Thomson Dam, a trillion-litre lake in the Gippsland hills that would more than double Melbourne's water storages; it was duly built, but too late to be any help in the next drought. He promised a range of schemes to help first-home buyers get into the market, including $5,000 low-interest loans for low-income families, modest interest-rate subsidies in the initial years for lower-middle-income buyers, and an injection of state funds into co-operative housing societies. And his third big pledge — to replace separate rail, bus, and tram tickets with a single ticket, issued by a unified public-transport authority that would replace the separate rail and tramways boards — proved so futuristic, and threatened so many bureaucratic and union empires, that it was only partially implemented in Hamer's time, leaving it to the Cain government to create the system we have now.

The real spice in the campaign came from the DLP's leader, Jim Brosnan. He claimed that, before the 1973 election, Hamer had promised the DLP he would introduce a touch of proportional representation in the Upper House, so that any party gaining 10 per cent of the vote would get at least three seats in the council. Brosnan said the promise had been made in exchange for DLP preferences, but that, after the election, Hamer had welshed on the deal. Hamer denied this, pointing to his 1973 policy speech, in which he pledged simply that the Liberals would consider the idea. They had done so, he said, and had rejected it. The evidence was inconclusive; but it would not be the only time that Hamer made statements which meant one thing to a hopeful listener, but were full of lawyer's caveats that qualified the apparent commitment. Brosnan attacked Hamer publicly as weak, ridiculing his 'marshmallow leadership', and the DLP refused to stand in marginal Melbourne seats, where its votes traditionally propped up the Liberals. In country seats, it directed preferences to the National Party.

In its final pre-election editorial, *The Age* described Victorians' attitude to state politics as one of 'vast apathy … this newspaper has received fewer letters on the election for the whole of this [six-week] campaign than we received for an average day during the last federal election'. Although caustic about the government's 'clutch of conservatives … boring us witless with catchcries that belong to another age', the paper endorsed the Liberals for another term:

> The Liberals have one force that Labor cannot match, and that is the singular character of Mr Hamer himself. He is well-liked and deserves to be. He is rare in politics: a transparently decent man. There is no ugly grasping at power, no obvious enjoyment of power and its trappings, no spite; there is real concern for the quality of life in this state. In a sense, Mr Hamer represents the progressive arm of the Liberal Party … But some other qualities which stem from his character — his unobtrusive leadership, his search for consensus, his denial of the Bolte style of political pugilism — perhaps also explain some of the weaknesses of his government. It has not moved fast enough; it has not moved decisively enough. Sometimes it has just not moved.
>
> We think he must make things happen this time. We think he should shake the government out of its torpor. We think he should reshape his Cabinet with men more attuned to his own beliefs. To do anything else would, we think, be a fearful misreading of a mandate. It would also be a fearful waste of Mr Hamer's personal talents.[3]

The electorate gave Hamer an even bigger victory than the Liberals had expected. The party's vote climbed to 45.9 per cent — the highest vote that the Liberals had received at any federal or state election in Victoria since the Great Depression. Bolte's best result had been 39.6 per cent in 1964. The DLP vote collapsed from 13.3 per cent in 1970 to 2.6 per cent in 1976, but most of its former voters had crossed to the Liberals; Labor's vote rose just 1 per cent in that time. On the federal parliamentary library's figures, the Liberals and Nationals (taken together) won 55.8 per cent of the vote after preferences; Labor, 44.2 per cent. In the *Financial Review*, Robert Murray commented that the result 'is confirmation that a non-charismatic, non-showy, non-firm politician ... can be a huge success, provided he is seen as competent, constructive and decent ... There is no doubt that most Victorians approve of Mr Hamer's quiet style of the slightly better-educated gentleman next door.'

The expanded houses, the favourable redistribution, and the strong vote saw the Liberals win a record 52 seats in the assembly, and 26 in the council. In two elections under Hamer, the party room had swollen from 61 members to 78. Of those, 22 were new MPs. A new force had entered the party room.

The 1976 election was the high point of Hamer's political success. It would also prove to be the start of his decline.

In 1955, when Bolte romped into power with dozens of new MPs, he was quick to assert control, lay down the rules, and set up party committees to keep them busy. That was not Hamer's style. Bolte also saw to it that MPs had no taxpayer-funded offices in their electorates, and that their Parliament House offices were shared with other MPs, so that any conversations could be overheard. Hamer had broken with that, paying for MPs to set up their own electorate offices. He also approved the building of what he hoped would be temporary offices at the back of Parliament House, in a building that became known by MPs as 'the chicken coop'.

Glyn Jenkins, then one of the party whips, notes another important point. The vast bulk of the class of 1955 were returned servicemen, used to obeying orders. In 1976, only two of the 22 new Liberal MPs were old enough to have served in the war. Most either ran their own businesses or were self-employed professionals; they were used to giving orders, not taking them. Their average age was just 40. All but one were male. Most of them were loyal Liberals who put the party first, but a few were highly ambitious men who wanted a ministry, and wanted it soon. 'They thought they were the answer to Victoria's problems,' Rob Knowles recalls, naming medico-businessman Ralph Howard and economist Kevin Foley as prime examples. They were not prepared to serve their time loyally and wait.

The first sign of the Young Turks' intentions occurred immediately after the election. One new MP — no one seems to remember who — convened a barbecue for the newcomers on the Mornington Peninsula to propose that they vote as a bloc to try to get one of their own into cabinet. As one MP recalls, Charles Francis was to be the candidate. The plan fell apart when they realised that, under the exhaustive-ballot system, which eliminated candidates one at a time, they might end up with the other 56 MPs voting as a bloc to keep him out. Instead, the core of the group decided to throw their weight behind candidates from the right to push the party in that direction.

In the leadership ballot, Pat Dickie defeated Alan Hunt in the contest to replace Murray Byrne as government leader in the council. Upper House backbencher Digby Crozier, a Casterton grazier, vaulted over more senior candidates to take Byrne's place in cabinet. The acerbically witty Robert Maclellan was another elected early, while senior ministers were still sweating on their places.

Hamer had a list of three backbenchers he wanted in the ministry: Geoff Hayes, who had chaired an inquiry that produced an impressive report on residential land shortages; Walter Jona, one of Hamer's closest friends in politics; and Haddon Storey, who had stayed in the Upper House, and whom Hamer had earmarked to be the next attorney-general. When the party room had elected its 15 ministers, all the vacancies had been filled, and all ministers had been re-elected, but none on Hamer's list had won a place. Uncharacteristically, he then decided to impose his will on the party room; in the light of the party's record victory, he would increase the size of cabinet to 18, and appoint three ministers rather than the two he was previously allowed. The real beneficiary was Storey, since the Constitution limited the Upper House to five ministers, and Hamer decided to raise it to six. 'I was as surprised as anyone when he made these announcements,' Storey recalls. 'Typically, he had never discussed any of this with me, nor had he ever told me he wanted me as attorney-general. But I can only assume he wanted me as A-G, and had worked out this was the only way to achieve this outcome.' He became widely seen as one of Hamer's best appointments.

Some of the newcomers found themselves thrown in the deep end. Hamer was worried that if Alan Hunt stayed in the planning portfolio and saw through the Western Port conservation plan, Doug Jennings and his supporters could deny him preselection in 1979. At Hunt's suggestion, he gave planning instead to Geoff Hayes, and threw him housing as well. Digby Crozier found himself in Byrne's portfolio of state development. Lindsay Thompson was left in education for his fourth consecutive three-year term, but Alan Scanlan was demoted from the health portfolio to take a new ministry of special education, with Vasey Houghton promoted to take his place. Joe Rafferty, already 65, was given the demanding job of transport. Some felt that he and energy minister Jim Balfour, 61, should move to the backbench to make room for fresh blood; but as MPs' superannuation entitlements were based on their final salary, there was a powerful disincentive to engage in voluntary demotion.

Hamer's biggest problem was how to deal with the 22 new MPs. Or, rather, he had three problems: getting to know his new MPs and channel their energies; dealing with Jeff Kennett; and dealing with Doug Jennings and Charles Francis.

MPs interviewed for this book agreed that Hamer was always accessible, so long as you booked an appointment with him. Ministers could always ring him and get straight through. But there were few informal opportunities for MPs to chat to him as they had with Bolte. Charles Hider recalls that, unlike Bolte and Rylah, Hamer and Thompson would rarely be at the bar having a beer after parliament ended. Nor did Hamer frequent the billiards room, where Bolte spent much of his time. In particular, there were few opportunities for new MPs to get to know their leader, and Hamer's relations with many of them remained distant. Geoff Coleman, a stock and estate agent who won the marginal south-eastern suburban seat of Syndal, says that when they met in the corridor, Hamer always called him Charles, apparently unaware that that was a first name he did not use. Rob Knowles, later health minister in the Kennett government, says he had only about three conversations with his leader in his first three years in parliament. James Guest and Graeme Weideman urged Hamer to schedule regular lunches with the new backbenchers; Guest offered to organise them himself, but Hamer insisted he would take care of it. 'We did it just the once,' Weideman recalls. 'I got the impression from that that he wasn't that good one on one. He was reserved and hard to read. He left himself vulnerable by getting out of touch with the backbench.' David Hamer recalled in his memoirs that Malcolm Fraser, by contrast, made a practice of inviting small groups of backbenchers to dinner whenever parliament was sitting.

Geoff Coleman says a schism developed between the class of '76 and the older MPs, in part because so many of the newcomers found themselves housed together in the chicken coop:

> There were virtually no private conversations. Simply by the nature of things, it led to the formation of a group. There was Francis, Jennings, Kennett, [George] Cox, [Lou] Lieberman, Weideman, Coleman, [Neville] Hudson, [Peter] Macarthur, [Phil] Gude, [Don] Mackinnon, [Tom] Reynolds, (Rob) Knowles. The building had a very big common room, right at the back of it. Out the back was an oak tree called the Federation Oak, because it was planted at the time of Federation. There were some really raucous barbecues out there. Hamer could have come, but that wasn't his style.[4]

In some ways, the Liberals in the chicken coop became closer to their Labor neighbours than they did to their Liberal colleagues housed inside the building. We will hear more of that.

Jeff Kennett has made such an impact on Victorian politics that it is difficult now to understand how others saw him in 1976. He was just 28 years old. Colleagues remember him as full of energy and ideas, but difficult, pushy, abrasive, and habitually abusive towards others. In interviews for this book, few had good words to say for him at that early stage of his career. 'Many in the party regarded Kennett as just a bloody nuisance,' one recalled. Richard Alston, who became state party president in 1979, summed up nicely the pros and cons of the young Kennett:

> The thing I noticed about Jeff was that he was hyperactive, and Dick was surrounded by old men. Jeff was a breath of fresh air. He was a phenomenon. He would bounce into the room and take over. He'd go out of his way to offend people, and Dick seemed to be quite happy with all that.[5]

The young Kennett was never willing to accept a role as a junior member of the chorus, doing what he was told. He was always stepping out of line. Colleagues remember him as a loudmouth, one of the most disruptive members in an increasingly disruptive party room. From early on, Kennett joined Ralph Howard, Kevin Foley, James Guest, and several others to form a ginger group of pro-market reformers who constantly bombarded the government with policy ideas. Hamer's staff recall Kennett positioning himself each morning on the ground floor of the Premier's Department by the stairs, which gave him a minute or so to walk upstairs and along the corridor with Hamer to the premier's office, and pass on his latest idea about what the government should do. At the 1979 election he solicited funds from business to run his own Liberal Party advertising campaign, and gave up the idea only when the state executive ordered him to desist. While Kennett became something of a favourite of Hamer's, politically they were far apart, as the young MLA made clear in a barely veiled criticism of his leader in parliament in March 1978:

> I live with the fear … that we are slowly but surely becoming a socialist state. That is happening not because of the efforts of our political opponents, regardless of their political colour, but because

> of the disinclination of anti-socialists to defend the principles in which they believe. Governments that believe in free enterprise and freedom of choice for individuals have allowed those principles to be eroded over the years at the expense of the long-term interests of the people of this country ... If we do not wish to drift into a socialist state, those who are of the anti-socialist view must stick much more closely to their beliefs ... Already the average Australian working man supports a wife, two children, and three bureaucrats.[6]

Kennett was lucky that he entered politics when Hamer ruled. Had he come in a decade earlier, Bolte and Rylah would have teamed up in the party room to beat the brash young MP into submission, or, if that failed, would have treated him with such scorn that he became a political leper. But Hamer tolerated Kennett's maverick behaviour and opinions, condoning what others saw as continual breaches of discipline and disloyalty to colleagues.

The young Kennett gleefully made enemies among his fellow Liberals, but he did Hamer little damage in public. As we will see, it was a very different story with Jennings and Francis.

The subtle changes in the Liberal Party created by the class of '76 were little noticed by journalists or the public. An exception was an analysis by *The Herald* state political reporter Bruce Baskett on 2 August 1976. Doug Jennings, Baskett noted presciently, was not alone among the new MPs in his opposition to planning, or in his wider ideology:

> The ideas of non-interference, anti-planning and laissez-faire for a person's home and property are shared by others in the Parliamentary Liberal Party. It is not a junta, but it could develop into a grouping which in time would be a base of discontent within the over-large parliamentary section of the party.
>
> There are some very ambitious new men in State Parliament this time who believe they can and will be ministers, and a few who think they are more than capable of moving to the very top very quickly.

Several years earlier, Hamer told an interviewer he thought that the best years to be engaged in public life were between the ages of 45 and 60. He had seen Bolte's energy and self-discipline flag in his sixties, Rylah's health crack under the strain, and several ministerial colleagues overstay their time. On 29 July 1976, Dick himself turned 60. His original plan had been to serve just six years as premier, and then hand over. But, like Frodo in *The Lord of the Rings*, he would find the ring of power difficult to give up.

Part IV

The Hamer Years: 2

CHAPTER EIGHTEEN

Newport

In 1967, the State Electricity Commission decided to build a state-of-the-art 1,000-megawatt gas-fired power station at Newport. It had no reason to expect its decision to attract any controversy, as there had been power stations on the banks of the lower Yarra for almost 50 years. The heart of the SEC's generation system was in the Latrobe Valley, where a set of power stations pumped out electricity 24 hours a day. They burnt Victoria's moist brown coal, which is two-thirds water, and they worked most efficiently when they were kept going around the clock, as 'base load' stations. To meet the fluctuating 'peak load' demand, the SEC ran small hydro-electric power stations in Victoria's mountains, shared the electricity generated by the Snowy Mountains scheme, and ran some small old power stations in Melbourne fuelled by oil and gas — one of them in the heart of the city, in Spencer Street opposite *The Age*. Now it proposed to add a station to cater for the daily plateau created by the 'intermediate load', the extra demand created from the time consumers get up in the morning to the time the evening meal is cleared away at night. Esso-BHP's discoveries in Bass Strait in the early 1960s indicated that Victoria had plenty of natural gas, a relatively clean fuel compared to coal or oil. The station would be built with a chimney roughly 100 metres high to pump its waste gases into the atmosphere, so they would add little to pollution at ground level. In 1971, the design was complete. The plan was approved by cabinet, and legislation to build it sailed through parliament with the support of all parties.

But in 1972, as political observer Jean Holmes noted, public opinion had come alive in Victoria: 'something [was] stirring out there in Muggsville' — and the SEC's plans for Newport ran straight into it. Melbourne had discovered pollution, and had become concerned about it. These were the early, evangelical days of the environment movement. As we have seen, the World Health Organisation, which set the global standards for air quality, erred on the side of stringency, and cities like Melbourne discovered they had world-class smog. Most of that was due to unregulated car exhausts, but industry contributed. The government shared the public concern about pollution; it had set up the Environment Protection Authority as a watchdog to tackle it. The EPA regime required major polluters to obtain a licence, which allowed the authority to spell out the standards that Newport would have to meet. But to some — including senior figures at the EPA — this was not enough. If we are concerned about air pollution, they said, why add to it by building a power station in central Melbourne that would pump out 785 kilograms an hour of oxides of nitrogen, a principal ingredient of photochemical smog? And why are we proposing to use relatively scarce natural gas to generate electricity, when we have endless supplies of brown coal? In 1972, some Labor MPs and union leaders joined Williamstown residents and the environment movement to criticise the plan. Then, in November, the Builders Labourers Federation leader, Norm Gallagher, imposed a black ban on building Newport.

Bolte would have taken this as a declaration of war, and looked immediately for ways to strike back. Hamer put his faith in clarifying the issues, to persuade the station's opponents to back down. His government announced that the EPA would hold a public inquiry into the environmental impact of Newport's emissions on air and water quality. The inquiry took up much of 1973, during which community opposition spread. Ultimately, EPA director Alan Gilpin, who was no government stooge, concluded that the risks did not warrant blocking the project. Rather, he proposed that the chimney's height be doubled, and that it be required to shut down whenever pollution in Melbourne got to danger levels. The SEC accepted those conditions. Gallagher lifted the BLF's ban. It seemed like the skirmishing was over, and that work would soon begin.

In fact, it would take almost four years before the first work began on the Newport site. It would be seven years before it supplied any electricity to the grid. The long delay was one of the factors that changed public perceptions of Dick Hamer, especially in business circles. People came to see him as too soft, too trusting, a ditherer, forever opting for talks when action was required. Newport became a running sore that weakened his authority in the Liberal Party, and in the wider community. It is worth understanding how this happened.

When the BLF lifted its ban in 1973, five unions from the Socialist Left stepped in to impose their own. The public face of their ban was John Halfpenny, state secretary of the Amalgamated Metal Workers' Union. Halfpenny was an articulate communist who thrived on debate, so he became the union leader that conservative politicians blamed for the ban. But it was not his work. The AMWU was primarily a manufacturing union, even though it seemed to have members in every workplace. Halfpenny was its spokesman, but in this union the communists were the moderates — Halfpenny was a classical-music buff, passionate about cooking — while the real power lay with the Socialist Left (or SL) whose leaders came from the old hard-left Victorian ALP of the 1960s. The driving forces behind the ban were men such as Percy Johnson of the AMWU, Charlie Faure of the Electrical Trades Union, Sammy Williams of the Federated Engine Drivers and Firemen's Association, and George Crawford of the Plumbers and Gasfitters Union, who was ALP state president, and later a Labor MP. Part of their motivation was simply to expand their power by creating an issue they could use to regain their lost dominance in the union movement and the ALP. Some also feared that the SEC would use Newport to counter the clout of the militant shop stewards in the Latrobe Valley power stations, who had become a law unto themselves, able to call strikes that shut down the state's power supplies. While Newport was intended to operate 14 hours a day, it could be used 24 hours a day in a crisis — such as that caused by a strike in the Latrobe Valley.

The stalemate continued into 1974, fuelled by the fact that the EPA's own report appeared divided over whether or not Newport should be built. Much of the detail of the report appeared at odds with the decision to give it a green light, which reflected divisions within the EPA on the issue. Environmentalists appealed against the ruling, first to the EPA itself, and then to a special appeals board. But both appeals were rejected, with appeals board chairman Philip Opas, QC, declaring flatly that Newport 'represents no actual or potential threat to health'. One might note that the union movement took no part in any of these hearings; the five unions who had imposed the ban simply ignored them, and instead leant on other unions to join them.

Faced with either confrontation or negotiations, Hamer chose to negotiate. He was no fan of the union movement, but neither was he keen to undermine it. He and his ministers had a high regard for Ken Stone, the secretary of the Trades Hall Council, who, like former prime minister John Curtin, was a reformed alcoholic, respected across the board as an honest moderate. Stone was confident that the SL unions would eventually back down if the dispute was handled the right way, and put his own prestige on the line to try to get the Newport ban revoked. Hamer also had an unofficial industrial-relations advisor he held in high regard. Bob Hawke's son Stephen went to Melbourne Grammar with Dick's son Alastair, and sometimes on Saturday mornings the premier and the ACTU president would discuss issues privately while watching their sons play cricket. (One Saturday, Hamer recalled, they were the only two parents there.) Hamer knew he would have to make concessions to get the SL to back down; but, even as he negotiated with the unions, events were moving against him. Labor, seeing an opportunity to turn up the heat on the government, swapped sides to oppose building the station in Melbourne. The building unions also swapped sides, and in November 1974 the Trades Hall Council imposed a full union ban on the project. Solidarity had outmanoeuvred sense.

What could Hamer do? There were no easy choices. The most promising weapon in the statute books was the Essential Services Act, which gave the government power to declare a state of emergency if supply of an essential service were threatened, and empowered the minister to give directions that had to be obeyed, under threat of fines or jail. But in 25 years on the statute books, that act had never been used in any dispute, even by Bolte. Ministers feared that to do so would risk turning union leaders into martyrs, and give the militants an issue they could use to unite the whole labour movement behind them. At the 1988 conference of the H.R. Nicholls Society, David Russell, QC, later federal president of the National Party, reviewed the history of the act and its interstate counterparts, and concluded that because of the political difficulty in implementing it:

> Essential services legislation has not provided, and is unlikely in the future to provide, any practically useful response to misuse of trade union power in essential service industries, and is inferior to a common law regime or a statutory formulation embodying common law principles.[1]

In fact, the act was used successfully in 1981, soon after Hamer stepped down, when Bill Borthwick, backed by Lindsay Thompson, used it to end a milk carriers' strike called by the Transport Workers' Union. But politically, milk was in a class of its own. In Newport's case, there was also doubt as to whether an act designed to force people to operate a power station could be used to make them construct one. David Russell's paper suggested that sections 45D and 45E of the Trade Practices Act could be used to recover damages against unions — as has happened since. The government and the SEC considered taking civil action, but SEC assistant general manager Jack Johnson related later that their lawyers warned that 'the courts would make every effort to avoid ruling in the matter — because of the political overtones'. Even if the SEC won, he said, 'counsel believed that the damages could be negligible', and the unions could find a way around court orders. Few of those who kept urging Hamer to get tough with the unions were any help in telling him how.

Moreover, the anti-Newport coalition was divided over what,

if anything, it would accept as an alternative. The unions favoured a gas-fired station in some other part of the state. But the SEC demonstrated time and again that it had looked at all the other sites, and rejected them on both economic and environmental grounds. The Conservation Council of Victoria, the umbrella group of the environment movement, argued against using natural gas, a premium fuel, to generate electricity when Victoria had so much brown coal. But when the EPA had to set the rules for Loy Yang A, a brown-coal-fired station in the Latrobe Valley, the CCV opposed that, too, because it would add to air pollution in the valley. Hamer looked hard at building a pump storage hydro station in the hills of Trawool, south of Seymour, as part of a possible peace deal, but had to conclude that it could never operate on the scale of Newport. Victoria had wandered into an impasse that seemed to have no way out.

The government's initial response to the Trades Hall ban was to act stern, without any hint of its next move. Cabinet reaffirmed its determination that it would build Newport, and ruled out any alternative. Halfpenny responded: 'If the government wants the power station completed, Mr Hamer and his cabinet colleagues will have to don overalls and do the job themselves.' The minister for fuel and power, Jim Balfour, made a ministerial statement to parliament, declaring that Newport was two years behind schedule, and that, unless it was built, Victoria faced the risk of power shortages. The SEC took out full-page ads in the papers to warn Victorians: 'You need Newport.' But Hamer soon decided that the issue could not be solved by confrontation. He returned to the negotiating table with the SEC and a panel from the Trades Hall executive, and the issue disappeared from public view. In June 1975, Bruce Baskett, state political correspondent for *The Herald*, reported that the premier 'always responds "No comment" when the matter is raised at press conferences'. Similarly, the government refused to background journalists on the issue: Newport disappeared into a cone of silence.

Shreds of information leaked out occasionally: to reassure unions that Newport would not be used as an alternative to the brown-coal stations, Hamer offered to cut its natural gas allocation by 25 per cent, to end the competitive price war between the SEC and the Gas and Fuel Corporation, and build a pump storage station. The unions agreed that natural gas should be the fuel. But as time ticked on, the SEC had to make plans to fill the looming demand gap by building two relatively expensive, small gas-fired plants at Jeeralang in the Latrobe Valley. Halfpenny grew concerned at the implications of potential power shortages for the Victorian economy; he quietly pressed for an end to the ban. He also warned his colleagues that if they left the government no way out, and made it a fight to the end, the government, as the stronger force, would inevitably win, setting the union movement back for decades. Just before the 1976 election, he informed Hamer that the unions had agreed on a position, but would not reveal it until after the election. The entire campaign passed with virtually no mention of Newport by either side.

On 5 April, the Trades Hall executive declared its support for what became known as the 'Halfpenny-Hamer deal'. It would halve the size of the power station to a single unit of 500 megawatts, greatly reducing its role in the system, and would rule out any more power stations in Melbourne. But rather than claim a moral victory, Halfpenny's allies decided to block the compromise deal. Their opposition forced the Trades Hall to defer a final vote for a month. The old left within the AMWU took on their state secretary, and 'rolled' him; his own union decided to reject the plan. In one of those acts of bastardry that give union politics its inimitable flavour, Halfpenny, as the union's spokesman, was then ordered to present its argument to the council meeting, calling for the defeat of the plan he himself had written. On 6 May, the council rejected its executive's recommendation and reaffirmed the ban.

Once again, the government was trapped, with no way out. Pat Dickie, during a stint as acting premier, brought back the Bolte–Rylah style, calling on unionists to rise up and 'throw out the miserable gang of traitors at the Trades Hall'. Hamer, on the contrary, always assumed that his opponents were men of good will, open to reason. 'People are far too quick to question the motives of others,' he once told an interviewer. 'As far as I am concerned, a person is believable until proven otherwise. I think people in politics are motivated by a desire to serve, to do something constructive.' But now he was dealing with an exception to that rule, and he was neither armed for nor skilled in such combat. The government simply stepped up its rhetoric about the risk of future electricity shortages, and the damage they would do to the state. Public opinion, at first evenly divided, now started to swing the government's way as this argument sank in. Bolte chimed in with implicit criticism, telling a Melbourne City Council dinner that Hamer had been more patient than he would have been. A consensus grew that, whatever the merits of the original decision, Victoria needed a power station, and Newport had to be it.

Another deadlock followed, there were more negotiations, and another attempt by Stone to get the council to back down. It failed again. On the evening of 11 November 1976, the full Trades Hall Council rejected its executive's plan by just four votes out of 400 or so. The next morning, cabinet convened at eight o'clock to draw up its battle plan. It decided to wage war on two fronts. First, it would introduce new legislation, the Vital State Projects Act, that would make it illegal for a person or organisation to 'hinder or obstruct anything done or intended to be done in connection with a vital state project'. The new laws essentially took the still-unused powers of the Essential Services Act and applied them to bans on the building of vital infrastructure, rather than the operation of it. Second, the government itself went on strike in retaliation, announcing a list of hundreds of construction projects for which no new tenders would be called until the Newport dispute was over. If its 'capital strike' proceeded, it would gradually lead to huge job losses in construction, electrical, and plumbing work — and the workers would be likely to blame their union bosses. On 23 November, the government suspended work on 299 contracts for projects worth $417 million, on schools, roads, hospitals, water supply, railways — and, especially, electricity. It was controversial, but Victorians were fed up with the delay, and ready to back the government.

Labor became worried. Opposition leader Clyde Holding and state ALP president Peter Redlich (partners in the law firm of Holding Redlich) banged union heads together to get agreement to another circuit-breaker. A panel of four members would be set up to examine all the issues and report to both the government and the Trades Hall Council. It was chaired by the former vice-chancellor of Monash University, Sir Louis Matheson, a former engineering professor, and included two widely respected state officials, EPA chairman Jack Fraser and Gas and Fuel chairman Neil Smith, and Trades Hall Council president Jack ('Paddy') Ellis, from the left. Both sides agreed to be bound by the panel's conclusions. The Vital State Projects Bill was passed by parliament, but not proclaimed into law pending the inquiry.

But the inquiry's first report, in March 1977, failed to reach a conclusion: it found that even a half-strength Newport would add frequently to Melbourne's air-pollution problems, but that no alternative would be a good substitute. 'If a better site than Newport was available at reasonable cost,' it mused, 'then that site should be chosen. The problem is to determine what is a better site, and what is a reasonable cost.' The panel said these were value judgements it could not make. This was widely seen as a cop-out. Hamer retorted that those were the judgements the panel was set up to make, and sent it back to work. A month later, it produced a second report, finding by a 3–1 majority (Ellis dissenting) that there was no acceptable alternative at reasonable cost — so Newport it had to be.

Once again, the Trades Hall executive recommended that the union ban be lifted. Once again, the full council refused. The news of its rejection of the deal reached parliament late on the final night of the autumn session, on Thursday 5 May, as Hamer was about to fly out to lead a Victorian business mission to the Middle East and Europe. Hamer was defiant, telling parliament: 'We have no option now as a government but to take all necessary steps to ensure that the power station is built.' But the next morning he flew off on his business mission, leaving Lindsay Thompson in charge to decide, along with cabinet, what those next steps should be.

The first two steps were predictable. Cabinet quickly decided to proclaim the Vital State Projects Act, and then recalled parliament to pass a motion declaring Newport a vital state project. For the unions, this greatly raised the risks of action. While it would be politically risky for the government to prosecute the unions and their leaders, the potential fines of $50,000 and jail terms were enough to induce a new caution among union militants. The question now was how to get Newport built. Thompson's autobiography provided this answer:

> On the Saturday after the special session of Parliament, while walking home from the football in the rain, I came to the conclusion that the only way to build Newport was to use the labour of people who were prepared to work voluntarily, and preferably enthusiastically, on the project … [five days later] senior officers of the SEC informed me that to make a fresh start on construction work, 21 men would be needed … I requested that the Minister for Public Works, Robert Dunstan, be requested to attend the meeting … I told him that it would be necessary to recruit our own labour force and that we would advertise in the following day's paper for 21 tradesmen in the defined categories … Those interested were asked to apply in person to the personnel branch of the Public Works Department at 8.30 a.m. on the Friday morning … At 9 a.m. I was informed that 50 men had applied, and by midday the number had grown to well over 100 … On Monday 23 May 1977, work recommenced at Newport.[2]

They say success has many fathers, while failure is an orphan. In interviews for this book, several other ministers and MPs claimed it was their idea to recruit the workers by just putting an ad in the paper. But whoever deserves the credit, it worked. The union response was surprisingly muted, possibly because of fear of the Vital State Projects Act; possibly because most union leaders also wanted a way out of the mess. At first, the site was picketed by demonstrators who made sporadic attempts to stop the busloads of workers getting in and out; but police reported that most were student radicals and resident activists, not unionists. Indeed, according to Thompson, after a while union leaders sought access to the site to sign up workers, with little success. By the end of 1977, there were 300 men working on the site, and not a single minute had been lost in industrial disputes. By 1979, more than 1,000 men were working there, and the tower of the smokestack had become a new Melbourne landmark. On 7 August 1980, Newport was complete and connected to the grid.

Four-and-a-half years of failure had ended with success, but only partial success. The SEC was unhappy that it ended up with only half the power station it had planned; in 1987, Jack Johnson, who had charge of the project, said the extra costs of running the smaller gas-fired plant would add $600 million to Victorians' electricity bills over the life of the project. This was a significant cost, which contributed to the hefty price rises Victorian electricity consumers endured in the 1980s.

Moreover, since the unions could not hit back against Newport, they hit back elsewhere. At the site of the Arts Centre, an already chronically bad industrial-relations environment got even worse: the architect, Sir Roy Grounds, complained to Howson that the building unions were deliberately slowing construction in retaliation for their failure to stop Newport. In the Latrobe Valley, shop stewards brought Victoria to its knees, calling a strike that shut down the baseload power stations for ten days, supposedly over a pay claim that was completely outside the official wage guidelines. Only when 250,000 factory workers had been stood down because the power was off did the shop stewards reluctantly allow their men to return to work. The brown-coal stations had often shut down unexpectedly — miraculous improvements in their operational availability were recorded once they were privatised by the Kennett government — but the early years of the Yallourn W plant set new records for breakdowns. In the four years between 1976 and 1980, the first two units of the plant were out of order for 11 months and nine months respectively, on top of the time lost in scheduled maintenance and union strike action. And construction work slowed to a dawdle on the second two units; by 1981, they were two years behind schedule, and the new Loy Yang project was already six months behind schedule.

These were bad years for industrial relations in Australia — the worst period of the second half of the century. But they were particularly bad in Victoria, and worst of all in its public sector. This was not a problem that Hamer and his government wanted to face up to. It may be a mere coincidence that Thompson was in the chair when the government took the action that would end the Newport dispute at last. But many Liberals did not see it that way: Thompson's stocks rose, and many hailed him as a true leader who had acted where Hamer had merely dithered. It may also have been a mere coincidence that it was only after Thompson became premier that the federal and state governments agreed to set up a royal commission into the BLF, which ended up with Gallagher being sent to jail for corruption, ending his ability to hold the Victorian government and taxpayers to ransom. And there was something in the *Zeitgeist* that was not unique to Australia. This was the period when Arthur Scargill and his coal-mining union caused chaos in the UK, and strike activity reached epidemic levels in France, Italy, and other Western countries. But neither Hamer nor Fraser had an answer to it. The breakdown of wage indexation (which Hamer had supported, but Fraser opposed) ushered in a period of reckless wage rises that were the prime cause of the 1982–83 recession. It was only when the Hawke government took office that its accord with the ACTU — essentially, offering the union movement a place at the policy table in return for wage moderation — and the jailing of Gallagher gave Australia relative industrial peace.

But the union movement never regained the public trust it sacrificed in those years of bullying and mayhem. In the decades since, as opinion polls and declining membership have shown, unions have lost massive public support. They have paid a heavy price for having indulged the tough guys in the 1970s.

CHAPTER NINETEEN

The land deals

The scandal that most damaged the Hamer government was self-inflicted. In 1973, when Tom Uren proposed setting up a government land commission to compete with the private sector and bring down land prices, Pat Dickie as Victoria's minister for housing decided to head him off at the pass. Hamer had banned the Housing Commission from building high rises, so Dickie spent its money instead to amass a large stockpile of urban-fringe land. His aim was to make Uren finance the Housing Commission's land developments, rather than set up a rival land-development agency. The prime reason for the land deals was that Dickie saw himself in a turf war, and wanted to win it.

There was no shortage of willing sellers — particularly, sellers of land that had been locked up in one of Hamer's green wedges, or which had been given a 'corridor' zoning, implying eventual urban development, at some distant time. Such land was not highly valued, but could become very valuable for owners or developers with an option over it, if the Housing Commission could be persuaded to buy it — at urban prices.

Sunbury had developed along the west bank of Jacksons Creek, the main tributary of the Maribyrnong River. On the east bank were steep cliffs, and high up above them was a dairy farm, 'Goonawarra', owned for generations by the McMahon family. In 1970, Brighton property developer McGregor Aulsebrook (Greg) Kean and Adelaide financier Lensworth Finance negotiated an option to buy the farm, zoned rural at the time. But a year later, the Board of Works set out what land would be zoned for redevelopment, and what would stay rural. The McMahons' farm, and all the land on the east side of the creek, was zoned as a permanent green belt. That left Kean and Lensworth two choices: cut their losses and go elsewhere, or try to pull strings to get the zoning changed. They chose the latter.

At Pakenham, 1971 was a year of floods. One of the farms flooded was 'Pakenham Park', a farm owned by the Duncan family to the west of the town on Toomuc Creek. Undeterred, in late 1971 the Board of Works included most of the farm in its 'corridor' zone, implying urban development in the long term. A Sydney investor named Crichlow, whose silent partners included Toorak developer Harold Weeden, bought part of the farm, and acquired an option over the rest. Kean and Lensworth then bought the farm next door.

At the same time, Lensworth started amassing a huge parcel of rural land north of Craigieburn, to become known as Mount Ridley. It was all part of a new wave of activity by speculators in the wake of the board's zoning decision — which, at that time, earmarked the Mount Ridley site for eventual (but not imminent) urban development. But in 1974, when Alan Hunt trimmed the number of urban corridors from eight to five, the zoning for the Merri corridor changed to rural.

In Melton, the board's zonings envisaged the city growing to the east, towards Melbourne, with land to the west being a longer-term option. But in late 1972, property investors Peter Leake and Colin Cooke, trading as Nandina Investments, began amassing land west of the town for the Lewis Land Corporation and its financier, Cambridge Credit, trading as Welmac Pty Ltd. The Victorian manager of Lewis Land, Paul Day, later told an official inquiry that he had brought in Nandina as a consultant because Leake, its co-owner, was also Hunt's campaign manager. Companies associated with the Welmac bid donated $12,000 to Hunt's 1973 election campaign; there were allegations that this went into a secret 'slush fund' rather than to the Liberal Party. But no one produced any evidence that this gave Leake inside knowledge of the government's plans. To the contrary, it became abundantly clear that Dickie had kept Hunt in the dark about the commission's plans — and that when Hunt found about them, he hit the roof and did his utmost to try to stop them. But when his connection with Leake became public, it looked bad.

Pat Dickie was a punter, and he liked to back his judgement. In March 1973, he announced that the Housing Commission was looking to buy land in up to 12 towns around Melbourne, including Melton, Sunbury, and Pakenham. Wheels quickly began to turn. Potential sellers, or middlemen acting for them, approached the minister, the commission, and Bob Dillon, principal of Dandenong estate agents Dillon and Inkster, an otherwise obscure firm that was used by the commission in virtually every purchase it made. Property developer Brian Durston later told the County Court that he and Dillon, whom he called 'my partner', had 'engineered' the sale at Melton by introducing Welmac to the Housing Commission. He had been paid a 'consultant's fee', and Dillon an 'agent's commission'. At Sunbury, another developer, Graeme Hill, whose partners in land deals included opposition leader Clyde Holding, got in on the act, to make doors open for Lensworth. It was never clear how all these various threads came together, but the pattern they made was amazing.

The Pakenham deal came first. In January 1973, the official record shows that the Duncan family's agents approached Dillon and Inkster, the commission's agents, offering to sell the farm for $2,700 an acre. That was quite a price to ask. The previous year, the Duncans had sold the part closest to Pakenham to Crichlow for just $800 an acre. Three years earlier, the shire of Pakenham had valued the land at $364 an acre. Since then, the shire had confirmed a rural zoning over most of the farm, and farmland was not expensive. But in that time, Crichlow and his silent partners had taken out an option over the farm. As Labor MP David White argued in parliament, almost certainly it was they who instigated the deal. After Dickie's statement in March, the commission responded, and sent out a valuer. The valuation did not mention the floods, the rural zoning, or the option taken out over the property. It valued the land at urban prices — $2,800 an acre. A week later, the commission decided to buy it, without even waiting for the engineer's report, which arrived the following day, warning it that some of the land was flood-prone. Too late; the commission bought the land for the $2,700 an acre that the middlemen asked for — almost $2 million in all. Labor MP David Bornstein alone voiced dissent, criticising the commission as 'grossly irresponsible' for paying so much, and for buying land not zoned for development. The issue died.

In mid-1973, middlemen acting for Lensworth Finance — Graeme Hill, estate agents Moore Williams (Kean's firm), and the ubiquitous Bob Dillon — approached the commission to suggest that it buy the McMahons' dairy farm at Sunbury. On 17 July, Dickie urged the commission to do so, telling it not to worry about the fact that the land had been zoned for rural use. After the Pakenham purchase, Hamer had ordered all departments to consult with local planning authorities before making land purchases, but Dickie simply ignored the order. Hunt got wind of what the commission was up to. On 8 August, he wrote to Dickie to seek an assurance that the commission would consult the planning authorities before making any offers, and asked Dickie to phone him. Dickie ignored the letter. Instead, everyone pulled out all stops to close the deal. On 8 August, Lensworth appointed Dillon as its estate agent to sell the property for $3,400 an acre. On 9 August, the Valuer-General's Office gave the commission a valuation of $3,500 an acre, with the caveat that this assumed 'prior knowledge of residential rezoning'. Commission officials instructed the valuer to use that assumption, even though the planning authorities had recently confirmed its rural zoning. On 13 August, Dickie sought Hamer's approval for the purchase; Hamer, clearly giving it little thought, signed the approval without consulting Hunt. The next day, Dickie finally replied to Hunt, telling him that the premier had approved the purchase, and that the planning authorities now had to co-operate in bringing the land to market.

Lensworth exercised its option, and bought the land from the McMahons for $1,850 an acre. Two days later, it sold the land to the commission for $3,400 an acre. The middlemen reaped a profit of almost $1.5 million. They had bought land at rural prices, and sold it to taxpayers at urban prices. Lensworth kept 40 per cent of the profits, Kean and his partners took 40 per cent, and the other 20 per cent was split among their various helpers in getting the commission to buy the land — Hill, Moore Williams, and Dillon, who somehow was simultaneously acting for Lensworth, the vendor, and the Housing Commission, the buyer.

In September, while the Sunbury deal was going through, the Welmac consortium at Melton received an offer from Lensworth to buy their land for $2,550 an acre. It would have given them a quick million-dollar profit, since they had bought the land only months earlier at between $800 and $2,000 an acre. But Welmac declined the offer. It knew it was about to get a much better price from the Housing Commission.

Dickie was proud that he directed the commission specifically to buy the Welmac land. In 1977, he told parliament:

> I live seven miles away from that land … I walked the Melton area when Melton was a township of a couple of hundred people … I know the country closely and well … The (Welmac) parcel of land … would be perfect for our concept of development with a social mix … This area of land had views to the north-west that were quite magnificent. It looked out over the mounts of Bullengarook, Macedon and Blackwood, and the Great Dividing Range … As Minister for Housing, I made the decision to buy that land, and I stand by it.[1]

The first approach to Welmac came from Dillon and Durston in July 1973. But the commission wanted to compare a number of sites, and delayed a decision, until the minister stepped in. On 9 October, he upbraided the commissioners for looking for land south of Melton, and told them to buy the Welmac land instead. The next day, Bob Dillon, as the commission's agent, got together with Cooke and Leake, for Welmac, to compose a formal letter on behalf of the commission offering to buy the land for $3,750 an acre — land that Welmac had bought just a few months earlier for between $800 and

$2,000 an acre. At that stage, the commission had not examined the land, commissioned any planning or engineering studies, or sought a valuation. Yet two months later it bought the land, for $3,700 an acre — just a tad below the price that Dillon had made up with Welmac's agents.

Welmac's accountants calculated the profit on the deal as more than $2.5 million, even after $100,000 was paid to Dillon and Durston. It had bought the land for a bit over $2 million, and had sold it to taxpayers for $4.675 million.

By now, the commission had spent $10.6 million, of which $4.7 million was profit for the middlemen. None of the land it bought was zoned for urban development; indeed, at Sunbury and Pakenham, the authorities had made it clear that they opposed urban development in the foreseeable future. In each case, taxpayers had paid urban prices for rural land, in transactions that appeared to have been driven by a small group of middlemen who turned up in purchase after purchase. The checks and balances prescribed under the system had not worked. The Valuer-General's Office in each case valued the land at or above the amount asked by the vendors. Dickie and the commission simply ignored Hamer's directive that they consult with the planning authorities. And Hamer himself as treasurer approved each transaction without asking any questions. Something in those deals smelt to high heaven, and the smell was bound to leak out.

It did so in June 1974. Ben Hills and Philip Chubb of *The Age* investigative team broke the story of the Melton deal, highlighting the huge profit made by the Welmac consortium, and the dual role of Peter Leake as developer and as campaign manager for the minister for planning. The story rang alarm bells in some quarters. Police assistant commissioner Bill Crowley began a cursory inquiry; but, for reasons that are unclear, he abandoned it without even speaking to people quoted in the article. At Liberal headquarters, Noel Tennison was worried; he invited Hills to dinner, and offered to pass on to Hamer in private anything more that Hills could tell him. He did so, but nothing appeared to happen. Tennison then raised it with Hamer in person. 'I've looked into the matter,' Hamer told him sharply.

'Everything seems to be above board. Forget it!'

In May 1975, another investigative reporter with *The Age*, Lindsey Arkley, exposed the fact that the Pakenham land was flood-prone. But in public, the issue died. There was no more money for the commission to buy land; indeed, there was no money for it to develop the land it had already bought. The land boom of 1973 had turned into the bust of 1974–75. For developers, things got very tough — and some looked for scapegoats.

After *The Age* exposed the Melton deal, the middleman Brian Durston told the County Court later, he began to get anonymous phone calls threatening to kill him, and accusing him of being a 'f— squealer' who had 'spoilt millions of dollars worth of future business'. In February 1975, he was punched up outside the Dandenong Club by three men who told him that by talking about the deal, he had created a situation where there would be no more business. In June 1975, Durston said, he had met Weeden at the latter's Toorak home, where questions were asked that made him think Weeden might be the source of the continuing harassment. In September, he got a mate, Graeme Holden, to invite Weeden to discuss a business deal at the Hallam pub. When Weeden arrived, Holden lured him into his car, produced a gun, and threatened to kill him. Weeden was bound, gagged, blindfolded, and driven to Durston's farm at Na Nar Goon, where the kidnappers demanded $490,000 for his release, only to then realise that there was no way they could be paid the money without being detected. While his captors were sleeping, Weeden worked himself free and escaped. Durston was later jailed for three years. At the trial, Weeden denied having anything to do with the prior harassment of Durston. He told the court: 'From my experience, I don't think anyone makes enormous profits selling to the Housing Commission.'

Others disagreed. Where the police had failed to act, four new Labor MPs decided to investigate.

John Cain was 44 when he was elected to parliament in 1976. The son of the former premier and Labor legend, he was seen as a potential Labor leader even before he had a seat. Cain had studied law at Melbourne University, set up a suburban law practice in Preston, served a term as president of the Law Institute, and, in the 1960s, along with future federal ministers John Button and Michael Duffy, bank employees' union leader Barney Williams, and others, was one of the leaders of the branch-based 'Participants' group who fought doggedly to reform the authoritarian, union-based hard-left leadership of the ALP. By 1976, Cain was finally in parliament, and determined to make an impact. As an experienced solicitor with a keen eye for the shonky side of life, he began going back over the land deals, examining corporate and land-title records.

Three other new MPs, Steve Crabb, Jack Simpson, and David White, formed a team working in parallel with Cain to ferret out what had really happened. Crabb was 33, a Scottish migrant and actuary, who won the marginal seat of Knox against the trend in 1976, making himself noticed by organising his supporters to monitor prices at the local supermarkets. White was 32, the bright son of working-class parents; he grew up living above a shop in North Melbourne, but earned himself a commerce degree, accounting qualifications, and an MBA before deserting money for politics. He had been Holding's one-man research team for years before winning preselection. Simpson, 47, a former Essendon and VFA footballer, brought the experience of a generation of running his own family business in Moonee Ponds, and a long study of human nature. All three became ministers in the Cain governments of the 1980s. Moreover, in mid-1977, Clyde Holding resigned as opposition leader to stand for federal parliament, and his deputy, Frank Wilkes, took over, giving Labor a fresh face at the top.

The Age also returned to the issue in 1977. I teamed up with the late David Wilson, one of the finest investigative journalists Australia has produced, to revive its investigative team, aided on some articles by Lindsey Arkley and Stephen Mills. In January 1977, we reported that Lensworth Finance was set to receive a $9.2 million bonus as a result of cabinet's decision just before Christmas to approve the rezoning of farmland to allow the development of a satellite city of 130,000 people at Mount Ridley, north of Craigieburn. While this would be a private development, it was another case of the same developers pulling strings to get rural land rezoned as urban, and pocketing the profits. By then, Geoff Hayes had been appointed as minister for planning and minister for housing, and relied heavily on the advice of his 'can-do' permanent head, Neville Haynes. The Mount Ridley plan was taken to cabinet when Hunt was away on holidays, and was approved in principle. It was a breathtaking reversal of Hamer's own green-wedges policy, under which the Merri corridor was zoned rural. It raised serious questions about the integrity of the government's planning policy.

Several months later, Cain suggested that we investigate Lensworth's sale to the commission at Sunbury, which until then had been given no publicity. We discovered that Lensworth had made a $1.5 million profit on the sale; it had bought the land for $1.86 million, and then sold it to the commission 20 days later for $3.42 million. Moreover, the commission had curiously awarded the contract to develop the land to three men with no track record as developers: one of them was Peter Stirling, a prominent Liberal who had been Hamer's private secretary for six years. No one seriously suggested that Hamer himself had played any role in handing the contract to his longtime right-hand man. But to any normal person, it looked highly suspicious. Along with other stories that *The Age* was breaking — including the government's decision to award a $7 million contract for Geelong's state government offices to Geelong builder and Liberal Party fundraiser John Taylor, without even calling for tenders — it added to growing evidence that a small group of insiders were using their influence with the government to siphon money from the public.

Labor's four sleuths were also hot on the trail, and brought out new details about the deals. Police started investigating the Sunbury deal, and then extended their inquiries into Melton and Pakenham. *The Age* revealed the central role of Dillon in all three transactions, and of Kean as Lensworth's silent partner. We revisited the stories of Peter Leake's dual role at Melton, and Durston's revelations at his trial. The pieces of the jigsaw were falling into place; political pressure for action was building up. Finally, Hamer decided to appoint an inquiry into all three transactions. Retired Supreme Court judge Sir Gregory Gowans, 72, politically aligned with the DLP, was appointed as a one-man inquiry with Michael Dowling, QC, as counsel assisting, and support from the Fraud Squad.

The inquiry uncovered a lot of detail, but the only new element of significance was a corrupt relationship between Dillon and the Housing Commission's chief purchasing officer, Neill Riach. In all, Dillon had paid Riach $31,568 between 1973 and 1977, partly as a slice of the profit from the Melton deal, and partly as payment of travel expenses and a contribution towards a car for Mrs Riach. That was, however, the only corruption uncovered by the royal commission: a relatively small amount, given the sums involved, paid to a middle-ranking official. Dickie claimed vindication, telling parliament that the findings squashed Labor scuttlebutt that he had been paid a $20,000 bribe. Dillon and Riach were later sent to jail — years later, since the first royal commission was followed by a second, into other Housing Commission deals, which finished up sitting until 1981, and their trial had to wait until it was over.

The unanswered question was whether the Dillon–Riach relationship was the only corruption involved in the land deals. It's possible that it was. In his report, Gowans criticised Dickie for failing to ask the relevant questions of his officials. A report by management consultants Cresap McCormick and Paget was scathing about the commission's organisation, declaring: 'The pattern of executive leadership, responsibility and authority is confused and unclear.' The commission, they said, had no clear lines of responsibility, paid little attention to policy issues, and did little self-examination to monitor the effectiveness of its work.

But given the huge amount of money the middlemen stood to make, given Riach's relatively modest status, and given the paucity of resources allocated to the Fraud Squad investigation — a number of potential witnesses were never questioned, and at least one accused of receiving money was never asked to produce his bank records — it is also possible that there had been further corruption higher up the ladder, and that the inquiry simply failed to uncover it.

Politically, the Gowans inquiry also failed in a second important task: to deliver a clear finding as to who, if anyone, should be held responsible. Hamer had given the judge terms of reference that required him specifically to report back on 'whether any person was guilty of any impropriety, breach of law or duty, negligence, or act of dishonesty in relation thereto'. But Gowans did not report back in those terms. While criticising the credibility of Dickie's evidence, and his lack of attention to detail in the Pakenham purchase, Gowans declined to say whether this amounted to negligence or a breach of duty. As a result, Hamer claimed in public that Gowans had found no breach of duty or act of negligence by Dickie, whereas Nationals' leader Peter Ross-Edwards read the report as 'seriously questioning whether Mr Dickie is a fit and proper person to be a minister of the Crown'. Many in the community expected Hamer to force Dickie to resign. But that was not in Hamer's nature, and no minister had been sacked in Victoria since 1919. On the contrary, he wrote to Liberal branches insisting that there was no reason for Dickie to resign. Instead of a catharsis that would have allowed the Liberals to put the nightmare behind them, there was a stalemate. It swung more voters towards the view that Hamer was too 'weak', too trusting, to remain as premier.

Richard Thomas, an active Liberal progressive who had been mayor of St Kilda, and an experienced corporate public-relations operator, had joined Hamer at the start of 1978 as his media chief. He says that the land deals hurt Hamer more than he showed:

> One of the problems was that Dick trusted people. He accepted the assurances he was given, and believed them to be true. In a sense, he managed to have an extreme degree of naivete for a man with so much commercial and legal experience. [2]

Interviewed by Christopher Sexton in 1992, Hamer was defensive about his failure to demand Dickie's resignation:

> I thought for a long time whether I should require the minister, Vance Dickie, to vacate. I was surprised he didn't. Frankly, I would have. I had no doubt that in the circumstances, I would have resigned, although I would have expected to be back in the ministry before too long.
>
> But to require a minister to resign is another thing. So it became necessary for me to decide whether I would advise the governor to withdraw his commission: not because of any wrongdoing at all, not really on the ground of any carelessness either, personally, because he acted on the recommendations of the commission. The commission in turn seemed to be acting properly, on the basis of valuations. And the so-called Westminster tradition requiring the minister to take responsibility doesn't apply too well in the case of these quangoes, the quasi-autonomous corporations. It cuts across the whole idea of ministerial responsibility when the whole idea is that he doesn't interfere.

Yet one thing the Gowans report did make clear was that the Housing Commission was not a quasi-autonomous corporation, but very much under ministerial direction. In Gowans' words:

> The Minister regarded his views as requiring compliance, and involving recalcitrance if not obeyed … The chairman, Mr Gaskin, was 'the Minister's man', who would regard a suggestion from that quarter as as good as a direction.[3]

It is possible that Hamer was wary of taking on Dickie at a time when he needed at least a solid chunk of the right to support him in his battles with Doug Jennings. Yet while Dickie remained in cabinet, the land deals remained a problem.

The first decision that Hamer made was about his own future. In 1976, he had intended this to be his final term as premier; he would resign in good time for his successor to establish himself before facing the voters. By 1978, however, the land deals and the Jennings–Francis saga had left him determined to stay. At the start of April 1978, just after the release of the Gowans report and after his failure to have Jennings expelled by the state executive, Hamer told a dinner with backbenchers that while he had planned to retire from politics at the end of May, he had now decided to stay on to see the issues through, and lead the party into the next election. In May, he made his decision public. Most in the party were relieved; while Hamer certainly had critics in cabinet and the party room, the evidence suggests that few wanted a change of leader. Yet the Liberals were losing ground. The land deals and the party infighting had weakened their credibility as a government. Wilkes had proved a solid if unexciting opposition leader, and the dramatic improvement in Labor's frontbench had given it credibility as an alternative. The government was sitting on a powderkeg, and one loose cannon was about to ignite it.

Roberts Dunstan was one of the characters of the Victorian parliament. Born in late 1922, the son of a Mount Eliza solicitor, he was 17 when France fell. He promptly joined the army, and lied about his age so he could be sent overseas. He, too, fought at Tobruk, where an Italian shell blasted off his right leg. He was only 18. Discharged from the army as unfit to serve, he then applied to join the Air Force, arguing that once he had climbed into the plane, having only one leg was no disadvantage. He became the only Australian air gunner in the entire war to receive a DSO, and received wide publicity as an embodiment of Aussie courage. After the war, he spent one Christmas crossing the Alps on his crutches, and another in Italy as the house-guest of the gunner who blew off his leg. He became the film critic for *The Herald*, a local councillor on the Mornington Peninsula, and then the MP for Mornington, a safe Liberal seat. He continued as a film critic for another decade while serving as an MP, until he got serious about his political career, gave journalism away, and was elected to cabinet.

A spirited, liberal, witty man who liked a drink, Dunstan was part of the B-team in cabinet, serving for six years as minister for public works — until the night of 8 August 1978, when, no doubt with glass in hand, he telephoned *The Age* to give it his opinion of the prime minister. This might not have mattered had the prime minister been of the opposite party; but, since the prime minister was the leader of Dunstan's own party, and Dunstan himself was a state minister of that party, it was seen as impolitic of him to declare that the PM had 'gone mad' and was 'f—ng the economy', and that the building industry was being killed because of the cuts to capital works 'by the five farmers running the government' (presumably Fraser, Doug Anthony, Ian Sinclair, Tony Street, and Peter Nixon). The next morning, Dunstan awoke, read what he had said, and cheerfully offered to walk the plank. No minister had been sacked in Victoria since 1919, as we have seen, and Dunstan was one of Hamer's strongest supporters. But the premier knew he had no alternative.

Once tradition had been broken, and a minister sacked, Dickie was exposed. The ambition faction of the backbench was pushing for a complete ministerial spill, hoping that some of their group might be elected to cabinet — and, possibly, inject new life into the government. James Guest, one of the '76ers, took the initiative to gauge party opinion. As he recalled:

> If we'd had a vote in '78, Dickie, Granter, Houghton, and Balfour would all have been replaced. I spoke to 45 or so backbenchers and three ministers, and all but two were in favour of Dickie going. I took Dick a letter declaring that. He sat on the edge of his chair and looked nervous, but he didn't say anything.[4]

Others, including Alan Hunt, were giving him similar advice. Finally, Hamer called in Dickie, told him it was in the interests of the party that he should go, and gave him the weekend to think about it. At 9.00 a.m. on Monday 14 August, Dickie met Hamer and told him he would resign immediately, for health reasons. Keen to avoid a by-election, Hamer pressed him to stay on as a backbench MP, but Dickie knew this would cost him dearly in lost pension entitlements, so he quit parliament. He told *The Herald* that no Liberal had asked him to retire, that he was proud of his ministerial record, that he was retiring solely for health reasons, and added, 'I don't believe I've ever made a mistake.'

Others took a different view. An ANOP poll in October found that many voters saw the government as tired, incompetent, indecisive, lazy, and corrupt. The same month, David Wilson of *The Age* reported that middlemen had reaped more than $250,000 from seven other land purchases by the Housing Commission. One involved a company formerly part-owned by Liberal MP Vernon Hauser, who had unwisely lobbied the commission on its behalf. The government paid the company, Tamar Holdings, more than twice as much as Tamar itself had paid for the land a year or two earlier. Moreover, Geoff Hayes as housing minister had directed an ex gratia payment of $25,000 to Tamar, despite Hamer as treasurer earlier ruling that its claim had no merit. One of Alan Bond's companies made a similar killing on land it sold to the commission in Ballarat. Evidence to the Gowans inquiry revealed that Dillon and Inkster had been the vendor's agents in 24 major land sales to the commission in the previous eight years, in 12 of those as co-agents with Kean's firm, Moore Williams.

John Cain and his Labor colleagues were relentless in pushing for a royal commission. Hamer held off until after the 1979 election, and then appointed his energetic young ally Brian Dixon as minister for housing. Dixon took one look at the mounting pile of allegations about the Housing Commission's other land purchases, went to cabinet, and demanded and got a royal commission into all of them. The commission, headed by former judge Sir Sydney Frost, was meant to report in six months. It did not report for almost three years, until Labor was about to take power. By then, the damage to the government was irreversible. An editorial in *The Age* summarised the royal commission's findings:

> [It] found 'a lack of discipline, widespread ineptitude going far beyond anything which could be regarded as a normal or usual incidence of error and misjudgement … no proper ordering of priority according to need, inadequate budgeting procedures …' and so on … The [Housing] Commission bought land it could not use, it bought land it had no authority to buy, it bought land far in excess

> of need. It insisted on buying through agents paid by the vendors, a curious and highly compromising arrangement. It allowed builders seeking commission contracts to carry out underpriced work on the commissioners' homes. It bought without proper valuation of the land, disregarded valuations, or twisted them to suit its own purposes. Time and again, the taxpayers were diddled, and land bought above market value. When Mr Hamer as Premier insisted on certain procedures being followed, commission staff ignored them, and simply lied when reporting back to him. The commissioners and successive Ministers did nothing to stop them.[5]

Eventually, most of the land was developed. The Sunbury land became the Goonawarra estate. The Melton land opened the way for the development of West Melton. At Pakenham, while much of the land became lakes, parks, and sports grounds, most is now swallowed up in that rapidly growing town. Alan Hunt, interviewed for this book in 2011, was philosophical about the long-term merits of the planning issues he had fought for:

> Although a number of the purchases were questionable at the time, in the long term, they didn't make much difference … At Sunbury, I am now convinced that development would have split over Jacksons Creek [to Goonawarra] in any event … At Melton, I was very angry at the time, but in any event, that would now be urban land … At Pakenham, there's no doubt, looking back, that that area would have been developed. So if you look at the result 30 years after the event, it's less significant than it seemed at the time.

The corruption and gross incompetence, however, were things that the passage of time did not heal. The land deals became the issue that fatally eroded support for the Hamer government. Ordinary taxpayers felt that they had been used by shysters. They were right.

CHAPTER TWENTY

The economy, Malcolm Fraser, and the New Federalism

In 1974, Australia's long post-war economic boom suddenly ended. For more than a quarter of a century, growth had averaged almost 5 per cent a year. Unemployment had averaged less than 2 per cent. Prosperity was created, and shared, at a pace never matched before, or since. The boom was not confined to Australia: it happened all through the Western world, at much the same time. And then it ended at much the same time, all through the Western world.

The good times ended for Dick Hamer, too. He became the first premier since Sir Albert Dunstan to have to cope with a permanently weak economy — low growth, high unemployment, high inflation — and falling government revenues in real terms. The first half of his period as premier took place during a time of rapid expansion of government spending. The second half would become a period of austerity, and, for investment in infrastructure, contraction.

Victoria's economy suffered with the rest. In 1974–75, Australia's manufacturing activity slumped by 10 per cent, and Victoria was the key manufacturing state. The Whitlam government's 25 per cent tariff cut in 1973 collided with average wage rises of 30 per cent. Workers were laid off in their tens of thousands, as factories simply shut down, or slashed staff levels to survive. In 1974–75 alone, more than 100,000 jobs were lost in manufacturing nationally. Unemployment soared from 2.1 per cent to 4.8 per cent. By August

1978, almost 200,000 manufacturing jobs had been wiped out in five years: one in every seven factory jobs in Australia had been eliminated, a jobs massacre that would be repeated between 1988 and 1993 as the Hawke and Keating governments pushed through even bigger tariff cuts in the middle of a recession. Victoria specialised in labour-intensive manufacturing, particularly in textiles, clothing, and footwear (TCF) factories. The Hamer government's payroll-tax rebates helped keep alive most of those in country towns, but many others went under. The snowballing impact of the 25 per cent tariff cut became a headwind slowing the Victorian economy for the rest of Hamer's time in office. It significantly damaged his campaign to decentralise industry. He lobbied Fraser endlessly to reverse the cuts, with minor success. Hamer had never been a free-market zealot, but the massive job losses in Victoria from the tariff cuts made him an enemy of economic rationalism for the rest of his life.

His government's problems doubled when the largesse of the Whitlam government was replaced by the austerity of its successor. The Fraser government, installed by the governor-general in November 1975, and confirmed in a landslide at the election a month later, had no choice but to rein in federal spending, which had risen 115 per cent in three years. The real problem was that it lacked a viable strategy to get the economy back to solid growth; in the years that followed, the Australian economy remained stuck in third gear. The brunt of the spending cuts fell on the states; ironically, after all their complaints about Whitlam, state governments found themselves worse off under his successor.

Dick Hamer had known Malcolm Fraser for many years before they became premier and prime minister: he was the Fraser family's lawyer. Hubert Hamer had been solicitor to Sir Simon Fraser, Malcolm's grandfather (and best friend of April's grandfather). Dick in turn had been solicitor to Malcolm's father, Neville, executor of his estate, and director of the family's private companies. In his role as executor, he remained a director even as premier, which caused him embarrassment when it became public. But the two men were not close. Hamer was an unpretentious nice guy whom almost everyone liked; Fraser was a stern patrician, aloof and demanding. Hamer was to the left of the party; Fraser in those days positioned himself to the right. Hamer believed in a democratic, hands-off leadership style; Fraser was hands-on, skilled, and tireless at manipulating those whose support he needed. Patrick Weller quotes Hamer as saying that at times he felt that in discussions with Fraser, 'he was listening with attention in order to tell you where you were wrong'. Hamer was criticised by many for lacking willpower; no one could ever have said that of Fraser.

Their relationship as premier and prime minister was complex. Hamer was publicly loyal to Fraser when it really mattered, as in the crisis in 1975 when he endorsed Fraser's actions in public despite his private reservations. But, like Bolte, he asserted his right to criticise actions by his federal colleagues that hurt Victoria. He became a frequent critic of Fraser's 'fight inflation first' policy, a frequent supplicant for more money, and a frequent opponent of federal cuts to social programs. He was not alone in that: all the premiers weighed in to attack the Fraser government, on all sorts of issues. Political scientist Patrick Weller concluded that for Fraser, Hamer was in fact the most co-operative (or perhaps, the least unco-operative) of all the premiers: Fraser copped far worse criticism and obstruction from the right's Sir Joh Bjelke-Petersen in Queensland and Sir Charles Court in Western Australia, and from Labor premiers Neville Wran (New South Wales) and Don Dunstan (South Australia). Howson's diaries record that while Fraser frequently complained in private about Hamer's public advice to him, he consistently opposed any moves to unseat him as premier.

Fraser and his senior colleagues — such as treasurer Phillip Lynch, or employment minister Tony Street, who handled Victorian party issues for the PM — never criticised Hamer in public; they sent out a lesser gun to do that. In April 1977, Hamer seriously irritated Fraser by demanding a radical shift in economic policy to tackle inflation via a wage-price freeze, cuts to indirect taxes, and a national conference on the economy. Parts of this resembled the policy being advocated by the man Fraser feared most, ACTU president Bob Hawke. Perhaps

Hawke and Hamer had swapped ideas while watching their kids play cricket, or maybe both were taking advice from the Melbourne Institute of Applied Economic and Social Research, whose director, poverty expert Professor Ronald Henderson, influenced Hamer's economic thinking. Whatever the origin of Hamer's ideas, Fraser sent out the young John Howard, then minister for business and consumer affairs, to give the premier a very personal dressing-down. At a press conference in Canberra's Parliament House, Howard accused Hamer of having 'done another Newport' by giving in to union pressure to urge a change in economic policy. Howard said federal ministers had already explained to Hamer that it was not feasible to cut taxes to offset price rises, and if he wanted to reduce inflation by cutting taxes and charges, he should do it himself in Victoria by cutting 'the burden of workers' compensation charges' (which, as Hamer quickly pointed out, he was doing already). In *The Age*, Michelle Grattan noted that Howard's attack on his party's Victorian leader 'clearly carried the authority of Mr. Fraser'.

Fraser, like Hamer, was sceptical of Treasury advice, but saw no alternative to its strategy to 'fight inflation first': fix inflation, the theory went, and investors would gain the confidence to go out and build, and that would take care of unemployment. But how did you reduce inflation? Treasury's approach was to slow economic growth: that created unemployment, which would then reduce unions' wage demands, which would then reduce price increases. And the way to slow economic growth was to cut federal spending, which would also reduce the budget deficit.

In his autobiography, written with Margaret Simons, Fraser recounts that the day after his ministry was sworn in, he wrote to all ministers:

> Our overriding task during the months and indeed years ahead is to rein in the rate of growth of government spending and to reduce the relative size of the government sector. This task is central to our whole economic and social strategy.

Ministers, he added, would have to 'face up to many very hard options and take many very hard decisions'. Fraser was convinced that Australia was living beyond its means, and that was a further reason for cutting government spending. But while Fraser spoke the language of smaller government, he had to face up to the same dilemma that Ronald Reagan was to discover as president: when he got up close, there was not much his own government was doing that he wanted it to stop doing. Reagan's solution was to tell the Congress to find spending cuts, knowing that it wouldn't do so. Fraser's solution was to force the states to cut their capital expenditure — knowing that unless they took up his offer to collect a state income-tax surcharge, they would have no choice. A 'razor gang' headed by Lynch axed most of Whitlam's urban programs, and made some cuts elsewhere. Commonwealth spending edged down gradually as a share of GDP, from 24.3 per cent to 23.4 per cent, until the 1982–83 recession blew it up to a new record of 25.8 per cent.

The policy did slow inflation, for a while, and reduced the budget deficit. Inflation fell from 16.9 per cent in mid-1975 to 7.9 per cent in mid-1978, but only to rise again. Unemployment climbed as intended, to 6.5 per cent in early 1978, but that did little to slow the growth of wages or prices. Average hourly award wages grew by 9 per cent in 1979–80, and 12 per cent in 1980–81. Inflation climbed back above 10 per cent by the end of 1979, and was 11.5 per cent when the Fraser government lost office in March 1983. The budget deficit was whittled back, eventually reaching a small surplus (on today's definition), but that was the only area in which the policy achieved its goals. Over the seven years from mid-1976 to mid-1983, economic growth averaged just 2.3 per cent, less than half its level over the long boom. Unemployment averaged 6.5 per cent, more than three times its old level. The resources boom of 1980–81 saw mining investment lift Australia out of its sluggish growth, but it also sparked a wages free-for-all, which, along with a deteriorating international environment, higher oil prices, and a slump in private investment, catapulted the economy into recession in 1982.

Hamer had little interest in economics, and resented the

constraints it placed on him in government. His instincts were essentially a mix of populism, genuine economics, and self-interest. When the first discount liquor stores began to erode the viability of pubs' bottle shops, he slapped on a minimum beer price — putting the welfare of the pubs ahead of that of drinkers. (He backed down when it became clear that most Victorians had different priorities.) His opposition to the Fraser government's economic policies primarily reflected his interests as a premier who wanted more money from Canberra, not less. To the federal Treasury, cutting federal grants to the states and reducing the amount states could borrow allowed Canberra to reduce the 'public sector borrowing requirement', its obsession at the time; if governments borrowed less, it argued, interest rates would fall, and the private sector would borrow more. As economics, it was simplistic; as a policy in the late 1970s, it was a failure. Many economists outside Treasury opposed both it and the 'fight inflation first' policy, including Hamer's advisor Ronald Henderson and his colleagues at the Melbourne Institute. To Hamer, it simply meant that fewer patients could be treated in public hospitals, fewer homes connected to sewerage, and fewer houses built for the 10,000 people on the Housing Commission's waiting list. In 1977, Victorian housing approvals plunged 22.5 per cent, to their lowest level since 1965. Hamer became a frequent — and, to Fraser, unwelcome — participant in national economic debate, urging his federal counterpart to abandon or soften the 'fight inflation first' policy, give equal weight to tackling unemployment, seek consensus with the unions, loosen restrictions on state borrowing, and give the states more money to spend.

What most annoyed Fraser was that Hamer supported the unions in arguing for full wage indexation, whereas the Fraser government kept asking the Arbitration Commission to discount wage rises to help bring inflation down. In April 1977, Hamer broke from this briefly to propose a freeze on wages and prices for three months as a circuit-breaker to reduce inflation and expectations of future rises. He enjoyed a moment of success when Fraser and the other premiers formally endorsed his idea; but the unions would not agree to a wage freeze, and without commitments to a price freeze, neither would the Arbitration Commission, which set wages. At the end of 1978, Hamer annoyed Fraser further by hosting a national jobs conference in Melbourne at which Hawke and other union leaders were given a prominent role. Youth unemployment was then at very high levels, and Hamer was genuinely concerned to tackle it. While his economic policies were mostly ineffective, he did introduce incentives for employers to offer apprenticeships and training places to 'the jobless generation'. The state government led by example, increasing its apprenticeship and training intakes, and financing job-intensive projects in rural areas with high unemployment.

But, essentially, Hamer allowed Victoria's budgets to be dictated by federal government policy. Bolte began releasing the fiscal brakes after the Dandenong by-election in 1969, and in his final budget in 1971–72, the McMahon government's decision to hand the states the power to levy payroll tax saw him hike taxes and spending substantially. Hamer and Whitlam between them then sent taxes and spending soaring. Statistics at the time showed that Victoria shared with South Australia the biggest increase in taxes of any state, and the biggest increase in government employment. The Fraser years put an end to that: the running costs of government were contained, while federal grants and loan limits for capital works were halved as a share of GDP (excluding special projects such as the Loy Yang A power station, which were exempt from the limits). The impacts of Whitlam and Fraser respectively are clear when you compare Victoria's budget spending in 1969–70 (Bolte's last austere budget), 1975–76 (the last of the Whitlam years) and 1980–81 (the last year of the Hamer government), as a share of Australia's GDP:

	1969–70	**1975–76**	**1980–81**
	% GDP	**% GDP**	**% GDP**
Spending			
Education	.75	1.26	1.24
Health	.27	.60	.58
Transport	.21	.37	.30
Other	.89	1.59	1.74
Total recurrent	**2.12**	**3.82**	**3.86**

These figures come from the 2011–12 state budget papers, and are on the same definitions used today: they show that the state's recurrent spending peaked at 3.97 per cent of GDP in 1977–78, then slid back to roughly its 1975–76 level for the rest of the Fraser government. There is no modern data set for capital works, funding for which was essentially under Commonwealth control. Budget figures published at the time, which were fragmentary, showed the main stream of Victoria's capital works funding shrank from 0.51 per cent of GDP to 0.27 per cent in the same five years; the Bureau of Statistics reported a similar decline. Gross borrowing by the entire Victorian public sector shrank from 1.07 per cent of GDP to 0.61 per cent by 1981–82. In each of its first two years, the Fraser government lifted loan funds for the states by just 5 per cent, well below the rate of inflation. The next year, John Howard's first budget as treasurer held loan funds flat in nominal terms, and then, in 1979–80, Howard cut them by 13 per cent. In real terms, which measures what money actually buys after taking account of inflation, the Victorian Treasury estimated that in three years the Commonwealth had cut its loan allocation by almost a third — 31 per cent. Today it seems absurd that the federal government should have the power to decide how much state governments could borrow, but that arrangement lasted until the 1990s. Many projects that Hamer had announced in the good years were deferred forever: the North Wing of Parliament House, the Doncaster rail line. Fraser's austerity drive became another factor stopping Hamer from making it happen.

Health funding was among the areas targeted for cuts, as it was growing particularly fast. The Commonwealth's 1977–78 budget ordered a 5 per cent cut in hospital operating costs. In 1978, it ordered a freeze on all plans to expand hospital facilities and services pending a review. But the review did not report until 1981 — and then Fraser and his ministers seemed interested only in the proposals they could use to justify further cuts. New wings of hospitals were left empty because the Commonwealth would not approve the money for them to operate. In 1978, the Alfred Hospital left 200 beds empty because it had run out of money for dialysis services. Capital-works funding for hospitals was cut sharply. Hamer, feeling too squeezed by Canberra himself to have room to manoeuvre, passed on all the federal cuts to the hospitals, ordering a staff freeze in 1977, then leaving them to find the savings.

By and large, Hamer duplicated in his own budgets the policies he complained about in federal ones. For all his public concern about having to cut capital works, he chose to cut taxes rather than using state revenue to keep up investment in roads, rail, schools, hospitals, and so on. He followed other states in introducing de facto tobacco and petrol taxes by charging their sellers licence fees proportional to their sales; but unlike Bolte, he was no innovator on the revenue side. Gradually, Victoria adopted a regime of fiscal retrenchment. In his final budget in 1978–79, he reported with pride that the state had reduced its workforce by 200 the previous year; it would fall by a further 160 in 1978–79, and by 1072 in 1979–80. But he also highlighted the duplicity of Howard's claim that Commonwealth outlays in 1978–79 would increase by only 7.7 per cent. Some 40 per cent of those outlays, he said, were payments to the states: they would increase by only 5.2 per cent, while the Commonwealth's own spending would rise by 9.3 per cent. A year later, Thompson, as treasurer, highlighted a similar double standard: Howard's 1979–80 budget lifted the Commonwealth's own spending by 10.7 per cent, and yet raised funding for the states by just 6.4 per cent. The Hawke government was guilty of similar duplicity in the late 1980s, when its much-acclaimed spending cuts fell mostly on the states.

A different premier might have responded to federal spending cuts by leading a root-and-branch review of government activity to find efficiencies to save money. But that was not Hamer's nature — and, in fairness, the federal cuts got deeper with each year, and the whole strategy of forcing the states to make cuts was not flagged in advance. He and his ministers looked for cost savings, certainly, but mostly through broadbrush measures: cutting the capital-works program, and imposing first a freeze on hiring, and then on staff ceilings (which were criticised by the Public Service Board for their rigidity). He set up a cabinet budget committee, and an economics unit within the Premier's Department. He supported transport minister Joe Rafferty in replacing trains with buses on 17 little-used country rail lines. But most of the cost-saving initiatives in that period came from individual ministers. Ian Smith as minister for agriculture sold off the government's loss-making abattoirs and cold-storage plants. Brian Dixon, as minister for housing from 1979, sold off the Housing Commission's big construction-materials factory at Holmesglen. And Robert Maclellan, when he became transport minister in 1978, bit the bullet in style by slashing the chronic overmanning in the railways:

> I can remember Hamer exploding over the growth of the public sector, and saying to us: 'You've all got to lift your game!' I managed to reduce the staff numbers in public transport by 3,000, by making sure that every new position had to be approved by [Alan] Reiher [then chairman of VicRail]. But that was not his [Hamer's] plan; it was mine.[1]

Few ministers in the Hamer government were taking the lead in that area. As treasurer, Hamer did not have the time, or possibly the desire, to focus on how to make his government do more with less.

For all that, Hamer always depicted the Victorian economy as doing well. In his 1979 campaign policy speech, he told Victorians that there were 'clear signs of a recovery in our economy', and declared, 'I have not known a time in Victoria of such major activity in planning and construction.' He listed $3 billion worth of projects in the planning stages, most of them resource-based, ranging from Esso-BHP's oil and gas developments in Bass Strait to a range of industries attracted by Victoria's cheap gas and electricity — aluminium smelters, petrochemical plants, steel mills, a pulp mill, and Holden's new engine plant. He ran through a series of indicators in which Victoria led Australia: the highest average family incomes, 'easily the highest personal savings', consistently the lowest unemployment, the highest home ownership in the country 'and probably the world', and so on. Indicators such as these were part of the background of Victorian politics in that era: they gave Victorians the sense that they were doing well, thanks to a well-governed state. Since then, the political ascendancy of the free-market camp, and the Reserve Bank's high-dollar policy, has forced many of the industries built up in those years to close.

Two issues exemplified the gap between Hamer's approach to government and that of the new free-marketeers who were starting to become the key force for change in the party: third-party insurance, and the role of the Gas and Fuel Corporation.

The insurance issue is a microcosm of the way that politics worked. By 1970, consensus was growing that Victoria should replace its costly, time-consuming adversarial system of third-party car insurance with a quick, simple no-fault system. Politically, the argument was irresistible: chief secretary Ray Meagher told parliament in 1973 that most of the money paid to claimants did not reach them until more than three years after their accidents, and that one-sixth of all payouts were consumed in legal fees. In 1970, Rylah supported the idea of no-fault insurance, but the detail was the problem. What entitlements would be paid? Who would pay for them? Would they continue until complete recovery? Bolte as treasurer was wary, and the legal fraternity, especially the Labor law firms, insisted that victims also had to retain their right to sue.

In 1972, Hamer wanted to show that his government was acting to protect motorists. He agreed to a no-fault scheme with generous terms: accident victims would have all their hospital, medical, and ambulance bills paid, and would be compensated for 80 per cent of their lost income and bills for post-hospital care. Moreover, victims would retain the right to sue for additional damages. The Royal Automobile Club of Victoria warned that the scheme would require a 20 to 25 per cent increase in premiums. Hamer denied this, but the RACV's estimate proved to be a severe understatement. Claims and payouts escalated rapidly, and private insurers abandoned the field in droves. By January 1974, with only three insurers left, the government had to hike premiums by almost 50 per cent. By

October, they had almost doubled. In July 1975, the State Premiums Committee recommended a further 70 per cent rise for premiums in the city and a 93 per cent rise in the country. The government was required by law to table the recommendation within three weeks, but it failed to do so for nine months, tabling the recommendation only after the state election. It then agreed to increases of only 27 per cent, thereby making third-party insurance totally unprofitable. Now even the RACV pulled out, leaving the State Insurance Office as the only insurer. It could not be subsidised by the budget, since the budget itself was in strife. An economist would have urged reform of the scheme to reduce payouts, and/or hiking premiums to make motorists pay the bill; no doubt that was the advice Hamer was getting from the Victorian Treasury. But those options were electorally unpalatable; instead, he backed the SIO's alternative option: that it be allowed to enter the profitable field of general insurance, so it could cross-subsidise its losses on third-party insurance.

Peter Howson's diaries trace the growing division in the wider party organisation over the issue. But the right could not agree on an alternative, so Hamer won the fight. His government went on to make a determined bid to reduce the cost of the scheme by limiting the right to sue to cases where the victims had suffered 'substantial' damage. However, this led to a war with the Trades Hall Council, repeated strikes, and repeated negotiations, ending in a compromise that set the threshold as 'material' damage, leaving the courts to decide what that meant.

The Liberal right was even more angry when the government allowed the Gas and Fuel Corporation to start searching for gas in Bass Strait. In the early 1960s, the Esso-BHP consortium had discovered oil and gas in the Gippsland shelf of Bass Strait. At the time, the states controlled offshore waters, and Bolte bargained ruthlessly to buy up the gas cheaply to give a competitive advantage to Victorian industry. Esso-BHP could make big money from selling the oil, but the gas had to be sold to the Gas and Fuel Corporation, who sold it to industry. (Bolte's values were those of supporting national development, a long way from those of the free-market ideologues in power today.) It turned out that there was plenty of gas, and by 1978, Gas and Fuel (as it was generally known) had locked in a long-term price formula that gave it as much as it wanted at well below world prices. But this left Esso-BHP with no incentive to explore for more gas in Bass Strait, and its competitors were similarly wary. Gas and Fuel's executive chairman, Neil Smith, wanted to secure the corporation's supplies for the very long term. In his younger days, Smith had been private secretary to old John Cain as premier; in the 1960s, he ran Ansett's airline business; and in the 1970s and 1980s, he was one of Victoria's wiliest bureaucratic operators, with a track record of getting what he wanted. He tried to interest Shell, Woodside, Esso-BHP, and Mobil in joint ventures to explore for gas, without success. So, in 1977, Gas and Fuel applied for an exploration permit itself, in partnership with Beach Petroleum, a subsidiary of BHP's traditional rival, the Collins House group.

Esso-BHP cried foul, claiming that the corporation had offered it a worse deal than the one it signed with Beach. The new free-marketeers in the Liberal Party were outraged. They wanted to roll back the state; now, instead, a Liberal government was allowing it to expand further into private-sector turf. Howson's diary reports that rising young business tycoon John Elliott, by then a vice-president of the Victorian party, exploded in rage when party leaders were told. Elliott urged that the corporation be privatised. Hamer gave back as good as he got, telling Elliott that, in Howson's words, 'a gas monopoly was inevitable, and it was better that it be government than private'. Cabinet was divided, but Hamer won the battle. In November 1978, the Liberal state council opposed the government's decision, urging it to sell Gas and Fuel's exploration arm, and to consider selling the corporation itself. But Gas and Fuel stayed in the business until it was privatised years later by the Kennett government. In 1979, the partnership discovered the North Paaratte gas field, and, in 1981, Wallaby Creek. The wells that proved the value of the Otway Basin had been put down by Beach Petroleum on behalf of Victorian gas consumers.

On one important issue, Hamer and Fraser saw eye to eye, at least at the outset. Few things mattered more to Hamer than reform of federal–state relations — the 'New Federalism' that Fraser had promised. He had campaigned for it since he had been a backbencher; now, as premier, he was determined to try to make it happen. Under a policy to which Hamer contributed, Fraser proposed a two-stage reform of federal finances. In the first stage, the states and local government would be allocated a guaranteed share of income-tax collections. In the second, the states would also be given the right to levy their own income-tax surcharge, to be collected by the Commonwealth. Specific-purpose payments would be scaled back and replaced by general-purpose grants. And an advisory council on inter-governmental relations would be established to review the overlap in Commonwealth and state functions, and to propose a simpler division of tasks.

On paper, Fraser carried out his promises. From 1976 to 1977, the states and local government were given a guaranteed share of personal income-tax collections — with the added safeguard that for the first four years, they were guaranteed to receive at least as much as they would have under Whitlam's formula. The Fraser government also passed legislation allowing the states to impose their own income-tax surcharge. And yet, virtually nothing changed, except that special-purpose payments to the states were reduced. By and large, the states continued to be paid according to Whitlam's formula, not by their tax share. And no state imposed its own tax surcharge. What went wrong?

First, income tax grew by less than Treasury had expected. As one of the big reforms in the 1976 budget, Fraser and his treasurer, Phillip Lynch, had indexed the tax scales for inflation. In the past, income-tax revenue was swollen each year by bracket creep, as inflation pushed people into higher tax brackets that took a larger slice of their income. In the three Whitlam government budgets, despite Australia going into recession, income-tax revenue grew by 125 per cent. In the first three Fraser budgets, despite a modest recovery, income-tax revenue grew by just 39 per cent. The low growth of income-tax revenues also reflected lower than expected growth in employment; the economy, too, had failed to fire as forecast and, initially, inflation fell faster than expected. All this meant that Fraser and his team found their budget was under much more pressure than they had assumed in the idealistic days of 1975. They gradually abandoned tax indexation to give priority to getting the budget back to surplus.

Second, when the states' tax share was converted into a share of the previous year's income, the formula adopted by Fraser — giving the states 39.87 per cent of the previous year's income-tax revenue — failed even to match their share under the formula set by the Whitlam government, which the states were guaranteed until 1980. The concept of tax sharing, like that of tax indexation, was noble; but the implementation of both became subject to chiselling that quickly saw them end up as broken promises. It was typical of the atmosphere in which federal–state relations were conducted that Fraser set the states' share of income tax at 39.87 per cent of receipts. Why 39.87 per cent? Why not just round it off at 40 per cent? Because setting it at 39.87 per cent saved Canberra $15 million a year. In 1981, Howard came out of a Premiers' Conference chortling, because he had managed to keep $70 million that he had been holding back to offer the states as a last-minute concession.

Third, no state wanted to take responsibility for levying its own income tax. In retirement, Hamer maintained with some passion that the Fraser government had welshed on an unwritten understanding that it would unilaterally cut its income-tax rates, so the states could then move in to fill the gap — rather than adding a new surcharge on top of existing taxes. In 1982, Hamer told me: 'We had discussions on federal–state relations when the present federal government was in opposition, before the 1975 election — and there was quite widespread agreement that this was the way to do it.' He blamed federal Treasury for persuading the Fraser government not to do it: 'They believe their control over the economy is limited anyway, and therefore they are reluctant to let any area depart to the states, which they can't control.'

When interviewed for this book a generation later, Alan Hunt,

Victoria's minister for federal affairs from 1976 to 1979, also insisted that there had been an understanding at the political level that Canberra would cut its taxes first to force the states to act. This offered a win/win approach, since the federal government could claim electoral kudos for cutting taxes. But it was also possible that when voters saw the states raise their income taxes by the same amount that Canberra had cut them, they might feel they had been conned, and might take it out on both governments. To cut federal income tax would also cut across the priority that Fraser had given to tax indexation, and to getting the budget back in surplus. Hunt, too, blamed Treasury for talking Fraser into breaking his promise. If so, it's not hard to see why.

For his part, Fraser flatly denies that there was ever any such agreement. He told me that the states simply were not willing to bear the odium of imposing their own income taxes. They found it easier to leave it to Canberra to raise taxes, and then complain that their state was being given a bad deal. It is certainly true that while Bolte and Hamer wanted the states to raise more of their own revenue, this was not a priority for the other premiers. And the 1975 Liberal policy statement said nothing about the federal government 'making room' for the states; nor was it part of the 35-point public agreement that the Commonwealth and the states signed in 1976.

And finally, while the federal government delivered the funding promised by the Whitlam formula, it simultaneously clawed back money from the states in almost every other way it could. Economists Russell Mathews and Bhajan Grewal estimated that while tax-sharing grants to the states rose from 4 per cent of GDP to 4.5 per cent under the Fraser government, thanks to the Whitlam formula, that was far outweighed by the deep cuts to specific-purpose payments, which shrank from 5.4 per cent of GDP to 3.6 per cent. Only education held its ground. Hospital funding failed to keep pace with inflation even before most of it was rolled into general-revenue grants, while most other specific-purpose programs either were eliminated or suffered severe funding cuts. Fraser and Howard did the same to Loan Council authorisations for state borrowings: while the states were allowed to borrow to build power stations, the core state-budget sectors (such as health, education, and transport) had their borrowing programs halved as a share of GDP: from 1.7 per cent in Whitlam's last year to 0.8 per cent in Fraser's last budget. When Hamer complained in public that this forced him to make cuts, the Fraser government briefed journalists to point out that Hamer himself was cutting taxes, with the same effect.

The combined effect of all this was to sharply cut resources flowing from Canberra to the states: Mathews and Grewal estimated that they fell from 12.5 per cent of GDP in Whitlam's last budget to 10.5 per cent of GDP five years later, in Hamer's last budget. The total resources flowing from Canberra to state government had shrunk dramatically, relative to the size of the economy. This was not what Hamer had anticipated from the 'New Federalism'.

Yet, in the end, what is clear is that the Fraser government did give the states power to raise their own income tax, and that no state was willing to do it. By cutting their resources, it gave them a good reason to take the plunge. Had Henry Bolte been given the same opportunity, one suspects that this story would have had a very different ending.

CHAPTER TWENTY-ONE

Two key reforms

Hamer's premiership appears to fall neatly into two halves. In the first four years, to mid-1976, he reigned supreme over Victorian politics, a widely respected premier pushing through his reform agenda, with or without party support. Yet in the final five years or so, his own agenda seemed to disappear from sight: he seemed to be constantly on the defensive — over the land deals, the economy, and Newport, or against the new right-wing hardliners on his own side. Yet his reform agenda did continue. This period saw two of his government's most important reforms enacted: the Equal Opportunity Act, which legislated equal rights for women, and the Crimes (Sexual Offences) Act, which decriminalised homosexual acts.

Hamer was an instinctive feminist all his life. His mother, grandmother, aunt, and cousins were women who went out of the home to do things: running hospitals, running charities, and writing books. (His cousin Gwen Swinburne's anthology of historical documents, *A Source Book of Australian History*, is back in print almost a century after she compiled it.) In wartime Britain, he was delighted to find women flying planes and doing other jobs previously reserved for men. In the late 1940s, his sister Alison was one of the first women to combine teaching at Melbourne University with raising young children. As minister for local government in the 1960s, one of his priorities had been to encourage women to stand for their councils. Years later, he commented: 'As a community, we were scandalously dissipating the intelligence and the talents of half the population.' When the new wave of feminism broke on society in the late 1960s and early 1970s, he was ready to ride it.

His first chance came in 1971. The elite administrative division of the public service, from which all senior appointments were made, was exclusively male. In late 1970, an enterprising young woman used just her initials when applying. She was invited to sit the entrance exam, which she passed with flying colours; but when her gender became known, she was refused admission to the division. In one of his first acts as chief secretary, Hamer intervened, overruled the decision, and pledged to remove gender discrimination from the Victorian public service. It was the first of many changes he would make to transform the Victorian bureaucracy, which for decades had been an anachronistic male Masonic fiefdom: the Premier's Department included just three graduates; women required permission to stay in the service after they married; promotion was usually by seniority; and membership of a Masonic lodge was decidedly helpful in most areas, whereas in others, one close observer concluded that the main criterion for appointment seemed to be membership of the Catholic church. Hamer's reforms took the public service a fair part of the way towards becoming a modern corps of skilled, professional advisors, male and female. Under his government, graduates, formerly rare in the administrative division, made up most of the appointments to it; departments were reorganised along functional lines; talented officers were recruited from the Commonwealth to rebuild the service; and a research unit was established within the Public Service Board. These were reforms of a kind that were beyond Rylah's imagination.

There was still much left undone, allowing the Cain government to complete the job, but Cain himself, interviewed for this book, freely acknowledged that Hamer and his team did the spadework to modernise the Victorian public service:

> He commissioned the Bland report [on the public service] and then brought in a package of reforms. He brought in the senior executive service [the elite corps of top officials], and evaluation of work

> done. Public records reform dates from his time. Ron Cullen [the reforming chairman of the Public Service Board] was brought in by Dick … If Dick was around today, he wouldn't be impressed by the emphasis on making the public service operate like business units!
>
> But he didn't take on freedom of information legislation — he left that to us. The Director of Public Prosecutions was another reform we brought in. They didn't go all the way on gender equality and promotion on merit. As for cabinet records, they made a start: in those days they would take a file into the cabinet room and write a note [of the decisions] on the back of it. Since our time, every government has had public servants in the room to take notes.

In 1972, the revised Liberal platform prepared under Hamer's leadership committed the party to 'the implementation of measures designed to achieve full equality for women'. Legislation to abolish gender discrimination in the public service went through in early 1973. Extending the same principle to the private sector, however, took much longer. After all, the private sector was not just the workplace, but included society's social and recreational life, much of which was organised into gender-separate lines. Should the male-only Melbourne Club be required to admit women as members? Should the female-only Lyceum Club be required to admit men? Should golf clubs leasing Crown land be required to remove the distinction between (male) members and (female) associates?

The Liberal Party was divided on the whole idea of feminism. At one end was the influential Women's Electoral Lobby, a non-party feminist-advocacy group set up in 1972, and headed by Eve Mahlab, herself a Liberal. On the other was the women's section of the Victorian party, a formidable force largely made up of older conservative women who saw feminism as a threat. A typical example was the East Malvern women's branch, which proposed a motion at state conference in 1975 denouncing 'Women's Electoral Lobby propaganda' in the party newspaper, *The Australian Liberal*, as an example of 'subtle types of indoctrination used to promote Socialist objectives'. In 1975, Hamer had set up a Women's Advisory

Bureau within the government's Community Service Centre, and the Public Service Board appointed a young feminist, Penny Ryan, to run it. Within three weeks, the Stonnington women's branch of the party had met with Hamer's permanent head, Ken Green, to inform him that Ms Ryan had been a communist, once wrote an article for a student newspaper on her experiences of masturbation, was not a mother, and was clearly unsuitable for the job. A campaign spread around Liberal women's branches to demand her dismissal; Hamer initially stood firm, but then allowed her to be white-anted into resignation.

Hamer pressed on, cautiously. In 1975, he appointed a committee on the status of women, headed by Dr Eva Eden, principal of Janet Clarke Hall, to report to the government on 'measures to promote equality by legislative changes, reorientation of community attitudes, and changes to any discriminatory regulations and practices'. The result of its work was the Equal Opportunity Bill, which Hamer himself introduced in the Assembly in October 1976:

> ... it prohibits discrimination on the basis of sex or marital status by employers and bodies or authorities connected with employment; it prohibits discrimination by educational authorities; it prevents discriminatory practices in the supply of goods, services and accommodation.
>
> The Bill provides for the appointment of a Commissioner of Equal Opportunity and an Equal Opportunity Board. The commissioner will investigate allegations of discrimination and seek to resolve them by conciliation. When, but only when, the commissioner is unable to settle a complaint by conciliation, he [*sic*] is required to refer the complaint to the Equal Opportunity Board. It is expected that the great majority of cases would be settled by discussion and conciliation.[1]

On one hand, the bill narrowed the scope of the reforms proposed by the committee on the status of women, focussing only on tackling discrimination in the workplace and in educational opportunities, leaving aside the thorny issues of discrimination in social and recreational fields. It explicitly exempted, among others, religious orders, single-sex schools, 'any sporting activity organised for persons of the one sex, (and) any club set up for, or mainly for, persons of the one sex'. Clyde Holding criticised Hamer for leaving the clubs out. Interviewed for this book, Yolande Klempfner, Hamer's advisor on women's affairs, said that she argued for them to be included, but added: 'Dick understood that politics is the art of the possible: gently, gently, catchee monkey.' In retirement, Hamer said publicly that he regretted not having included clubs using Crown land. Less noticed was that the bill broadened the legislation to apply also to marital status, providing new protection to single mothers and unmarried couples, especially in the rental market. Fay Marles, who had taught history with Alison Patrick at Melbourne University, was appointed as the first commissioner. Deirdre Fitzgerald became the first chair of the Equal Opportunity Board. And Hamer put the Penny Ryan controversy behind him by appointing Klempfner, a successful commercial lawyer (and mother) to his own office as full-time women's advisor.

The new regime soon found itself with an explosive test case. No businessman in Melbourne was more powerful than Sir Reginald Ansett: he owned the biggest transport company in the southern hemisphere, television stations in Melbourne and Brisbane, and had wide-ranging investments. He was close to Bolte, who in 1960 had stopped the State Rivers and Water Supply Commission from building a dam on Ansett's farm, and in 1972 had shielded Ansett's empire from a takeover bid by setting up a select committee to inquire into it. After his retirement, Bolte joined Ansett's board. At the 1977 federal election, Ansett personally paid for TV commercials in which Bolte attacked the new Australian Democrats, claiming: 'A vote for the Democrats is a vote for Labor.' In 1978, Ansett was nearing 70, used to getting his way, and adamant that no women would fly his planes.

Deborah Lawrie (then using her married name of Deborah Wardley) was a 24-year-old science teacher with a passion to be an airline pilot. She had taken out a private pilot's licence at 18, a commercial pilot's licence at 20, had logged 2,600 flying hours, and was a flying instructor at Moorabbin. For two years, she kept applying to join Ansett's pilot-training program, but was rejected while her male counterparts were accepted. If Ansett embodied the old world, she embodied the new. In August 1978, she took her case to the Equal Opportunity Commission.

Fay Marles (the mother of Richard Marles, later a Labor minister in the Gillard government) was still new to the job, sharing her office with the board that oversaw her, and discovering that Hamer's keen support for equal opportunity gave her unusual clout:

> Dick Hamer was fantastic to me … The other [interstate] commissioners all had trouble with their governments. I didn't have any trouble with him … He had a personal commitment to the issue, and everyone knew he was really interested in it, and that gave me status: 'You don't play around with me.' There were a lot of people who didn't like equal opportunity, but with his protection, I was able to work without a lot of obstructions getting in my way.[2]

But Ansett believed he had far more clout, and would not be told what to do by a bunch of feminists. Marles recalls:

> I went to see Ansett. He had my letter, and he said to me: 'This will be on the premier's desk tomorrow.' I told him the premier already had it … I didn't talk to him [Hamer] about the case — that would have been dynamite. But I would warn him if something like that was going to land in his lap.

When Marles' conciliation failed to move Ansett, Hamer tried himself. In the early 1990s, he told interviewer Christopher Sexton:

> Ansett was very adamant. A number of his executives told me they were appalled. I remember ringing him up, because I knew him very well.

> I said to him, 'Reg, you're surely not going to let this case go before the Equal Opportunity Board, because it's a very bad case. It *is* discrimination!'
>
> He said, 'Yes, it is discrimination.'
>
> I said, 'How are you going to defend it?'
>
> He said, 'I've got to defend it … I'm not going to have a woman pilot sitting up there. I'd lose all my passengers. They'd be very alarmed.'[3]

Ansett was unmoved when Hamer recounted his favourable wartime experience of having been flown by a female pilot in the Royal Air Force. Wardley's complaint went to the board, where it was upheld. Ansett's lawyers appealed to the Supreme Court on the grounds that a procedural error by the board gave reason to fear it was biased against the tycoon. The court ordered the government to appoint a board of outsiders to hear the case. It did, and that board also found against Ansett. He then took the case to the High Court, where he lost 4–2. Hamer's old classmate Sir Keith Aickin and his fellow-conservative Sir Garfield Barwick both found for Ansett, relying on an extreme reading of federal powers, but all the other judges upheld the state's right to legislate. Fay Marles recalls that after the case, Hamer threw a party at Monomeath Avenue for the commission team.

The Supreme Court had ordered Ansett to take Wardley into the next intake. When she graduated from classroom training, however, he would not allow her into flight training. But by then Ansett himself had become an employee: rival transport tycoon Sir Peter Abeles had teamed up with Rupert Murdoch to take over his company, and Hamer refused to intervene to protect Ansett, as Bolte had done seven years earlier. Wardley appealed to Murdoch's brother-in-law, John Calvert-Jones, whom she had taught to fly. Two days later, Murdoch issued an order overruling the old boss. Wardley became an Ansett pilot, flew with the company until the pilots' strike of 1989, then moved to the Netherlands and, as Deborah Lawrie, flew with KLM for years before returning to Australia as a pilot, first with

Jetstar, and then with Tiger Airways. But she remains one of very few female commercial passenger pilots in this country.

Outlawing sex discrimination was relatively easy. Repealing the laws against homosexuality was politically more difficult. Passing a law to recognise prostitution would be more difficult still. None of these were issues that Liberal governments traditionally tackled. Hamer's move to outlaw sex discrimination had been made roughly simultaneously with New South Wales and South Australia, but they were Labor states. Governments of the right normally do nothing on such matters, leaving them for governments of the left to fix. One of the things that made Hamer unique was that he tackled them from the conservative side of politics, and did so by patiently persuading the party to come with him.

Sexual attitudes had changed dramatically since 1960, but the laws governing them had not. Yet when societies change, tolerance can replace intolerance at bewildering speed. A generation after the US civil rights movement, you could see virtually no sign anymore of the racism that the movement had fought against: the former white racists had either embraced racial tolerance or hidden their views. Similarly in Australia in the 1970s, a society that even a decade earlier found homosexuality abhorrent came to accept it with astonishing speed. In 1967, a Morgan Gallup poll found that only 22 per cent of Australians wanted to reform the laws against homosexuality, while 64 per cent wanted to keep them. Yet by 1976, Morgan found that 68 per cent favoured legalising homosexual conduct, and just 26 per cent were still opposed. In recent years, the polls have found a similar rapid reversal of attitudes to gay marriage. But in the 1970s, as now, cautious politicians lagged behind the community, held back by minority pressure groups who saw liberalisation on these issues as a threat to what they stood for.

The lead in homosexual-law reform came initially from Canada, whose prime minister of the 1960s and 1970s, the cool Pierre Trudeau, famously declared: 'The State has no place in the bedrooms of the nation.' South Australia led the way in this country, after its conscience had been shaken by a shocking tragedy one night in 1972 when three Vice Squad detectives on the prowl threw a gay man, Dr George Duncan, into the River Torrens, unaware that he could not swim. Another factor in changing South Australian attitudes was the fact that premier Don Dunstan, while very popular, was widely (and rightly) thought to be gay.

In Victoria, police did not patrol the bedrooms of the state. The real issue for gay men was police entrapment. Graham Carbery's brief history, *Towards Homosexual Equality in Australian Criminal Law*, published online, recounts that in the summer of 1976–77 alone, police using entrapment methods arrested more than 100 men for homosexual offences at Black Rock beach, 'a well-known meeting place for homosexual men'. The controversy this provoked led Hamer to declare his support for legalising homosexuality, and he asked Haddon Storey as attorney-general to review what should be done. The situation in the party room was now too fractious for him to try to bulldoze his way through, as he had in abolishing capital punishment. He and Storey knew that this time they had to bring the party with them. Storey recalls:

> It took a while to get through, because I decided to workshop it very carefully through a party committee. There was a lot of consultation, and we had some pretty conservative MPs on that committee. But they were all people who were prepared to sit down and work through the issues. People were becoming more educated about it over time.[4]

Activists had formed a Homosexual Law Reform Coalition, and their goal was nothing short of full equality in the law between homosexual and heterosexual behaviour. That was a big ask from the Liberal Party room, but time was on their side. Gradually, society's attitudes changed, and Storey's patient persuasion permeated through to the backbench.

One complication was that Hamer was also under pressure to take action on prostitution. As sexual liberation spread, so did brothels, in the guise of 'massage parlours' that began operating openly throughout the suburbs. In September 1975, the government banned massage parlours from residential areas. But enforcement was a problem, and with opinion polls showing that most Victorians supported legalisation of prostitution, police had more urgent priorities to tackle. In 1978, Brian Dixon, as member for St Kilda, publicly called for brothels to be legalised, and privately pushed within the party for reform. Chief secretary Pat Dickie and backbencher Bill Campbell prepared a report on the issue, but discussion of it was kept to the party room. Hamer decided that the time was not right to tackle liberalisation of either homosexuality or brothels, and both issues were postponed until after the 1979 election.

As a backbencher, Storey had chaired the party committee that recommended the Equal Opportunity Bill. Now, as attorney-general, he applied the same principle to his new sexual-offences bill:

> The underlying theme was that there shouldn't be any distinction in the Crimes Act on the basis of gender. What wasn't an offence for women shouldn't be an offence for men. We scrubbed what was in the Crimes Act and rewrote it in gender-neutral terms. And the result was that homosexual offences disappeared from the Act.[5]

One of the oddities of the old Crimes Act had been that it outlawed male homosexual behaviour, but was silent on female homosexuality. Legend has it that when the British parliament originally decided to outlaw 'the abominable crime of buggery', ministers left out female homosexuality because they felt it too indecent a subject to be mentioned to Queen Victoria when presenting the bill for royal assent. The effect of introducing gender equality was to remove what had been male-only offences.

Storey's bill went far wider than simply removing buggery from the statutes. It introduced a common age of consent for boys and girls, increased penalties for sexual offences committed against young people for whom the perpetrator was responsible, outlawed rape in marriage (at least for separated couples), broadened the definition of penetration, and classified offences into different grades, with stiffer penalties. The bill sailed through the council, but struck trouble in the assembly. After half-a-dozen Liberals crossed the floor to vote with the Nationals against deleting buggery from the statutes, Robert Maclellan, handling the bill in the Lower House, moved an amendment to make it an offence to solicit 'for immoral sexual purposes' in a public place. Cain warned in vain that the words had 'a dangerously wide meaning', but the Liberals lined up loyally to support the amendment, which police sporadically applied against homosexuals until the Cain government deleted it in 1986.

Prostitution, however, proved too tough a nut for the party room to crack. Hamer left it for the Cain government, in its 1986 reforms to sexual laws, to bring the law into line with changed community standards.

Even so, Storey's sexual-offences act was a vanguard reform. It helped to redefine Victoria as a tolerant, broad-minded state in which real issues were talked about and tackled. It eventually forced the Wran government in Sydney to follow — although, Graham Carbery recounts, it took until 2003 for New South Wales to fully match Storey's gender-neutral reforms. Victoria was the only state in which a Liberal government ever led the way in making homosexual acts legal. In the other mainland states, Labor governments carried out the reforms; in Tasmania, reform was finally achieved by a private member's bill moved by Greens MP Christine Milne, who went on to become her party's federal leader. The 1980 legislation was one of the most important reforms of the Hamer era; and, unlike the party's split over capital punishment, Storey's careful approach ensured that he brought everyone with him.

In his six years as attorney-general, Storey pushed through a large reform agenda that maintained the pace of Hamer's early years. He introduced residential-tenancy reform to create greater equality of rights between landlords and tenants. He took the first steps to transfer all of the state's land-title records to computer files — a project that, despite its large potential cost savings, was completed only under the Brumby government, 30 years later. The age of legal majority was reduced to 18, and the conduct of rape cases was reformed to, among other things, prevent defence counsel from cross-examining the victim on her previous sexual history. As so often, however, judges ganged up with defence counsel to get around the new law.

Another important reform was the establishment of the Legal Aid Commission. Legal aid to the poor had been pioneered in the 1960s, with Rylah's support, by the legal-aid committee of the Law Institute led by solicitor Jack Heffernan. By the late 1970s, Storey recalled:

> We had a scattering of legal-aid providers: the Commonwealth body for Commonwealth cases, the legal-aid committee, operating with limited resources, voluntary legal-aid centres and pro-bono schemes by solicitors. We had discussions with the Law Institute and with the Commonwealth Attorney-General, Peter Durack, and got a good deal by which the Commonwealth and the state both contributed money to fund the Legal Aid Commission. Julian Gardner [a founder of the volunteer-run Fitzroy Legal Service] was the first chief executive.

This was a time of competitive reforms, when Victoria, New South Wales, and South Australia virtually competed to lead the way, each setting the pace in different areas. One example was the race between Victoria and New South Wales to establish relationships with Chinese provinces. Hamer got in first: in 1977, even before China had opened up to Western investment, Victoria began seeking a sister-state relationship with Jiangsu, the relatively developed coastal province north of Shanghai, home of historic cities such as Nanjing and Suzhou. By August 1979, Hamer was in Nanjing to sign the deal. Two weeks later, New South Wales premier Neville Wran signed a similar agreement with the southern province of Guangdong. Yet while Hamer returned to Nanjing in 1980, this time with a delegation of 111 business leaders and officials, it took a long time for the sister states to develop a meaningful relationship. Hamer established a similar relationship with Aichi prefecture, home of Japan's third-largest city, Nagoya, and also the home of Toyota, which was then expanding its manufacturing presence in Melbourne.

In 2011, Ted Baillieu as premier visited Jiangsu, which has developed into an economy as big as Indonesia or Spain, to reinvigorate the relationship by stepping up people-to-people exchanges, including up to 50 'Hamer Scholarships' for Victorian postgraduate students to live in Jiangsu to study Chinese. By then, China had become Victoria's biggest trading partner, and by a very long way. In an interview for this book just before his trip to Jiangsu, Baillieu ranked the decision to initiate ties with China, right at the outset of its extraordinary development, as one of the three great legacies that Hamer left Victoria, along with his reforms to protect the state's heritage and develop the arts. 'He not only backed it at a time when few saw China's economic potential, but he chose Jiangsu, the province west of Shanghai, and the Yangtze delta, which has become a huge economy, with a growing share of China's GDP,' Baillieu said. Monash University and Caulfield Grammar School, he said, were able to establish their campuses in Suzhou and Nanjing respectively, partly thanks to the long relationship that had developed between Victoria and Jiangsu.

One area in which Victoria was well out in front of other states was tackling the road toll. At the 1976 election, Hamer pledged to introduce random breath tests for drivers. Labor opposed it as a breach of civil liberties, as did the chairman of the Australian Law Reform Commission, the future High Court justice Michael Kirby. But by now Victorians had made it clear where their priorities lay in the choice between road safety and civil liberties. The road toll had kicked back up, and more than one in four drivers tested after being involved in accidents had a blood-alcohol content above .05 per cent. The National Party voted with the government, the bill passed in June 1976, and the state's road toll resumed its rapid decline, shrinking from 938 in 1976 to 657 by 1980.

Hamer remained an enthusiastic sponsor of change wherever it made sense to him. From 1977, every new numberplate issued in the state carried the slogan 'Victoria — Garden State'. As slogans go, it was pleasant, aesthetic, ordinary, and unthreatening: it was utterly characteristic of Hamer, the gardener of Monomeath Avenue, and it exemplified what so many Victorians liked about him. In the same year, the Victorian Film Corporation came into being. Henry Handel Richardson's schooldays' novel, *The Getting of Wisdom*, was its first big hit, with Susannah Fowle in the lead role, and young hopefuls Kerry Armstrong, Noni Hazlehurst, and Sigrid Thornton among the students; the VFC (now Film Victoria) then showed its diversity by backing *Mad Max*. Bingo was legalised, overturning a 23-year ban. Werribee Park, the mansion that Hamer had bought in 1973 for $1.5 million, opened its gates to become *the* park of the outer south-western suburbs. Smoking was banned on public transport.

Energy conservation became one of his new causes. The SEC and the Gas and Fuel Corporation were prodded to offer consumers home insulation on credit, which people could pay off over time from savings on their electricity or gas bills. Hamer set up a solar energy council, and preserved the option for nuclear power to be a future source of generation. He ordered all government departments to start buying four-cylinder cars (Australian-made, of course). He decreed that new public buildings had to have windows that opened (a commonsense feature that his own office, built in the 1960s, sorely lacked, making him reliant on air conditioning). And Brian Dixon produced a Melbourne bike plan to follow up the success of the Yarra bike path.

While the pace of activity slowed as the federal government restricted the supply of loan funds, Hamer was pushing on as fast as he could to build new transport links. In 1977, his government was simultaneously building the underground rail loop, the West Gate Bridge, and the Eastern Freeway. It extended the East Burwood tramway to Middleborough Road — the first extension of the tram network for decades — and made plans to extend the East Preston line. New tracks were laid on the Frankston and Dandenong lines to allow more express trains. In 1978, the government chose a compromise 12-kilometre route down the Gardiner's Creek valley to link the South-Eastern and Mulgrave freeways, while keeping the road away from the creek. But it ran into a stalemate with the Fraser government over the proposed route for the Albury-Wodonga freeway bypass: the states and the locals wanted the freeway to go through the town, where it would be most useful, while the feds insisted it take the cheaper route by going around the town. It took 25 years for Canberra to admit it was wrong: the freeway through the middle of Albury opened only in 2007.

Of all the projects dear to Hamer's heart, none became more of a trial than the Victorian Arts Centre: the combination of concert hall, theatres, and spire he had pledged to build by the Yarra at Melbourne's southern entrance. The history of the project is a fascinating story beyond the scope of this book; Vicki Fairfax's history, *A Place Across the River*, is a worthy treatment of it, from which this summary is drawn.

After years of procrastination by his predecessors, Bolte had built the National Gallery building (1968), the first stage of the centre. He agreed to build the rest of the centre, but as the projected cost skyrocketed — from $11.76 million in December 1966 to $25.7 million barely a year later — he got cold feet, for good reason. Much of the site turned out to be unsuitable for major buildings. In the words of a subsequent report by engineering consultant John Payton, of John Connell and Associates:

> Below ground at this particular location is beyond belief … The site is underlaid by soft ground and Coode Island silt. Below the silt is gravel, which forms the old bed of the Yarra, and below that, the basalt rock that flows along the bank of the river.[6]

The National Gallery was built on solid mudstone, which once formed the cliff overlooking the Yarra gorge. The Concert Hall would sit on a basalt outcrop. But the theatres and the spire would be sitting on '40 metres of treacherous silt'. And the architect, Sir Roy Grounds, had designed the theatres to sit underground.

Bolte shelved the project. In 1970, the West Gate Bridge collapsed, killing 35 people; some years earlier, the King Street Bridge, too, had collapsed. Bolte was not going to risk a third collapse with the Arts Centre. He told Grounds and the centre's building committee, headed by Kenneth Myer, then boss of Myer's, that if they could come up with a simpler design that was above ground, with less complex engineering, then 'we might take another look'. Grounds' design was scrapped, and he had to refund $500,000 — a fortune at the time, because the committee blamed him, in Vicki Fairfax's words, for 'having designed a building that was almost certainly unworkable'.

By the end of 1971, Grounds came back with a new plan, and persuaded the building committee and the government that the theatres and spire could be built for $28.5 million. In 1973, agreement was reached to build the concert hall for $10 million, and workers sunk the first of a series of 60-metre steel piles, reaching down to the bedrock to hold the whole complex in place. Then they discovered that the groundwater running through the site was full of acid: possibly from salt water deposited millions of years ago; possibly from a car-battery factory that had operated there in recent decades. BHP had to design a special steel that would corrode more slowly; the piles were enclosed in concrete sleeves; and a 'cathode protection system' of electric currents was installed to try to neutralise the acid.

Next, cracks appeared in neighbouring buildings, for which the owners blamed the excavations at the Arts Centre. Then drillers digging a lift well hit an aquifer that flooded the site. And then, as if all this wasn't enough of a trial, Norm Gallagher decided that since the premier wanted the Arts Centre so much, it would be an ideal site to be the pacesetter in improving building workers' wages and conditions. Vicki Fairfax tells the story:

> By early 1977, the BLF had installed overtime bans on all their sites, which by July had also been taken up by the carpenters. Thug tactics and blatant blackmail were the order of the day … At one stage the plumbers broke off the taps and sawed the spindles off the water valves. They then went to the Department of Health and complained that, as the site had no water, it was a health risk. As the only people

who could fix the taps were plumbers, the situation was at an impasse. The stand off was to last six months.

If anyone delivering materials to the site did not have a union ticket, Fairfax recounts, 'the site would be declared black for 24 hours. Then, without fail, the men would reappear at the weekend and work overtime.' Black bans were often called in the middle of strategic concrete pours, because 'they knew that stopping them in the middle would mean having to jackhammer out what they [had] already done, and start again'. Project engineer Michael Hipkins estimated that industrial unrest held up construction for four years and added more than $25 million to the cost of the project. It ended up costing taxpayers $225 million. Taxpayers had to pay for not only the sabotage committed by the workers, but for 'mud money,' height allowances, travel time, over-award payments, union picnic days, and, most grating of all to project managers, cash payments to get workers to return from strike. One wonders how Bolte would have handled Norm Gallagher, had their times overlapped. He certainly would not have kept agreeing to pay up, as Hamer did.

That Hamer kept his faith in the project through all this shows how much the Arts Centre meant to him — and how hard it is for governments to walk away from projects once they've adopted them. In the end, Melbourne ended up with an arts complex of which it could be proud, and which has repaid the city by attracting people to come to its shows. An older, wiser Jeff Kennett, interviewed for this book, said Hamer's support for the arts was his great legacy to Victoria:

> Dick was a real patron of the arts, and his government was in that tradition. He nurtured them, he provided them with money, he provided them with his personal involvement. And I don't think you can have a modern city if it doesn't have a strong cultural heart … To me, his greatest contribution was the cultural base which he gave this city, where hundreds of thousands of people enjoy the arts — not only the locals, but visitors from interstate and overseas.

Fairfax concludes that Hamer's tripartite role as premier, treasurer, and minister for the arts was crucial in seeing the project through:

> Without his sustained personal support, [it is unlikely] it would have had the form and administrative structure it did … Hamer knew that he could trust Myer's judgment to tell him what he needed to know, and equally, to be aware (in his words) of 'what I didn't want to know'.[7]

His Labor opponents recognised his key role in the project with two unusually generous gestures. In 1982, as premier, John Cain invited Hamer, as the political father of the project, to open the concert hall, which was the first half of it to be completed. And after Hamer's death in 2004, premier Steve Bracks decided to rename it as Hamer Hall, as a lasting reminder of a good man who had made Victoria a home for the arts.

CHAPTER TWENTY-TWO

Planning and the Liberal Party

A key reason the Liberal Party lost the 1982 election is that voters react against parties at war with themselves. And a key part of the story of the Hamer government is one of a gradual descent into open disunity, which ended up destroying the government.

A little disunity does little harm. It can keep ministers on their toes, raise issues which ought to be noticed, give vent to legitimate viewpoints which ought to be voiced, and help to create a climate in which people are judged by their performance, not by their position. But there's a difference between a dog giving its owner a gentle nip to alert him to something, and a dog biting its owner aggressively and treating him as its enemy. Bolte experienced some of the former from party-room rebels like Alex Taylor. Hamer experienced the latter from Doug Jennings, Charles Francis, and others.

The liberal takeover of the Liberal Party naturally sparked animosity from the conservative wing of the party, especially when it set out to destroy the Country/National party, which the Liberal right saw as its ally. On both sides of the party, there was a lack of will to work together. The new rulers on the left of the party saw their role as being to keep pressing on to retain the political middle ground, rather than slowing down to bring the right with them. By 1975 no one was in control, or able to hold a divided party together. When Leo Hawkins was sacked as state secretary, his deputy, Trevor Fairbairn, declined the job, and Dr Tim Pascoe was brought in from the federal secretariat as a temporary replacement. But after a year Pascoe, too, quit because of the factional infighting, complaining to Howson of the problems he faced in 'trying to be friends with all the factions in the Liberal Party', and that he was 'getting out before things get too difficult'. (Others frequently complained to Howson about the intensity of party infighting; but, as one of the worst culprits, he blithely ignored them. Hamer wanted to be everyone's friend. Howson was the type who preferred to be your enemy.)

Graham Jennings (no relation to Doug) was appointed state secretary. He, too, lasted little more than a year, upon which Neville Hughes, a Volvo executive, took over. Hughes managed to last six years, which was quite an achievement. He recalls:

> Membership levels were not a big problem, but the party was in a desperate financial position. There was a very substantial deficit run up for the 1976 state election. They employed me to try to bring it into some sort of order ... Hamer was totally aloof from the party's financial position. I did establish a good working relationship with him, but I always felt that there was a chasm between his role and ours ... And [I was] always having to bear with the capriciousness of the party.[1]

Despite repeated attempts by the right to unseat him, Peter Hardie saw out his three-year term as state president. He handed over in July 1976 to Joy Mein, who defeated Howson in a state council ballot (according to Howson, by 318 votes to 258). Mein, too, had to cope with constant destabilisation from the Howson camp, and from the ambitions of businessman John Elliott, who became a key figure in the party from the mid-1970s on. But she, too, saw out her term, and in July 1979, barrister Richard Alston came through a crowded field to win. Alston was also on the left of the party in those days, but was seen by the right as someone they could work with. One of the first of the new wave of Catholics in the Liberal Party, he was to move to the Senate in 1986, and was minister for communications from 1996 to 2003 in the Howard government.

In June 1976, the Liberal state executive learned that party members investigating the Western Port preselection had discovered that in two pro-Jennings branches, someone had inflated membership numbers by falsely enrolling people who were not Liberal Party members, thus giving the branches preselection votes to which they were not entitled. One branch, Pearcedale-Langwarrin, would not have been entitled to send any delegates to the preselection were it not for the last-minute 'enrolment' of 21 people on a single day, including local matriarch Dame Elisabeth Murdoch. The executive ordered an inquiry, and word leaked out to Dan Webb of Channel 7. *The Age* spoke to more than 20 people listed as members of the Hastings and Pearcedale-Langwarrin branches who denied that they had ever joined either branch. Three belonged to some other branch; one lived 150 kilometres away; a prominent local government identity said he had never heard of Langwarrin until questioned by party officials; and Dame Elisabeth said she supported the Liberal Party, but had never been a member. (Peter Hardie told Victorians she was added to the membership list because she had donated money to the party. But given her generosity, if Dame Elisabeth automatically joined every organisation to which she gave a donation, she would have become a member of almost every cultural and charitable group in Victoria.)

The party organisation closed ranks in public. In November, the official investigation concluded that at least 16 delegates at the preselection (which Jennings had won narrowly) were ineligible to vote, as three branches had insufficient members to be eligible to send delegates. But it blamed only 'poor administrative procedures in the state secretariat,' held no one responsible, and cleared Jennings from allegations of branch stacking. Yet the party refused to release the report, or to show it to Jennings. When the story first appeared, Jennings broke off the leash, telling one newspaper that he had been threatened with blackmail and murder, another that bureaucrats had 'taken over the state' since Hamer became premier, and a third that most MPs were 'yes men interested only in getting a portfolio', and it was 'quite abnormal to find one who is honest and straight'. Invited to speak at the Royal Australian Planning Institute, he told the planners:

'People are getting sick and tired of this meddling in their affairs. Either you've got to have freehold land and the rights that go with it, or you've got socialism.'

The party stayed silent, hoping it would go away. For a while, Jennings reverted to silence, but it didn't last. In October 1976, Charles Francis lined up with Labor to call for the Beach report into police corruption, then under wraps, to be released publicly. It was hardly the stuff of insurrection, but Hamer decided to make an example of him, and gave him a dressing-down in the party room. Francis resented it. By 1977, readers of *The Australian* and the *National Times* were being treated to verbatim accounts of what had been said in the Victorian Liberal Party room, at such length that many assumed the meetings had been tape-recorded. Out in the new members' 'chicken coop', Labor Party MPs were learning things, too. As the land deals scandal progressed, it became an open secret that Liberal MPs were leaking damaging material to Labor and the media. Colleagues whispered that Morris Williams, an eccentric economist who came to parliament from the Institute of Public Affairs, used to go straight out of the party room and get on the phone to a journalist. In 1992, Labor's industry minister, David White, told the Legislative Council that Francis had been one of Labor's best sources on the land deals: 'He was extremely helpful,' White smiled. 'That was well known to everybody on both sides of the House.'

Their party colleagues grew fed up: while many in cabinet and the backbench shared Jennings' view that planning was blocking important developments, they could not tolerate disloyalty. 'Jennings and Francis were like burrs under the saddlebag,' Digby Crozier recalled in an interview for this book. 'It got to the point where not only were divisions in the party room being leaked, but they were being quite open about it.' In one speech, Jennings told his colleagues: 'People are beginning to think we're a bunch of crooks.' Hamer was initially reluctant to expel them from the party room, fearing they might do more harm outside the tent than within it. But on 6 September 1977, when Wilkes moved a motion of no confidence in the government over the land deals, Jennings abstained from the vote. Francis had been paired with an absent Labor MP, but he walked out with Jennings, and Hamer and the cabinet decided that both should go. They were expelled from the party room, by a vote of 69 to 4 in Francis' case, although it took some months to obtain the overwhelming majorities needed in the state executive and state council to expel them from the party.

Jennings hit back with a rambling 65-page 'personal explanation', tabled under privilege, which recounted his version of dozens of conversations and accused dozens of his former colleagues of being corrupt, cynical conspirators. Hamer referred the document to the solicitor-general, future High Court judge Sir Daryl Dawson, who concluded that: 'There are some conversations (that is, hearsay evidence) related in the document that are said to support some of the allegations but, apart from this, there is no evidence in the document itself other than the assertions it makes.' Jennings' own credibility by then was eroded, even in his own electorate. At the 1979 election, he was beaten into a distant third place by Wonthaggi builder Alan Brown, who within a decade would be Liberal leader. Francis lost even more easily in Caulfield, where the young Ted Tanner reclaimed his father's old seat for the Liberals. Jennings returned to Queensland, joined the National Party, was given a seat, and became a loyal backbench supporter of Sir Joh Bjelke-Petersen — until, one day in 1987, attendants found him dead in the parliamentary sauna, apparently from a heart attack.

The Jennings maelstrom distracted attention from a more significant development that was underway. A widespread, low-key rebellion was growing in the party against Hamer's determination to preserve the best of Victoria's heritage and environment. It was a central part of his agenda, which won him widespread praise from the community. But his values collided with those of interests that the Liberal Party has traditionally supported: property developers, speculators, and landowners who feel they should be free to use their land as they see fit. We saw earlier that, as minister for local government, Hamer introduced the green-wedges policy, which overnight reduced the value of speculators' land and options to buy property in corridors designated as non-urban wedges. In theory, this meant that developers should abandon their options or sell the land back to farmers. In practice, however, it meant that they often sought to use political influence to get the zonings changed. It was a similar story when minimum subdivisions were introduced to prevent urban sprawl in areas such as the Dandenongs, the Mornington Peninsula, the Yarra Valley, and along the state's coastline. Those who lost potential development rights tried to regain them through political influence.

If the building or landscape in danger was seen as being of great importance, Hamer bought it. By the end of his reign, the state government had bought dozens of historic buildings or natural landscapes to protect them for the future. The best-known example was the Windsor Hotel, Melbourne's grandest 19th-century hotel, which stood directly opposite Parliament House in Spring Street. It was one of the first buildings to be listed on the Historic Buildings Register, and the listing came as the hotel's board applied for permission to build a 38-storey office tower next door. Entrepreneur Gordon Barton proposed an alternative plan: a consortium of other hotel owners could buy the Windsor and turn it into a classy casino. When both ideas were squashed — the first by Hamer and Hunt, the second by the Liberal Party room — the owners went on strike and refused to pay their rates and taxes, claiming that the hotel was unviable, and that they should be allowed to demolish it. In the previous 15 years, Melbourne had already lost most of its grand old hotels: the Menzies, the Federal, the Oriental, Champion's, Scotts, and the Cathedral hotels were all demolished in the 1960s or early 1970s. The fate of the Windsor became a test of the government's credibility. Hamer stepped in, bought the hotel for $4 million, and leased it to Federal Hotels. The lease was later transferred to the Oberoi group, which renovated the Windsor and ultimately bought it, fully justifying the government's intervention.

But the owners, and those of libertarian bent, argued that if planning imposed restrictions on owners' land use, and the state was not prepared to buy them out, they should be paid compensation for the development opportunities they had lost. Hunt rejected this, arguing that there had never been a legal right for owners to use land as they chose or to subdivide it. But when he was replaced by Geoff Hayes after the 1976 election, the direction of planning swung around, under the influence of the department's can-do secretary, Neville Haynes. In December 1976, while Hunt was away on holidays, Hayes not only won cabinet approval in principle for Mount Ridley, a vast new satellite city to be built north of Craigieburn on land that formed part of Hamer's green wedges, but quietly revoked council planning controls over a 45-hectare site at the foot of Mount Dandenong to allow US developers Kaiser Aetna to build a 400-home subdivision on land zoned rural. Bill Borthwick, as the local MP and minister for conservation then trying to reverse inappropriate subdivisions in the Dandenongs, led a council delegation to tell Hayes that his action was inconsistent with the government's own planning policies. *The Age* got wind of both stories, and ran them prominently; under pressure, the government would eventually reverse both decisions.

The party's planning committee wanted an independent inquiry into landowners' right to compensation for unfavourable planning decisions. In 1976, James Gobbo, later to become governor of Victoria under the Kennett government, was appointed to head a three-man inquiry into the issue, along with influential planning consultant Les Perrott (who had lobbied Hamer to approve Mt Ridley) and prominent investment banker and racehorse owner David Hains. There was no expert on the committee to represent the public interest in planning. Architectural historian and National Trust activist Miles Lewis noted that Gobbo had frequently appeared in hearings as counsel for the owners of historic buildings, and Perrott as a witness for them. Their report, delivered at the end of 1977, recommended that owners of historic buildings and natural landscapes who were denied 'reasonably beneficial use' of their property due to planning or heritage restrictions should be entitled to receive compensation, and a tribunal should be set up to assess compensation claims. They did not, however, support compensation for owners affected by rezoning decisions.

The right of the Liberal Party was delighted with the Gobbo report. Howson records that, while it was still confidential, Robert Maclellan invited him into his office to read it, then kept him informed about its progress in cabinet. Hamer, however, refused to table the report until the government had decided its response — which it kept delaying, and delaying, as different voices in the power structure put conflicting views to it. The report was eventually released by opposition leader Frank Wilkes; once again, someone had leaked it to the enemy. While Maclellan kept giving Howson positive reports about what cabinet was likely to decide, and even Hamer kept assuring party officials that the government would implement the report, its deteriorating financial position made this more and more difficult. If cabinet wanted to compensate landowners for preserving historic buildings in the city, or beautiful landscapes on the urban fringe, Treasury pointed out, it would have to pay for this by cutting existing spending somewhere, or raising taxes, or both. Hamer gradually turned against the plan. By August 1978, Hunt was back as planning minister, and he had no time for it. The Gobbo report was shelved forever. Influential CBD property owners who had been counting on compensation took this as evidence that Hamer was against them, and could not be trusted.

By then, discipline was gradually breaking down throughout the party, and disunity was breaking out in public. In November 1978, the right moved successfully for the state council of the party to urge the restoration of the death penalty, opposing one of Hamer's key reforms, and got the council to oppose his decision to allow the Gas and Fuel Corporation to explore for gas. The 125 motions listed from branches were a microcosm of the Liberal Party at the time, from the thoughtful and visionary — urging the state to step up remedial tuition for children falling behind, and the Fraser government to 'take the necessary steps to initiate the formation of an Australasia Pacific Economic Group' — to motions calling on the government to scrap fluoridation, and consider abolishing penalty rates. The Victorian Liberal Party was a broad church, but an unhappy one. Howson's diaries report hundreds of conversations with Maclellan and others that exemplify the saying of former New Zealand leader Mike Moore: 'In politics, your opponents sit on the other side of the chamber. Your enemies sit on your own.'

Howson's own attitude to Hamer by now was close to pathological hatred. 'I do not see much difference at the moment between Hamer and Whitlam,' he wrote after one state executive meeting, at which he attacked Brian Dixon for the 'extravagance' of his 'Life. Be in It.' campaign. Jennifer McCallum, whose movement, People Against Communism, held rallies to try to stir up grass-roots support for the right, claimed in 1978 that Sir Robert Menzies had written to her offering his support for the movement, 'because we have such a hopelessly inadequate State Government'. (Menzies' son Ken and biographer Allan Martin later cautioned, however, that his harsh views on others in his final years reflected the psychological impact of the disabling stroke he had suffered.) Howson made no secret of his antagonism to Hamer. At the end of 1978, when, in another role, he had to host a delegation of Chinese officials at a dinner at the Melbourne Club, it must have taken all his aristocratic nerve to invite the premier to be his guest — and all of Hamer's self-discipline and his vision of the future importance of relations with China for him to accept. The colossal potential of China seems to have been the only thing these two Liberals agreed on.

By the end of 1978, the political climate in Victoria had changed sharply, and so had the mood in the Liberal Party. Richard Alston sums up the problems he was about to inherit as party president:

> Dick was a class act, and his brand of small-l liberalism worked well when the times were good. But towards the end, things were getting a bit tougher, and he was reluctant to move to stronger economic policies. As things got bad, Dick's lack of focus on economics became a problem with lots of people … He became more fallible with the passage of time, ministers got tired, things went wrong … And these things [party disunity] are often about frustrated ambitions.[2]

Or, as Digby Crozier put it: 'Initially, incumbency is an advantage. But, over time, there comes a point when incumbency becomes a handicap.'

By 1979, against a refreshed Labor opposition, the deadweight of incumbency was starting to weigh down the Hamer government.

CHAPTER TWENTY-THREE

Hanging from a cliff

The year 1979 was one that changed the world. The year began with the Vietnamese invading Cambodia to oust the bloodthirsty Khmer Rouge regime, arguably the worst government since Hitler; yet the world responded with hostile sanctions rather than gratitude. A month later, Muslim activists forced the Shah of Iran into exile; their spiritual leader, the Ayatollah Khomeini, returned to lead the authoritarian, backwards-looking 'Iranian revolution', and by November, militants had seized the US embassy and taken 53 diplomats hostage. And on Christmas Eve, Russia's ageing dictator, Leonid Brezhnev, made the fatal mistake of invading Afghanistan, a decision whose consequences arguably led to the fall of the Soviet Union, and reverberate still.

Australians were not happy. For three years, the focus of economic policy had been to 'fight inflation first' and get the federal budget out of deficit. Yet inflation was still above 8 per cent, building activity remained stuck at recession levels, growth was sluggish, and unemployment had risen to 6.4 per cent. In August 1978, the first budget of Malcolm Fraser's young treasurer, John Howard, had ended universal health care, imposed an income-tax surcharge, lifted petrol taxes to impose world-parity pricing, and scrapped the half-yearly indexation of pensions. Not surprisingly, the Fraser government's popularity slumped, while frequent union strikes to immobilise public transport or turn off power supplies fanned public discontent.

For the Hamer government, the campaign for the 1979 election began with the resignation of Roberts Dunstan and Pat Dickie from the cabinet — and in Dickie's case, from parliament — in August 1978. The ensuing cabinet election was a victory for the old guard against those wanting a new look: Jim Ramsay, the cabinet secretary, moved up to fill one vacancy; Tom Austin, the unofficial leader of the rural faction, took the other. Austin came from the famous family of Western District squatters who introduced rabbits to Australia in 1859; he himself had been part of the team that got Henry Bolte elected to Hampden in 1947. A solid conservative who enjoyed general respect, he might have ended up as premier himself in other circumstances; but while he always had influence, he never sought the top job. These were safe appointments, but not the rejuvenation of cabinet that some felt was needed. Hamer did reshuffle portfolios, and for the better: he promoted Maclellan to minister for transport, returned Hunt to the planning portfolio, and left Hayes as minister for housing. Hamer announced that, to prevent conflicts of interest, he would require ministers and MPs to list their assets in a register kept by parliament. It was a popular move, but Liberal Party polling found the party was in trouble, especially in the outer suburbs.

A by-election in Ballarat was also unwelcome — particularly as it had to be fought on the old 1965 boundaries, to elect someone to see out the last eight months of Dickie's term. In 1976, the Liberals had won by a comfortable 8.9 per cent, but the party's popularity had collapsed since. An *Age* poll taken just before Dickie and Dunstan departed found a landslide two-party swing to Labor of about 7 per cent. In marginal Liberal seats, the swing averaged 9 per cent. The underlying indicators of voter support were much better: the Liberals led by 49 per cent to 37 per cent as the party seen as best able to manage the state, and by 51–35 as the party seen as most likely to provide strong and stable government. Nonetheless, after preferences, Labor was running equal with the combined Liberal–National vote. Up to 20 government seats were at risk — as, indeed, was the government itself.

Since 1955, despite its political dominance, the government had lost five of the 19 by-elections held in Liberal seats. Just a year earlier,

Labor had won back Greensborough with a swing of 6.25 per cent — at a by-election that saw Pauline Toner elected as Labor's first-ever female state MP, and the new Australian Democrats win 18 per cent of the vote, most of which flowed on to Labor. (In 1982, Toner would become the first female minister in a Victorian government. She would also be the only practising Catholic in John Cain's cabinet; in his father's last cabinet, almost half the ministry were practising Catholics.)

Ballarat had been a Labor town before the Split, and a new generation of activists, including a young economics teacher, Steve Bracks, was determined to make it one again. (In 1999, Bracks as Labor leader would bring down the seemingly invincible Jeff Kennett as premier, with a strategy that focussed on winning support from country towns such as Ballarat.) Labor's candidate for the by-election was David Williams, Bracks' former economics lecturer at the University of Ballarat (then Ballarat CAE). Everything was running Labor's way. They won the seat with a 9.6 per cent swing.

Just as Bolte did after his by-election loss at Dandenong, Hamer met with cabinet on the Monday morning and offered his resignation. But according to Howson, reporting what his wife was told by Robert Maclellan's wife, 'there was a chorus, led by Lindsay, to persuade him to stay'. Someone suggested that Joe Rafferty should step down to allow more fresh blood into cabinet; Rafferty retorted that if he were forced out of cabinet, he would quit parliament, forcing another by-election in his marginal seat. Howson's diary records that many in his circle thought Hamer was looking tired; he himself thought that Hamer's powers of concentration seemed less sharp than they used to be. Maclellan told Howson that part of the problem was that too many ministers were unwilling to make decisions, and instead kept handing their tough issues to Hamer to solve. Little had gone right for him in 1978. The Christmas–New Year break was particularly welcome.

The Hamer government entered 1979 with the polls suggesting it would be fighting for survival at the election due in March. At best, it would have to form a coalition with the Nationals; at worst, it could be thrown out for a Labor government. Liberals on the right were pessimistic: retired Senate president Sir Magnus Cormack told Howson that the result would be like 1952 (when the Liberals were left with just 11 seats). Hamer was one of the few who remained optimistic that the Liberals would win in their own right.

His secret weapon was himself. The Liberals' market research told them that, despite everything, Hamer was still their brand advantage. *The Age* poll in August 1978 found that, while his popularity had taken a dive, 80 per cent of Victorians still rated his performance as premier as either good or fair; only 17 per cent rated it as poor. By contrast, 57 per cent of voters polled couldn't name the opposition leader when asked, and when told it was Frank Wilkes, few had strong views on him one way or the other. Pollster Gary Morgan, always a shrewd judge, told a disbelieving Howson that Hamer's image with the public remained strong. The Liberals' advertising agency, Masius Wynne-Williams, decided that, for the third election in a row, the Liberals should focus their campaign on Hamer, with the slogan 'Hamer: Vital for Victoria'. The ad campaign was unusual in that most of it was positive, highlighting the Hamer government's achievements. Masius had prepared negative ads attacking Labor as controlled by socialists, but the Liberal hierarchy dumped them unused, judging that, with Labor headed by a man as ordinary as Wilkes, the ads would fail the reality test in suburban living rooms. The Liberals also distributed a 16-page booklet, *More than Meets the Eye*, extolling the government's record in detail across all portfolios.

Boldly, Hamer decided to run a three-month campaign, ignoring party advice to engage in a shorter fight. On 6 February, he announced that the election date would be 5 May. His strategy was twofold: he wanted to give Labor as much time as possible to make mistakes under pressure, and himself as much time as possible to demonstrate to voters his superiority over Wilkes. Parliament was not allowed to sit — that would have given Labor an ideal forum — but, in a first for Victoria, he agreed to take part in two TV debates, one with Wilkes alone, and one with Wilkes and Ross-Edwards, so long as they were run live and uncut (he did not trust the ABC current-affairs team, whom he saw as Labor partisans).

The long campaign also allowed the Liberals to make the most of their usual advantage in fundraising: in radio and TV advertising, the Liberals outspent Labor by almost three to one. *The Herald* reported that a single fundraising dinner with Hamer for 25 donors at the Toorak home of trucking tycoon Lindsay Fox raised $62,500; it allowed them to beef up their advertising in the final days, when Labor was almost out of funds.

The Liberals had few new policies to offer: Hamer had been rolling his policies out for the past seven years. His out-of-character attempts to paint Labor as a socialist tiger were abandoned after they inspired more ridicule than fear: 'Can Mr Hamer really believe that the conservative Mr Wilkes is a closet revolutionary, or that … he would endorse the nationalisation of everything in sight?' asked *The Age* in a mid-campaign editorial. But the paper also summed up his opponent's message as: 'Vote Labor — you'll hardly notice the difference.' The lack of a fresh message might have been a problem for the Liberals, were it not that Labor eventually created a new topic of conversation by proposing a radical policy. Rather than the state standing by helplessly in the face of high unemployment, Wilkes argued, it could free up $400 million of funds for job-creating programs by raiding the 'hollow logs' — bank accounts and government bonds — in which semi-government authorities stashed away spare money they were not ready to use. If they were required instead to store the money with a central Treasury-run fund, the bigger pool of funds would require less of a safety margin, and the surplus funds could be invested to get the state economy moving again.

It's hard to imagine how a plan proposed by financial-market specialists could become the central issue of an election campaign. Hardly anyone understood it, which made it an easy target for the Liberals to attack. Kevin Foley devoted his economic expertise to tearing Wilkes' arguments apart. Using Foley's material, Hamer argued that there was no surplus money there, and that by confiscating the funds of authorities such as the Board of Works and the railways, Labor risked sending them bankrupt or leaving them unable to finance essential works. There was, in fact, a much stronger argument for Labor's case than either side realised at the time: country water authorities had been borrowing money from the government at a subsidised rate of 3 per cent, and then lending it out in the markets at far higher rates. This was not only ripping off taxpayers, but depriving the state of money that was meant to be employed in building useful things, and keeping the economy growing. A Keating might have won the argument for Labor, but Wilkes was no Keating. The money from Lindsay Fox's fundraising dinner was soon paying for Liberal ads on TV and radio attacking Labor's policy as a risk. Polling suggests there was a sizeable shift back to the Liberals in the final fortnight of the campaign.

Yet the state Treasury was already doing something similar. Between 1976 and 1979, as the Fraser government repeatedly cut Victoria's borrowing limit in real terms, the Treasury secretary, Sir Ernest Coates, and his successor, Ian Baker, found a new source of funds by reducing the state's financial portfolio and using that capital to finance its works program. What was radical about Labor's proposal was that it proposed doing the same to the semi-government authorities. At the time, few Victorians understood, let alone cared, that this would essentially spell the end of a long Victorian tradition of relying on quasi-independent expert authorities, boards, and commissions to provide their water, sewerage, electricity, gas, trains, trams and buses, roads, and so much else. Labor was proposing to take away the financial independence of these 'quangoes' (quasi-autonomous national-government organisations). The Cain government would also remove most of their operational independence, while the Kennett government would go much further by selling the state's electricity and gas businesses to private (mostly overseas) firms, and privatising the delivery of public transport (and much else). By and large, by 2010 only Victoria's water and country-rail services were still delivered by the semi-government authorities that for so long had dominated the state.

Hamer's gamble on holding two televised debates paid off: he was widely seen as the winner. His own campaign promises were a strange mix of ideas, reflecting the swirling ideological winds of the time, and the Liberal Party's shift from the centre to the small-government agenda of the right. He pledged to legislate to require secret ballots of union members before strike action could take effect. He would set up a parliamentary expenditure-review committee to scrutinise departmental spending, review public service staffing, increase penalties for drug dealers, abolish death duties altogether, allow citizens to set public policies through referendums, as in the US, and introduce 'sunset' legislation under which laws and agencies would expire after a fixed time unless renewed by a fresh mandate. More in the old Hamer style, he also pledged to expand domiciliary nursing services, day hospitals, and elderly citizens centres, and provide a state-funded home-renovation service to allow more old people to be cared for while staying in their homes. World War I veterans would be given free travel on public transport, while pensioners would be given discounts on motor-car registration and third-party insurance. A new Olympic pool would be built on Batman Avenue. And despite the fiscal straitjacket imposed on him by Canberra, the premier promised to increase public funding of non-government schools from 20 per cent to 25 per cent of the cost of educating a child in the equivalent grade of state schools.

Labor needed a swing of 9 per cent to win government, and 5 per cent to force the Liberals into coalition with the Nationals. Against expectations, it achieved neither. In an unusual result, Democrat voters gave most of their preferences to the Liberals; they felt they had more in common with Hamer than with Wilkes. The election result hung in the balance for ten days, until Brian Dixon emerged as the winner in St Kilda by just 81 votes. The Liberals had won a bare majority, with 41 seats in the 81-member House, to 32 for Labor and 8 for the Nationals. They had lost ten seats to Labor and one to the Nationals, but survived to govern in their own right. In the south-eastern suburbs, part of the Liberal heartland until then, Labor picked up five seats — Glenhuntly, Bentleigh, Oakleigh, Heatherton, and Springvale — in a regional campaign directed by architect Evan Walker, who would go on to be one of the key ministers in the Cain government of the 1980s. In Glenhuntly, Labor was aided by DLP preferences, directed against Charles Hider, whom the DLP remnants saw as embodying the small-l liberalism they hated in Hamer's Liberal Party. But Labor failed to make any gains along the Ringwood corridor, where Box Hill, Mitcham, Ringwood, and Monbulk all held for the government. And the Ballarat by-election turned out to be just a by-election: the Liberals held three of their four marginal seats in the provincial cities, and regained the Ballarat upper-house seat they had lost six months earlier. The bias of the electoral system against urban voters also played a part; for the first time since 1952, Labor won most of the seats in Melbourne. If votes in Melbourne had the same weight as votes in the country, mathematical probability suggests Labor would most likely have won an extra seat at the Liberals' expense, forcing them into coalition.

The election outcome was a reprieve for Hamer. But, arguably, it was a reprieve that weakened his government rather than strengthened it. Going into coalition with the National Party would have meant an abrupt shift in Hamer's style; it would have been unwelcome to the ambitious backbenchers who wanted places in cabinet and a new focus on deregulation and smaller government. But it might have shifted the government's priorities to focus on economic development sooner than otherwise happened, and perhaps with less trauma and indecision. Ross-Edwards was close to Hamer; he, too, had been to Geelong Grammar, Trinity, and the Melbourne University law school. An intelligent man with good human understanding and streaks of liberalism, he freely conceded that had he lived in the city, he would have been a Liberal. But having survived boarding school with a speech defect, he had developed into a tougher man than either Hamer or Thompson; as deputy premier, he would have been a force for discipline. As Digby Crozier put it: 'Ross-Edwards was a street fighter, and he could be very tough — and very effective.' The Nationals would have claimed three or four cabinet positions, but most likely the Liberal casualties would have come from the timeservers of the ministry, not the high performers. Against that, the cost would have been a shift to the right on social and environmental issues; this might have jeopardised Haddon Storey's landmark reforms of sexual offences, as well as Hamer's campaign for a casino.

With the government now hanging on a single-vote majority, however, and potentially facing more losses ahead, relations with the Nationals moved to the top of Hamer's agenda. Some Liberals had already been quietly advocating a merger of the two parties to stop them fighting each other so they could focus instead on fighting Labor. Now Hamer and Ross-Edwards quietly began negotiations aimed at achieving a formal alliance, and potentially an eventual merger. Their talks progressed swimmingly until they came to confront the next step: what would happen if the Liberals lost another by-election in the new parliamentary term? Ross-Edwards wanted agreement that if the Liberals became a minority government depending on the Nationals to survive, it would form a coalition with at least one National (presumably himself) in the ministry. Hamer declined; he felt he could not concede publicly that his party might lose its hard-won majority. The negotiations broke down at this point.

But in Hamer's final term, as Labor became a party preparing for government, the Nationals became a party preparing for coalition. On key issues, they usually voted with the government. The Liberals' majority became less precarious in 1980 when Nationals MP Neil McInnes swapped sides to join the Liberals, lifting their majority to three. Hamer genuinely believed in a merger of the two parties; in March 1981, he told incredulous Young Liberals that 'the non-socialist cause' would be best served by a single party. Ross-Edwards was to remain the Nationals' leader until after the 1988 election, but refused to enter a coalition with Kennett, for whom he had no time. The two parties finally negotiated a coalition only after Alan Brown became Liberal leader in 1989.

Hamer's close victory did nothing to unify the party. Kennett, the unofficial leader of the class of 1976, launched a new campaign to get some of them elected to cabinet. As Walter Jona wrote in his autobiography:

> I can recall, on many occasions, Jeff making it known that he didn't intend to be around in politics for a long time, but he did intend to make his time in it both memorable and contributory. Prior to the 1979 state election Jeff had his eyes on the shape of the new ministry … Knowing how meticulous Jeff was in his planning, I was not surprised to be informed by some of his close colleagues that he was organising a few days away together on the Murray River with his proposed voting block, during which they would decide on their preferred new nominees for Cabinet and on those ministers they intended to replace …[1]

Under a revised agreement, the party room was to elect the four leaders and ten other ministers, while the premier would appoint four. There were only two vacancies: Joe Rafferty had been given the plum post of agent-general in London, and Alan Scanlan had lost Oakleigh to Labor's Race Mathews. This meant that at least two ministers would miss out on being in the ten to be elected. When the ballot began, Jona's fears were confirmed. The first ballot elected not Bill Borthwick, the party's usual first choice, but Lou Lieberman, a Wodonga solicitor who had taken Benambra from the Nationals in 1976 and now headed the '76ers ticket. The power of the new boys had been proved dramatically — so dramatically that it led to defections which wrecked the chances of the rest of their ticket. 'The list suddenly dissipated, and there was no discipline to keep to the arrangements,' recalls Rob Knowles. Lieberman was the only member of the class of '76 to be elected. Alan Wood, who had taken Swan Hill from the Nationals in 1973, was the only other new face elected.

Hamer then had four ministers needing his support to hold their places, plus all the candidates on his supporters' ticket, organised by Alan Hunt. To the dismay of some on both sides of the party, he reappointed the veteran Jim Balfour for a sixth ministerial term, as well as Vasey Houghton, who had struggled with the health portfolio, and Walter Jona. Only Geoff Hayes was dropped from the lineup, taking the blame for poor planning decisions that had cost the government support. It is not clear why Hamer picked Norman

Lacy in his place. While Lieberman certainly earned his stripes as a minister, the new cabinet was hardly the rejuvenation that the Hamer government needed — or that its 'ambition faction' was demanding.

CHAPTER TWENTY-FOUR

The casino

Sue Calwell didn't fit the stereotype. Young women of her age were meant to be feminine and demure, and to let the men take charge. She was bouncy, brash, and keen to take charge herself. She had left school early, got a job, went to work overseas, and then came back to Melbourne in her mid-twenties, 'young and pretty ambitious'. When the owners of Melbourne's big hotels, headed by Bruce Matear of the Hotel Australia, decided to set up a bureau to attract meetings and conventions to Melbourne, and advertised for its inaugural executive director, Sue Calwell walked in the door and talked her way into the job. One bit of the world was about to change:

> The first day I turned up to work, I found my office was in the basement. I had a secretary who resented that another woman younger than her had got the job. I wandered down Collins Street knocking on doors, trying to get companies involved, trying to get people to understand the potential of the meetings business. But there was no 'tourism industry' in those days, no tourism marketing. I wanted Melbourne to have the first conference centre of [international] standards in Australia ... but after a year, I felt I was not getting anywhere.
>
> Dick Hamer was going on one of his trade missions to San Francisco, New York and all that. I wrote a letter under Bruce Matear's name to Dick Hamer, saying that tourism needed to

> be represented on this trip. The next morning, I got a call from Geoffrey Smith [Victoria's chief of protocol] to say that Bruce would be welcome on the mission. I said no, I would be going. He was very uncomfortable with that, and also I had no money. I was winging it ... [but after some lobbying on her behalf] they said they would accept me.
>
> We had a meeting in the cabinet room. When it got to my turn, I stood up and said I was really sorry, I would have to withdraw from the tour, because I had no resources, and we can't get any support from governments ... I calculated that it would be harder for them to take me out of the tour than to leave me in.
>
> Then doors opened. I got on the plane. Hamer came and sat me next to him in business class, and said: 'I'd like to know why you are here. What do you hope to achieve from it? And how come I'm paying for you?' ... I talked to him all the way to Honolulu. We got on like a house on fire. He told everyone on the delegation to support me.
>
> I don't think there had been any women on these missions before. Dick always loved young women — and young men — of vitality and energy. We'd go out nightclubbing and dancing. Dick Hamer was a good dancer, and he loved to dance, so we'd sweep the floor together.
>
> When we got back, he called in Digby Crozier [the Minister for Tourism], and said, 'We're going to make this sing, and market Melbourne as a tourist destination.' He agreed to the funding I'd asked for [to set up a Melbourne Tourism Authority, with the state paying two-thirds of the cost].[1]

Thus, in February 1977, began a friendship that was to change the direction of the Hamer government. Hamer became a convert to the idea of building a world-class convention centre in Melbourne to attract tourists — which then evolved into a plan to build a casino by the Yarra to pay for it. He was far ahead of other politicians of his time in grasping how important tourism would become in Australia's economy, and the wider benefits that could flow from the state investing in this area. By then, he had already bought two of Victoria's grand old hotels, the Windsor in Melbourne, and the Shamrock in Bendigo, to protect them from demolition; he had bought them to preserve the state's history, but deciding what to do with them introduced him to the tourism industry's agenda. Yet the idea that the government should facilitate the development of a casino — and promote gambling — to subsidise a loss-making convention centre was anathema to many Liberal MPs, including some of Hamer's closest allies, and to many Victorians from all areas.

To some, it didn't help that the main proponent of the plan was an irrepressible, vivacious, attractive young woman who seemed to have a special relationship with the premier. They were frequently seen together, even dancing together late one Saturday night at a Liberal Party state council meeting in Geelong. Hamer loved to dance with attractive women; Sue Calwell was far from alone in that respect. But people talked, and — rightly or wrongly — drew conclusions. What might have been just insider gossip reached a wide audience when a throwaway scandal sheet, the *Toorak Times*, run by undischarged bankrupt and con man Jack Pacholli, insinuated repeatedly that the premier and the lobbyist were having an affair.

Most of the paper's readers may have been unaware that Pacholli was a criminal who was indifferent to the truth of what he published, loved to have his paper talked about, and knew that his bankruptcy made it futile for anyone he defamed to sue him. Pacholli didn't know whether any rumours he heard were true or not, and didn't care: people liked to read them, so his practice was to treat rumours as fact. The rumour that the premier was having an affair was only one of hundreds of unsubstantiated rumours that were elevated into fact in the *Toorak Times*. But many grass-roots Liberals assumed that because the story was in a newspaper, it had to be true. Party members and even MPs began to believe that the premier was having an affair with the convention centre's lobbyist, and that was why he wanted to build a casino and convention centre. Liberal state director Neville Hughes recalled that the party's female members were particularly incensed, with many expressing sympathy for April. True or false, the rumours became part of the mix of factors that began to undermine Hamer's authority as leader.

Only two people really knew whether or not they had an affair. One, Dick Hamer, died in 2004. The other, Sue Calwell, flatly denied it when interviewed for this book:

> Look, Dick was an innocent. I was living at the time with Dennis Gowing [better known as used car tycoon Kevin Dennis]. I was young and attractive, and I was a real person, a free spirit. In those days, young women just couldn't be left like that … I was never going to win [against the rumours].
>
> I was part of Dick's light side. He was fun, he was gregarious, but he really was a gentleman. He was like a father figure to me. My own father taught me ballroom dancing, and I loved dancing with Dick. People raised eyebrows, we would dance crazy, and people would say, 'It's very inappropriate, in front of chairmen and managers, all these business people.' And I got away with anything. I had the support of the premier; no one was going to mess with me.

People were not used to seeing young women in positions of influence, she argued; many assumed they must be there because they were having an affair with someone important. During her 20 years as a tourism executive, Calwell says she was often rumoured to be having affairs with different men. One of them was one of Hamer's younger ministers, well known for his obsession with women, who kept pestering her to go out with him — 'so I used to take someone along whenever I had a meeting with him.' She blames the rumours on the sexist assumptions of that era of transition in women's role in society, and on the malevolent yellow journalism of Pacholli and the *Toorak Times*. But in a parting aside at the end of our interview, she conceded that she and the premier had enjoyed an unusual relationship: 'We didn't have an affair. But he might have been obsessed with me.'

Certainly, Hamer became obsessed with the idea of building a convention centre in Melbourne. When it became clear that this would not be economically viable by itself, he became obsessed with the idea of building it alongside a casino whose profits could subsidise it. Like his obsession with turning the Latrobe Valley's coal into oil, it became one of the main themes of his last years as premier. But whereas his coal-to-oil dream was a visionary but implausible diversion, his pursuit of a casino, while more plausible, split the party, and his own supporters, at a time when it needed to stand united.

After the 1979 election, Hamer, for the first time, included himself in the ministerial reshuffle. He handed over the Treasury portfolio to Lindsay Thompson, which was seen as a strong hint that he planned to hand over the reins to Thompson during that three-year term. But he also gave up his beloved hobby, his portfolio as minister for the arts, to cabinet newcomer Norman Lacy — which freed him to appoint himself as minister for state development, decentralisation, and tourism. The appointment attracted virtually no comment at the time, but it was a strange choice of priorities. Hamer was interested in all three areas of the portfolio; but then, he was also interested in most other portfolios, and, as premier, he could involve himself in any issue he chose. The new portfolio tied him down to administrative and ceremonial tasks that would have been better delegated to a minister, so that as premier he could focus on key issues. Digby Crozier, who found himself moved out to be minister for local government, says he was 'very surprised' that the premier wanted to take the portfolio for himself:

> It was probably a good move, because it put him in the box seat to drive the state's reputation as a place to do business, and as a place to invest in. He'd always had views on how it should be handled. But there was no new investment comparable to Alcoa [the Portland smelter] in that term.[2]

Hamer's seven years as minister for the arts was an indulgence, but one that consumed little time and reflected his intense interest in the area. It is possible that putting himself in charge of tourism was, again, an indulgence. But that was not how Hamer saw it. He argued that, with rising productivity in agriculture and manufacturing, employment growth in future would rely on growth in service industries — and, above all, in tourism. Under fire in March 1980, he responded in parliament with unusual passion:

> It is the fastest-growing industry in the world, and by the end of this century it is believed that it will be the largest industry in the world. If we are interested in the progress of Victoria, and in its growth and development, we must give attention to how we can build up this industry ... It is in person-to-person services that mechanization is less likely to take place, and where job opportunities for young people will occur in future. That is my interest in the promotion and expansion of tourism; it is my interest in one aspect of that industry, which is the provision of a proper convention centre in Melbourne. About 25 per cent of all tourist travel involves attendance at conventions and conferences ... It is the people attending conventions who spend the most money and stay the longest of all types of visitors.
>
> Therefore it is very much in Victoria's interests to promote and encourage the development of convention centres. I make no bones about that ... I propose to continue to involve myself in such discussions and to give what support I and the Government can to major developments in the state. That is the plain duty of the Government.[3]

Two plans became major priorities. The port of Melbourne was shifting downstream to accommodate bigger ships. The Melbourne Harbour Trust proposed building a World Trade Centre on the vacated site of North Wharf — on the Yarra, at the edge of the CBD, by the Spencer Street Bridge. Similar centres had mushroomed across the US, providing offices for companies and government authorities involved in trade and shipping, together with halls that could host meetings and conventions. But they usually ran at a loss. Studies indicated that a trade centre in Melbourne would be unlikely to pay its way. Nonetheless, Hamer became an early supporter of the plan, and when Malcolm Fraser agreed to allow the states to nominate a couple of vital infrastructure projects that would be exempt from Loan Council constraints, there was some amazement when the two projects Hamer proposed were the Loy Yang A power station and the World Trade Centre.

His choice exposed him to heavy criticism, from the ALP and *The Age* in public, and from his own economic advisors in private. Treasury opposed the trade centre, warning that it would not be viable and would be a drain on the budget. A report by consultants Baker, Suttie and Co., commissioned by the government but then kept secret, predicted it would lose millions of dollars in its first decade or two. Over lunch at Dame Elisabeth Murdoch's home 'Cruden Farm' one day, former Treasury secretary Sir Ernest Coates told Howson he had tried very hard to talk Hamer out of it. Coates feared that borrowing to build a loss-making project would damage Victoria's credit rating, and make it more expensive and difficult to raise funds in future. (In view of later Victorian governments' insistence on maintaining a AAA credit rating, it is worth noting that Coates regarded a AA rating as acceptable.) Hamer compromised by agreeing to build the World Trade Centre without a convention centre, but it still lost money. Later, ironically, the Cain Labor government added a hotel and convention centre next door, which occasionally hosted large conferences, and was used by the Kennett government for a temporary casino until the Crown Casino opened.

The World Trade Centre was eclipsed by a much more exciting project. In 1977, Hamer had set up the Melbourne Tourism Authority, along the lines suggested by Sue Calwell on that flight to Honolulu. She became its first director; and, in a partnership with the tourism industry, the government paid two-thirds of the cost. Hamer then appointed Calwell to head a committee to examine potential sites for a world-class convention centre. Another member of the committee was John Haddad, managing director of the Federal Hotels group. Haddad had built Australia's first casino at Wrest Point in Hobart, where he overturned decades of opposition to casinos, and proved that they could be run as legitimate business operations. Now he was keen to create a world-class casino in his hometown. He had already made two attempts to win support for a bold plan to put a casino in the historic Windsor Hotel. Each time, Hamer had supported it, as had then tourism minister Murray Byrne, but it was killed off by the social conservatives in the party room. Calwell, Haddad, and the committee then looked at five different sites for a convention centre, including North Wharf, the Exhibition Buildings, the Jolimont railyards, and the new Museum station, then under construction. But the site that caught Haddad's imagination was just across the Yarra from Flinders Street station. It was a block of offices, next to the site of the Arts Centre, right on the river, in the area we now call Southbank. It was the head office of APM, Australia's biggest papermaking firm, but it was willing to grant him an option to buy so long as it became a partner in the project.

Federal Hotels came up with a new offer: let us build a casino, Haddad said, and we will build a convention centre next door. Sydney architect Kevin Curtin, who had designed Wrest Point, came up with a startlingly imaginative design for a nine-storey glass pyramid on the south bank of the Yarra. It was a beautiful work of art, which predated by several years I.M. Pei's design for his famous (but much smaller) glass pyramid in the forecourt of the Louvre. In an interview for this book, John Haddad was deeply nostalgic as he lovingly displayed a portfolio of Curtin's plans:

> I wanted to build a magnificent casino-hotel-entertainment centre. It would have been one of the most beautiful casinos in the world if it had got approval — as good as or better than Monte Carlo, Wiesbaden, or Baden-Baden. It would have been a pyramid entirely of glass, reflecting the Yarra, reflecting the sky, all over … It was only half the size of Crown [the casino that Melbourne built in the 1990s], but it had a shopping complex, exhibition hall, and international convention centre. It would have had a footbridge over the Yarra, and been totally integrated into the riverside.

The casino was to occupy the second floor. The nightclub was given the top floor. Between the two would be a 1,250-seat cabaret, a disco, restaurants, a licensed club (with no gaming), a retail plaza with coffee shops and cinemas, and office suites. There would be no poker machines; Hamer made it clear he would not allow them. There would also be no bedrooms: Haddad knew he would need the united support of his fellow hotel-owners if he was to overturn Victoria's traditional hostility to gambling venues. A people's plaza would connect the casino to the Arts Centre and St Kilda Road. All this was designed and thought out long before the Cain government created Southbank, even before *The Age* initiated its 'Give the Yarra a Go!' campaign in 1980. It would have been a spectacular building, and a great neighbour for the Arts Centre.

Haddad's trump card was to pledge that if the casino were approved, Federal Hotels and APM would build a four-storey convention centre next door, able to seat up to 3,000 delegates. The state government would be offered free use of the centre to stage conventions. In effect, the casino's profits would subsidise the convention centre's losses. No government funds would be required.

Hamer loved it from the outset. 'Dick was attracted to the look of it, and the way it would complement the Arts Centre and the spire,' Haddad remembered. 'He knew it would become a catalyst for tourism.' The casino and convention centre would offset the ridicule that Hamer had suffered over his failed Melbourne Landmark proposal — a global competition set up to design a landmark for the city to be built over the Jolimont railyards. A panel chaired by entrepreneur and former lord mayor Ron Walker, and including Sue Calwell and ad man/columnist Phillip Adams, among others, was asked to award a prize of $100,000 for the best proposal. A brave idea ended in failure: no proposal was thought worth building, no prize was awarded, and Melbourne comedians had a field day with the more ludicrous entries.

But the glass casino could have become Melbourne's real landmark, a building that could identify the city worldwide. John Haddad knew that it would be a tough battle, but thought they could win over the party room:

> It was generally well received. Labor didn't put up much opposition. The National Party was OK. *The Age* was the only paper that gave us a hard time. We had a strong record in running casinos. Wrest Point had introduced a rule of no tips, to avoid collusion. We brought in a count room, where the government's people and our people counted the dollars, so there would be no risk of being infiltrated by people using the casino to launder money or cook the books. The winners received their payouts only by cheque, so it was all open and clean. And there were to be no poker machines.

In the debate that followed, it was widely accepted that Federal Hotels had run an impressively clean operation at Wrest Point. But some argued that was because Hobart was a small town; in a bigger city like Melbourne, organised crime would muscle its way in to use the casino as a front for other activities. And even with no poker machines, many in the Liberal Party and the churches worried that vulnerable people would be drawn like moths to the flame, gambling beyond their means and sending their families sliding into poverty.

The plan to allow a casino became a new source of division within an already divided party. It cut across the usual left/right lines. Some of the right-wing radicals who caused trouble in the party room, such as Jeff Kennett, endorsed the plan. But some of Hamer's closest allies, including Lindsay Thompson and influential backbencher Don Saltmarsh, a former Methodist minister, opposed any expansion of gambling opportunities, fearing the impact on family budgets.

Hamer won the first round. On 31 July 1979, with many members on leave, the party room reversed its blanket opposition to casinos, and agreed to commission a feasibility study of the project. Hamer had prepared his ground by personally briefing the editors of the three newspapers — a tactic he rarely employed — and other potential sources of opposition. On 2 August, he went public, declaring that the government had endorsed the 'Southgate' plan in principle, subject to negotiations over the details. But it was only deep into a long press release on the benefits of the new convention centre and entertainment venue that the premier mentioned that the project also involved approval of a casino. He knew how sensitive the issue would be — not least because the National Mutual insurance company had bought the historic Rialto building in Collins Street, and was trying to get government approval to build a casino and convention centre there. Its chairman, Gerry Niall, a man of trenchant conservative views, was a friend of Alan Hamer but a longtime critic of Dick; the premier's obvious support for the Southgate casino over his own plan turned Niall from Hamer critic to Hamer enemy.

On 9 October, the party room at full strength set up a committee headed by Thompson to inquire whether casinos should be legalised, and if so, under what conditions. Six weeks later, the committee implicitly gave a green light to Southgate — and, potentially, the rival $140 million plan by National Mutual for the Rialto and its neighbours — by concluding that casinos would generate tourism and employment. It urged that they be built in conjunction with an entertainment and convention centre, rather than as smaller stand-alone clubs, or as stand-alone casinos in regional Victoria (for which there were also many bidders). The party room endorsed the recommendation on a show of hands, but the debate was far from over. Niall complained publicly that Hamer had associated himself closely with the Southgate bid, to the disadvantage of the Rialto plan. In the wider community, Russell Skelton commented in *The Age*, 'an effective behind-the-scenes campaign [was being waged] by Melbourne's churches, including the Uniting Church, against casinos in any circumstances'. Parliament was bombarded with petitions against a casino. Eastern suburbs Liberal MPs grew worried. The situation called for skills in political infighting that Hamer had never bothered to acquire. Fraser would have worked tirelessly on the phone and in one-on-one meetings to swing the crucial votes his way, and would have got his supporters to do the same; Hamer had never done that, and wasn't about to start. Labor, having uncorked the issue by declaring its support for a casino during the 1979 election campaign, now tried to focus the debate on allegations that Hamer had given the Southgate group favoured access and support. In an important concession to his critics, especially Niall, Hamer pledged that an independent committee would be set up to decide which proposals, if any, would be given casino licences.

But on 22 April, the Liberals folded under the pressure. The party room decided it would not consider legalising casinos until there was 'a demonstrable community demand for them'. Hamer beat a strategic retreat, moving successfully that the issue of a casino be considered separately from that of a convention centre. 'The party is not prepared to give the go-ahead at this juncture because of the overriding public opinion that has expressed itself,' he told reporters. It was left to Haddad to point out what the decision meant. 'It is impossible to launch a privately funded convention and entertainment centre,' he said. 'You cannot ask people to buy shares in a scheme that is going to run at a loss.'

Hamer's government began exploring the option of adapting the Exhibition Buildings to be Melbourne's convention centre, but that got nowhere. Inspired by *The Age*'s 'Give the Yarra a Go' campaign to revitalise the lower Yarra and its environment, he also commissioned a senior planning official, John Lawson, to come up with plans for renovating the south bank of the Yarra next to the proposed casino and convention centre. When the government swung right in December 1980 to adopt the pro-business 'New Directions' agenda, Federal Hotels decided to try again. It engaged a PR firm, and commissioned an opinion poll that found 54 per cent of Victorians were in favour of a casino. The Young Liberals, reliably pro-Hamer and pro-casino, were recruited to send telegrams to Liberal MPs urging them to drop their opposition to casinos. It was this lobbying that provoked Box Hill MP Don Mackinnon to move in the party room on 11 March 1981 that it was the prerogative of MPs to decide whether there was demonstrable support for a casino. The motion was designed as a challenge to the casino's supporters. They took up the challenge: Hamer, Brian Dixon, Ian Smith, and Jeff Kennett all urged the party to open the door to a casino. But by 38 votes to 30, the party voted to shut the door for good.

Hamer's defeat on the casino had long-term consequences for the state. The Haddad plan would have given Melbourne a beautiful architectural showpiece on a site that now hosts some of Southbank's dullest architecture. A casino without poker machines would have weakened the case for a casino with poker machines, as the Kirner government later chose. Hamer's opposition to legalising poker machines was unequivocal; back in 1971, he moved a motion that won unanimous support in the Liberal Party room:

> This party never under any circumstances will approve the introduction of poker machines in Victoria. Government opposition is largely based on the belief they take money that would normally be spent on food and clothing, and the families who are hardest hit are those who can least afford it.[4]

Future Victorian governments would have different principles.

The defeat of his casino plan was a serious blow to Hamer's prestige. Bolte would not have let himself be seen to be on the losing side; Hamer had been seen publicly to lose twice in 12 months on the same issue. It was democratic but, unquestionably, it undermined his authority. And that authority would be undermined even more when Ian Smith announced five days after the Mackinnon motion that he would move a private member's bill to overturn the party room's decision. In a sense, it was the beginning of the end.

CHAPTER TWENTY-FIVE

1980

When Dick Hamer chose to stay on as premier in 1978, rather than retire and see it interpreted as a concession of defeat to some enemy or other, it was because he assumed his problems were temporary: he had to just see them through, normal times would resume, and then he could retire on top. The reality was just the opposite. Few things got better for him after 1978. Most things got worse.

First, the competition became more formidable. The 1979 election gave Labor a second influx of new talent: 20 new MPs, including three who would become key ministers in the Cain government. Evan Walker, one of Melbourne's most successful architects, and an energetic critic on planning issues, went straight into Labor's leadership team. Rob Jolly, formerly Hawke's research economist at the ACTU, became shadow treasurer; and Race Mathews, former federal MP and secretary to Gough Whitlam, became an articulate Labor voice on a range of issues. Labor MPs described themselves as 'a party preparing for government', and they were. Wilkes was still a minor liability as leader: in April 1980, John Cain launched his first bid for the post, only to see the Socialist Left MPs line up solidly behind Wilkes, the least socialist leader Labor had ever had. But most observers thought it was only a matter of time before Cain took over.

The Liberals gained just nine new members in 1979: two of them, Alan Brown and Don Hayward, were to become key ministers in the first term of the Kennett government, and Brown, who had won back Western Port from Doug Jennings, served an important period as party leader from 1989 to 1991. Yet perhaps the biggest transformation was that, in a diminished party room, the election trebled the number of female MPs, with Joan Chambers winning Ballarat South and Gracia Baylor becoming (with Labor's Joan Coxsedge) one of the first two women elected to the Upper House. Jeanette Patrick was elected as party secretary in 1979, putting her in contention to become the first woman in a Victorian ministry. But one of the few backbenchers who could have really refreshed the ministry in 1979, Athol Guy of Seekers fame, quit politics due to serious bronchial illness. Overall, the 1979 election made Victorian politics a far more even contest.

Second, Hamer's control of the party had always rested on the perception that he was its best vote-winner. The Liberals' narrow escape at the 1979 election made that assumption less certain. As the government slid further in the opinion polls, his authority in the party eroded. With each public defeat at the hands of the party room on the casino, his authority in the community eroded. His critics became more forthright, and more determined to force a leadership change. In September 1979, *The Age* reported that Ian Smith was considering challenging Hamer for the leadership. Smith had courage and ability, but he was widely seen as insensitive, vain, and too interested in women to ever have a serious chance of winning the numbers. Nor was there any obvious alternative to Hamer. His deputy, Lindsay Thompson, was far too loyal to mount a challenge, and, after 12 years as education minister, seemed worn out. Robert Maclellan was too abrasive and too far to the right of the party. Brian Dixon was too earnest and too far to the left. Alan Hunt was in the wrong house, and had many enemies. Bill Borthwick was probably the Liberals' best option, but he, too, was loyal to Hamer, and came from the same stream of the party. To have a leadership change, as a rule, you need a challenger. Howson's diaries reveal that, to the very end, Hamer's enemies on the right could never agree on who they wanted as premier.

Third, Australia's economy failed to shake off either high inflation or high unemployment, relative to the good years of the long post-war boom. A new wave of mining investment from 1980 lifted the national economy, but made Victoria's performance look worse by comparison to the states where it was happening. For years, Bolte and Hamer in turn had boasted that Victoria had Australia's lowest unemployment rate. But in late 1979, New South Wales streaked past it, and by late 1980, Queensland and Western Australia had virtually drawn level. In Hamer's first five years in power, Victoria accounted for 26 per cent of the nation's housing approvals. In the next five years, its share was just 19 per cent, and the slump in home construction flowed through to many industries. Interstate migration figures showed that a flood of Victorians were leaving for Queensland and Western Australia. In the nine years of Hamer's premiership, in net terms, Victoria lost more than 100,000 people through interstate migration. In his last year as premier, Victoria's population grew by just 33,000; Queensland's, by 79,000.

Most of this, however, was due to factors that no state government could control. It was hardly the fault of the Hamer government that Queensland had a warmer climate than Victoria. It was not its fault that New South Wales and Queensland had black coal, and WA had iron ore, and Victoria had none of that. Moreover, in 1980, wage indexation was finally pushed over the cliff by a coalition of its opponents, from the left and the right. Wage growth surged back over 10 per cent, and the Fraser government tried to contain inflation by allowing the dollar to rise, which damaged manufacturing. All of this hurt Victoria, and the state's unemployment rate climbed to over 6 per cent. Yet the opposition and media reporting fuelled the impression that it was because of the Hamer government that Victoria was falling behind — and this interpretation was embraced by the Liberals' usual allies in business. It became common for business to complain that the Hamer government was stifling development; indeed, it became almost *de rigueur* for business leaders to do so. Yet rarely were Victorians given any examples of how it was stifling development. Rather, the impression relied on the vibe emanating from the obvious examples: the indecision over the casino, the Alcoa plant, and ICI's plans for Point Wilson (of which, more later). A sense of malaise began to hang over the state, and whether it was justified or not, it accelerated Hamer's loss of authority.

Fourth, perhaps the deepest problem was that Hamer himself had almost run out of an agenda. He had begun with a series of social, environmental, and consumer reforms which picked the low-hanging fruit, in political terms. The reforms left undone became more difficult to bring off as his political capital became depleted. He had seized the initiative, and gained authority by that. Whitlam's largesse had helped him make things happen; but when that ran out, he seemed helpless to counter the investment cuts forced on him by Canberra. From 1976, the new problems were mostly economic ones, and economics was not his field. He was getting older, and more tired. As time went on, he seemed to be increasingly reacting to what others said or did, rather than leading the way himself.

Hamer did become obsessed with three potential economic projects that appealed to him: had even one of them come to fruition in his time as premier, the record of his latter years would appear more rewarding. But the first was the casino/convention centre, where his reluctance to use his position to win over his critics saw him lose a battle he could have won. The second was his crusade to attract foreign investment to turn Victoria's massive deposits of brown coal into oil. And the third was Alcoa's decision to build a world-class aluminium smelter at Portland.

In 1973, the oil producers' cartel OPEC (the Organization of Petroleum Exporting Countries) ended the West's long economic boom by doubling global oil prices overnight. In 1979, OPEC doubled prices again, throwing much of the Western world into recession. Companies and governments everywhere scrambled to search for alternatives. South Africa had survived OPEC's trade embargo by turning its black coal reserves into oil. Hamer was already obsessed with the prospect of doing the same with Victoria's moist brown coal. In his last years as premier, he made repeated trips to Japan, Germany, and elsewhere to try to put together consortiums with the financial and technical clout to turn brown coal into oil or related products. Visitors to his office were met by a little phial of black goo that sat permanently on the premier's desk: it was solvent refined coal from the Latrobe Valley, a halfway product in the liquefaction process. Hamer's lively mind was excited by the prospect of turning coal into oil; as a boy, he probably listened to Monash recounting how the State Electricty Commission had overturned the conventional wisdom that brown coal (which is two-thirds water) was too wet to be used to generate electricity. It was technically feasible to turn coal into oil; but to be economically viable, it needed oil prices to keep soaring, and to stay up. To most insiders, that never seemed likely, and while he did attract four separate consortiums to carry out R&D on coal liquefaction in the state, none of them led to any commercial development. No one doubted Hamer's conviction on the topic, but many thought his priorities were askew.

The Alcoa smelter at first seemed a dream project for Hamer and Digby Crozier, his minister for state development. In Australia in the 1970s, few developments made more sense than building aluminium smelters. Australia already had three of them, including Alcoa's smelter at Point Henry, near Geelong. It had abundant deposits of bauxite, cheap coal-fired electricity, and deep-water ports. Bauxite is refined to produce alumina, which is then smelted down to make aluminium, in a process requiring huge amounts of electricity. As soaring oil prices pushed up electricity costs in the rest of the world, the global aluminium giants descended on Australia to find sites for new smelters. The states competed to offer them land, ports, and cut-price electricity contracts. Queensland snapped up Comalco (part of the Rio Tinto group) to build a smelter on Boyne Island, near Gladstone. New South Wales won the French Pechiney group and the Australian–Swiss consortium Nabalco to Newcastle, then discovered it would not have enough electricity to supply them both, and dropped the latter. All three companies had investigated Victoria, but passed it over. When Alcoa showed interest, the Hamer government was only too willing to make a deal.

Alcoa's original smelter at Point Henry was mostly supplied by a power station it built itself at Anglesea's coalfields, with SEC power used as a backup. But in 1979 the company's goal was to build a new world-class smelter, much larger, and located at a deep-water port for ease of shipping. Victoria had two deep-water ports: Hastings, in Western Port, just 30 kilometres from the SEC's main transmission line from the Latrobe Valley to Melbourne, and Portland, about 360 kilometres away in the far corner of the state. At Western Port, there was a vocal conservation movement that opposed the industrialisation of Hastings. At Portland, the state had spent $40 million already to develop the harbour so as to attract business to the town, with little success. It was government policy to charge the same prices for electricity throughout the state, regardless of the cost of supplying different locations. But that policy had never been applied to a consumer the size of Alcoa, which, if it built four potlines as envisaged, would use up to 25 per cent of Victoria's electricity. Building a transmission line to Portland would cost at least $100 million; building one to Hastings would cost a small fraction of that. If Alcoa chose to go to Portland, who would pay for its transmission line?

It was a test of the Hamer government's policy priorities, made more difficult by local factors. Employment in the Western District had collapsed in the 1970s as farms mechanised and consumers began shopping in regional cities rather than at the local store. Portland had been rejected by so many companies in the past that another loss would have been taken hard. Alcoa preferred to go to Portland, where it was welcome; it did not want the smelter to become another Newport. Portland was part of Digby Crozier's electorate. And had the government insisted that Alcoa pay for the transmission line, it would have been inconsistent with the policy it applied to other users, and almost certainly would have seen Alcoa dump Portland, and go instead to Hastings, or interstate.

Yet there was no justice in making other electricity users or taxpayers pay the cost of Alcoa's transmission line. Moreover, as a rule of thumb, about 10 per cent of electricity generated is lost in transmission; on the long line to Portland, those losses would be greater, and the SEC had no way to recoup them. Alcoa early on had negotiated an electricity price that critics estimated could be below the cost of supply. And since the unions were taking revenge for their defeat on Newport by disrupting the SEC's construction program elsewhere, the SEC was in serious financial trouble. It was in no position to afford cross-subsidies.

Treasury told the government that Western Port was 'a far better site', and urged that Alcoa be pressured to accept it. It estimated that the Portland site would cost the state \$11 million a year, or \$12,200 (almost the average wage) for each job it created. Failing that, it suggested, Alcoa should be urged to build up its Geelong smelter instead. But the government feared another Newport. Instead, it signed off on a deal in which the SEC would pay 58 per cent of the cost of the transmission line to Portland, while the state and Alcoa paid 21 per cent each. It also agreed to refund Alcoa all the electricity turnover tax it would pay in the first ten years of its life, expected to be \$50 million. In effect, ordinary Victorians would have to pay almost 80 per cent of the cost of a line built essentially for Alcoa's benefit, while exempting it for ten years from a tax everyone else paid. Many Victorians did not like that deal, and even more didn't like it when in August 1981, the SEC, squeezed financially from all sides, hiked power prices by an average of 20 per cent. Alcoa was the most unhappy of all, because its power tariff was raised 33 per cent. World aluminium prices were falling, construction costs at Portland were rising rapidly, and the overvalued dollar was squeezing its profits. Moreover, the rare Mellblom's spider orchid had been discovered on the site, and the local Gunditjmara tribe had taken legal action to try to stop the project, saying it would desecrate their sacred sites. In the face of all this, Alcoa mothballed the project. Work would not resume for another three years, until the Cain government, under political pressure, signed a 1,500-page agreement in which it took a stake in the project, and offered the company an innovative floating subsidy, which has proved to be a godsend to Alcoa, and a burden to every Victorian government since. It was a classic example of the damage done when governments — sometimes harried by oppositions and the media — allow politics to dictate what should be hard-headed decisions made on financial grounds.

There was a silver lining to the Alcoa deal: years later, its transmission line became useful in other ways. It now links Victoria's grid with South Australia's, giving both states greater security of supply than they had before; that was part of the original plan, although it took years to take effect. What was quite unforeseen in 1979 was that, 30 years after it was built, Alcoa's transmission line opened the way for a new generation of gas and wind power stations in western Victoria to join the national electricity grid. This has given the state a more diverse and reliable mix of electricity, generated at more diverse locations, and with lower greenhouse-gas emissions. The old SEC men would have felt some consolation.

The Point Wilson story also began well. In February 1979, ICI Australia announced plans to build a $900 million petrochemical complex at Point Wilson, near Avalon airfield. Hamer tried to keep a distance from the project, for good reason: his brother Alan was joint managing director of ICI Australia. The two brothers agreed never to discuss the issue; Dick ensured that it was handled by other ministers. ICI was attracted to Victoria by its cheap gas, and to Australia by the Fraser government's pro-manufacturing stance. Point Wilson was a relatively remote spot on Port Phillip Bay, home to little more than an ammunition depot, a wharf, the odd fishing shack, and thousands of birds in wintertime. ICI envisaged a world-scale plant to produce a range of chemicals for domestic use and export. It would be the largest of a stream of petrochemical plants intended for Victoria at that time.

But then the problems began. One of the species that wintered at Point Wilson was the orange-bellied parrot, an endangered species in the wild. Bill Borthwick's last big reform as conservation minister had been to require an environmental-effects statement for any major development. Experts agreed that a chlorine plant and an endangered parrot would make bad neighbours. Then ICI, like Alcoa and other manufacturers, became hit by Australia's deteriorating competitiveness: soaring wages, an overvalued dollar, falling prices, and a construction workforce that was an employer's nightmare. To top this off, the Fraser government reneged on a promise to shelve an inquiry into protection of the chemicals industry. For ICI, that was the last straw. In October 1981, Point Wilson, too, was deferred indefinitely; unlike Portland, it was never revived.

Hamer's critics on the right ridiculed the orange-bellied parrot and Mellblom's spider orchid as examples of how Victoria was driving industry and jobs away by its effete concern for things of trivial importance. But, in reality, neither the parrot nor the spider orchid played a decisive role. For both Alcoa and ICI, there were far more important economic factors that dictated both decisions. And while the role of environmental-effects statements and other environmental controls caused sharp divisions in Hamer's cabinet in his final months, one might note that years later, in May 1997, under the pro-business Kennett government, Robert Maclellan as planning minister refused permission for the Coode Island chemical-storage facility to be relocated to Point Lillias, just around from Point Wilson, because of concerns on environmental, occupational health and safety, and Aboriginal-heritage grounds. What seemed way-out in 1980 had become mainstream by 1997.

For all the tensions between their governments, Hamer threw himself into Fraser's campaign for the 1980 federal election, held on 18 October. But the election outcome was a disaster for Victorian Liberals. Fraser won re-election — with just 50.4 per cent of the two-party preferred vote, he managed to win a 23-seat majority — but in Victoria there was a landslide swing to Labor. For the first time since 1929, Labor won a majority of Victorian seats in the House of Representatives. In 1977, the coalition had won 23 of Victoria's 33 seats, and Labor just ten. In 1980, the coalition won 16, and Labor 17. Labor won 50.7 per cent of the two-party preferred vote — its best performance in Victoria since the Split. The swing to Labor after preferences was 6.2 per cent, twice the 3.1 per cent swing in the rest of Australia. Seven of the 12 seats the coalition lost were in Victoria.

Someone had to be held to blame, and Fraser was determined that it wouldn't be him.

A closer look, however, showed that the Victorian losses reflected a mix of factors. Four of the seats lost — LaTrobe, Hotham, Holt, and Henty — had been held by very small margins, and would have fallen in even a modest swing. Two seats were lost because the re-formed DLP switched its preferences to Labor: in Ballarat, because Labor's candidate was a former DLP member, John Mildren, and in McMillan, because its small-l Liberal MP, Barry Simon, had organised the defeat of a motion that would have blocked Medibank payments for abortions. And in Isaacs, Liberal MP and ex-publican Bill Burns had been caught drink driving and had lost his licence in a blaze of bad publicity. Nonetheless, *The Age* estimated that the same voting on state boundaries could see Labor pick up a net ten seats. A repeat of that vote would put Labor into government.

Within days, an unsourced story appeared in the *Sunday Press* quoting 'influential Liberals' as blaming the losses in Victoria on the Hamer government, and putting pressure through the media on him to resign as premier. Howson and his friends decided to ask Sir Henry Bolte to tell Hamer it was time to go. The plan backfired when Bolte said he would tell Hamer to stand firm, and that any cabinet changes would be seen as a sign of weakness. But Hamer was given a very different message by a delegation of senior Liberals, led by John Elliott: they told him that his government was now seen as anti-business, and that there had to be changes to both its people and its policies. Sir Robert Law-Smith, head of the AMP Society, warned publicly that the building unions were making it uneconomic to invest in Victoria, and that the AMP would take its investment elsewhere. Hamer was used to getting unwelcome advice from the party and ignoring it. This time, he decided to act.

Sources closer to home were also urging him to adopt a big package of pro-business reforms. The parliamentary committee set up under Kevin Foley to review public-sector bodies found Victoria's public sector had 8,000 quasi-autonomous organisations, or 'quangoes', working without clear directions or lines of authority. In cabinet, an unlikely left–right alliance had developed between employment minister Brian Dixon, a St Kilda liberal, but an economist, and agriculture minister Ian Smith, a young Western District conservative once seen as Bolte's heir. Both had carried out significant privatisations — Dixon selling the Housing Commission's prefabrication unit, Holmesglen Constructions, and Smith selling the state's network of abattoirs and cool stores. As minister for agriculture since 1973, Smith had pushed through unpopular reforms in a range of rural industries to reduce costs; but after seven years in that job, he told people he was experiencing 'male menopause' and wanted a new challenge. Dixon as assistant education minister had led the reforms to shift power from the bureaucracy to principals and school councils, giving them a growing funding allocation under their own control.

In late 1980, Smith and Dixon joined forces to press for a change of policy tack. 'We wrote a paper on what could be improved in Victoria's economic policies,' Dixon recalled. 'Smith and I worked together on the issues, and we recommended ourselves to be the ministers for economic development, and employment and training.' Both believed that Victoria's economic growth and employment levels were being held back by red tape, unnecessary regulation, and 'the web of government', as Smith called it. They wanted bold reforms to create a better environment for business to grow in, and for Victoria to attract investment. A backbench committee of Don Hayward, Ralph Howard, and Ted Tanner was set up to write a new economic platform. But what reforms could the government make without dismantling the planning and environmental controls that Hamer, Hunt, and Borthwick had created over the previous decade?

December 1980 was a fateful month for the Hamer government. On 8 December, Robert Maclellan announced that the government would close four suburban train lines, end passenger trains on seven country lines, and close a number of freight lines. On 11 December, the premier unveiled an eight-page action plan setting out his government's new pro-business policies, under the label 'Jobs from Growth'. On 17 December, he reshuffled his cabinet, with a surprising new minister. And on 23 December, he appeared to sack the Melbourne City Council, announcing that it would be replaced by administrators until a new, smaller council was elected on new, smaller boundaries.

It was meant to be a month of decisive action that would turn around the government's fortunes. On the findings of the Morgan Poll, so it did — but in the wrong direction.

Labor had called for a new transport plan. In late 1979, Robert Maclellan decided to produce one, and appointed a retired BHP executive, Murray Lonie, and one of the Country Roads Board's top men, Robin Underwood, to draw up a blueprint. Delivered in September 1980, its official name was the Victorian Transport Study, but it became known as the Lonie Report. Its central conclusion was that rail was old technology in terminal decline, whereas roads were modern, flexible technology, able to take people wherever they wanted, at reasonable cost.

Rail patronage had dwindled to 86 million passengers a year in Melbourne, and 3.2 million in the country, and would at best stabilise at around those levels, the report predicted. The way Victoria had to go in the future, it said, was to replace rail with road in most areas, keeping rail only for certain long-distance freight and highly patronised passenger services. In Melbourne, the report proposed scrapping seven suburban rail lines — Sandringham, St Kilda, Port Melbourne, Williamstown, Altona, Upfield, and Alamein — and cutting off the Hurstbridge line at Eltham. At least six tram lines would also be scrapped, with bus services expanding to replace the trains and trams. In the country, all rail-passenger services would be replaced by buses, except on the Geelong line; all freight restrictions on road transport would be scrapped; and much of the freight network would be shut down.

This was the opposite of what Hamer had set out to do a decade earlier, when he argued that rail transport would become more important as the city grew, not less so. That was why he had built the underground rail loop. This time, he seemed to offer no resistance, other than to shield Liberal-held seats from cuts. On 8 December, Maclellan announced the government's decision. It would close four suburban lines, all running through Labor electorates, while keeping the four that ran through Liberal seats. Two of them, the Upfield line through Brunswick and the Port Melbourne line, he envisaged being torn up to become freeway routes. The government would close passenger services on eight smaller country lines, but keep services going on the core trunk lines.

Three days later, Hamer announced his government's 'New Directions for Economic Growth'. It was a thin document, seen on all sides as full of pious aspirations, with little detail as to how they would be achieved. Victorians were told that planning administration would be streamlined to speed up the process of gaining approval for new factories. The government would take action to end demarcation disputes between unions, which had held up work on many building sites, including the Arts Centre and AMP's Collins Place development. Important developments would not be blocked by minor environmental issues. Factories would be encouraged to recycle their waste heat in the plant, and those generating their own power would be allowed to sell it to the SEC. The Department of State Development, Decentralisation and Tourism would be replaced by a new Ministry of Economic Development, and a new Ministry of Employment and Training would be created. But there was hardly any detail on just how the path of development would be made easier.

Next came the cabinet reshuffle. In 1979, Hamer had rescued Balfour after he had failed to win re-election to the ministry. The old dairyfarmer was now 66, and had spent a third of his adult life in cabinet: a gentleman of politics who had left no significant mark on events. Hamer now called in the favour he had extended 18 months earlier. Balfour accepted his fate and retired to the backbench, and the party demanded that the premier be the one to choose Balfour's successor. The obvious pick was the cabinet secretary, Glyn Jenkins, an accountant from Geelong who was capable and ideologically in the centre of the party. Some urged Hamer to promote Jeanette Patrick to become Victoria's first female minister. But there was also a push from the '76ers for a third candidate. 'Glyn Jenkins was the one in line for cabinet, but a few of us had a discussion with him (Hamer)', recalled Rob Knowles. And to widespread astonishment,

Hamer chose Jeff Kennett to be the new minister. One of his staff recalls that when someone told him the news, he assumed it was a joke.

Kennett had reminded Hamer that in 1975 he had told the Liberals in Burwood that he would stay in parliament for only two terms. If Hamer needed him in the ministry, he said, he would stand again, but if he stayed on the backbench, he would fulfil his promise and get out. Hamer had always been impressed by Kennett's energy: he saw him as someone who could make a difference. Glyn Jenkins accepted his decision: looking back, he says, 'Dick saw in Jeff Kennett a man with a future.'

The reshuffle promoted Smith to be minister for economic development, taking over Hamer's extra portfolio, and Dixon to be minister for employment and training. Lou Lieberman replaced Balfour as minister for minerals and energy, with a brief to help drive the reforms, while retaining his day job as minister for planning. Tom Austin moved into agriculture, and Kennett became minister for housing. For the first time, Hamer's only portfolio was as premier.

Two days before Christmas, Hamer sprang one more surprise. Needled by widespread criticism that his New Directions policy lacked substance, he announced that the Melbourne City Council would be sacked and replaced by a team of commissioners, and then reconstituted to represent a smaller area. Hamer said that the council was too factionalised, and had been indecisive on planning issues. Some asked if, on these criteria, the government was planning to sack itself. There was further embarrassment when it emerged that the council could not be sacked without enabling legislation. It remained in business until late April, with former lord mayor Irvin Rockman running an effective campaign to challenge the reasons for the decision.

Before any of these decisions were made, the Morgan Poll had reported at the start of December that the Liberals were polling better than at the 1979 election, with Hamer holding a commanding lead over Wilkes. It was the last good polling news that Hamer would ever receive.

CHAPTER TWENTY-SIX

Decline and fall

Early in 1981, Dick Hamer confided to his deputy, Lindsay Thompson, that he planned to retire as premier in July or August that year. He would turn 65 in July, and would bring up nine years in the job in August; only Bolte and Albert Dunstan would have lasted longer in the top job. It was well known in the party that Hamer wanted Thompson to succeed him. Thompson had been unfailingly loyal as his deputy, and had become as close a political friend as Hamer allowed. The Hamers and Thompsons frequently dined together, often with Walter Jona and his wife, Alwynne. Hamer's retirement plans were secret, but insiders generally assumed that he would retire rather than fight another election. Hamer, however, kept his plans close to his chest.

'I suspect the only people he told were Lindsay and April,' said Richard Thomas, his media advisor. But Thomas knew his boss well enough to guess his plans, and arranged to move to a plum job in the private sector while he was still media advisor to the premier, rather than the former media advisor to the ex-premier.

But to prevent speculation on retirement dominating his final months, Hamer told his principal private secretary, Richard Mulcahy, to brief journalists that he would stay on to lead the Liberals into the 1982 election. In the situation, it was a risky strategy. When the media reported that Hamer planned to stay on, those who wanted a change of leadership decided they would have to destabilise him to force him out. Moreover, even Thompson was left uncertain about what Hamer really intended to do. That uncertainty might well explain why he ordered MPs to retreat to the sidelines at the crucial moment when Hamer was attacked by one of his own team.

The release of the New Directions strategy brought the government no bounce. The favourable Morgan Poll in December was soon overwhelmed by a hostile reaction to cabinet's decision to end passenger services on 11 train lines; the government provided no figures to justify its choices, and people assumed, rightly, that they were politically driven. The decision to sack the Melbourne City Council became a fiasco; the council was still in business, and Irvin Rockman was making a good case for it to stay that way. The Teachers' Tribunal embarrassed the government by awarding school principals a 15 per cent pay rise; the government had told its representative, Jack Baker, that he would not get another term on the tribunal, and this was his way of returning the favour. Then came the party room's fateful decision on 11 March, when, upset by pressure from the Young Liberals and a public-relations firm to support a casino, MPs voted to rule it out completely.

Ian Smith, three months into his new role as minister for economic development, was frustrated and angry. Turning the vague aspirations of New Directions into real policy changes was proving difficult. Cabinet had made little headway down the path of deregulation. It had approved extending shopping hours for tourist precincts 'in principle'. Jim Ramsay, the minister for labour and industry, had promised to come up with a policy to try to unwind penalty rates in tourist industries. A subcommittee was drafting a bill to legalise casinos, until the party room killed it. Lieberman was meeting with insurance firm Colonial Mutual to seek a compromise that would retain the historic town house at 1 Collins Street, while allowing the insurer (which wanted to knock it down) to build a new tower behind it. Smith was impatient with change taking place at a gradual, consensus speed. He wanted to be an economic czar, able to overrule decisions by his colleagues so that developments could go ahead without environmental or planning issues getting in the way. But when he tried that line on his cabinet colleagues, they slapped him down unceremoniously. And now the party room had blocked a casino plan that, according to one poll, enjoyed majority support.

Smith decided to take fate into his own hands. He went to see Hamer, and told him he was thinking of moving a private member's bill to authorise a casino, just as Hamer had done in 1975 to abolish hanging. Smith argued that as Labor's policy was to support a casino, it would have to vote for the bill, so that, even if most Liberals opposed the bill, it would still pass. Smith said he thought that Hamer indicated support for this plan. Hamer said he did nothing of the sort. At the same time, backbencher Ralph Howard, Smith's most open supporter, told *The Age* that the party had to actively consider changing its leader; a senior minister was said to be organising support for a challenge.

On 14 and 15 March, the Liberal Party state council met at the Pharmacy College in Parkville. About midday on the Sunday, Smith declared in a statement that he would move a private member's bill to legalise casinos. Hamer met immediately with the leadership team (Thompson, Hunt, and Storey) and Richard Alston, the party president. With their backing, he ordered Smith to issue a second statement to say that, rather than introduce a bill, he would put his plan to cabinet and the party room. Smith refused. Hamer then sacked him from the cabinet, and called a press conference to announce the decision. In a brazen attempt to upstage his leader, Smith entered the room and sat next to Hamer. The photo shows Hamer, normally the most placid of men, seething with rage at Smith's impudence; when a reporter directed a question to Smith, Hamer walked out. It was an act of unprecedented rebellion by the very minister whom Hamer had put in charge of the government's new direction.

Initially, public opinion sided with Hamer. Peter Ross-Edwards summed up a widespread view, calling Smith 'a man of great ambition but not very much political judgement'. But Smith's rebellion lasted only two days. Lindsay Thompson, always a peacemaker, persuaded him to apologise, and Hamer to take him back into the ministry. A tearful Smith withdrew his plan 'unequivocally', withdrew his claim that Hamer had approved his action, and praised his leader as 'a very big man'. But Hamer's backdown did him more harm than Smith's rebellion had. In sacking a minister who had brazenly defied cabinet solidarity, he had shown a strength of leadership that he had been lacking. To back down on that decision just two days later seemed to confirm that he was weak and vacillating. This was further confirmed in early May when Smith, utterly unrepentant, called for Hamer to set a retirement date.

The party didn't need a pollster to tell it that it had problems. But George Camakaris did so anyway, delivering a report that began in Shakespearean tones: 'Now is the winter of our discontent.' Hamer had lost 'RESPECT,' he informed the party in capital letters; the premier was not seen as standing up for his state in the way that Neville Wran or Bjelke-Petersen stood up for theirs. Victorians were discontented about many things, he reported; not all were the government's fault, but the voters were blaming it, 'just as a person annoyed at work will go home and kick the dog'. Liberal supporters had 'lost the sense of direction, of unity, and of pride in their team'. Camakaris offered no advice on who should lead the party, but urged that:

> whoever it is must have support from the Liberal Party — even if it hurts. Questions of whether or not one agrees with a particular point must be weighed against the need to preserve the respect for the Premier — for the voters, the latter is the more important.[1]

It was a warning to those who had been undermining Hamer. Like earlier warnings, it was ignored.

The Victorian economy was not doing as badly as Hamer's business enemies claimed. In January, APM announced a $200 million expansion of its Maryvale plant, and Nissan and Toyota both announced plans for new assembly lines. The government announced plans for new ski resorts at Dinner Plain and Mount Stirling; the SEC began planning for a 4,000-megawatt coal-fired station at Driffield, next to Hazelwood; and the first trains ran through the underground rail loop. The Driffield power station was never built, but the rest was real. In February, politics was knocked off the front page by controversy over Greg Chappell's decision to tell brother Trevor to bowl underarm to stop New Zealand hitting a six, and by the Alice Springs coroner finding that baby Azaria Chamberlain was taken by a dingo. In March, the government announced that the 1956 Olympic Pool would become a basketball centre. The first bits of the new regime were put in place: Dixon decided to outsource all future housing construction, Smith set up the Victorian Economic Development Corporation to lend money for business expansion, and the Melbourne City Council was finally sacked. But while Victoria was not standing still like South Australia and Tasmania, its economy was losing ground to the other three states, and the psychological malaise deepened.

By now, the leaders of all Australia's insurance giants — the AMP, National Mutual, and Colonial Mutual — had decided to stop investing in Victoria, mostly because the anarchy of the building unions had made new projects too risky to embark on, but partly because they were angry at their inability to knock down or redevelop historic buildings. On 9 April, Howson records, his friend Gerry Niall, chairman of National Mutual, invited him to a meeting with John Elliott, Stephen Kimpton, chairman of the Commonwealth Bank, and Sir Charles ('Dave') McGrath, head of car-parts manufacturer Repco, to discuss how to get a new Liberal leader and who it should be. On Howson's account, only Elliott disagreed with that agenda, but the meeting ended without a strategy. Niall tried to persuade Lindsay Thompson to challenge Hamer, but was rebuffed. On 29 April, Niall, Kimpton, and Howson met with Sir John Anderson, a leading importer and former state president and party treasurer, described by Peter Blazey as 'Bolte's closest extra-parliamentary confidant'. Anderson told them he had tried to persuade Hamer to stand down, without success; that meeting, too, ended up with more complaints than solutions.

On 29 April, Malcolm Fraser finally took the initiative to try to end the lawlessness on Victorian building sites. He announced that the Commonwealth had asked the states to join in joint action to deregister Gallagher's Builders Labourers Federation — the first move in trying to end its control over the industry. Hamer did not reply. In the skimpy records of Victorian cabinet meetings in May 1981, there is no indication that the subject was even discussed.

The beginning of the end was the Premiers' Conference on 5 May, the one at which Howard told journalists afterwards that he held back $70 million that federal cabinet had authorised for the states. The impact of the resources boom, large wage rises, and the end of tax indexation had lifted income-tax receipts by 17.5 per cent in 1979–80 and a further 16.6 per cent in 1980–81. But the Commonwealth offered the states only an 8 per cent rise, later lifted to 9 per cent, in tax-sharing payments. Inflation in the government sector was running at 12.5 per cent. Essentially, after all the years of rhetoric about the New Federalism, Fraser and Howard had decided to use the Commonwealth's revenue windfall to try to get their own budget out of deficit. Hamer was on his own. He had already told ministers to plan for across-the-board 3 per cent cuts in their staff ceilings. Now he had to find further savings.

Hamer was nearing 65, and his energy was running down. 'In those final months, I felt he looked very tired, and dispirited,' observed Race Mathews, a sympathetic opponent. But when Hamer sat in his usual seat by the assembly table on Thursday 7 May, very few knew it would be his last day in parliament. Friday was another sitting day; and, besides, his staff had said he would be staying to fight the election. Hamer answered a string of questions on the Premiers' Conference, on the state of the economy, government spending on advertising, and whether the school dental program would be spared from budget cuts. He made a ministerial statement on the Premiers' Conference, giving no hint that this would be his final speech in parliament. He voted in divisions arising from his statement, and on a bill to ever-so-slightly liberalise shop-trading hours, and then he went home. He skipped the next day's sittings, and did not plan to come back. On 15 May, he took off to lead a large business delegation on a month-long trip to the United States.

They had got only as far as Los Angeles when the first bombshell burst. On 19 May, *The Age* published a letter that Kennett had earlier sent to Hamer, urging him to cancel his trip and stay home 'to lead the state's fight for a better redistribution of federal funds'. He also called on Hamer to reverse other decisions that cabinet had just made: the new cabinet committee to review all programs — 'the cold chisel gang', comprising Thompson, Smith, and Dixon — should be reformed with Hamer as chair and a different cast of members. Hamer had received the letter and ignored it, as he ignored most of Kennett's suggestions. But this time Kennett had copied the letter and sent it to all the other cabinet members. And somebody very helpfully passed it on to Philip Chubb, state political reporter for *The Age*.

There was much speculation as to who had leaked it. Was it Smith? Kennett himself? Some third minister? Smith denied any involvement. Interviewed for this book, Kennett gave a rueful smile and shook his head:

> It certainly wasn't me. In hindsight, it [the letter] was obviously not a good idea. That was part of my naivety. There were a number of issues confronting our government. I didn't think it was the best time for our leader to be away. He rang me up and said: 'I've read your letter, but I've decided I'm going, and that's that.' And then a week later, it was leaked.

The irony, says Chubb, is that even 30 years later, he himself does not know who leaked the letter to him:

> Whoever it was, they just put it in my pigeonhole, in an envelope addressed to me. I rang Kennett to verify that he had written the letter, and he essentially confirmed that. The story took off — and in a way, the fact that the leaker was anonymous made it all the more vicious.[2]

What is clear is that the leak was intended to damage Hamer, and possibly Kennett as well. Both the letter and the leaking of it highlighted the disunity of the government. It exemplified the malaise that Camakaris had described: a party at war with itself, and an electorate losing patience with it.

But worse was to come. The following day, four of the eight units at Hazelwood power station broke down simultaneously. It was during a cold snap, and at a time when other power-station units were out for scheduled maintenance. For the first time in years, the SEC had to cut off power — not because of a strike, but because it had so many units out of action. The rules of the time dictated that it had to cut off supply to industry to protect domestic supply; as a result, some 250,000 workers were laid off. It was the worst breakdown of the system for decades, and it happened while Hamer and SEC chairman Charles Trethowan were in the US trying to get more energy-intensive investment in Victoria. Power was not fully restored until Saturday 23 May. And by then, an even bigger storm had crashed down on the government.

Jim Clarke was editor of the *Warrnambool Standard*, Ian Smith's local paper. At a dinner with Smith, he had arranged to do a long interview with Smith at his farm on Saturday 9 May, to be published as a feature article in the paper two weeks later. It was hardly a background chat: Clarke had come with another reporter and a mutual friend, and the interview began with Smith testing the sound level on the tape recorder to ensure that his words would be heard. And, in keeping with Smith's character, he did not hold back.

Hamer, he declared early in the interview, was 'a far-left-wing leader'. Bolte had been 'excellent' for his era in politics, and so was Hamer, 'up until recently', but his era was now 'finished'. Hamer's achievements, he said, had become entrenched in people's consciousness — 'people don't want to go polluting the atmosphere' — and it was time to end that emphasis, and shift to a more flexible approach. Smith told Clarke he had always had disagreements with Hamer's priorities, but went on:

> I decided to wait within the system, and try to reform it from within … I always had the ambition to be Minister of Agriculture, to do a whole lot of things. I got to be Minister of Agriculture at 33, and [eight years later] most of the things I wanted to do have been done. I've got to a stage of male menopause; I've got to set new horizons for myself.

> Hamer has got a ton of energy, and, to his credit, he's the most democratic individual I've ever come across. But the sort of democracy he runs is that he listens to everyone, and agrees with them all — and where does that leave you? No one knows where they're going. What it needs is a much clearer, more tightly defined set of objectives and goals.
>
> Roughly half-way between Bolte and Hamer is the next era. I think in personal style, there's an enormous craving for Bolte back, perhaps without his rough edges, in that, if someone wanted to do something that was a legitimate project and they discussed it with the Premier, and he said 'yes, let's go ahead', then it would go ahead. Now, if you get that undertaking, he [Hamer] allows too many other people to have a say.[3]

Smith gave the example of the copper deposit discovered by BP and Western Mining in the remote north-east mountains near Benambra, in an area proposed to be part of the Alpine National Park. You could just excise that land from the park, he argued, mine it, and buy some other land to add to the national park. (In fact, something like that did happen; a copper mine opened under the Kirner government, only to shut down after four years, leaving taxpayers to foot the bill for $5.8 million of remedial work to secure its toxic-waste tailings. At the time of writing, there are plans to reopen the mine.)

Smith complained of 'the web of government … [the departments of] conservation, planning, local government, labour and industry' that were blocking projects. He argued that the leader should be free to make a snap decision after listening to the proponent of the project, without needing to wait for, let alone take account of, studies of the impact of the project. One can understand his frustration with the time taken to get decisions, but his solution was like the Queen's rule in *Alice in Wonderland*: 'Sentence first — verdict afterwards.' With some lapses, such as his decision to hand Victoria's biggest building contract of 1976 to a Liberal fundraiser without calling for tenders, Hamer was committed to following due process.

Clarke's main interest was in Smith's line of argument. But he could only have been startled at the *obiter dicta* that Smith freely volunteered. The Liberal Party, Smith joked, was 'numb with fright' at the prospect of Hamer leading them into the next election. Hamer, he said, was a man of enormous ego, 'and he doesn't have a retirement ego yet'. The turmoil in March had hurt Hamer, not him: 'Except for a few backbenchers, I don't think I've done myself any damage at all … It did the Premier a lot of harm, but nevertheless he recognises that he has to rely on people like me to get things done … We've now got to clean up the job that he wasn't able to do, and can't do.' The premier, he quipped, spent most of his time reflecting on his philosophy. 'Hamer has almost lost his identity. He has been so pummelled, pushed around and led about, that I don't think he knows whether he's coming or going'.

It is certain that Smith did not intend those comments to be published. Yet the tape of the interview reveals that while he declared some other comments off the record, he put no such injunction on anything he said about Hamer. Politicians and journalists talk a lot, and politicians often say things to journalists that both instinctively know are off the record. Bolte rarely bothered to tell journalists at his morning press conference that something he said was off the record; the journalists were just expected to *know*, or, if you were a new boy, to ask one of the old hands. But that requires a good understanding between the politician and the journalist. Smith was unlucky, but it is a bit reckless for a politician speaking into a tape recorder in a formal interview with a journalist he does not know well to assume that criticisms of his leader will be treated as off the record. That Smith's criticisms of Hamer were published was the result of a misunderstanding, but ultimately one for which he had to take responsibility: all he had needed to do was to say that those statements were off the record. In comments to the *Warrnambool Standard* 25 years later, Smith implied that he thought Clarke was a loyal Liberal who would protect his interests in deciding what to publish. With a tape recorder running, it would have been wise to check.

Clarke knew he had a big story, even if he couldn't publish it for two weeks. The *Warrnambool Standard* was owned by David Syme

& Co Pty Ltd, publishers of *The Age*, for whom Clarke had worked before going to Warrnambool. He told *The Age* what he had, and it sure told its readers. It held nothing back in a story that ran across the front of page one on the morning of Saturday 23 May: 'Smith lashes Hamer.' Philip Chubb, who wrote the story, had been given a transcript of the interview. Transcripts make irony and jokes dangerous: when you hear the tape of the interview, it is clear that Smith was joking when he said the party was 'numb with fright' about the prospect of Hamer leading it into the election, but *The Age* reported it as a plain statement of fact. Smith was one of those arrogant guys whose style of humour was to shock you by saying things in a brazen way. Inevitably, those nuances disappeared in *The Age* version of the story: rather than a minister who was a bit full of himself letting loose with his views in a jocular tone, it seemed that a senior minister had launched a full-frontal attack on his leader.

Frank McGuire, now Labor MLA for Broadmeadows, was then a state political reporter for *The Herald*. That Saturday morning he read *The Age* story, and, at 7.01 a.m., rang acting premier Lindsay Thompson at home. A sleepy voice answered. When McGuire explained why he was calling, Thompson woke up very fast; he promised to ring back shortly. He did so, but only to say 'No comment.' That Saturday, Richard Alston was the only Liberal whom McGuire could find who spoke out in defence of Hamer. Thompson, the instinctive bridgebuilder, must have realised quickly that this bridge was now destroyed forever. On his instructions, Liberals interviewed by the media pulled down the shutters. A reader got the sense that they were preparing for change.

Cabinet, minus Smith, met informally at Thompson's home over the weekend. Late on Sunday, Thompson rang Smith to demand his resignation. Smith said he would comply if he was allowed first to speak frankly to cabinet about why he felt as he did. Thompson agreed. Eventually, Thompson spoke out publicly to support his leader, while Hamer's old friend and ally, the tireless charity worker Dame Phyllis Frost, rang the media and gave it a piece of her mind, calling on Victorians to support a man who had been such a good premier. The silence was deafening. Newspapers reported AMP chairman Sir Robert Law-Smith saying that the insurance giant would invest no more in Victoria. Now Gerry Niall went public with his criticisms of Hamer's leadership, calling on the Liberals to elect a new premier.

The army had not prepared Hamer to govern in a climate of disloyalty from his troops. Party loyalty was one of those things you took for granted in the Bolte era, like a strong economy. Richard Mulcahy recounts that they were still in Los Angeles at the time:

> In Melbourne, Chris Diprose, his PA, would check up on gossip about what was going on. He told me by phone that Storey and Dixon were saying it was time to move on. Hamer said: 'That can't be true. They're very loyal ministers.' Sue Calwell was in his room, and she piped up: 'No, that can't be true. Everybody loves Dick.'
>
> They flew on to New York. I had the weekend free, so I went to South Carolina. When I got to Columbia, I was paged at the airport: they told me to ring Melbourne, and ring the premier. I rang him first. He said: 'Richard, there's trouble in Melbourne. Lindsay says we've got to go home.' Don Hughes, the chairman of Cadbury-Schweppes, took over leadership of the mission.
>
> On the way from LA to Hawaii, he told me that Ian Smith had been in the cabinet room, and had been allowed to voice all his grievances. He felt he'd been undermined, but didn't want to admit it. We stayed at the Royal Hawaii; Dick stayed at Lindsay Fox's place. We were calling around our contacts on the backbench, and the bottom line was that it was falling down: he either had to resign or he would get voted out. Dick didn't look happy when I told him. Then Neil [Mooney, Hamer's new press secretary] said something similar. So he said: 'Right, that's it.'
>
> We were going out to dinner at the Outrigger Canoe Club, but first we went to a hula show at the Sheraton Moana Hotel at Waikiki. Here we were, on the verge of a political coup, and the premier got up and started dancing like a 20-year-old. Then we took off for dinner with Lindsay Fox and his wife.

> On the plane back, I sat with the premier. I looked over, and saw he was writing out his resignation speech. He still hadn't said anything to me or Neil about it. He asked me to make an appointment with the governor. When we got out of the airport, he went straight home to Canterbury for a shower. Then we went back to Government House, where he had a cup of tea with the governor [Sir Henry Winneke]. Then we went back to Treasury Place. We had to fight our way through the underground car park to get to the private lift — it was quite disorderly, the way it unfolded.[4]

Fox had arranged for his private jet to take them from Sydney to Essendon, to escape the media waiting (with Thompson) at Tullamarine. In the scramble, they forgot their passports, which were left behind in Sydney. After arriving at his office, Hamer met with Thompson and Alston, then with his personal staff, and then with cabinet. Hamer had given no interviews since the story first broke. Amazingly, word of his decision had still not leaked out when he faced the media at Treasury Place — first in his office, with reporters only, and then at a formal press conference with so many cameras and journalists in attendance that people were tripping over each other. Hamer, given the circumstances, was astonishingly composed, even vigorous and upbeat, as he read his statement:

> After 19 continuous years as a Cabinet Minister, and nearly nine as Premier (the second longest unbroken term in Victorian history) I have decided that the time has come to step down.
>
> I will accordingly be resigning my commission to His Excellency the Governor of Victoria next Friday, 5 June. I will be asking the Parliamentary Liberal Party next Tuesday to elect a successor …
>
> I have not come to this decision by reason of recent events. I had fully intended to step down in any case in August since I will not be seeking a further 3-year term as a candidate for the Liberal Party in Kew … and I wished to give my successor ample scope to establish the identity and capacity of the new government before the state election next year … But recent events have certainly caused me to

bring forward the date of my retirement as Premier …

Throughout my political life, I have regarded unity in the pursuit of our goals as vital. Only through unified and dedicated teamwork can the great Liberal aims of care for the individual in a free society, and the increase of community wealth as the basis for all other programs, be achieved.

Today the unity is more important than ever. It is in the interests of that unity that I am now stepping down.

There is a further reason. I have always believed that institutions, including governments, benefit from change and new ideas, and that upward movement ought to be encouraged. This particularly applies to those with youth and vigour, who are the true inheritors of all that we do, and I have always sought to encourage those elements, both within and outside the Parliament.

In politics, as in many other realms in life, teamwork, and loyalty within that team, are essential. Those who do not give loyalty cannot expect to attract or require it from others.

I have served in many governments in my 19 years as a Minister of the Crown, and always, until now, there has been an attitude of mutual trust and confidence and a willingness to sink individual views and aspirations in the interests of the team as a whole, and loyally support decisions democratically taken together as a joint responsibility by those who share our great Liberal beliefs. This principle cannot be allowed to flag or fail.

I am grateful for the great friendship and support of my colleagues in Cabinet and the party over many years. We have achieved much together, including many things of enduring value to our state.

Victoria has immense potential and a bright future, well recognised by all except by the few who choose to downplay and denigrate. Victoria has the highest average family incomes, the highest per capita savings, the highest rate of home ownership, the highest rate of job creation (ABS figures for the year to April 1981), the lowest road toll and generally the lowest (or second lowest) unemployment rate in Australia.

> Those are solid achievements, and form a firm basis for Victoria's assured future. The New Directions policy, adopted by the Government earlier this year in its *Strategy for the '80s*, lays out the path by which that future will be realised. But it will require the guidance of a strong unified government, dedicated to free enterprise, and the creation of jobs from growth, especially for our young people.
>
> Victoria has been in the forefront of many fields, especially in the programs broadly labelled 'Quality of Life'. Much has been achieved in recent years in the preservation of our natural heritage and historic buildings, in the dramatic increase in national and other parks, in the protection of our air and waterways from pollution, in the new range of choice and opportunity in the arts, sport and passive recreation, in the care of physically and mentally handicapped people, and help for our elderly citizens.
>
> These 'Quality of Life' issues will not become less important in the future; they are securely built into our lifestyle now, but they must not be allowed to be manipulated by extremists to the detriment of sensible growth and development, so essential for job creation.
>
> I am proud to be a Victorian, and to have had the privilege of leading a Victorian Liberal Government for so long. I thank all those who have given me loyal and dedicated support over those years; especially am I grateful for the friendship and dedication of the Deputy premier, Lindsay Thompson, over the whole period of my Premiership. No leader could have asked for more reliable or unstinted support.
>
> It now remains to establish a new Liberal Ministry which will lead Victoria forward in the '80s. I wish the new government team every success in its task, and I call on all true Victorians to give them their confidence. It goes without saying that I pledge them my full support.[5]

He fielded 30 questions from the media, with his usual succinct answers. 'Not one person' had asked him directly to step down.

Smith had made no complaints to him since being reinstated. He did not regret having given Smith a second chance, but 'criticism from a colleague' was the most disturbing aspect of it all. He had stayed in Hawaii to get 'an overnight break and a good sleep'. He would not be canvassing votes for any candidate for leadership. And he said over and over that he had already decided to retire soon, and this had merely brought it forward a couple of months.

His composure and dignity was extraordinary, in both press conferences and in the TV interviews that followed. He had been harried into early retirement, and yet, columnist Les Tanner wrote in *The Age*, he looked relaxed, a winner. But April did not hide her emotional distress, telling Frank McGuire of *The Herald*: 'They butchered him when he couldn't defend himself ... It's a savage game, and often a dishonourable game. I just think Dick was an honourable man playing that game.' She told *The Australian*: 'I must be very naïve. I was surprised almost no one spoke up for Dick ... No one called me at all — no one was interested in my reaction, or how I was feeling.' Her only support had come from Thompson and Dame Phyllis. She refused to speak to *The Age*, which the anti-Hamer right had used as its mouthpiece.

Attention quickly turned from Hamer to the leadership battle. The result was exactly the same as in the deputy leadership contest back in 1972: once again, Thompson defeated Borthwick by a single vote. Peter Howson recorded in his diary a list of which MPs he was told voted for Thompson and which for Borthwick. If his list is correct, Thompson's support came mainly from the longstanding Liberal MPs, who felt that such a decent man deserved his turn at the top. Borthwick's support, by contrast, came mostly from MPs elected in 1976 and 1979, who felt that the Liberals' electoral position had deteriorated so much that they needed a change, not another leader like Hamer. Labor was hoping for a Thompson victory, and they got it. Bolte claimed later that it was too late for Thompson to turn the ship around, but there was a bigger problem: he did not want to turn the ship around. Like Hamer, he was worn out. He had been a minister for 23 years, 12 of them in education; he seemed much older than he was. Borthwick was only a year younger, but seemed fresher, more dynamic, with a lot of personal charm. Whether he could have saved the ship, we will never know. Several MPs who voted for Thompson said in interviews for this book that, in hindsight, Borthwick might have given the party a better chance of holding on to power. He certainly was the driving force in the dispute that was to mark the high point of the Thompson government: when it used the Essential Services Act to force striking milk drivers back to work. Bob Hawke mused privately that if the Liberals were ever going to win the next election, they should have called it during that dispute — but Lindsay Thompson was far too decent to think this way.

Hamer never got to sit on the backbench again. In the middle of the milk dispute, on 18 July, he quietly slipped away, resigning as MLA for Kew. In an editorial headed 'Farewell, Mr Hamer', *The Age* for once was generous:

> Few people in our history have stepped down with such good reason to be proud of their achievements. The disappointments in some areas should not obscure the significant legacy, in style and substance, that he has left the community after nine years as Premier and 19 as a Minister.
>
> For Mr Hamer has been more than just a successful politician. He has been a scrupulously fair one, a man who embodied humane values, and a leader of social concern and foresight. He was wrong at times; he often pursued misguided priorities; he was not an ideal leader. But neither is anyone else; and he suffered from our tendency these days to make leaders into scapegoats for social problems that have far more complex causes.
>
> It is partly due to Mr Hamer that Victoria in 1981 has a growing network of national and urban parks, some protection for our finest buildings and landscapes, a flourishing artistic and cultural life, and that homosexuality is no longer a crime here or the gallows a punishment. For these and other reforms, and his personal example of courtesy under pressure, he deserves the warm thanks of the community in his retirement.[6]

Coda

CHAPTER TWENTY-SEVEN

Life after politics

To be stripped of power is a traumatic experience for any political leader. The greater the power, the more traumatic the loss of it. It was no accident that Jeff Kennett founded Beyond Blue to publicise the problem of depression after he himself had been dumped from power: in some form or other, depression is the normal experience of leaders who have been rejected. Since he had set his sights on a political career in the late 1940s, Dick Hamer had taken all reverses in his stride. But to be forced out, as he was in 1981, broke through all his psychological defences. The next few years would be the worst of his life, as he struggled to find a new role for himself. He made uncharacteristic errors of judgement, fell in with thieves, jeopardised his marriage, and, in some ways, lost his sense of purpose.

At first, the pain was offset by an outpouring of public support. More than a thousand letters flooded in from people all over Victoria, and from political leaders interstate, expressing support for Dick and April, and gratitude for what he had done as premier, and the way he had done it. Some were more or less formal letters of thanks from Liberal Party branches, local councils, or business groups. A sprinkling of letters came from some of Hamer's enemies in the party or in business, such as Sir Charles McGrath and Bob Ansett of the Melbourne Chamber of Commerce, perhaps writing to expiate a sense of guilt. Even the AMP Society, through its Victorian chief and future managing director, Ian Salmon, wrote to apologise for the political impact of his chairman's remarks that the AMP would no longer invest in Victoria: 'We are sorry for any hurt that our unwitting role has caused you,' Salmon wrote. 'I have a very high respect and regard for you.'[1]

But most were heartfelt messages, written with sincerity and emotion. Some came from old friends, among them very warm letters to April from Dame Edith Bolte, and to Dick from Dame Elisabeth Murdoch. Shirley Haynes from the Parliamentary Dining Room wrote to tell Dick: 'It has been an honour to serve you and your family over the years, as you all endeared yourselves to me.' Some came from political opponents who respected him, such as Barry Jones, and Peter and Joy Ross-Edwards. Some came from business leaders who genuinely admired Hamer and had been appalled to see other business leaders denounce him because he had not given them what they wanted. And many letters came from total strangers who had trusted and admired him, shared his suffering and grief in their own homes, and wanted to let Dick and April know how much people appreciated them.

Dick's old mentors wrote to congratulate him on what he had achieved. Sir James Darling, his old headmaster at Geelong Grammar, and also Ian Smith's old headmaster, wrote in praise of one of his former students and in scorn for the other. Professor 'Mac' Ball, his former politics lecturer, wrote to tell Dick he had been the best premier of Victoria in his (Mac's) lifetime. From Sydney, his old army commander, Sir Victor Windeyer, long retired from the High Court, wrote to tell him: 'I have been well aware of, and have admired, the wisdom, moderation and sense of reason and true values that you brought to your performance in your political duties.' And from distant Wiltshire, his old friend 'Jumbo', the former governor Sir Rohan Delacombe, wrote that he and his wife were 'most distressed' by the way Dick's career had ended, and ended on a cheerier note: 'Come and visit us in the UK.'

Travel would indeed become one of Dick's preoccupations in retirement, but finding something to do in Melbourne was his first priority. Soon after he resigned, he was invited out to King Street's fashionable Underground disco, which had been set up in 1977 by Brian Goldsmith, and was in those days the coolest nightclub in town. It employed female door staff — 'it's hard to hit a girl,' Goldsmith said — threw people out if they started annoying others, and had a sign warning those seeking entry: 'No tiaras. No tattoos.' Goldsmith remembers the night he first met Dick Hamer: 'He was in a casual shirt, dancing, having a wonderful time. And I thought, *That's the sort of man I'd like on my board*.'

He rang Hamer to offer him a board position. Hamer said later it was the first position anyone had offered him since he'd lost the premiership. He had heard good things about Goldsmith and his disco, so he accepted. It developed into the closest friendship of his post-political life. April remarked later: 'Dick and Brian had a very good friendship. I think they had fun together. It must have been a case of opposites attracting.'

Other appointments gradually followed. In the commercial field, his friend Sir Donald Trescowthick recruited him to join the board of his company, Charles Davis Ltd, which by then owned Harris Scarfe in Adelaide, a range of Tasmanian retail outlets, and was expanding into areas from mining to hotels, motels, property development, and auto-parts distribution. Hamer became chairman of the Victorian arm of one of the country's biggest financial-advice firms, the Burns Philp Trustee Company. In the arts, he became chairman of two institutions he had been most supportive of: the Victorian College of the Arts, of which he was the political father, and the Victoria State Opera, where as premier he had been more like a fairy godfather, giving it the resources to meet at least some of its ambitions. The VSO became the main single focus of Hamer's energies in retirement.

His retirement from politics opened the way for another woman to enter parliament: Prue Sibree (now Prue Leggoe), a young mother of three who also ran her own city law firm, defeated 14 other candidates to win Liberal preselection in Hamer's old seat. Sibree was prominent in Hamer's wing of the party, and her victory gave the Liberals four women in parliament, as against Labor's two. But it also gave Labor a new leader. At Kew, for the first time since 1973, the

Liberals had gained a swing at a by-election. For the Socialist Left, it was the straw that broke the camel's back: fearful that it would be blamed if Labor lost the election under Frank Wilkes, it shifted its support to John Cain, who was elected Labor leader on 8 September, and soon pulled well ahead in the polls.

Hamer took no part in the 1982 election, choosing to keep out of Lindsay Thompson's way. But the new premier made few changes. In early 1981, Hamer had quietly put on hold the proposed cuts to suburban railway lines; Thompson as premier abandoned them. The party room continued to fight against reforms, this time dumping a proposed pre-Christmas trial of later shopping hours. Labor under Cain looked ready to govern, and the election on 3 April turned out to be the annihilation that the Liberals had long feared. The party lost 18 of its 42 seats in the assembly: Labor took 17 of them, and Gippsland South returned to the Nationals. Labor won 50.04 per cent of the vote, the first time since 1917 that one party had won most of the votes cast. The massacre took out almost a third of the cabinet, including Bill Borthwick and Brian Dixon, as well as newer ministers Norman Lacy (targeted by the DLP for allowing sex education in schools), Glyn Jenkins, and Graeme Weideman. Backbenchers to lose their seats included Hamer's arch-critic Ralph Howard, the economist Kevin Foley, and Don Saltmarsh, a leading campaigner against a casino. In two-party terms, the federal Parliamentary Library estimated, the swing averaged 4.3 per cent; but in outer-suburban Melbourne, where most of the marginal seats were, it was roughly 7 per cent. Democrat preferences this time swung to Labor, which won 53.8 per cent of the vote after preferences, its best vote since 1952. Thompson remained Liberal leader for a few months, and then retired: the Liberals, hoping for a short-cut back to power, took a punt by making Jeff Kennett their new leader. He eventually led them back to power, but only after three elections and ten years.

Thompson did make one change for his old friend and leader. In the New Year's Day honours in 1982, Dick became Sir Rupert Hamer, and April became Lady Hamer. It caused surprise, on two grounds. Dick had never used the name Rupert before, but this time, he had no good alternative. Moreover, he himself had refused to hand out political knighthoods after criticism from *The Age*. After 1975, the only retiring cabinet minister to receive a knighthood was John Rossiter (also known as Jack or 'Punchy', from his boxing days), who persuaded Dick that he needed it to uphold the prestige of his position as agent-general in London. Murray Byrne was farewelled with a CMG, the highest honour below a knighthood, while Ray Meagher and Vernon Wilcox had to accept a CBE. Hamer's knighthood was one of the last awarded by a Victorian government. The state had no power to award Order of Australia honours, and the Cain government refused to award imperial honours, so its election ended Victoria's own honours system.

Hamer withdrew from any direct role in politics, apart from a streetwalk in East Yarra in 1983 to support Mark Birrell, a future Kennett government minister. But as an ex-premier, he was invited to give a lot of speeches, and, after having given so many dull speeches in office, he produced some quite lively ones out of office. His 1981 Kemsley Oration to the Royal Australian Planning Institute sharply denounced the legal mission-creep of the Town Planning Appeals Tribunal (now VCAT), and called for it to be stripped back to basics, as he had intended back in 1965. His 1982 Deakin Lecture to the Melbourne University Liberal Club was a trenchant critique of how the Commonwealth had used the powers given it by the High Court to transform the Federation in its own interests, along with proposals for reform. He was usually happy to oblige when invited to speak, and he had a talent for finding interesting aspects in apparently humdrum issues or events; he would have made a great governor. A classic example came when he was invited to open the Greek–Australian International Legal and Medical Conference: rather than bore into the intricacies of issues where medicine meets the law, Hamer decided that Greek–Australian professional people would enjoy an account of Australia's role in the Battle of Crete in 1941. It was a riveting speech, even if it had nothing to do with their conference.

In mid-1982, he and April left for overeseas, heading to Florence for an intensive two-month course in Italian language and culture. (It was initiated by April, who had already sat and passed Year 12 Italian.) They were to go on many overseas trips in retirement, often with the educational tour agency Australians Studying Abroad, and Dick loved recounting their travels to friends and family. His daughter Julia recalled:

> He was such a fact collector! He loved information, and he loved learning about new things … He had a beautiful clarity of mind. In explaining anything, he would do it step by step, leaving out unnecessary detail, in clear, plain language without jargon, and at a measured pace, so that you could grasp the meaning as he went along, of even quite complex things. It was another lesson in how to do things extremely well. I think this must have been one of his great strengths in public life.[2]

By now he was on a range of boards and committees: apart from his business interests and his roles in the arts, he became vice-chairman of two of his favourite creations as premier: the Fountains Trust, which raised money to build fountains in Melbourne, and the board of Werribee Park. He twice drew up outlines for an autobiography, and wrote the first chapter of an autobiographical novel set in the war, but neither project progressed. The University of Melbourne honoured one of its distinguished sons with an honorary LL.D. In an interview with me in mid-1982, he professed to be loving retirement:

> It's enabled me to do all the things I've contemplated from year to year, but couldn't get time to do. The biggest change is reading things other than reports! I read novels, which I haven't been able to do for 22 years. I play tennis with friends two afternoons a week. I walk around, I enjoy the countryside, I visit friends, have them here — and feel the better for it.[3]

Yet, despite the appearance that all was well, Dick was a disturbed man, and it showed in untypical behaviour and a series of bad decisions. Christopher Sexton, at one point recruited to be his biographer, remembers him drinking heavily at formal dinners at Trinity College, where Hamer had been made a Fellow. Sue Calwell recalls that every time she went to the Underground, it seemed, 'Dick was always there, with young girls, sitting around talking … I think it was probably harmless, but he hung around there a lot.'

A friend of Brian Goldsmith's talked him into lending his name to a project to grow jojoba beans in central Queensland. The promoter, a smooth-talking rogue named Fritz (or Freddie) Mader (or Maeder), had previously been married to Rupert Murdoch's first wife, Patricia Booker, and engaged to one of the Kidman girls. 'He was a pillar of Adelaide society, went to St Peter's College, mixed in the top social circles in South Australia, largely with the wine families', Goldsmith recalls. Mader first met Hamer over lunch at the Underground. He saw the marketing value of the Hamer name; he flew to Florence, where Dick and April were studying, and talked Dick into becoming chairman of his core company, Jojoba Management Ltd. Mader had already been charged by Queensland's Corporate Affairs Commission with failing to issue a registered prospectus for his jojoba plantation, yet Hamer trusted him, and went on roadshows to promote the company to investors. But even to one of his trusting nature, there was something wrong with the business. 'If there's some money, spend it — that's Freddie,' he told *Australian Business* later. Essentially, Mader was running a Ponzi scheme, distributing investors' money in huge commissions and salaries to salesmen, executives, himself, and his family, while investing too little in the plantations for them to meet revenue goals. The new investments had been used to pay the costs of servicing the old, and the trusted Hamer was the figure used to attract them. 'My face was appearing all over the place,' Hamer said. 'I suppose I must have fallen in with thieves.'

But one scam soon led to another. Mader talked Hamer and Goldsmith into joining him in another scheme, to do a Mount Ridley: buy rural land at the back of the Gold Coast while it was cheap, hang on to it in expectation of rezoning, and then cash in and make profits when the rezoning happened. Hamer was again named as chairman of the company, Land Bank Estate Pty Ltd — without his knowledge, he says, while he and April were in France. Once again, Mader sought money from investors using Hamer's name, and without issuing a prospectus. Fate had it that the local MP was Doug Jennings: Jennings had scores to settle with Hamer, and the Queensland parliament was a perfect venue for it. Jennings' last speech before his death in the parliamentary sauna was a scathing attack on Hamer and the Land Bank. By then, Mader was no longer there to smooth the waters. Charged in court over his conduct of the jojoba business, he had skipped bail and absconded to Spain. Hamer was left to account for the Land Bank in a Brisbane court, where he was cross-examined by prosecutor Patrick Keane, now a judge of the High Court. Hamer and Goldsmith had to repay investors from their own pockets.

It was not the worst mistake he made in those days. In 1983, Sue Calwell asked Hamer and Goldsmith to represent the Melbourne Tourism Authority at a travel conference in Mexico. At a dinner party in Los Angeles, they met a blonde named Julia Stock, who claimed to be friends with half of Hollywood's A-list. 'She had ideas of establishing herself as a theatrical agent for actors and musicians who would come to Australia to perform and record,' Hamer said later. 'Brian and I encouraged her to come to Australia, and I even loaned her the airfare at her request.' Clearly, that was not all that happened between them. In March 1984, the Murdoch-owned scandal sheet *Truth* reported that Stock was demanding $100,000 from Hamer; she told the paper they had been lovers, but he had jilted her after attracting her to Australia by promising to divorce April and marry her. Even *Truth* in the end concluded that she was an untruthful gold-digger, but there was no denying the authenticity of Hamer's handwriting in a warm love letter published with her story. For Dick and April, it was the worst moment in what was otherwise a long and happy marriage.

The Melbourne arts scene was where Hamer made his most fruitful contributions in retirement. Music was his passion. He had the administrative skills, experience, and contacts that artistic companies desperately need. There was a synergy to it that proved a happy fit. 'All those committees and boards allowed him to find himself again,' says his daughter Julia. 'When he died, we got lots of letters from people who had worked with him, telling us what a wonderful trouble-shooter he had been, and what a calming, practical influence he was on their board.'

The Victoria State Opera became his main focus. It had been founded in 1962 by conductor Leonard Spira as the Victorian Opera Company, and in 1970 a very young Peter Burch was recruited to manage both the opera and the Victorian Ballet Guild. He recruited retired opera diva Joan Hammond to chair the company, they appointed the young Richard Divall as musical director, and then they asked Hamer as the new premier to increase its $500 annual grant to about $20,000. The federal government subsidised the Australian Opera as the national opera company; but, like its current incarnation, Opera Australia, it was essentially a Sydney-based company, coming to Melbourne for just a couple of months a year. Hamer saw merit in giving Melbourne its own opera company, even if it could never match the resources of its Sydney counterpart. As premier, treasurer, and minister for the arts, he had kept increasing its grants — to $165,000 by 1975 — allowing it to become a fully professional company, with an innovative repertoire. In 1976, Ken Mackenzie-Forbes was recruited as general manager, and, with Hamer's approval, it became the Victoria State Opera.

Soon after resigning as premier, Hamer joined the board of the company, and in 1982 became its chairman. One of his strengths was the respect in which he was held by John Cain and Race Mathews, the arts minister in the new government. Late in 1982, this was shown in an unusual way: Cain invited Hamer to open the first part of the Arts Centre to be completed, the concert hall overlooking the Yarra. In interviews for this book, Cain and Mathews said it was their way of paying tribute to Hamer's persistence against so many obstacles in getting the centre built. 'He was delighted when I asked him,' Cain said. 'But, frankly, I don't think it would have been built at that time without him.' Mathews paid a generous tribute to his predecessor:

> The arts scene in Melbourne was very much his creation. The Arts Ministry had been shaped by Hamer and [Eric] Westbrook. He had conceptualised it, and presided over its implementation. The Victorian College of the Arts was an important part of his design. The VSO in a way was another of his creations, and it flourished under his patronage. They set up the tapestry workshop, a print workshop, the Meat Market crafts centre, and we had half-a-dozen flourishing theatre companies, most of them started up in the Hamer years … I don't think I made any changes at all in the arts bureaucracy. I think he was grateful, maybe surprised, that his legacy remained intact.[4]

Cain and Mathews gave strong support to the VSO, increasing its annual grant eventually to $1.1 million. In 1984, the company moved into its new home when Cain opened the State Theatre complex, the final stage of the Arts Centre. But the VSO seemed to be everywhere: they performed *Aida* at the Carlton football ground, they performed *La Boheme* on ABC television, and they made several recordings, including *Lohengrin* with Alberto Remedios in the title role, and Berlioz' grand opera *Les Troyens*, with Margreta Elkins. The company was starting to become, as Hamer envisaged, a genuine Melbourne rival to the Sydney-based Australian Opera.

But the VSO's finances remained precarious at best. Its venue was the State Theatre, which boasted a far bigger stage than the Sydney Opera House, but was expensive to rent. The large stage tempted it to mount lavish, expensive productions. Its innovative Australian-commissioned works played to empty seats. The company received little federal funding, and as Victoria's finances were squeezed by the Hawke government's cuts, its state grant was to remain unchanged for a decade. Low subsidies and high costs meant its prices were higher than those for Australian Opera productions in Melbourne, which led to a loss of audience. When it went to the other extreme by offering very cheap seats to young subscribers, that worsened its bottom line. In 1985, Hamer as chairman complained that the company had been kept afloat only by the financial success of its production of *The Pirates of Penzance*, which toured nationally to huge audiences.

In 1990, for a host of reasons — far more than most analysts mention — Victoria crashed into a deep recession. Opera patronage and sponsorship were badly affected. Yet in 1991 the VSO moved its administration from a cheap building in Fitzroy to expensive new premises on Southbank, in the arts precinct. According to an audit carried out later, the fitout alone cost $2.5 million, and the rent was $660,000 a year. The VSO was not making enough money to pay for a home like that. In 1991, it posted a loss of $1.5 million, a large loss for such a small company. That was followed by a further loss of $1.7 million in 1992. When the Kennett government took power at the end of that year, the VSO was a financial basket-case. Kennett, too, was cutting spending, but he and his arts minister, Haddon Storey, felt loyalty to Hamer, and shared his vision for the company. 'The VSO had become an important part of Victoria's performing-arts infrastructure,' Storey said. 'If it failed, it would have detrimental flow-on effects to the Victorian arts world … and would diminish Victoria's standing in the arts.' They provided a $2.4 million grant, which Hamer and Mackenzie-Forbes used to pay off debts. But in return, the company accepted a cut in its annual grant from $1.1 million to $800,000. It abandoned plans to mount a Melbourne production of Wagner's *Ring* cycle, which triggered the resignation of Richard Divall, its longtime artistic director.

Still the company kept living beyond its means, and the fire alarms were ringing. Labor MP Bob Ives told parliament:

> There is disquiet within sections of the arts community that, despite considerable artistic success, the management of the Victoria State Opera has been marked by a lack of financial discipline, self-indulgence in the staging and production of operas — the most notable example being the recent production of *The Tales of Hoffmann* — and negligent planning and self-deluding grandiosity

in the acquisition of its building. There are fears that those past practices will continue.[5]

In 1995, Mackenzie-Forbes was moved out of the general manager's desk, and Hamer, by then 78, stood down as chairman. In 1995, the VSO posted another $1.2 million loss. In May 1996, Kennett bailed them out a second time with a $5 million grant, intended to serve as a capital fund, but asked his friend Graeme Samuel, chairman of the rival Australian Opera, to 'sort out the mess'. In October 1996, Samuel dictated the terms of what was officially called a merger, but was really a takeover. The VSO was no more. The Australian Opera was renamed Opera Australia; its low-budget trainee company, Oz Opera, became based in Melbourne, but the state had lost its opera company.

These were bad times for Hamer's business affairs, too. In 1989, the Estate Mortgage trustee company became the first of many Victorian financial houses to get into trouble because of their own incompetence. The Burns Philp Trustee Company, of which Hamer had been Victorian chairman, was trustee to Estate Mortgage, but had failed to raise the alarm at its clearly unsustainable strategy; within a year, Burns Philp Trustees itself was forced to close. In 1992, Hamer was chairman of the McEwans hardware chain when it, too, went into receivership. Owned and run by the Luxton family for decades, it had been through a series of owners in its last years: first Repco, then Sir Donald Trescowthick's Charles Davis group, of which Hamer was a director, and then half of it was sold in a management buyout. Hamer went with the deal as chairman, but one wonders what relevant expertise a 75-year-old ex-premier could bring to a business changing as rapidly as hardware retailing. In 1993, the receivers sold the chain to Bunnings, which closed many of its stores. Hamer remained a director of Charles Davis until 1994, by which time it, too, was selling off many of the businesses it had acquired in the boom years. In 2001, Charles Davis also went into receivership.

None of this affected Hamer's public standing; in 1992, he was honoured again by being named a Companion of the Order of Australia. And as his business career failed, Hamer came back to politics. In the 1980s, he had been reluctant to enter political debates: 'I don't think that old wrestlers should wrestle again,' he quipped in 1986 to *The Herald*. But he made one exception: constitutional change. The most significant political role that Hamer took on in retirement was to be one of six prominent lawyers appointed by the Hawke government to review the Constitution. The Constitutional Commission was set up in 1985 with Sir Maurice Byers, former Commonwealth solicitor-general under both sides of politics, as chairman; the other commissioners included Gough Whitlam, law professors Enid Campbell and Leslie Zines, and Justice John Toohey, who withdrew after being promoted to the High Court.

The commission's final report, released in 1988, was an extraordinarily ambitious document, proposing dozens of changes to a Constitution that had proved extraordinarily resistant to change in the past. One wonders what Hamer was thinking when he joined the others in proposing so many changes that his pragmatism and past experience must have warned him would be impossible to deliver. The most important of their many recommendations were that:

- Federal parliament should move to a four-year term, in which the Senate would be unable to block Supply in the first three years.
- The principle of 'one vote, one value' should be enshrined in the Constitution, and apply to states as well as the Commonwealth.
- A new section should be added to the Constitution to enshrine basic human rights, such as freedom of conscience and religion, freedom of thought, expression, association, and peaceful assembly; freedom from racial, sexual, or political discrimination; the right to a fair trial, and many others.
- State governments should be formally empowered to levy excise duties (as, in effect, they were already doing).

There was no bipartisan support for the commission from the outset, nor was there for its recommendations. John Howard was then federal leader of the Liberal Party, and Peter Reith its shadow attorney-general. Howard was a conservative; Reith was from the radical right. Both were longstanding enemies of Hamer — in Reith's case, from his childhood, when Hamer as minister for local government had intervened to stop his family building a holiday home overlooking Phillip Island's penguin parade — and they did not accept him as representating the Liberal side. Despite their opposition, Bob Hawke put parts of the first three proposals, and a fourth to formally recognise local government, to a referendum in September 1988. Every proposal was rejected in every state.

Hamer returned to the political stage during the 1993 federal election campaign, when he wrote a series of commentaries in *The Herald-Sun* supporting John Hewson and his Liberal–National coalition. Hamer remained a Liberal Party member all his life, but played no significant part in it. He was not a member of the Melbourne Club, and sought no role in the party organisation. Jeff Kennett did not consult him; and in office, he overturned many of Hamer's policies. Yet, as a loyal team man, Hamer never criticised the Kennett government in public; for its 1996 election campaign, he wrote a series of commentaries in *The Age* supporting its re-election. And in 1999, he endorsed Kennett's tourism minister, Louise Asher — in younger days, his intended biographer — in a bitter preselection contest between the Kennett faction and the Kroger–Costello faction for the seat of Brighton.

On issues outside state politics, he felt free to speak out. In 1993, he joined former federal health minister Neal Blewett and others to urge governments to stop treating drug use as a crime, and to treat it instead as a health problem. He became one of the first to advocate a trial of supplying heroin to users, while offering them treatment for their addiction. In his last years, when he aired his views through letters to *The Age*, it was the subject he raised most frequently, trying to break through the knee-jerk response that supplying free drugs would only make the problem worse.

His best-known cause was the republic. In 1988, at Melbourne University, he had debated his old friend Manning Clark on the issue of whether Australia should become a republic: Clark was for it; Hamer, against. But as on capital punishment, his views changed. When prime minister Paul Keating put the republic on the agenda after the 1993 election, Hamer joined New South Wales premier Nick Greiner as one of the few prominent Liberals to support the change, while emphasising that he wanted Australia to remain in the Commonwealth, with the Queen at its head. When the Howard government called a constitutional convention in 1998 to design a proposal to be put to a referendum, Hamer agreed to stand as an Australian Republican Movement candidate from Victoria. With 16 conventioneers to be elected from the state, Hamer was allocated seventh place on the ARM ticket, which gave him a chance of election if the ARM dominated the poll. But with 158 candidates from 60 groups, that was unlikely; and in the campaign, the ARM's minimalist model of change — in effect, changing the governor-general for a president chosen the same way — lost ground to the Real Republic ticket headed by social-justice campaigner the Rev. Tim Costello, which called for an elected president. Although he was well down the ARM ticket, Hamer scored the eighth-highest personal vote of the 158 candidates; but at 81, his last tilt at election fell short.

It certainly did not end his interest in the republic. In 1999, he wrote a powerful article for *The Age* highlighting the differences between the rather complex model that came out of the convention, which allowed for widespread input by various groups, and what he considered the Howard government's misleading description of it on the referendum ballot paper as 'a president chosen by a two-thirds majority of both Houses of Parliament'. The referendum ballot failed in Victoria by fewer than 10,000 votes, but Victoria was the only state in which it came close. Even before the 1988 fiasco, Hamer had warned that referendums could pass only if both major parties supported them. This had last happened in 1977, when the Fraser government successfully put four referendums to ensure that no future opposition could come to power the way it had.

Another of Hamer's favourite causes was the fight for pragmatic economic policies against economic rationalism. One of his tennis partners was Ernest Rodeck, a bright, charming, public-spirited engineer who had been transported to Australia in 1940 as one of the Dunera boys — the Jewish refugees from Hitler who were shipped to Australia because the British, inexplicably, thought they might have Nazi sympathies. After the war, Rodeck co-founded the Fler furniture company in Melbourne, and then became a senior executive at Pacific Dunlop. In 1990, he founded the Society for Balanced Trade, later renamed the Society for Australian Industry and Employment. Hamer became its patron, and argued through letters to newspapers, chapters in books, and other means for a reorientation of economic policy to give greater emphasis to encouraging production in Australia, rather than providing a level playing-field for consumers. He applauded Howard's decision in 1997 to ensure long-term support for the car industry in Australia. He would have been appalled by the policies of Labor and Liberal governments, and the Reserve Bank, which have combined since to drive it out of Australia.

In his seventies and eighties, Hamer was involved in any number of liberal, environmental, artistic, and humanitarian causes. He was on everyone's guest list, everyone's committee. Steve Bracks, premier from 1999 to 2007, recalls that even as in old age, 'he always looked young: intellectually broad-minded, and still very engaged. There was always warmth about him.'

In the early 1990s, he was not only chairman of the Victoria State Opera, but more or less simultaneously national president of the Save the Children Fund, president of the Friends of the Royal Botanic Gardens, president of the Friends of the ABC, chairman of the Cancer/Heart consultative council, chairman of Greenhouse Action Australia, president of the Melbourne Foundation Day Committee, member of the MCG/Olympic Park Trust, member of the Yarra Bend Trust, council member of the Victorian College of the Arts, and many other bodies. It is astonishing that he could arrange his schedule to fit in so many committee meetings. He wrote letters to *The Age* in support of recycling urban water and putting irrigation channels in pipes, and to argue for an apology to Aboriginal Australians, a national Bill of Rights, a fountain in Federation Square, a Melbourne-based opera company, the protection of Point Nepean, and so on. Late in life, he wrote out a list of all the organisations of which he was patron; he managed to remember 71 of them.

Few issues stirred him more than those he saw as threatening the Australian ethos of a fair go. He was appalled by Pauline Hanson's attempt to create a 'mainstream Australian' racist backlash against Aboriginals and Asian migrants, and by prime minister John Howard's indulgence of it. On 8 December 1996, he gave a speech to the Rally Against Racism held in the Treasury Gardens, which put strongly his core beliefs:

> Today we declare our common humanity. This cause cuts across politics, across all age groups, across all backgrounds.
>
> We claim to be a civilised nation. Let us act like one.
>
> Let us reject and condemn attempts to divide us — based on ignorance and blind prejudice — and declare and uphold the true belief that all people are equal, that all discrimination on grounds of race, colour, religion or sex, is totally obnoxious — in Victoria, not only unacceptable, but unlawful.
>
> Here in Australia, we are all migrants or descendants of migrants — yes, even our indigenous people. We have four million Australians who were either born in other countries or whose parents were born abroad. Right here in Melbourne, we have Australians who come from over 70 different nations.
>
> We have accepted an obligation under the United Nations to shelter political refugees; we have provided a safe and secure haven for many thousands of displaced persons from many countries. They have made immense contributions to our skills, our cultural life and our resources. It is a proud record. Let us all be proud of it.
>
> Of course we are a multicultural society. It is a historical fact.
>
> As a young man I spent five-and-a-half years fighting in a war against the evil and ugly Nazi tyranny, arrogantly asserting the superiority of one race above all others and cruelly suppressing millions, especially the Jewish people.
>
> We upheld a better faith — humanity, tolerance, mutual respect

> for all. I have always believed that we *are* a tolerant people, that we *do* welcome and respect diversity, that we *do* uphold freedom and equality for all before the law. There are times that we need to declare this faith, and this is one of them.
>
> I firmly believe that if we uphold these basic beliefs, we can be an example to the whole world of a truly tolerant multicultural society, where real freedom breathes and abides.

For Australia Day 1997, asked by *The Age* what he loved best about his country, Hamer singled out five attributes:

- the variety, beauty … and this splendid climate invite an outdoor lifestyle and the enjoyment of nature.
- [its] broad tolerance and hospitable spirit have offered a welcome and a home for many thousands of refugees from misery and oppression.
- [its] citizens include millions from 140 countries, whose diverse cultures have enriched our lives.
- [it] respects its heritage of personal liberty, freedom of speech and assembly, democratic institutions and the rule of law.
- compassion, mateship and voluntary effort in support of community causes are valued and recognised.

Two causes became particular preoccupations in his later years. In the late 1980s, the violist Marco van Pagee suggested that Melbourne should host an international chamber-music competition. As music critic Michael Shmith of *The Age* recounted, Hamer was enthused; so was Kenneth Tribe, the former chairman of Musica Viva, Australia's chamber-music entrepreneur; so was Bernt Schlickum, the 'committedly cultural' managing director of Mercedes-Benz Australia; and so was Hamer's great friend Dame Elisabeth Murdoch. In 1989, they set up an organisation, with Hamer as chairman. The first competition was held in 1991, with the main prizes going to Britain's Gould Piano Trio and Russia's St Petersburg Quartet; both ensembles now enjoy worldwide renown. Further competitions have been held every four years since; from 1997, they have been supplemented by what was initially an Australian national competition, now extended to an Asia–Pacific competition, also held every four years. In 2009, five years after Hamer's death, the Asia–Pacific competition was won by a young Melbourne ensemble called the Hamer Quartet: violinists Cameron Hill and Rebecca Chan, violist Stefanie Farrands, and cellist Michael Dahlenburg. Proteges of the conductor William Hennessy, they named their quartet in Dick's honour, and performed as an ensemble for three years, enjoying considerable success before their careers took them separate ways.

One of the organisations that Dick had been proud to help in its early days was Albury-Wodonga's famed Flying Fruit Fly Circus. In 1995, he lent his support to set up the Melbourne Institute for Circus Arts, with eight students located in an unrenovated warehouse at the Docklands. Swinburne University took them under its wing, and it is now the National Institute of Circus Arts, with an elegant home on Swinburne's Prahran campus, financed with the help of the Pratt Foundation. Dick was inaugural chairman of the institute. Surprisingly, among the many activities he pursued in retirement, this was his only active connection with Swinburne University, apart from an occasion in 1995 when he became the first to receive an honorary doctorate from the technical school that his uncle and aunt created.

As Dick moved into his eighties, he gradually reduced his involvement in his community, and increased his involvement in his family. In 1994, he and April finally moved out of Monomeath Avenue to a modest home high on a hill in Kew. (The new owners promptly demolished their old home to build something grander.) Dick and April spent every second weekend at an idealistic 'village farm' at Tallarook, 'Lyndale Park', where they, Brian Goldsmith, and others had holiday houses on a jointly owned 200-hectare farm. They became hands-on grandparents, especially to the youngest of their eight grandchildren, the family of their youngest son, Alastair, and his wife, Megan. 'He was a clown with children, and would have them screaming with laughter,' his daughter Sarah remembers. 'He would swipe something from their plate, and pretend nothing had happened.' Julia has similar memories. 'He used to play tricks on them, silly things, and to the boys, it was just hilarious.'

He remained active in the chamber-music competitions and the Institute of Circus Arts. He continued to write letters to *The Age*, variously warning the West in January 2003 against invading Iraq, urging that irrigation water be enclosed in pipes to reduce the waste through evaporation, and urging the state government to establish a new Victorian opera company. And he became involved in one last political cause, urging the Howard government to reverse its 'shameful and inhuman' policy of locking up asylum-seekers. Just before Christmas 2003, he penned his final political statement:

> The spirit of Christmas, as well as ordinary compassion, demands action to end the continuing horror of the refugees. So many Australians feel diminished and ashamed, and call for intervention by the Minister on humanitarian grounds.
>
> If there are no terrorists among the hundreds of refugees still behind barbed wire, their continued detention offends against many of the very principles which most Australians uphold and take pride in, best summed up in the basic principle of a 'fair go'.
>
> The women and the children (94 in detention centres in Australia, 90 in Nauru) have not committed any crime. They should be released immediately, subject to any appropriate conditions.
>
> If any refugees cannot physically be returned to their homeland (Afghanistan for instance seems as dangerous as ever in parts) they should not be imprisoned indefinitely, but released while their applications are reconsidered. Many would make very good Aussie citizens.
>
> Let us press for a Christmas gesture which would make us proud to be Australians.[6]

Towards the end, Julia recalls:

> Over the last year or two my father became increasingly gentle and affectionate, remarkably so … I think he had been reflecting on his

> approaching death, and had come to value his connections with the people who loved him above almost all things — that, and public service, trying to improve life for everyone. Also, he was slowing down.[7]

Dick was now 87. On the morning of 23 March 2004, he told April he was not feeling well. Nonetheless, he went into town to attend a parliamentary lunch in honour of a visiting US Muslim leader. He then came home, lay down for a rest, went to sleep, and never woke up.

Melbourne came together to celebrate one of its favourite sons. There was standing room only in St Paul's Cathedral for his state funeral, where his life was commemorated with a particularly powerful tribute from Lindsay Thompson, looking frail but sounding stentorian, followed by others from Richard Divall and Fay Marles. The Reverend Ron Browning, son of his cousin Margaret (Swinburne), delivered the eulogy. A piper played the Scottish lament 'The Flowers of the Forest'. Joan Carden sang the Alleluia from Mozart's *Exsultate, jubilate*. The Flinders Quartet played the adagio from Haydn's 'Sunrise' Quartet. The Trinity College choir sang the hymns and psalm. Steve Waldron, writing in *The Age*, remarked that it seemed 'the most natural thing in the world to see … political rivals Joan Kirner and Jeff Kennett sitting together. Labor premier Steve Bracks and Prime Minister John Howard shared a forward pew — an unlikely "front bench"'. Dick's daughter Sarah Brenan read from Tennyson's *Ulysses*:

> Much have I seen and known; cities of men
> And manners, climates, councils, governments,
> Myself not least, but honor'd of them all;
> And drunk delight of battle with my peers,
> Far on the ringing plains of windy Troy.
> I am a part of all that I have met;
> Yet all experience is an arch wherethro'
> Gleams that untravell'd world, whose margin fades
> For ever and for ever when I move.

> How dull it is to pause, to make an end,
> To rust unburnish'd, not to shine in use!
> As tho' to breathe were life.

It was testimony to the bipartisan respect and affection for Hamer that Labor premier Steve Bracks took the unexpected step of naming the concert hall of the Arts Centre 'Hamer Hall', calling it 'a symbol of the qualify of life issues which he pursued'. It was a fitting tribute: to Hamer's crucial role in getting the Arts Centre built; to his contribution, in so many roles, to Melbourne's musical life; and to his achievements as a reforming leader who helped to make Victoria the tolerant, well-educated, well-run state it is today.

CHAPTER TWENTY-EIGHT

Dick Hamer: an assessment

Some governments simply govern; others lead. At its best, the Hamer government was one of the latter: it led the way to a different Victoria. There was no change of party when he took over as leader, yet it led a change in policies and political culture that makes it the watershed between the Victoria of the past and the Victoria of today. Hamer came out of a post-Victorian world of affluence, elegance, hard work, and civic responsibility. Yet he became the first Victorian premier to belong to the modern world, which assumes its leaders to be gender-neutral, multicultural, free of prejudice, environmentally responsible, and socially and economically inclusive. Hamer was comfortable with all that, as few of his contemporaries were: he helped to create that world in Victoria. To some of his liberal colleagues, it was a weakness that he was so open-minded, so forward-thinking, so quick to see and consider the merit in alternative views. They dismissed him as 'trendy', failing to grasp that these were not passing fads, but a permanent shift in social values. The trendy things in the 1970s were wide lapels, bell-bottomed jeans, and platform shoes: they came and went. Feminism, environmentalism, and racial equality were not trends: they had come to stay. Hamer saw that when his opponents in the party did not, and he was comfortable with it, because they were his own values.

The first reason for his enduring political success is that voters embraced his policies. Victorians did not want another Bolte-style government. Most of them wanted a government that took consumer rights and women's rights seriously, did more to protect the vulnerable, gave priority to protecting the things they wanted to keep, improved public transport rather than just kept it going, and created new opportunities for their leisure hours — good parks in the outer suburbs, bike paths along the city's creeks and rivers, arts venues and quality companies to perform in them. Hamer promised all that, delivered, and took possession of the political middle ground.

None of this was against Liberal values, although it was against the values of some 'big-L' Liberals, as the conservatives sometimes called themselves. The Liberal Party in Victoria was a broad church. In the 1970s, the early feminists and environmentalists, and the art-lovers, were just as likely to vote Liberal as Labor. Many of them were higher-income people who thus, like Hamer, belonged to the Liberal tribe. While the party room was predominantly conservative, the party organisation was predominantly liberal, at least until the 1975 conservative groundswell against Whitlam shifted the balance. In Melbourne, the grassroots of the party remained predominantly liberal throughout Hamer's time. In some ways, the Victorian party still is, to the extent that some of the Liberal constituencies that Hamer represented would have trouble feeling at home with the federal Liberal Party of today, as he himself frequently found himself in opposition to policies of the Howard government.

The second reason for Hamer's success was his own character. He loved to read and quote Marcus Aurelius, the Roman emperor and Stoic philosopher, whose *Meditations* set out an ideal that, at the end of this narrative, sounds familiar to us:

> [Claudius] Maximus was my model for self-control, fixity of purpose, and cheerfulness under ill-health or other misfortunes. His character was an admirable combination of dignity and charm, and all the duties of his station were performed quietly and without fuss. He gave everyone the conviction that he spoke as he believed, and acted as he judged right … Kindliness, sympathy, and sincerity all contributed to give the impression of a rectitude that was innate

> rather than inculcated. Nobody was ever made by him to feel inferior, yet none could have presumed to challenge his pre-eminence.[1]

Hamer's political success came not only from what he did, but from how he did it. Victorians saw him as not only intelligent, but genuine and fair-minded. He exuded some remarkably reassuring qualities: an impregnable courtesy, a sense of quiet competence and authority, a natural warmth and kindness, an unfailing self-discipline. Some perceptive observers realised that his ability to shrug off criticism as he did, and constantly forgive his attackers, stemmed from, as Don Hayward put it, 'a self-confidence that bordered on hubris'; he might have been a better politician had he felt the stings and blows of political combat more than he did. There was something old-fashioned to it: he was probably the last premier to have had a classical education, and he always carried a sense of *noblesse oblige*. Yet one of the reasons that Hamer won three elections as premier was that Victorians trusted him, and they trusted him because they saw him as an intelligent, reliable, hard-working man who was genuinely concerned about ordinary people and made decisions in their interest.

A third thing that made Hamer stand out from other political leaders was his integrity. Amid the more than 1,000 letters that Dick and April received after his resignation, one from Cheryl Saunders, later professor of constitutional law at Melbourne University, summed up what made his government different:

> Under your leadership, the government of Victoria has been more civilised and rational, and less preoccupied with narrow party advantage, than any other government in Australia.[2]

Many others saw him that way. Hamer was no Utopian idealist; he barely took a step without sizing up its political implications. He knew as well as any that politics is the art of the possible. But he assessed the long-term interests of the state and its people, and steered in that direction, rather than trying to manufacture issues, or direct debates for short-term political gain. You could not imagine Hamer setting up a royal commission whose goal was to embarrass his political opponents. He saw himself as a trustee for all the people in the state. That is why he inspired so much admiration from Victorians. Some colleagues wanted him to be more like Bolte — quick to seize the political advantage and turn the public against his opponents. That was not the way Hamer governed, and Victorians liked him that way.

A fourth factor in Hamer's political success, especially in earlier years, was his determination and energy. He was very bright, able to handle a very heavy workload, and able to generate the momentum for reforms. As minister for local government in the 1960s, his drive was one of the things that made him stand out from Bolte's other ministers, and made the party look to him as the obvious successor. Even at the end, when he was almost 65 and visibly tiring, his former press secretary Richard Thomas told him: 'Probably only your personal staff have any idea of the enormous workload which you carried in recent years.' He shared with John Howard an extraordinary ability to keep on top of all the issues his government faced, and at times, a determination to ram through reforms if he could not bring the party with him.

That was not, however, his normal approach. Critics from both sides of politics said that he relied too much on patient persuasion and on getting consensus; many felt he would have been a better premier had he been tougher and bolder, more hungry to get his way. But apart from his decision to abolish capital punishment — clearly an emotional decision for him, as a legacy of the Ryan hanging — Hamer's approach was normally to go at the pace that the party room would accept. If he could not get all he wanted, he would try again for what he could get. Critics saw him as passive; yet, as an earlier Victorian Liberal leader, Trevor Oldham, put it, reform was never achieved 'by sitting down calmly and waiting for something to turn up'. And Hamer was very much a reformer.

But he was passive in dealing with difficult people and, sometimes, difficult problems. Richard Thomas, the staffer who got closest to him, was constantly amazed by his understanding of tangled policy questions and 'his prodigious memory, especially for people', but added: 'If Dick had faults, one of them was he was too ready to see good in people, and too little prepared to believe ill of them.' Hamer had grown up steeped in Christianity, from his father's side, and from Geelong Grammar. As he grew to adulthood, his rational mind rejected first the miracles, and ultimately the belief that there was a Supreme Being ruling the universe. Yet his values always bore the strong imprint of the ethic of the Gospels: treat others as you would like them to treat you; show generosity to the poor and the suffering; and forgive those who strike you, and turn the other cheek.

Because Hamer was so trusting, he did not smell danger as soon as he should have, in government, and especially in retirement. He and his government paid dearly for his readiness to sign off on the Housing Commission's land purchases without checking that it had consulted with the planning authorities, as he had ordered after the Pakenham deal. On Newport, the union ban on building the station left him without good policy choices; yet, in hindsight, it was not enough for him to negotiate with Ken Stone and John Halfpenny, and trust that they could bring an unruly union movement with them. In the end, it was a question of who was running the state, and the government should have played it tougher, sooner, to force the unions to back down. The Liberal Party paid dearly for allowing a loose cannon like Doug Jennings to become an MP, even after he had shown a preference for firing his cannon at his own team. And Hamer and Fraser both ignored for far too long the costs of the thuggish culture that took root in Victoria's building unions, and remains there still.

These failures helped to erode his and his party's dominance of Victorian politics, as did things that were not his fault: the renaissance in Labor's ranks, the failure of the economy to regain its former strength, and the federal government's decision to force the states to make deeper spending cuts than it was prepared to make itself. As Hamer's electoral position weakened, his authority in the party declined, and weaknesses that had not mattered earlier came to the fore. Like most in the party, he had resented the way that Bolte and Rylah manipulated outcomes in the cabinet and the party room; his own very different style of leadership was, in part, a reaction against that. But as times got tougher, his unwillingness to get involved in fighting for the issues he cared about became costly. At the moment of the greatest crisis in his career, when he was in Hawaii deciding whether to resign as premier or fight on, Hamer left it to two staffers, Richard Mulcahy and Neil Mooney, to find out the numbers in Melbourne, rather than doing it himself. Many former Liberal MPs interviewed for this book assert that, at this critical time, Hamer still had the numbers to stay on.

But that was how Hamer worked: he was hands-on when it came to thinking through policy issues; hands-off when it came to winning the party's support for them. Graeme Weideman, who took on Hamer's tourism portfolio in the Thompson government, concludes that Hamer had 'left himself vulnerable by getting out of touch with the backbench'. He spent too little time with them, one on one or in small groups, working to keep them onside; and he gave them too little to do, leaving them free to gripe and plot. In his early years, he kept control of cabinet and party meetings; later, as his position weakened and the party became more fractious, he allowed meetings to slip out of control. Liberal MPs who served under both Kennett and Hamer were almost unanimous in judging Kennett the better leader in the party room: he allowed room for real debate, but kept it tightly focussed. Don Hayward entered parliament in 1979 straight from life as a senior executive at General Motors, and was astonished by the contrast between the way that business operated and what he found in government:

> He tolerated ministers who really were not on top of the job; a lot of his ministers were relatively incompetent. To a large extent, the bureaucracy ran the show, and there wasn't really a sense of direction.
>
> Often party meetings were all over the place. People would get up and talk about their own pet things that really weren't to the issue — and Hamer would let it go on. At the end, he allowed Ian Smith to run riot. It was a failure of leadership on Hamer's part. Allowing indiscipline to become established was what brought him down.[3]

Hamer's commitment to democracy within the party, which had distinguished him so sharply from Bolte and Rylah, ultimately became his Achilles heel. The best example was his defeat by the party room on the casino issue. It inevitably damaged his leadership in the eyes of the public — and in the eyes of business. It was also a tragedy for Melbourne. Federal Hotels' plan for a glass pyramid on the Yarra bank was a stunning design; its plan for a casino-convention centre without any poker machines was a concept that maximised the benefits to Victoria and minimised the costs. It should have been built, and it could have been built, had the premier who promoted it been prepared to climb down into the political trenches to fight for it.

Yet that was the nature of the man; it was part of his strength, and of his weakness. One of the things that Victorians liked about him was that, unlike Fraser, he was not constantly in political combat, but seemed to stand above it, just doing his duty. Hayward was right to say that he tolerated incompetent ministers, yet that was even more true of Bolte. The difference was that in Bolte's time, the economy was cruising along, and Labor was a pushover. Hamer was the first Liberal leader to face a skilled opposition, and he was too slow to force his ministers and party to lift their game. He was also the first leader for decades to face an economy in which it was hard for a school leaver to find a job. By the late 1970s, the state needed to focus on rebuilding its economic and business strength. While Hamer did give high priority to getting school leavers into apprenticeships and training programs, he was a lawyer, more interested in people's rights and welfare than in running the state at peak efficiency, or creating the conditions for business to thrive. In the end, the economic and fiscal problems accumulated, and combined with chronic disloyalty in Liberal ranks to overwhelm him.

Many of those problems, however, crept up on him. In hindsight, we can see clearly how they developed, and point out better ways he could have handled them. But we should be wary of judging past actions merely from hindsight. It was not obvious at the time that the Trades Hall Council would repeatedly reject agreements on Newport reached by its leaders. There was nothing to flag to Hamer that the

Fraser government — 'theoretically on the same political team', as Josh Gordon of *The Age* has put it in describing the gulf between the Abbott and Napthine governments — would sharply reduce his government's ability to invest in infrastructure, or that it would cut recurrent grants significantly in real terms. In the 1970s, we had far less community debate than we have now. There was no internet, radio talkback was in its infancy, and television and the newspapers covered the news, but mostly left serious analysis to *The Age* — which itself was erratic in the depth and balance of its coverage. The scope for public debate was far less than we are used to now, as was its quality.

In hindsight, Dick Hamer stayed on too long. Had he stepped down in 1978, as originally planned, he would have been remembered without ambivalence as a highly successful politician: his two electoral successes were unassailable. Yet in 1978, apart from the Howson camp, there was no one demanding that he go — in fact, quite the opposite. The Liberals never had a better leader waiting in the wings, let alone knocking on the door. Hamer never had more than half-a-dozen top-class ministers; had he been more ruthless in discarding the poor performers, he would have led a stronger team, and achieved more. But he respected the party's democratic traditions, and he was generally soft on people: weak ministers were no exception.

It was a far-from-perfect government, as we have seen. It made serious mistakes; it had serious limitations. Yet it delivered substantial policy achievements, and, equally importantly, it won respect for the way it governed. Dick Hamer was the modern exemplar of integrity in politics. He was also the last Liberal premier in Australia to win three elections. Why was it then, that, by the end of his life, Hamer's legacy appeared to be respected more by his Labor opponents than by his own side?

To answer that question properly would involve a study of the Liberal Party that is outside the scope of this book. As the transition from Bolte to Hamer demonstrates, all political parties must transform themselves over time, to meet new challenges thrown up by a changing society and a changing world. When Menzies re-formed the conservative side of politics in 1944, he chose to call it the Liberal Party rather than the Conservative Party because he saw himself as a liberal, not a conservative. 'We took the name "Liberal" because we were determined to be a progressive party, willing to make experiments, in no sense reactionary, but believing in the individual, his rights, and his enterprise,' Menzies wrote in *Afternoon Light*. Menzies fully accepted Deakin's 'settlement' of regulating wage rises, tariffs, and immigration to lift real wages and workers' living standards. He expanded the welfare system and the size of the state, albeit modestly. The three achievements he was most proud of, he said, were maintaining a harmonious coalition with the Country Party (which threw him out of office in his first stint as prime minister), the expansion of Australia's universities, and the development of Canberra. These priorities had little in common with those of the federal Liberal Party today.

In recent years, the federal party has moved to undo the achievements of Liberal governments in the past: dismantling what remains of Deakin's policies, reducing the welfare system and the size of the state, making universities rely on income from foreign students to finance growth. Where Deakin, Hamer, and Menzies and Bolte, in different ways, tried to occupy the middle ground, today's federal Liberals work by taking up a position to the right of it, and trying to move the middle ground towards them. The political faultlines between Liberal and Labor have become less tribal, more ideological. At the risk of oversimplifying, one could describe the older Menzies and Bolte as economic and social conservatives, in that, by and large, they accepted the economic and social order they inherited, and did not try to change it. Hamer, too, was an economic conservative, but he was a social liberal, trying to create a more open, tolerant society. Kennett was both an economic and social liberal. But Howard saw himself as an economic liberal and social conservative, the exact opposite to Hamer. And, with some qualifications — especially in Victoria — that is the broad orientation of the Liberal Party today. In Victoria, the party still celebrates Hamer's legacy: Jeff Kennett commissioned the statue that now stands in front of his old office, and Ted Baillieu as premier established the Hamer scholarships for Victorians to study Chinese in China, out of respect for the leader who pioneered the Victoria–Jiangsu relationship. At the national level, however, the Liberal Party has moved away from Hamer, just as it has moved away from Fraser, Deakin, and, to some extent, even Menzies.

A fair reckoning would have to conclude that Hamer and his ministers left Victoria a substantial positive legacy. They made Melbourne a centre of the arts, gave women equal opportunity in the workplace, removed the laws against homosexuality, and ended capital punishment. They substantially reduced the electoral bias against Melbourne voters, and broke the barriers that kept the public service from recruiting and promoting the best people. They ended the demolition of inner suburbs, preserved the best of Victoria's buildings and landscapes, and, in a scientifically driven process, set aside large areas of diverse ecosystems as national parks. They reversed the population drift away from country towns, and channelled the city's outer-suburban growth along corridors served by rail. They built the underground rail loop, the Arts Centre, the Eastern Freeway, and the Thomson Dam. They greatly increased investment in the railways while scrapping the railways' monopoly of freight movements within Victoria, and tackling the overstaffing and overprovision of country services. They finished the West Gate Bridge, and started to link the South-Eastern and Mulgrave freeways with what we now call CityLink. They continued Bolte's heavy investment in making Victoria's education system second to none. They allowed the hospitals to meet rapidly rising expectations for treatment while coping with the increased costs of an all-salaried staff. And every regional city in Victoria has an art gallery, theatre, or library from the Hamer era.

Tom Harley, great-grandson of Alfred Deakin, was a prominent young Liberal activist in Hamer's time. Now a strategic consultant, he sees the balance of Hamer's achievements and failures as overwhelmingly positive:

> The tragedy of Dick was that he was a reasonable man, set on consensus-driven policies. He overcompensated for the Bolte era by seeking to run the cabinet process democratically, and that became his Achilles heel … He was run over at the end by the Young Turks. Some of them were capable, and some weren't. But they were all impatient. And he ended up carrying the can for people he didn't want. I think he got tired and self-indulgent towards the end.
>
> But the real measure of his time is what he did to the state, which is profound. He changed the state, and he did it against the will of the parliamentary party. Under him, the values embodied in quality of life issues became central to Victorian politics. If you cast your mind around state politics, there are very few people who make such an imprint.[4]

In a letter to Hamer on his retirement, Michael Collins Persse, then head of history at Geelong Grammar School and now the school's historian and archivist, told him he would also be remembered for something else:

> There is about you a dignity, an honour, a gentleness — and will continue to flow to you a gratitude — too scarce in a world where generosity of spirit too seldom prevails in public life.[5]

APPENDIX A

Hamer on Hamer

Dick Hamer never wrote an autobiography. Judging from his draft outline for one, evidently written in his eighties, had he done so, it would have been a very different book from this one. He wanted to focus on detailed accounts of what his government achieved in five key areas — the environment and planning, the status of women, the arts, youth and sport, and social welfare — and his thoughts on reform of the federal system, the role of government, and the future. Other than that, he intended to allocate just four chapters to cover his entire political career, and one for his life before politics. By then, however, his memory was no longer as sharp as it had been, and the project lapsed. His best piece of writing in retirement was his 1982 Deakin Lecture, 'The Future of the Federal Compact', a powerful critique of the way that successive federal governments had wrested power from the states; unfortunately, it can be found only in libraries.

In interviews that Hamer gave early in his retirement, and in his interviews with Christopher Sexton in the early 1990s, he took on some of the criticisms made of him, and looked back on his political career when his memory of it was still fresh. The following compilation of his views is drawn from an interview by Peter Ellingsen of *The Age* three weeks after he resigned as premier, a long interview he gave me for *The Age* a year later, and his later interviews with Sexton.

On the Ryan hanging

Over all the time I'd been in cabinet, in every case, even under Henry Bolte, the death sentence was commuted — with one exception. The exception was Ryan. Of all the cases that had come before us, I thought that was the least worthy of carrying out the death sentence. First, it was sort of involuntary. Second, it wasn't clear who had fired the shot. There was quite a discussion in cabinet; there were three or four members of cabinet who felt the same way. But thereafter, I couldn't bring myself to argue the case against it. I'd been changing my mind gradually, but that was the turning point.[1]

On the crisis of 1975

I made my views known [to Fraser]. But if I'd gone public, it wouldn't have been possible except as a private citizen. In any case, what it led to was a decision by the people, the electors. If it had been otherwise, I would have felt even more strongly. But that moderated my feelings.[2]

On ministerial failures

It's always been my view that the most efficient way to organise a big operation is to delegate to people clear responsibilities, and hold them responsible for the result ... I think, by and large, the people I chose for the job turned out well. There were two, for which it's hard to take any responsibility because I inherited them, who fell short of the highest standards in terms of efficiency ... I don't want to overemphasise that, because by and large the system worked pretty well.[1]

On consensus and delays

What I meant by consensus is not trying to get everyone to agree, but inviting participation from everyone who has views to express. In my time we never had a vote in cabinet, not one single vote. It wasn't necessary. Out of the discussions around the cabinet table there emerged a clear line of action, a 'consensus'.[2]

I have never been unwilling to make a decision where the thing has reached a stage where a decision can be made. But often I have held up a decision until someone or other could be consulted who has not been consulted. Many times [criticism] has been due to lack of full knowledge of what is really going on. On other occasions, it is due to self-interest — people get impatient because it is costing them money. Of course, there are inexcusable cases of delay. Normally they are down the line somewhere, where someone is faced with a difficult situation … and they will put it in the too-hard basket. It's a very common human failing … You haul them over the coals when you find this happening.[3]

On politics and the casino

You've got to accept that you will be a target of abuse. If you don't, you shouldn't be in politics … Every time you make a decision, you make an enemy or two. Some will be permanent until the day you die.

The worst moments are when you realise with hindsight that something's been handled all wrong, and it's got out of hand. Sometimes hares start running in the media and are very difficult to stop. The whole thing is misinterpreted.

If you want a recent example, I suppose the casino was handled all wrong. I certainly underestimated the degree of opposition — although when you look at it, it's coming from people who are never likely to use a casino — but it's still there, a sort of instinctive reaction which I think we should have disarmed beforehand with facts and informed opinion. And that's how it is in most cases. It's as though you've used the wrong club, overshot the green![2]

I have never lobbied or tried to round up the numbers. I have enough faith in the wisdom of people that, when they hear the arguments of both sides, they will arrive at a sensible conclusion. Almost never has that been unjustified.

I suppose if I had liked to lobby [for the casino], I could have procured a different result. But as much as anything, that [party-room vote] was a reaction from independent-minded people to what they regarded as pressure from outside: not from me, but from outside. It did not, in my view, reflect the true opinion.[3]

On his regrets

The thing that's caused me most regret is that we didn't get a better setup between federal and state governments. The whole financial relationship is a mess, a travesty really of democratic principles of responsibility — all the potential for [buck-passing] that goes on … It's difficult to see what you can do without good will at the centre [Canberra].

Was the solution for the federal government to make dramatic cuts to income tax and grants to the states, so they were forced to raise their own funds?

That's the only way it can be done. That's what we expected to happen after 1975. We had discussions when the [Fraser] government was in opposition … There was quite widespread agreement that this was the way to do it. The Commonwealth was to retire from part of the income tax field, namely the amount which went beyond the amount needed for its own responsibilities, and the states would be forced to collect their share … That's the only way to achieve it. It's no good adding or subtracting marginal state taxes on top of the existing tax: no state is going to take that on, it's just politically impossible.

Hamer said he also regretted not having used the Equal Opportunity Act to ban sporting clubs on Crown land from discriminating against women. He wished he had intervened sooner to head off Doug Jennings' entry into parliament, when allegations first surfaced that he had won preselection due to branch stacking. And he regretted taking Ian Smith back into cabinet in March 1981:

But at the time it seemed the right thing to do. He apologised and withdrew unreservedly. I thought then he had certain abilities — he has quite an inquiring and incisive mind, he expresses himself well, and he has some administrative ability when he likes to apply it — and I thought then he would serve as a sound member of the team.[2]

On his legacy

First of all, I think our physical surroundings, in Melbourne and throughout the state, have changed vastly. We have many more parks. Our heritage, both natural and man-made, is better preserved and in better shape than it was.

Secondly, I think the opportunities for people to find themselves, to enlarge themselves outside the daily grind, are much better. That runs through the whole area of the arts, libraries, the education system, pre-schools.

And thirdly, I think this society is much less prejudiced now than it used to be. The attitude to the migrant community is far better. Attitudes to handicapped people, especially the mentally retarded, have changed. And for the first time, we're beginning to use the wits, the intelligence, and the other attributes of half the population — the women.

specifically …

The whole idea of domiciliary services has always appealed to me. People who have trouble being in the mainstream of the community for all sorts of reasons ought to be maintained in their homes rather than being stuck away in an institution. Things like special schools, and day centres for the elderly have always given me great pleasure.

And I'm particularly proud of the development of the metropolitan parks. When you look around and see how the Yarra valley is developing, the Maribyrnong Valley, Jells Park — well, that gives me a lot of satisfaction. People are coming there by the thousands for active recreation, to walk, ride bikes, or just lie in the sun. That, I think, is something the community needs, and which gives me satisfaction to have helped along.[2]

APPENDIX B

Tributes to Hamer on his retirement

Diana Baillieu, mother of future premier Ted Baillieu (to April)
First of all, my thoughts are very specially with you today. You have been so marvellous, and truly, I think, it must be more difficult to be the *wife* of the Premier than to be the Premier! Every ball bowled up to someone you love, you would want to hit yourself; but you can't, you just have to be endlessly wise, tactful, restrained and dignified — and *silent*! For you both, I am sure it will be in many ways a relief to have a bit more of a peaceful life, after giving ***so*** much of yourselves, *in every way*, all these years …

Everard Baillieu, founder of Baillieu Allard, president of the Royal Humane Society, and former comrade of Hamer at Tobruk
I am disgusted and appalled by the events … The actions of certain sections of so-called 'big business' especially revolted me. Never have I seen a more splendid example of Christian behaviour and character than your own dignified announcement of your retirement. My warmest congratulations.

Ted Baillieu, premier of Victoria 2010–13 (on Hamer's death in 2004)
I believe there are four giants of the Victorian Liberal Party: Sir Robert Menzies, Henry Bolte, Jeff Kennett and Dick Hamer … Dick

Hamer was a decent, modest, determined and intelligent visionary for Victoria … So much of what we take for granted in Victoria is part of his legacy … the Arts Centre, a healthy Yarra, the city taking its face to the river, parks and gardens … equal opportunity, the underground loop, Werribee Park, fluoridation, or even the 'Life. Be in it.' Campaign or the dams, it is an extraordinary legacy … Dick Hamer made it happen. He made it happen with a cheery smile, a reassuring presence, and a supportive word for just about everybody.

Macmahon 'Mac' Ball, emeritus professor of politics at Melbourne University, and Hamer's former lecturer

In my view, you have been easily the best and most civilised Premier we have had for the last 60 years — as long as I have been interested in politics … [Ball urged him to write] a book of reflections that could be a basic source book for future generations of serious students. Please make sure you start on this without delay.

Jean Battersby, chief executive, the Australia Council

I really feel that what you have done for the arts in Victoria is historic, and that the way you have done it is, if anything, even more remarkable. To have a government leader prepared to help the arts without fanfare or embarrassment — as if such assistance should be taken for granted as an activity of government — has been a great example. I only wish the Federal help had been given with such grace as this.

Geoffrey Blainey, historian and chairman of the Australia Council

So much was launched, and so much was consolidated, that in time to come, it will be seen as a period of great significance in the arts.

Dame Edith (Jill) Bolte, wife of former premier Sir Henry Bolte

My dear April

When I heard the news yesterday, I almost felt like there was a death in the family. You have been so much in our thoughts. What a cruel thing politics are. [*sic*]

I thought you were so good on the TV, and I can't say how I would have reacted. The press have nearly driven me mad. Why they did not leave Henry alone, I can't think. April, words fail me when I try to express to you how we feel. There is only one good thing, you will be freer to be together more, and lead a more leisurely life.

Henry tried to ring Dick last night, but naturally you were out … When we come back, you and Dick must come up to the farm to visit us. We would love to see you both.

Give my love to Dick, who has dedicated his life to Victoria for so many years, and it is all very sad. Now you won't have to go to all those terrible annual meetings &c, but that is not much compensation for what has happened …

With fondest love, Jill

Lorna Boucher, Ringwood

I apologise as a member of the human race for the way you were treated … I am a Liberal voter. I feel so ashamed. You are a great man among men, and a fine example to us all.

Steve Bracks, premier of Victoria (in 2004)

Sir Rupert was a leader ahead of his time … He fought for socially just causes, he broke new ground and he never resiled from his commitment to pursuing the greater good in public life.

Janet Calvert-Jones, businesswoman, philanthropist, sister of Rupert Murdoch

I just want to add my own expression of admiration to what John [her husband] has said. I have always admired you, and all that you have stood for, so very much, and — like many others — have been much saddened by the events of the last few days. The way you have handled it has only served to increase my admiration.

Lady Maie Casey, author and widow of Lord Casey, former governor-general

I send you both my deepest admiration and affection … Your energy, ability and integrity have been recognised for many years. You will continue to remain an imperishable force.

Joan Chambers, Liberal MP for Ballarat South 1979–82 (to April)

The first time I really identified with the Liberals was when Dick became Premier, and we had a key politician who was obviously fair, compassionate and far-sighted. The ironic fact is that there are still vast numbers of us who feel that.

Manning Clark, historian and old college friend

I believe you stood for something worthwhile — and still do.

Ron Clarke, former champion athlete, future mayor of the Gold Coast

There are thousands of Victorians very disappointed [that] your fine period of stewardship of this state has ended in such a way. Those of us not affected by prejudice or pocket feel extremely sorry you have been so badly done by.

Sir James Darling, former headmaster of Geelong Grammar School

I have written you a long letter, which I have destroyed …

I am sure it is much easier to bully people and to bribe them, but it isn't the right way, and anyhow, we have to be ourselves in life, and to do things in the way suitable to our own character and taste. I am sure that you've done much more your way than you would have done any other way.

I am sorry about Ian Smith, but I never could understand how he got so far. Impetuous and lacking in judgment as well as incapable of humility — very odd! But he was always the same.

Thank you sincerely for all that you have done, and for showing that it isn't necessary for a political leader to be a thug.

Robert Doyle, then Liberal leader in Victoria, and later mayor of Melbourne (in 2004)

Dick was a legend … As a Liberal Premier, while continuing to promote the ideals of economic growth and self-determination, he brought to our party and to the office of Premier an energising perspective … which spoke to a broad range of Victorians. His renewed approach to the environment, the arts, urban planning and social welfare redefined our party's landscape … He was a visionary, and many of the decisions he made and the policies he put in place prepared us for the issues we face today.

Sir Llewellyn Edwards, then deputy premier and Liberal leader of Queensland

Leadership, in my limited experience, is a demanding, lonely and unpredictable responsibility — and recent events in your state proved this. But I do believe that, when history is written, the unnecessary events of these last weeks will fade for the records of your achievements.

Dame Phyllis Frost, chairman of the State Relief Committee, and tireless social campaigner

The Smiths of this world are soon forgotten, and Dick's accomplishments won't be.

Jack Galbally, former Labor leader in the Legislative Council

Dick Hamer, in my experience, was a rarity. He was a calm, well-reasoned man who observed the best principles of democratic government. He never abused his position and there was absolutely nothing devious about him. He was a gentleman who played the game fair.

Mrs J. Graham, Mill Park
You have always conducted yourself in a dignified and respectful way no matter how awkward or heated the situation, and you have my deepest respect.

Norman Harper, professor emeritus of history at the University of Melbourne and prominent commentator
Can I congratulate you on your dignity and courage … on your integrity and imagination in those long years of service? These are qualities so often missing from the makeup of most political leaders.

Shirley Horne, state president, National Council of Women
It is difficult now to imagine Victoria without the Equal Opportunity Board and Commission. This is surely an indication of the importance of the [Equal Opportunity] Act, which continues to change significantly community attitudes to women.

Graham Jennings, former state director, Liberal Party
I firmly believe that you would have had all necessary support for success if you had wanted to continue to lead the party. You and April have been magnificent — only those who really know you both can be aware how much strength and goodness you have brought to government in Victoria …

It remains my firm belief that the true Victorians would have supported you through thick and thin.

Barry Jones, former federal minister, ALP president, and state MP (in his autobiography* A Thinking Reed *(2006))
In my five years in State Parliament I observed him closely, with growing admiration … I think Dick Hamer was the finest flower in the Victorian Deakinite Liberal tradition. I worked with him closely on a number of causes, including the arts and the abolition of the death penalty. I admired him immensely.

Sir Alfred Kemsley, businessman, former chairman of the Town and Country Planning Board

It was not until your advent that those of us who pioneered [town planning] under difficulties experienced real achievements. [Frederick] Cook and I welcomed you so much.

John Kennedy, chairman of the Teachers Tribunal, and former Hawthorn captain and coach

In the various crises that, I suppose, form a part of political life for any leader, I was always most impressed by the fact that you remained true to yourself. I came to expect that your comments would be reasonable and intelligent, and expressed in a calm but forthright manner. I was never disappointed … I hope, Dick, that you will now be able to adjust your values correctly, and … enjoy the glorious freedom of total, mindless bias in favour of the Hawks!

Sir Phillip Law, former Antarctic explorer and head of the Victorian Institute of Colleges

The world of business is not the only world, and the state has other functions than simply helping selfish people to get money. Over a number of years you have successfully performed the task of maintaining some sort of balance between the material and non-material interests.

***Ranald Macdonald, managing director of David Syme & Co, owners of* The Age**

Perhaps the best thing anyone could hope for is for people to say 'He had integrity'. That is the way you will be remembered.

Ian Macphee, federal minister for immigration and ethnic affairs

You have given the Liberal Party a warmth which it never had. Your humane, honest, progressive and fair approach to government will become a model — not immediately, but perhaps not too far away.

Eve Mahlab, co-founder of the Women's Electoral Lobby
I have very much appreciated your concern for increasing the wellbeing of women, and I know that this is based on a genuine belief in social justice rather than political mileage … I really feel that all Victorians, not just women, have been enriched by the contribution you have both made.

R.J. Matthews and family, Moe

Dear Mr and Mrs Hamer
You're both still tops in our books. Even though we've never met you personally, people of your calibre are always our friends. We found your leadership as Premier to be just and fair … Like me, you're an ex-Desert Rat. If you're [coming] our way, we'll be honoured to put a cuppa on and trot out the cakes and scones. May God come between you and harm, wherever you run.

Ken and Marjorie Menzies, son and daughter-in-law of Sir Robert Menzies
We've been very sad about the events of the last few weeks, and would like you to know how much we've appreciated the magnificent leadership you've given. The Quality of Life that is mentioned so much with regard to you two is something we need to hold on to … Thanks for all you've given, and for the marvellous example you've both set — something for which we should all aim.

Sinclair (Mick) Miller, chief commissioner of the Victoria Police
May I say that in the 10 years in which I have come in reasonably close contact with you, I have never doubted your integrity or your dedication. You are one of the exceptionally few men I have met in public life who has never failed to keep a promise, and who has always been prepared to listen and to act upon the advice of others.

I will never forget your decisive response to my question about the alternatives between the hostages and the ransom demand at the time of the Faraday kidnapping.

My wife and I were deeply moved by the dignity and sincerity projected by you and Mrs Hamer, through media interviews, at what must have been the most traumatic time.

I consider myself a better person for having known you.

Dame Elisabeth Murdoch, philanthropist, widow of Sir Keith, mother of Rupert, and colleague of Dick in many artistic projects

My dear Dick and April
Unhappily, as I was in London at the bedside of my beloved dying sister, my sorrow was a natural and respectable grief, but when I heard somewhat belatedly of your retirement and the utterly disgraceful discreditable and incredible events leading up to it, my thoughts and feelings were far from respectable!

In some ways, I was fortunate to have been so far away and out of touch, but am very sad to have missed witnessing, what I heard on all sides, your superb dignity and greatness in the last scenes of the tragic drama.

You will have received a wealth of tributes, and I find it hard to adequately express my admiration and affection for you and my gratitude for all your fine achievements for this state of ours — you have stood head and shoulders above your colleagues — as a shining beacon for all that is good and true, and the influence of such a fine character in public life has surely been of incalculable value to Australia …

'It is not the arrival but the journey that matters'. Your journey has been long and often hard, but must be acclaimed as a truly admirable, successful and worthwhile one. Personally I have so much to thank you for, which I do, most warmly.

Baillieu Myer, chairman of the Myer Emporium (to April)

Sarah and I — and I am sure, millions of other Victorians — were distressed at your comments in today's paper. We are deeply conscious of the role that you and Dick have played in improving the quality of life in this great state over such a long period, and at such personal cost … Your contribution will be long remembered and respected. We share the views of one writer who said Dick was one of the few politicians who can be loved and admired.

A.R. Norton, Dandenong South
You are too nice a bloke to be Premier.

Sir Gustav Nossal, director, Walter and Eliza Hall Institute of Medical Research
Dick, you have been an outstanding and remarkable leader of this state over the last nine years. Your far-sighted humanity and compassion, and your intelligent, balanced and fair approach to problems has been appreciated by all thinking citizens. Your absolute integrity and steadfast refusal to allow issues to be clouded by personal animus or ad hominem polemics have significantly raised the moral standard of Australian politics: would that there were more people of your ilk in Canberra.

The strong support that both of you [April & Dick] have given to research and education has made my task more rewarding — and more pressing. It is certain that the brilliant new Hall Institute building would never have become a reality without your vigorous backing, and I hope you will consider it one of the monuments related to your 'reign'.

Dr Henry Nowik, former head of Mars confectionery, Master Foods, and Uncle Ben's in Australia, writing from Virginia
I do know that the impact of your leadership and statesmanship will long remain with those many people who were inspired by your dedication.

John Oldham, diplomat, brother of Trevor and Gordon Oldham
(After telling Dick he had implemented many of the reforms that Trevor Oldham had hoped to carry out as premier)

To my mind, you have maintained a dignity unfortunately lacking in Australian political life … History has a habit of putting accounts in a fair-minded perspective.

Michael Collins Persse, head of history, Geelong Grammar School

I truly believe that you will be remembered, with deep gratitude and affection, long after almost any other contemporary Australian politician, because you have consistently put humanity above commerce, principle above expediency, and perhaps even, when necessary, people before principle.

There is about you a dignity, an honour, a gentleness — and will continue to flow to you a gratitude — too scarce in a world where generosity of spirit too seldom prevails in public life.

As one who lives in, and for 25 years has tried to serve this school, and who cares for what might be called its ideal, I am very proud and grateful to think that so admirable a Premier and a man is to some extent a product of Geelong Grammar School.

Brian Powell, executive director, Victorian Chamber of Manufactures

I believe you can look back with considerable pride at what you have achieved for Victoria … Your approach achieves far more effective results than would often appear to a critical media and public.

Arthur Preston, superintendent, Wesley Central Mission

You have my unqualified admiration. Thank you … for your interest in the community services of the Mission, and for the generous assistance you have given us.

Jill Robb, film producer and founding chief executive of the Victorian Film Commission

Having had the privilege … of working for you, I was — and still am — appalled at the events preceding your resignation. My time with you was one of the highlights of my life.

R.B. Roscoe, chairman, Melbourne Underground Rail Loop Authority

It is a matter of great satisfaction that during your term as Premier, the Underground Rail Loop became a reality, and a physical reminder of the foresight and enterprise of the Government under your leadership.

Peter Ross-Edwards, leader of the National Party (in parliament, 1981)

He was a man for whom I have always had a deep respect: a man of outstanding intellect, great charm, and enormous capacity for hard work. Dick Hamer never let me down in any undertaking he gave … Future generations will benefit greatly from the land purchased for environmental purchases, and the buildings preserved for heritage reasons. What I admired most about him … was his capacity not to bear a grudge, and to ignore the insults, rudeness and unfair criticism which unfortunately are becoming more and more a part of political life today.

Lawrie Shears, director-general of education, Victoria

I want to thank you for the generous support you have given to the decisions that have made the decade one of the most significant in the history of education, and placed our state in the forefront of education in Australia.

Albert Shergold, director, Brick and Pipe Industries Ltd

Private enterprise is inclined to expect too much from government, and of course, it's always easy to blame others for one's own failures. [He then gave a long list of competitive strengths that Hamer had maintained for Victoria.] Frankly, I can find little cause to criticise your handling of the above matters … It does appear to me that you are possibly, too kind, too decent, too loyal, not ruthless enough to be a politician. Thus the very qualities which we most admire in a man could be the very qualities which bring this contemptible and empty criticism from many who have found it hard to equal you in anything.

Ray Steele, president of the Victorian Cricket Association

I am not a political person, but I am boiling over what has happened. Thank you for the job you have done as Premier of this state.

Freeman Strickland, chairman, Perpetual Trustees (and much else)

So many of us were greatly saddened by all that has happened … The business community of Melbourne must accept some of the responsibility. I just want to assure you that you had a host of supporters in commerce and industry; the pity of it was that action to close the ranks was taken too late. Events just moved too swiftly … I did form a deep and lasting respect for you.

David Tonkin, Liberal premier of South Australia

(My) Cabinet has voted to send a message of admiration for your magnificent leadership of the state of Victoria during some turbulent and often difficult years. I am sure that Victorians have still to realise the full extent of your achievement.

Sir Donald Trescowthick, executive chairman, Charles Davis group

I regret very much that two or three people from the business sector decided to make public comments which were slanted to become critical of you and your Government when, in fact, all they were doing was speaking from the hip pocket nerve. They will have to live with those comments, as will their companies.

I know I speak on behalf of the great majority of the business community when I say just how much we have appreciated the manner in which you have guided the state during the past nine years. Without your mature and even-handed approach, the business sector in this state would indeed be in a sad and sorry position.

I guess it's life … but it is annoying and most hurtful when people choose to forget the thousands of achievements and make great publicity out of one or two failings. How they expect a Premier to be infallible, when they are not, continues to escape me. I can assure you that there are many business leaders who have many skeletons in their corporate cupboards which they would not want ventilated.

From a personal point of view, and from my position in the business community in Victoria, I ask you to accept our apologies for the manner in which you have been treated.

Dennis Tricks, chairman, Melbourne Stock Exchange

You said to me not long ago that I was learning a few things about politics. But I very much regret that over the last few days, I have been further educated … You have certainly provided leadership, and you have a great number of admirers in the business community for the exemplary manner in which you have conducted yourself at all times, and especially during the recent political crisis. Your wisdom and fairness will be missed.

Bertram Wainer, pioneer of legalised abortion and campaigner against police corruption

I have admired few politicians in my life: Churchill, Menzies, Kennedy and yourself. I have, contrary to public belief, always been a Liberal … In the aftermath of the Beach inquiry, I know the problems you faced, and that politics is the art of the possible. By allowing the inquiry to have the [terms] of reference it did, you went further than any other Premier would have done…

I am ashamed that such a dastardly event could have been connived at, and I could not even raise my voice against it. I doubt that I shall live to see again a Premier whose every act seemed to be of care, concern, decency, democracy and service to the community.

A.N. Whittle, Elwood

Well done, thou good and faithful servant.

Sir Victor Windeyer, former judge of the High Court, and Hamer's old wartime commander

I cherish the recollection of your friendly and loyal help in those days … I have no knowledge of political events in Victoria, or squabbles there, but I have been well aware of, and have admired, the wisdom, moderation and sense of reason and true values that you brought to your performance in your political duties.

Archbishop Sir Frank Woods, former Anglican Archbishop of Melbourne

How horrified Jean and I have been to read of your being 'stabbed in the back' (as April quite rightly said). How thankful we are for all your liberal (in the non-political sense of the word) Premiership over these many years, and how we admire the dignity with which you met criticism … You stand for, and have maintained, moral and spiritual values which too few are standing for inside and outside Parliament.

Notes

Introduction

1 Parliamentary Debates, Victoria (henceforth called *Hansard*), vol. 308, 1972–73, pp. 174–75.

1/Beginnings

1 *The Argus*, 20 November 1883.

2 E.H. Sugden and F.W. Eggleston, *George Swinburne: a biography* (1931), pp. 123–252.

3 *op. cit.*, pp. 62–63.

4 *op. cit.*, p. 38.

2/Childhood

1 Alison Patrick, 'Born Lucky', pp. 194–217 of *The Half-open Door*, edited by Patricia Grimshaw and Lynne Strahan (1982).

2 *The Argus*, 10, 11, and 19 August 1925.

3 Patrick, *op. cit.*

4 David Hamer, *Memories of My Life* (privately published 2002).

5 Michael Collins Persse, *In the Light of Eternity: selected writings* (2011).

6 Jim Guest, interview, 2011.

7 All the quotations from Hamer presented in indented form in this chapter come from interviews with his daughter Julia in the late 1990s.

3/From law to war

1 Diana Dyason, untitled chapter in *Memories of Melbourne University: undergraduate life in the years since 1917*, ed. Hume Dow (1983).
2 All indented quotations from Hamer in the first half of this chapter, before the outbreak of war, come from his interviews with his daughter Julia.
3 Interview with the author, April 1979.
4 Interview by Hazel de Berg with April Hamer, 14 March 1980, for the National Library of Australia's oral-history project on Australian writers (in this case, her sister Anne Elder).
5 All indented quotations from Hamer in the second half of this chapter, after the outbreak of war, come from his diaries from 1939 to 1941.

4/Tobruk

1 Olbrich's report forms an appendix to *Tobruk: the great siege 1941–42*, by William F. Buckingham (2012).
2 Unless otherwise stated, all indented quotations from Hamer in this chapter come from his diaries.
3 Interview by Christopher Sexton with Hamer, 1992.

5/From El Alamein …

1 Unless otherwise stated, all indented quotations from Hamer in this chapter are from his interviews with his daughter Julia.
2 David Dexter, *Australia in the War of 1939–1945, Series 1 – Army, Vol. VI: The New Guinea Offensive* (1961).
3 *The Argus*, 2 March 1944.
4 Interview, April 1979.

6/… to East Yarra

1 All quotations from Hamer in this chapter, unless otherwise stated, are from his interviews with his daughter Julia.
2 Interview by Christopher Sexton with Hamer, 1992.
3 Comments by Professor Christopher Hamer in e-mail to the author.
4 Sarah Brenan, interview, 2011.
5 Lady April Hamer, interview, 2011.

7/Melbourne in the 1950s

1 Tom Prior, *Bolte by Bolte* (1990), p. 180.

8/Politics before Bolte

1 J.B. Paul, 'The Premiership of Sir Albert Dunstan', unpublished M.A. thesis, Melbourne University (1960).

9/Henry Bolte

1 Prior, *op. cit.*, p. 15.
2 Barry Muir, *Bolte from Bamganie* (1973), Foreword by Sir Robert Menzies, p. vii.
3 Walter Jona, *People, Parliament and Politics* (2006), pp. 85, 88.
4 Philip Ayres, *Owen Dixon* (2003), p. 259.
5 Prior, p. 30.
6 Jona, chapter 8, pp. 126–44, gives a persuasive inside account of how the world-beating legislation actually came about.
7 Interview with Mel Pratt for the National Library of Australia, 1976.
8 Glyn Jenkins, interview, 2011.
9 Muir, p. 158.
10 Ayres, p. 275.

10/Hamer enters politics

1 All quotations from Murray Byrne are from an interview in 2011.
2 *Hansard*, 23 March 1960.
3 *Hansard*, 21 October 1959.
4 *Hansard*, 3 October 1962.

11/Planning Melbourne

1 The Sir Alfred Kemsley Oration, Windsor Hotel, 10 November 1981.
2 Speech to planning seminar at Camberwell Civic Centre, 21 May 1986.
3 Ministerial statement on a New Town Planning Organisation for Victoria, 21 February 1968, *Hansard*, 1967–68, pp. 3244–50.
4 Dennis Simsion, interview, 2011.
5 Lady April Hamer, letter to *The Age*, 30 August 2011.

6 Speech to Building Industry Congress, 23 August 1968, 'Melbourne — 2000 AD'.

12/The succession

1 Interview with Mel Pratt, 11 February 1976, for the National Library of Australia's oral-history project.
2 Peter Yule, *Ian Potter* (2006).
3 Interview with Michelle Grattan, *The Age*, February 1971.
4 Prior, *op. cit.*, pp. 42, 153, and 175.
5 Jona, *op. cit.*, pp. 90–91.

13/Hamer the man

1 Correspondence in the Hamer papers, State Library of Victoria.
2 Julia Hamer, memories of her father written after his death in 2004.
3 Sarah Brenan, interview, 2011.
4 Lady April Hamer, interview, 2011.
5 Alan Hunt, interview, 2011.
6 Interview with the author, 1979.
7 Robert Maclellan, interview, 2011.
8 Haddon Storey, interview, 2011.
9 Murray Byrne, interview, 2011.
10 Digby Crozier, interview, 2011.

14/Hamer makes it happen

1 Jean Holmes, *Australian Journal of Politics and History*, vol. XVIII, no. 2 (1974), pp. 274–75.

17/The Liberals turn right

1 *The Age*, 28 July 1973. I was present.
2 Malcolm Fraser and Margaret Simons, *Malcolm Fraser: the political memoirs*, (2010) p. 293.
3 *The Age*, 19 March 1976.
4 Geoff Coleman, interview, 2011.
5 Richard Alston, interview, 2012.
6 *Hansard*, vol. 336, 9 March 1978, pp. 219–20.

18/Newport

1 David Russell QC, 'In Search of the Magic Pudding: Essential Services legislation', paper presented at the 1988 conference of the H.R. Nicholls Society.
2 Lindsay Thompson, *I Remember: an autobiography* (1989).

19/The land deals

1 *Hansard*, vol. 334, 19 October 1977, pp. 10478–80.
2 Richard Thomas, interview, 2012.
3 Sir Gregory Gowans, *Report of the Board of Inquiry into certain land purchases by the Housing Commission (1978)*, Parliamentary Papers 1978–79, no. 6.
4 James Guest, interview, 2011.
5 *The Age*, 'A Postscript to the Land Deals', editorial, 29 October 1981.

20/The economy, Malcolm Fraser, and the New Federalism

1 Robert Maclellan, interview, 2011.

21/Two key reforms

1 *Hansard*, vol. 329, 11 November 1976, p. 4078.
2 Fay Marles, interview, 2011.
3 Christopher Sexton, interview, 1992.
4 Haddon Storey, interview, 2011.
5 Haddon Storey, interview, 2013.
6 Vicki Fairfax, *A Place Across the River: they aspired to create the Victorian Arts Centre* (2002), p. 105.
7 *ibid.*, p. 120.

22/Planning and the Liberal Party

1 Neville Hughes, interview, 2012.
2 Richard Alston, interview, 2012.

23/Hanging from a cliff

1 Jona, *op.cit.*, p. 98.

24/The casino

1 Sue Calwell, interview, 2011.
2 Digby Crozier, interview, 2011.
3 *Hansard,* vol. 350, 26 March 1980, pp. 477–81.
4 Muir, *op. cit.*, p. 156.

26/Decline and fall

1 The Camakaris report is discussed at length by Stephen Mills in *The New Machine Men* (1986), pp. 34–37.
2 Philip Chubb, interview, 2011.
3 Ian Smith, interview with Jim Clarke, 9 May 1981.
4 Richard Mulcahy, interview, 2012.
5 Hamer's retirement speech was quoted in full by *The Age* and *The Sun*, 29 May 1981. The speech has also been posted on YouTube.
6 *The Age*, editorial, 21 July 1981.

27/Life after politics

1 The letters Dick and April received after his retirement are stored at the State Library of Victoria.
2 Julia Hamer, memories of her father written after his death.
3 *The Age*, 3 July 1982.
4 Race Mathews, interview, 2012.
5 *Hansard* online, 12 May 1993, p. 771.
6 *The Age*, 20 December 2003.
7 Julia Hamer, memories of her father written after his death.

28/Dick Hamer: an assessment

1 Marcus Aurelius, *Meditations*, book 1, passage 15.
2 Letter from Cheryl Saunders in the Hamer papers, State Library of Victoria.
3 Don Hayward, interview, 2012.
4 Tom Harley, interview, 2011.
5 Letter from Michael Collins Persse, Hamer papers, SLV.

Appendix A/Hamer on Hamer

1 Interviews with Christopher Sexton, 1992.
2 Interview with the author, reported in *The Age*, 3 July 1982.
3 Interview with Peter Ellingsen, reported in *The Age*, 30 June 1981.

For further reading

First, the internet. On most topics treated in this book, I found valuable information through Google (including its newspaper archive), Wikipedia, and the National Library's online treasure, Trove (www.trove.nla.gov.au), which includes, among other things, every article and advertisement ever published in Melbourne's former conservative daily, *The Argus*, from 1846 to 1957.

Second, many books also played a part in informing this biography. Some of the most important are:

HAMER FAMILY: Alison Patrick's all-too-brief memoir of her childhood, 'Born Lucky', in *The Half-open Door* (1982), edited by Patricia Grimshaw and Lynne Strahan, is beautifully done. David Hamer's *Memories of My Life* would make interesting reading, if it is ever published — as would Dick's own unpublished diaries, from 1939 to 1941.

The biography *George Swinburne* (1931), published after his death by his friends Edward Sugden and Sir Frederic Eggleston, is not only an attractive portrait of Hamer's uncle, but Eggleston also sneaks in a short history of Victorian politics up to that time. *Practical Measures: 100 years at Swinburne* (2007), by Peter Love, is a recent official history that recounts how Swinburne founded the college, and includes a lovely photo of Ethel, then 91, with students in 1959.

The National Library has a recorded interview with April in 1980 by Hazel de Berg, which focussed on her sister, the poet Anne Elder, but includes much on their family and upbringing.

GEELONG GRAMMAR has been well served by historians. Weston Bate's *Light Blue Down Under: the history of Geelong Grammar School* (1990) gives one perspective, while longtime teacher Michael Collins Persse provided another in *Well-ordered Liberty: a portrait of Geelong Grammar School 1855–1995* (1995). This chapter also draws on Persse's *In the Light of Eternity: selected writings* (2011).

MELBOURNE UNIVERSITY has had new histories and reminiscences published every generation or so. I drew mostly on Diana 'Ding' Dyason's chapter in *Memories of Melbourne University: undergraduate life in the years since 1917* (1983), edited by Hume Dow, and *A Place Apart, the University of Melbourne: decades of challenge* (1996), by Professor John Poynter and Dr Carolyn Rasmussen.

THE WAR: World War II, I suspect, has had more words devoted to it than any other episode in human history. Start reading wherever you choose.

VICTORIAN POLITICAL HISTORY, by contrast, is unknown to most Victorians. *The Victorian Premiers 1856–2006* (2006), edited by Paul Strangio and Brian Costar, is a good place to start, along with *150 Years of Spring Street* (2007) by Robert Murray, and Geoffrey Blainey's *A History of Victoria* (1981, revised 2006). *A People's Counsel: a history of the Parliament of Victoria, 1956–1990* (1992) by Raymond Wright, is an unusually lively official history, but weak on the Hamer years. Edward (Ted) Barbor served as press secretary to six premiers from all three parties: his memoir, *They Went Their Way* (1960), is worth reading.

Katharine West's *Power in the Liberal Party* (1966) is the classic account of the Hollway era, just as Robert Murray's *The Split* (1970) is the classic history of the catastrophe that Labor wrought on itself in 1955.

Peter Blazey's *Bolte: a political biography* (1972) tried to be objective; it underplays some of Bolte's strengths, but highlights the bad sides that made Hamer decide to be different. Barry Muir's *Bolte from Bamganie* (1973) is the official biography, written in response. Tom Prior's *Bolte by Bolte* (1990) is essentially an extended interview with Bolte, speaking freely in the last year of his life. Norman Abjorensen's *Leadership and the Liberal Revival* (2007) revisits him a generation later, trying to separate myth from reality.

Hansard, the record of parliamentary debates, is now online, although you can go and make yourself a cup of coffee while you wait for a single 1,200-page volume to download. Selected parliamentary papers, including the annual financial reports, are now online at www.parliament.vic.gov.au/vufind/

For both the Bolte and Hamer periods, the most valuable commentary on key events was in the regular updates of Victorian politics in the *Australian Journal of Politics and History*, especially from 1968 on, when Jean Holmes wrote them.

Peter Howson's diaries, for all their bias and bile, are invaluable as an inside glimpse into Liberal politics in this period. They run to many thousands of pages. Don Aitkin's 'best of' collection, *The Howson Diaries: the life of politics* (1984), focuses entirely on Howson's years as a federal MP. The full diaries (1956–1990) are in the National Library of Australia.

Several Liberal ministers wrote autobiographies. Lindsay Thompson's *I Remember: an autobiography* (1989) is rich in lively anecdotes, but can be found only in libraries. Walter Jona's *People, Parliament and Politics* (2006) is more substantial. Noel Tennison's *My Spin in PR* (2008) is a witty account of his career, including his two years working for Hamer and the Liberal Party. Tony Parkinson's *Jeff: the rise and fall of a political phenomenon* (2000) is valuable on Kennett's years as Liberal leader, but brushes over his early years on the backbench.

Barry Jones' autobiography, *A Thinking Reed* (2006) is outstanding; unfortunately, his five years in Victorian politics form only a small part of it. *Malcolm Fraser: the political memoirs* (2010) by Malcolm

Fraser and Margaret Simons, is very good on the 1975 crisis, but glosses over Fraser's relations with the states and gradual withdrawal from his New Federalism policy.

The best books on specific subjects are Mike Richards' *The Hanged Man: the life and death of Ronald Ryan* (2002), an impressively detailed narration of events leading to the Ryan hanging, and *A Place Across the River: they aspired to create the Victorian Arts Centre* (2002) by Vicki Fairfax, a similarly detailed record of the long struggle to build the Arts Centre.

There are a number of academic studies of this period. Jean Holmes' *The Government of Victoria* (1976) is dry and dense with facts, but covers a lot of territory. Peter Aimer's *Politics, Power & Persuasion: the Liberals in Victoria* (1973) studies the Liberal Party organisation in the Bolte era. *Anatomy of an Election* (1979), edited by Peter Hay, Ian Ward, and John Warhurst, collects 23 chapters by academics on the 1979 state election.

Essays on Victorian Politics (1985), edited by Peter Hay, John Halligan, John Warhurst, and Brian Costar, was published in the Cain era, but includes a lot of useful material on Hamer's years, particularly in chapters by Roger Wettenhall, 'The Public Sector in Victoria: how different?' and John Power and Nicholas Low, 'Hamer's Policy Seedlings: inquiries and ministries'.

The works of Russell (R.L.) Mathews are invaluable for understanding federal–state financial relations in this era. I relied heavily on his *Federal Finance: intergovernmental relations in Australia since Federation* (1972, with W.R.C. Jay) and *The Public Sector in Jeopardy: Australian fiscal federalism from Whitlam to Keating* (1997, with Bhajan Grewal).

For further viewing

Hamer Hall is the most significant of several memorials to Hamer in Melbourne, although not built for that purpose.

A statue by Peter Corlett stands, most appropriately, where the Premier's Department offices meet the Treasury Gardens. Alongside it are statues of John Cain junior, Sir Albert Dunstan, and Sir Henry Bolte.

The Heide art gallery, former home of John and Sunday Reed, which Hamer bought to make a gallery of modernism, has a Sir Rupert Hamer garden.

At Olinda, the Forests Commission long ago carved out 120 hectares from the wet Dandenongs forest to create the R.J. Hamer Arboretum, with almost 200 species of trees and numerous walking tracks linking them.

And for viewing at your computer, Malcolm Farnsworth of the website www.australianpolitics.com has posted a video of Hamer's 1981 resignation speech on YouTube.

Index